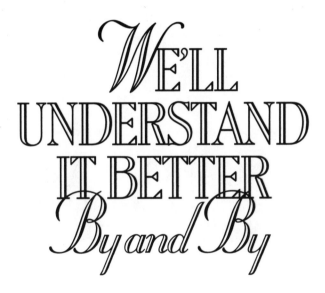

WE'LL UNDERSTAND IT BETTER By and By

PIONEERING AFRICAN AMERICAN GOSPEL COMPOSERS

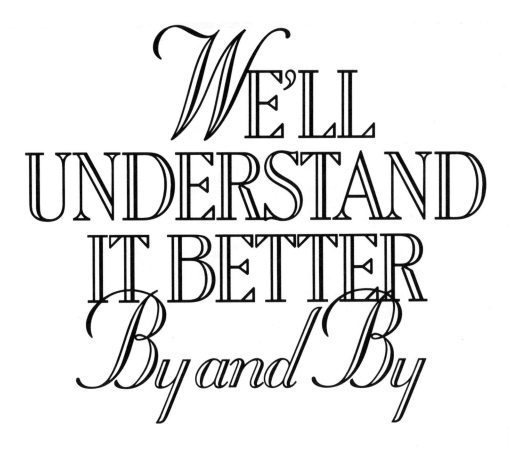

WE'LL UNDERSTAND IT BETTER By and By

Edited by Bernice Johnson Reagon

SMITHSONIAN INSTITUTION PRESS

Washington and London

© 1992 by the Smithsonian Institution
All rights reserved

Supervisory Editor: Duke Johns
Copy Editor: Judy Sacks
Designer: Janice Wheeler

Library of Congress Cataloging-in-Publication Data
We'll understand it better by and by : pioneering African American gospel composers / edited by Bernice Johnson Reagon.
   p.   cm.
   Includes bibliographical references and index.
   ISBN 1–56098–166–0 (alk. paper).—ISBN 1–56098–167–9 (pbk. : alk. paper)
   1. Afro-American composers—Biography. 2. Gospel music—History and criticism. I. Reagon, Bernice Johnson, 1942–
ML390.W274   1992
782.25—dc20   91–37954

British Library Cataloguing-in-Publication Data is available

Manufactured in the United States of America
99 98 97 96   5 4 3

⊗ The paper used in this publication meets the minimum requirements of the American National Standard for Permanence of Paper for Printed Library Materials Z39.48–1984

On the cover: Louise McCord, in performance at a Roberta Martin Singers reunion concert, Smithsonian Institution, 1981. The book's title is derived from Reverend Charles Albert Tindley's song "We'll Understand It Better By and By."

TO PEARL WILLIAMS-JONES

Pearl Williams-Jones was a pioneering scholar in African American gospel music who served as consultant to the Smithsonian Institution in conceptualizing and developing its decade-long research, documentation, and public presentation programs on gospel music history. A singer, pianist, composer/arranger, and teacher, Ms. Williams-Jones served as minister of music of the Bible Way Church and as associate professor of music at the University of the District of Columbia. Her work is represented here with two articles based on her Smithsonian-sponsored research on Roberta Martin and the Roberta Martin Singers. Pearl Williams-Jones died February 4, 1991, as the work on this volume was being completed.

CONTENTS

ACKNOWLEDGMENTS

It is an honor and a blessing to serve as medium—a way through which this story about gospel music could be passed. The team of scholars represented in this volume is like the visible tip of an iceberg. Over the ten years of this work, we have stood on solid ground supported in many ways. In this space, we offer thanks, acknowledgment, and credit to those who have surrounded us with their efforts, encouragement, advice, and resources.

First, there is the African American community, the creators and nurturers of the shout, the spiritual, the dance, and the clarion sounds of gospel music—song and singing. It is this rich, dynamic legacy of worship and tradition we celebrate in this publication.

The journey from the community through the academy by way of our national museum is layered with the work of those too numerous to call here. The names we share here are those who made specific contributions and as a collective symbolized the community of support that helped this project be realized. Two people served as administrative coordinators during the preparation of the manuscript. Lisa Ann Pertillar Brevard transcribed the conference tapes and served as liaison with the authors for two summers as a Smithsonian intern. For two years, Adisa Douglas assisted in the expanded coordination responsibilities and as copy editor was invaluable to the completion of this project.

The Smithsonian Institution gave this project a home, which became a place where scholars interested in this area could find support for their research. I acknowledge the work and support of the Smithsonian staff: the staff of the Program in African American Culture (formerly Program in Black American Culture)—Linn Shapiro, Niani Kilkenny, John Archambeault, Donna Hagler, Diane Green; Judy Moore, Harold Closter, James Weaver, John Fesperman, James Morris, James Early, Josiah Hatch; National Museum of American History Director Roger Kennedy; and the host of volunteers who staffed the conferences. The programming staff of Washington, D.C., area radio stations WYCB, WUST, WUDC, WHMM, WAMU, WETA, and WOL and of National Public Radio served as an invaluable link to the community in sharing the research and inviting the community to join and witness our work.

The last stages of preparing the manuscript were greatly advanced by Kathy Anderson, Helen Toni Douglas, and Arlene Sandifer.

The data base for this publication was developed through a network of informants who agreed to share their stories, scholars, researchers, and resource centers. These include Wayne Shirley, librarian, Music Division at the Library of Congress; Howard University's Moorland-Spingarn Research Center; Schomburg Center for Research in Black Culture, New York Public Library; Fisk University Library; *Washington Post* archives; Elsie Bailey, principal of Booker T. Washington High School in Memphis, Tenn.; the descendants of Charles Albert Tindley—Esther Jackson and William Robbins—and the Berlin Heritage Foundation, Berlin, Md., the Tindley Temple United Methodist Church community, Philadelphia, Pa.; Doug Seroff; Stuart Goosman; J. Edward Hoy; Anna Lois Brooks; and Jackie Alper. At the Smithsonian Institution Press, Daniel Goodwin, Duke Johns, and copy editor Judy Sacks became the team that carried the manuscript through its last stages to you.

I
OVERVIEW

PIONEERING AFRICAN AMERICAN GOSPEL MUSIC COMPOSERS

A Smithsonian Institution Research Project

Bernice Johnson Reagon

W ith this volume we present the results of a Smithsonian-sponsored, seven-year study in the history and development of African American gospel music. We have focused our efforts on the legacy left by the major pioneering gospel music composers, whose compositions and organizing efforts shaped the form for the first half of this century. Any study of African American sacred song and singing is a study of its host community in general and its worship community in particular. The African American worship community—the Black church in its largest expression—has been the nurturing institution for one of the world's greatest music cultures. Here we are looking not only at specific practices taking place over a two hundred–year period within organized religious services but also at the role of sacred music and worship in shaping the sound and rhythm of African American culture as a whole.

Today, it is African American music, in structure and often in content, that drives mainstream popular culture worldwide. Any honest discussion about the contemporary music culture of the United States of America is almost always also a discussion of the African American music tradition. However, participants, musicians and consumers, are woefully ignorant of the source of these expressions, performance traditions, and aesthetics. Whether the community of musicians and audience is American, European, or Asian, or whether the audience crosses class or culture, the way the voice is used, the way instruments are held and played, the way instruments sound when played, the way an audience responds in a contemporary concert, the way in which a performer has dialogue with the audience, all can be traced to the African American worship tradition created within the Black church. What is not present within this contemporary popular music community is a conscious awareness that its expressions are drawn from a culture whose music operates as a phenomenon far beyond entertainment categories.

The story of African American sacred music is much more than a story of how African American song and singing developed. It is the story of a people under stress searching for a more fertile ground for survival in a strange land. It is a Black story and an American story we tell about how one of America's major cultural communities in motion at the turn of the twentieth century created a new and powerful music tradition.

The American story of struggle and searching documented in the song culture of the African American legacy was the concern of W. E. B. Du Bois in 1903 when he wrote "Of the Sorrow Songs" in *The Souls of Black Folk*:

Little of beauty has America given the world save the rude grandeur God himself stamped on her bosom; the human spirit in this new world has expressed itself in vigor and ingenuity rather than in beauty. And so by fateful chance the Negro folk-song—the rhythmic cry of the slave—stands to-day not simply as the sole American music, but as the most beautiful expression of human experience born this side the seas. It has been neglected, it has been, and is, half despised, and above all it has been persistently mistaken and misunderstood; but notwithstanding, it still remains as the singular spiritual heritage of the nation and the greatest gift of the Negro people. (Du Bois [1903] 1961, 181–82)

DEFINITIONAL STATEMENT

African American gospel music is a twentieth-century phenomenon, born of a people moving from rural communities to the urban centers of this country. Black people left Southern rural communities that had limited promise and held experiences of social and economic terror. When African Americans moved to the city, they were looking for more space. As so often in the history of Black music, new situations fostered new sounds. The evolution of gospel music represents one of the most important and prolific contributions to American sacred music.

Into new urban communities, we brought dreams of change; we also brought as much of the past as we could carry—traditions that provided solid ground for uprooted families in strange, often cold, environments. The sound of Black America expanded to embrace this reality. The new dimensions of this expansion are most evident in the development of the urban church music that became known as gospel.

The new music evolved out of the African American repertoire and song style of the nineteenth century, which included hymns, arranged and congregational spirituals, shape-note singing, and a style of singing distinguished by a highly charged, emotional sound. The foundation of the culture which evolved within the nineteenth-century plantation slave community was African in structure and in process—in the how and the why things were done. The ingredients included African and European expressions and repertoire cauterized by the slave experience in this new world. As African Americans embraced Christianity and began to build their churches and the communities the churches served, they evolved a way of being and surviving that had a sound and function that continued as they moved through the twentieth century. Gospel is but one expression of this forward and expanding motion.

Gospel is both a repertoire and a style of singing. Gospel music can either be appropriated from a hymn or spiritual by a well-versed performance or it can be composed as a new song and performed in a variety of gospel styles. In writing about the performance tradition, gospel music historian Pearl Williams-Jones stated:

> The performing process is so intuitive as to be almost unteachable. The greatest gospel artists are usually those who were born nearest the source of the tradition. . . .
> There are two basic sources from which gospel singing has derived its aesthetic ideals: the free-style collective improvisations of the African American church congregation and the rhetorical solo style of the gospel preacher. Inherent in this also is the concept of African American folk rhetoric, folk expressions, bodily movement, charismatic energy, cadence, tonal range and timbre. (Williams-Jones 1976, 115–16)

The new gospel style of singing can best be understood as song delivered as a high-powered spiritual force, with increased emphasis on vocal rhythms and calculated use of vocal textures to create greater intensity. Basic gospel-song musical structures rest on the sacred-music traditions within the Black community: congregational style singing with its call-and-response forms, and slow-metered, lined-out Protestant hymns. Much of the new style of singing, with its driving rhythms and percussive instrumental accompaniment, was nurtured within the turn-of-the-century Black Pentecostal (sometimes called Holiness or Sanctified) church. As other African American denominations moved to a more structured, ordered format, in which the sermon stood as the highest spiritual point of the service and the music was used to set the stage, the new Pentecostal denomination used congregational singing as a way of achieving climactic experiences of spiritual transcendence. These experiences—called spiritual possession, shouting, or the holy dance—were considered evidence of the manifestation of God as the Holy Spirit within the individual believer. This powerful singing and its use as personal and community testament within the worship setting also influenced music within Black Baptist and Methodist denominations.

There were new songs whose spiritual texts were secular applications of biblical literature rather than expressions of commitment to a specific Christian doctrine. An interesting example is "If I Had My Way":

> If I had-a my way
> If I had-a my way, in this wicked world,
> If I had-a my way,
> I'd tear this building down
> I'd tear this building down

> Well you read in the Bible, you will understand
> That old Samson was the strongest man
> Well they tell me God almighty
> Rode on the wings of the wind
> And he saw old Samson and he called to him
> Said he whispered low into Samson's mind
> Said "Deliver my children from the Philistines."

The call-and-response form flourished in the new genre. Songs such as "In the Morning, When I Rise" rocked churches with a strong leader giving the call—"In the morning"—and the congregation thundering the response—"When I rise."

In addition to the new songs, best attributed to congregational composition with individual authors unknown, in the early part of the century songwriters consciously tapped into the compositional fervor of the new singing, using hymns and spirituals as musical framework. The music they created, which became known as gospel, is the subject of this volume.

Although gospel music is part of the African American oral tradition, pioneers in the field made innovative use of mainstream communications technology—print, radio, recordings, and television. Thus, we have a musical tradition with a history accessible to us in part because of the utilization of twentieth-century information technology. However, gospel does not hold center stage in any of those media. Instead, the technologies operate in service to the Black oral tradition. Radio, records, and sheet music became part of a network created by a new group of composers and singers who through their music served a cultural community in demographic flux from rural to urban, from South to North, from East to West.

Most people know that gospel music exists. However, gospel music practitioners are a specialized constituency, for gospel music is a blend of music and commitment to a body of beliefs and practices. For years, and even today, most people who have supported and created the music also have articulated a commitment to live a Christian life. It is by far the most vibrant, community-based musical genre within African America.

Although its development parallels the development of the recording industry and of jazz and blues forms, gospel music existed as a subterranean stream, only occasionally breaking through into mainstream popular culture. This is past. Today, African American gospel music is viewed by many as the source of inspiration for new musical and performing styles. We are no longer only feeling the presence of gospel music through the soul sounds of such master musicians as Ray Charles and Aretha Franklin. One can now find gospel selections on every major television variety show, and gospel songs are now considered in their own category in the Grammy Awards. Faced with the economic collapse of disco at the end of the 1970s, the recording industry is giving vigorous attention to the gospel music network of concerts and recordings and its history of maintaining healthy profits on low-budget productions.

It is in actual performance that the African American gospel song is fully revealed in its uniqueness and power. The music serves as a medium through which the congregation, singers, and listeners can transcend to higher emotional and spiritual levels. I use the word *listeners* cautiously, for in a gospel music environment, hearers of the songs must play an active role in order for the song, once raised by the singer, to grow to full bloom.

THE SMITHSONIAN PROJECT

This project, whose purpose was to study and document gospel music as well as to develop live performance programs and colloquia, began in 1977 as part of the work of the Smithsonian Division of Performing Arts (DPA), Program in Black American Culture (PBAC) (now the Program in African American Culture at the National Museum of American History). DPA was organized to present living expressions of American culture through concerts, sound recordings, lecture demonstrations, and festivals.

Within the PBAC, we developed a model that created the live performance program as a public offering of primary research and analysis. The infrastructure of the project rested on the administrative and production support of Linn Shapiro, who was followed by Niani Kilkenny as program coordinator and producer. James Morris, then director of DPA, suggested that I continue working with this new model for the presentation of my research, and he consistently supported the development and expansion of the effort until the division was reorganized in 1983 and our office moved to its current location at the National Museum of American History.

To conduct a study in the development of twentieth-century gospel music, the Smithsonian sought and supported the work of a loose community of scholars based in academic institutions throughout the nation whose research, publication, and teaching efforts had already revealed their interest in the gospel music field. The colloquium format of our conferences on the pioneering gospel music composers always featured the combined work of a team of scholars and informants with first-hand experience with the history of the composers. The live-performance events featured artists who had grown up within the tradition and contemporary musicians who accepted Smithsonian commissions to perform the traditional repertoire.

I had an initial discussion about organizing a multiyear effort in the research, documentation, and presentation of public programs in African American gospel music history with Pearl Williams-Jones. Williams-Jones served as consultant on our initial concert series and for our first major conference on the pioneering gospel music composers. This conference, held in 1981, looked at the contributions of Roberta Martin, the dean of the ensemble sound of classic gospel performance in singing, handling of text, and accompaniment. It set a standard and model for our live presentation work, for its clarion element was the reunion of nine singers who had performed in the Roberta Martin Singers from 1932 to 1967. Six scholars joined primary informants in panels and roundtable discussions, making the Smithsonian come alive with the life and work of this major twentieth-century American composer.

Pearl Williams-Jones had already done ground-breaking work in discussing the performance aesthetics in gospel music in her article "Afro-American Gospel: A Crystallization of the Black Aesthetic" (Williams-Jones 1975, 373–84). She introduced me to Horace Clarence Boyer, who served as composition analyst for each of the composers in this series and thus provided the largest number of articles (six) for this volume. For those readers who are musical score literate, Boyer's articles, great reading experiences, are also wonderful workbook exercises in basic gospel music composition.

Ethnomusicologist Portia Maultsby, whose specialty is the African American popular music industry, also worked on the team, bringing the perspective of the role the gospel music community played in the formation of post–World War II popular secular music. As we moved through the project, other scholars participated: notably, Reverend Charles Walker and Luvenia George on Lucie E. Campbell; Wayne Shirley, music librarian at the Library of Congress, on Reverend Charles Albert Tindley and Kenneth Morris; Michael Harris on Thomas Andrew Dorsey; and William Wiggins and Anthony Heilbut on Reverend William Herbert Brewster. Through it all, I served as coordinator, fundraiser, and conceptualizer of research and programming.

Seizing the opportunity to follow my own research interests, I conducted oral-history projects for Charles Albert Tindley, William Herbert Brewster, Roberta Martin, and Kenneth Morris. In my interviews with informants, I sought not only to obtain historical facts but also to create within the interview environment an invitation to traditional ways of sharing history, telling stories, and offering testimony. As a historian, I am as concerned with the "voice" as historical record as I am with the content data contained in the story. In developing articles based on this research, I continued to search for ways of presenting what is an oral process in a written form.

THE CONFERENCE MODEL: A LIVE PUBLICATION

The model we created for our public programs drew upon the Smithsonian Festival of American Folklife as well as an earlier project investigating and documenting the culture of the Civil Rights Movement. First, all of the programs had to accommodate a number of constituencies: (1) the scholarly field, because the content and analysis were based on primary field research and primary archival resources; (2) the informants, who in many instances had no experience with museums or mainstream cultural and educational institutions; (3) the lay public, which, in many cases, was being introduced to gospel music for the first time through the conferences; (4) the community that nurtured the forms within their church and civic organizations; (5) aficionados—collectors, recording entrepreneurs, and researchers who operate outside of the academy; and (6) the museum itself, which had historically seen public programs as a way to explain exhibit- and collection-based work of curators rather than as a publication of primary research and analysis whose data base often was oral, with little or no material collection exhibition. In this instance, we used the public program to stimulate interest within the museum community to collect and create exhibits in subject areas suffering from neglect.

Our conferences included a symposium-performance event, small exhibit components, and an outreach component, which included a small publication. In our outreach presentations, we used what would normally be thought of as PR to share the research with larger audiences. We used radio programs to introduce wider audiences to a particular composer and the music created by recording artists. Through our programs on radio stations devoted to gospel music we were able to reach the community where gospel thrives. We found this audience who knew and practiced the music as an integral part of their lives deeply interested in the history and cultural context of the music. The educationally driven museum experience served to expand how they knew what they had known for so long through worship. Each conference had a program booklet with an article by the primary scholars represented in this volume that served to survey the field covered by the conference. The idea was to give to each person who attended and those who inquired later a research-based document that would define and introduce the focus of the conference. The African American gospel music community was thrilled that their national museum was documenting and analyzing something familiar and integral to their lives. The project became an act of affirmation as highly trained members of the academy through their research proclaimed gospel music a major sacred music of twentieth-century America.

Each colloquium was composed of panels of scholars, informants, and performers. In this model, scholars presented the results of their data and analysis whenever possible to the data base from which they had pulled some of their findings. Informants and performers became specialists as they through oral testimony brought the audience closer to the subject area. For example, testimonies from the Reverend Laurence Roberts, record producer for Savoy Records, and Eugene Smith, tenor and narrator with the Roberta Martin Singers, exposed the gathered audience to a living field data base. The scholars had a new experience of reading papers to their colleagues, to people they had interviewed, and to an audience of practitioners and aficionados who held an intense relationship to the subject area. The experience was one of reporting to several fields at once. Having a number of scholars who had never lost their base within the African American community even as they excelled in various disciplines within the academy greatly enhanced the power of the colloquium panel experience.

Most of the live-performance programs were concerts. In some cases, we brought together the singers who had created the record: the Roberta Martin Singers reunion concerts; the Robert J. Bradley session, which included testimony and music on his work with his mentor, Lucie E. Campbell; and the session with Reverend William Herbert Brewster and his congregation from Memphis, which included the Brewstaires and a passion play cast. In other instances, we had to be more inventive. With Reverend Charles Albert Tindley, we commissioned a script written by Eleanor Traylor based on an oral-history project conducted among those who remembered Tindley. We commissioned contemporary singers, the Howard University Gospel Choir and the Philadelphia Ambassadors, to perform Tindley's songs in the style of the performers from the classic era. In this performance, which was initially held at the Smithsonian and then taken to Philadelphia and performed in Tindley Temple, the highly acclaimed actor Avery Brooks played the role of Tindley. Through the performance, we were able to have the songs come out of Reverend Tindley's sermons, which we found was the most effective way of sharing the original practice and performance context of this composer, whose works have traveled so far from their congregational base in Tindley Temple.

Every effort was made to document all of these public events with the hope of building an archive that could ground material collection as well as support the development of artifact collections. This publication is the result of this documentation.

THE HISTORICAL BACKGROUND

In its relatively young history during the twentieth century, gospel as a genre of music with a distinctive repertoire and performance tradition has already passed through several developmental stages. However, to understand the twentieth-century story, it is important to look at the evolution of the song, the singing, and the worship culture whence it sprang.

> Lord, I got a right
> Lord, I got a right
> Lord, I got a right
> I got a right to the tree of life.

This declaration song of freedom belongs to a body of musical literature unparalleled in documenting the voice of African American people struggling to battle the yoke of bondage. Today, these songs are called spirituals.

The importance of spirituals can be weighed in part by the tenaciousness of their survival in the twentieth century. The oral tradition that passed these songs from one generation to another was, and is, powerful and pervasive. As I grew up, the songs were everywhere. I envision that I began to learn them in the womb. "Didn't My Lord Deliver Daniel," "Cried and I Cried Until I Found the Lord," "In That Great Getting up Morning," "Go Down Moses," "Over My Head, I See Trouble in the Air," "I Got Shoes, All of God's Children Got Shoes," "Walk Believer, Walk Daniel," "Walk around Zion, I Believe," "Every Time I Feel the Spirit," "Witness for My Lord": My teachers taught them in the one-room schoolhouse I attended. I learned them in the country churches my father pastored in Worth, Mitchell, and Dougherty Counties, Georgia. I sang them as concert songs with full harmony arrangements in the high school and college choirs.

My early experience, post–World War II, was not unlike that of world-renowned concert tenor Roland Hayes, who was born twenty-four years after slavery and who wrote in the introduction to his collection of spirituals: "I have seen them (Aframerican [sic] religious folk songs) being born in our religious services at the community Mount Zion Baptist Church at 'Little Row' (now Curryville), Gordon County, Georgia. Here I heard great ritual sermons preached and prayers prayed, and I sang the Aframerican religious folk songs as a child with my parents and the church folk" (Hayes 1948, vii).

The African American choral-song tradition was nurtured in slavery. The enslavement of Africans in America and the resulting slave experience provided the breeding ground for African American culture in all its manifestations. Frederick Douglass felt that these songs presented a kind of documentation of a communal worldview held by these imprisoned people: "They told a tale which was then altogether beyond my feeble comprehension; they were tones, loud, long, and deep, breathing the prayer and complaint of souls boiling over with the bitterest anguish. Every tone was a testimony against slavery, and a prayer to God for deliverance from chains. . . ." (Douglass [1855] 1962, 99).

The sacred songs created during this period became known as spirituals as African Americans moved from bondage to establish themselves as free people. However, we do not use the terms *sacred*, *worship*, or *church* in the strict contemporary sense. Within the African American oral tradition, these terms function as larger and more personal concepts. Phrases such as "everyday with me is holy," "worship can take place anywhere," and "the church is in you" capture the way in which the arena of the sacred within the African American community is boundless and exists wherever it does. This is emphasized by Lawrence Levine in his ground-breaking study, *Black Culture and Black Consciousness:*

It is significant that the most common form of slave music we know of is sacred song. I use the term "sacred" not in its present usage as something antithetical to the secular world; neither the slaves nor their African forebears ever drew modernity's clear line between the sacred and the secular. The uses to which the spirituals were put are an unmistakable indication of this. They were not sung solely or even primarily in churches or praise houses but were used as rowing songs, field songs, work songs, and social songs. (Levine 1977, 30–31)

The sacred music of the slaves gives us a rich opportunity to look not only at the creation of this repertoire but also at its use and evolution. If we accept the premise that cultural products can provide a guiding and monitoring device through which one can follow the development of a people under new and changing conditions, then the spirituals would serve us well.

At Fisk University with the Fisk Jubilee Singers we get the next major evidence of the use of the songs outside of slavery and beyond the boundaries of the African American community. In 1871, the Jubilee Singers, led by George L. White, then treasurer of Fisk University, started on a tour to raise money for that institution. Their repertoire included art songs, hymns, and anthems, standards that would be expected of any choir of that period. A year earlier, for example, the Fisk Singers had performed the cantata of "Esther" in Nashville, Memphis, and Chattanooga (Marsh 1892, 13).

In 1871, White took the students on a tour. Although warmly received initially, the lack of financial income from their standard concert repertoire signaled a disaster. However, pushing forward, the group turned to the spirituals as their central repertoire, and the response to the music was phenomenal. The turnaround for the tour took place in Oberlin, Ohio, where they sang for a convention of ministers at the National Council of the Congregational Church. From Oberlin eastward, their fortunes changed. Their audiences were deeply moved by the power of the spiritual and responded to their pleas for funding for the economic salvation of their school, Fisk University.

The Jubilee Singers raised over twenty thousand dollars on their first tour. Theodore F. Seward issued in 1872 a publication of their repertoire called *Jubilee Songs* with forty of the sixty-one melodies harmonized (Seward 1872). The success of the Jubilee Singers prompted virtually every Black college to organize a group—a quartet or choir—to sing spirituals, and the early concert performance of spirituals became connected to raising money for Black education.

In 1874, Thomas P. Fenner from Hampton College took a group of Hampton Singers to the North and issued in that same year *Cabin and Plantation Songs*, a collection of spirituals with harmonies. In his introduction, Fenner, echoing in part some of the earlier value judgments of his body of songs, wrote: "There are evidently, I think, two legitimate methods of treating this music: either to render it in its absolute, rude simplicity, or to develop it without destroying its original characteristics, the only proper field for such development being in harmony" (Fenner [1874] 1901, iii).

With the advent of the spiritual for the concert stage, there began to be a stabilization of what was called the spiritual repertoire and a formalization of the harmony and arrangement patterns. In fact, many early composers saw the songs as raw material, ripe for development.

The two divisions in Fenner's statement also echoed the paths of evolution of the spiritual. The Fisk, Hampton, and other Black college traditions would increasingly follow a path based on developing the song by adding a Western harmonic structure. This established for arranged spirituals a tradition in which the melodies and lyrics were seen as jewels to be moved to a more polished setting. Within this tradition, there was a range of positions on how much adornment the songs needed. There were strong advocates of the simple setting, of doing as little to the structure of the song as possible.

The formalized settings altered the performance of the spirituals as well as the sound and the use of the voice. The qualities of the European classical choir were imposed on the music, creating smooth, rounded voices with a unity of sound; in performance, the singers assumed a formal stance, without motion, often with their hands clasped or held at their sides.

The other strand of the tradition of Black American choral singing continued as sacred song in the African American church. Especially in the Baptist, Methodist, and Pentecostal congregations, characteristically African aesthetics were maintained in choral singing. The expression of unity while maintaining the individual voices; the freedom to move the body as it experienced the song; the growth of the song directly out of the sermon rather than as a separate part of the service; the open-endedness that could result in improvisation, changing leads, varying moods and spiritual states of the entire congregation; the nurturing and feeding of the soul; and the unleashing of emotions through the power of sound on the body—these were all part of the work of Black congregational-style singing.

The Black choral tradition brought forth new songs as it preserved old ones. "Jacob's Ladder," "Swing Low, Sweet Chariot," and "Didn't My Lord Deliver Daniel" all kept their places in Black choral music. However, these songs were joined by new songs, such as "Jesus Is My Only Friend," "Let Me Ride, Jesus," and "Jesus Is on the Mainline," that maintained the strong musical and functional link to the older repertoire. Changes came in rhythm, instrumentation, and musical intensity, reflecting the changes occurring as Black people moved from the country to the city.

Spirituals, sprung from an African tradition that has its own standards for the performance and function of music, have served to steady and exalt Africa's people in America and enrich the wider society as well. For here we have a body of music that cannot be grasped solely through discussions of melody, harmony, and rhythm. Neither can we complete the picture by pursuing a strictly sociological discussion of the music's function and the ways in which it reflects the worldview of its creators. Understanding Black American spirituals requires a combined approach: one must study performance styles, musical qualities, and social function.

Spirituals record the struggle of a people to survive, but like no other histories, they also have the power to touch the souls and stir the emotions of the people who sing and hear them. The African American spiritual and its evolution within American society—like a great river shooting off hundreds of tributaries to be joined together somewhere further down the way—give us the richest opportunity to view the tradition in a way that unleashes the powerful human story it holds.

CONGREGATIONAL GOSPELS

During the post–Civil War years, the congregational style of singing was transformed by the new Pentecostal congregations, sometimes known also as Holiness or Sanctified. The style of worship in these churches included congregational singing performance that functioned to bring on "spirit" possession. The ethnomusicologist William Dargan has named the kind of songs used most often during testimony and tarrying services *congregational gospels*. He describes the turn-of-the-century period as a transition from the older slave-based repertoire to the rehearsed gospel song tradition (Dargan 1983).

Horace Clarence Boyer points to the driving cultural force of the Church of God in Christ Pentecostal denomination founded by Bishop Charles Henry Mason of Mississippi. Shout songs like "I'm a Soldier in the Army of the Lord" and the reformulation of the spiritual "My Soul Is a Witness for My Lord" into the overpowering shout "Witness" became staples in Pentecostal congregational-song services. These songs and this new singing with instrumental accompaniment were a departure from the Methodist and Baptist congregational styles. With tambourines and washtub bass, and later piano and other instruments moving as percussive forces in the musical compositions, there were all the fire and potential for invoking possession, a crucial ingredient in Holiness worship practices. Twentieth-century gospel had found its spiritual nurturing ground.

THE COMMUNITY QUARTET TRADITION

The repertoire and European-based performance style of the Black college and university groups greatly influenced the development of community-based quartets. Early groups were called *jubilee quartets*, and they adopted the college repertoire and aesthetic characterized by a smooth, restrained, one-voice style of choral singing. Two of the greatest centers of early quartet tradition were Tidewater, Virginia, influenced by Hampton Institute, giving the world the Golden Gate Jubilee Quartet; and Jefferson County, Alabama, with its connection to the Tuskegee Institute choral tradition (Seroff 1980).

The pioneers of the community-based jubilee quartets began to evolve musically, drawing in more elements from the folk church performance tradition. Shifts also made room for new intense, talented singers: tenors who created new lines that leapt out of the chord with bluesy musical curlicues, and basses who stretched into unconventional bass runs.

In the 1930s, solo leads evolved that mirrored the preaching tradition, and the jubilee quartet became the gospel quartet. This change saw the prolific creation of new songs and arrangement techniques. The 1940s and 1950s saw the top groups gain national followings and move from community-group status to full-time performing and recording artists. They included groups such as the Fairfield Four; the Spirit of Memphis; the Swan Silvertones; the Swanee Quintet; the Nightingales; the Five Blind Boys of Jackson, Mississippi; the Five Blind Boys of Alabama; the Dixie Hummingbirds; the Soul Stirrers; the Harmonizing Four; and the Pilgrim Travelers. This national culture was supported by thousands of local groups who performed the latest popular quartet tunes as well as creating their own. Today this tradition continues, for example, in the modern-jazz pop sounds of Take 6 (Reprise 25670, 25892).

THE PIONEERING COMPOSERS

Congregational and arranged gospel music was greatly advanced by the work of the pioneering gospel music composers. The earliest and most prominent of these composers was the Reverend Charles Albert Tindley. Born around 1851 in the Eastern Shore community of Berlin, Maryland, Tindley was a songwriter, preacher, publisher of songs and sermons, and pivotal force in the development of composed gospel songs. His compositions formed the base upon which the new Black gospel music was developed and influenced all the early gospel music composers: Lucie E. Campbell, Thomas A. Dorsey, Reverend William Herbert Brewster, and Roberta Martin. It is a tribute to his genius that many of today's singers consider his songs an integral part of the treasured pool of African American sacred music. His songs "Stand By Me," "The Storm Is Passing Over," "Nothing Between," "Leave It There," and others have become classics of the Black sacred music tradition and continue to be an important part of African American culture and song repertoire.

Tindley was followed by Lucie E. Campbell of Memphis, Tennessee. Performer, music director, composer, and teacher, Campbell was part of a small but influential group that set the standard for the performance of religious music in the Black Baptist church for over forty years. Her songs became classics within the new music published by the National Baptist Convention, U.S.A., Inc., the largest Black organization in the world, with over six million members. Born in Mississippi to former slaves, Miss Campbell became one of the best known and most influential women in this giant assemblage. Several of her compositions became gospel music classics: "In the Upper Room," made famous by Mahalia Jackson (Columbia C58804); "Jesus Gave Me Water," recorded by the Soul Stirrers (Specialty 802); and "Touch Me, Lord Jesus," a hit by the Angelic Gospel Singers (Mal 4381). Her gospel hymn "He Understands; He'll Say, 'Well Done'" became a funeral song, and her "Something Within" took the 1919 National Baptist Convention by storm and became a standard within the African American sacred music tradition.

Lucie E. Campbell helped create a rich musical environment within this expanding Black Baptist denomination that nurtured the young composers following her. She was a major songwriter and master organizer behind the flowering of the twentieth-century new sacred song.

There was a network among the new composers, and Lucie E. Campbell served as a crucial link. For example, she gave Thomas A. Dorsey, often called the "father of gospel music," his introduction to the National Baptist Convention and its large national audience. Dorsey wrote over one thousand songs. Among his masterpieces are "Peace in the Valley" and "Precious Lord," composed in 1932 as the result of the tragic death of his wife and newborn son.

During the late 1920s Dorsey began to turn to the church and its music. He began adapting blues and jazz rhythms to the writing of sacred verse and coined the term *gospel* to differentiate the new song form from what was the current sacred music.

By 1929, he had published the first gospel song in manuscript form as sheet music, "If You See My Savior." He went on to start his own publishing business and became a pioneer in the concept of selling gospel sheet music. By the mid–1940s, Chicago was the home of several gospel music publishing houses, and Dorsey's was among the best known.

Dorsey and Theodore R. Frye formed the first gospel chorus at the Pilgrim Baptist Church, and in 1932, Dorsey, Frye, and Magnolia Lewis Butts formed the National Convention of Gospel Choirs and Choruses, Inc., the model for all other gospel music conventions. During the 1930s, Dorsey became so famous that gospel songs of the period were known as "Dorseys" (Williams 1985).

In partnership with Sallie Martin and Theodore Frye, Dorsey founded what has been called the "Chicago school of gospel," a community of composers, publishers, and singers that also included Roberta Martin and Kenneth Morris. The Martin-Dorsey team developed gospel choirs in Chicago, Cleveland, on the East Coast, throughout the South, and in California. In 1940, Martin organized the Sallie Martin Singers and began working with Kenneth Morris in the Martin and Morris Publishing House (Martin 1986).

Lucie E. Campbell introduced the work of another gospel pioneer, the Reverend William Herbert Brewster of Memphis, Tennessee, at the National Baptist Convention. During one period, Brewster replaced Campbell as music programmer for the Convention. Brewster's career as composer provides an interesting link between the prolific Chicago community and Memphis. During the forties, Brewster worked with Chicago arrangers Kenneth Morris and Theodore Frye. It was Brewster who gave gospel music its first million-dollar sellers, "Move on up a Little Higher," recorded by Mahalia Jackson (Apollo 164), and "Surely God Is Able," recorded by Clara Ward and the Ward Singers (Savoy 7015).

Reverend William Herbert Brewster was truly a Renaissance figure in the tradition of Charles Albert Tindley and Richard Allen. He served as minister, composer, playwright, historian, educator, and pastor of East Trigg Baptist Church for over fifty years until his death in 1987. One of the most prolific and innovative of the pioneering composers, he wrote songs as a child and continued the practice as he moved into the ministry. He gained wider attention during the thirties as larger audiences heard the new songs he created for his church services, gospel-drama extravaganzas, radio ministry, and community-based performing groups. Through his collaboration with Chicago arrangers Morris and Frye and with Ward Publishing in Philadelphia, his songs became staples in an expanding gospel repertoire and performance circuit. The top names in gospel music came to his church and home in Memphis for his new songs: Queen C. Anderson, a native of Memphis who primarily sang Brewster songs; Mahalia Jackson; the Clara Ward Singers; Sam Cooke of the Soul Stirrers; and Rosetta Tharpe.

Brewster called his gospel songs sermons set to music. His poetic lyricism and his use of the preaching ballad form in the verse form followed by a swinging, thundering call-and-response chorus transformed the classic gospel song genre (Reagon 1983).

It was Roberta Martin who, through the group she founded in 1933, introduced and developed the choral sound for the classic gospel era. The sound was suited for mixed voices, and particularly for female voices. The arrangements were a departure from the *a cappella* quartet with four-part harmony structures. Martin created a choral sound in her ensemble that provided the model sound for the community-based church gospel choir (Williams-Jones 1982).

Martin was one of gospel music's most articulate and influential exponents. Not only did she excel as a singer, pianist, composer, arranger, and organizer of groups and choirs, but she went on to found and operate her own gospel music publishing house in Chicago.

Her first church position was as pianist for the Young People's Choir of Ebenezer Baptist Church. There she worked with Thomas A. Dorsey and Theodore Frye, both of whom helped guide her early career. In 1933, with the help of Dorsey and Frye, she organized the Martin-Frye Quartet. This group evolved into the Roberta Martin Singers in 1936. Until the late 1940s she traveled with the group. She was replaced by her protégée and stepdaughter, Lucy Smith-Collier. The Roberta Martin sound defined an entire era. Her unique combination of musical elements standardized what became known as the classic gospel period.

The Roberta Martin Singers embodied the choral and solo style for the classic era in gospel. This is the period of the great soloists and groups: Mahalia Jackson, Brother Joe May, Alex Bradford, the Clara Ward Singers, the Angelic Gospel Singers, the Famous Caravans, the Davis Sisters, and Madame Edna Gallmon Cooke, to name a few. Many who moved on to great careers in gospel and secular music, such as James Cleveland, Dinah Washington, and Della Reese, were former members of the Roberta Martin Singers, which served as a kind of "university" for talented young musicians coming through Chicago during that period (Reagon 1990a).

Kenneth Morris, a contemporary of Roberta Martin, was a publisher, arranger, and composer and was among the vanguard of musicians who began the evolutionary process that resulted in the major structural and organizational changes that occurred in gospel music during the 1930s and 1940s. Morris entered the publishing business as an arranger with the Lillian M. Bowles Music House in 1936. As an arranger he has over three thousand songs to his credit. While publishing, Morris composed his first gospel composition, "I'll Be a Servant for the Lord," which was recorded by the Wings over Jordan Choir. Some of his other compositions include "Dig a Little Deeper in God's Love" and "Yes, God Is Real."

CONTEMPORARY GOSPEL MUSIC

Today, the struggles of the gospel pioneers bear fruit as gospel enters a new era. If one visits virtually any American college with Black students on campus, one will find a gospel choir. The first college-based gospel choir was started at Howard University in 1965 by a group of brilliant musicians—Henry Davis, Wesley Boyd, and Richard Smallwood, all music majors who had been forbidden to play their music in the university's music practice rooms. Changes came only after Black students insisted on a curriculum that acknowledged the presence and contribution of African Americans and a revision in the treatment of African and African-based history and traditions, including gospel music.

It was during this period that Edwin Hawkins's recording of "Oh Happy Day" became a crossover hit. Contemporary gospel music dominated by choirs found a new place in the congregations and schools other than the Baptist and Pentecostal denominations, such as the Catholic, Episcopal, and Presbyterian churches, as well as Ivy League institutions like Harvard and Yale. The style is marked by a blend of classic gospel sound with Euroclassical and jazz ingredients in the accompaniment and voicings.

The Richard Smallwood Singers, with their (three) soprano voicings grounded by lower alto, tenor, and baritone lines, produce a choral effect that sounds like a Pentecostal shout. All of this vocal work is driven, enveloped, and caressed by a virtuoso piano accompaniment. Smallwood, a pioneer in the contemporary gospel sound, continues the network begun with Tindley and stretching through the Chicago school, for Roberta Martin and her protégée Lucy Collier-Smith greatly influenced his gospel piano style (Reagon 1990a).

Contemporary gospel is paced today by names such as the Clark Sisters, Vanessa Bell, Andrae Crouch, Jessy Dixon, Take 6, the Bobby Jones Singers, and the Winans and the Hawkins dynasties, gospel music families with a number of siblings—the Winans, Bebe and Cece; the Hawkinses, Edwin, Walter, and Tremaine. These composers and performers are charting a new course for gospel music, pushing the boundaries of secular and sacred song, exploring new ways to create blends of African-based and European-based musical elements, and achieving access to widening audiences beyond worship congregations.

Even as these newer sounds make their way across territory which in the past was reserved for secular music, the traditional gospel music audiences are demanding a continuance of the classic styles. Thus, for example, there is a resurgence in the careers of singers who learned their style of performance from the Martin Singers.

African American gospel song continues to be a strong community-based tradition with an expanding influence on the larger music culture. It is compelling because it communicates the determination and steadfastness of its creators. Into our songs, we African Americans have worked the full range and intensity of our legacy in this land that made us slaves. Into our singing, we have forged the sounds of a people of resolute spirit and fortitude in this land that debated our worth as human beings. Our singing tradition announces the presence of our community. It is a way in which we nurture and heal ourselves. It is an offering to the celebration of life and the lifting of the spirit.

THE IMPACT OF GOSPEL MUSIC ON THE SECULAR MUSIC INDUSTRY

Portia K. Maultsby

I've had a lot of offers to stop singing gospel and take up singing jazz and blues, but blues and jazz just aren't me. —ALBERTINA WALKER

Many of the past gospel hits of the [Staple Singers] crossed over into the pop charts, which is just another indication of the common roots from which black music sprang. —"SPECIAL EDITION"

Crossing over from gospel to pop wasn't hard because it was just a matter of changing words. —LOU RAWLS

Since the 1930s, Black gospel music has loomed from its status as the exclusive property of storefront African American churches to become a dynamic and viable force in the commercial music industry. It became an economic commodity in secular contexts when its performers were broadcast over network and independent radio stations; recorded by independent record companies; and showcased in large concert halls, coliseums, theaters, jazz festivals, and nightclubs. The exposure and acceptance of gospel music outside the sanctuaries of Black churches simultaneously expanded its consumer market and led to its appropriation by purveyors of secular idioms. The infectious rhythms, melismatic melodies, complex harmonies, call–response structures, and compelling character of this music permeate the vinyl of various popular music styles. Even the gospel message could not be contained within the walls of the Black church as former gospel singers rerecorded gospel songs under rhythm and blues, soul, and pop labels. While serving as a catalyst for new popular music styles, gospel music propelled the growth of a post–World War II, multibillion-dollar secular music industry. This essay will examine the commercialization of gospel music and its transformation into popular song.

THE COMMERCIALIZATION OF GOSPEL MUSIC

In a 1979 article on contemporary gospel music, scholar-performer Horace Clarence Boyer posed a question that continues to be debated among African American church congregations: "Is it possible that one day gospel music will no longer belong to the church?" (Boyer 1979a, 6). Eight years later, *Billboard* published a report on the status of gospel music that indirectly addressed the issue: "Perhaps the biggest news in gospel music this year [1987] is the stunning growth and wider acceptance of black gospel music. No longer an esoteric cultural phenomenon, it is now presented in many styles and is quickly becoming another popular form of black music without losing any of its message" ("Black Gospel: Rocketing to Higher Prominence" 1987, G–6). While this commentary accurately assesses the growth of a non-Christian and cross-cultural consumer market for Black gospel music, it totally misinterprets the continued existence of gospel as both a religious and a cultural phenomenon.

Over the last seventy years, gospel music has evolved from the improvised singing of congregations and from the traditional styles of Thomas A. Dorsey, William Herbert Brewster, Lucie Campbell, and Roberta Martin to the contemporary sounds of quartets, choirs, small groups, and ensembles. The coexistence and popularity of these diverse gospel styles among African American Christians and non-Christians suggest that gospel continues to be a vital form of expression in the African American community. In a study on gospel music, ethnomusicologist Mellonee Burnim concluded that "Gospel is not just a musical exercise; it is a process of esoteric sharing and affirmation. It is more than the beat; it is more than the movement; it even embodies much more than text, harmonies or instrumental accompaniment. All of these factors and others intertwine to produce a genre which represents a uniquely Black perspective, one which manifests itself in a cogent, dynamic cultural philosophy or world view" (Burnim 1988, 112). Gospel music therefore is a complex form that embodies the religious, cultural, historical, and social dimensions of Black life in America. The current misinterpretation about the religious and cultural significance of this tradition emanates from the exploitation of gospel music as an economic commodity.

Gospel music has been expropriated and used by the music industry to generate new consumer markets, giving rise to new functions and performing contexts. Repackaged and promoted as entertainment to a cross-cultural and non-Christian audience in non-traditional arenas, the spiritual message and cultural aesthetic of gospel were subordinated to the money-making interest of the music industry.

From the 1930s through the 1960s, performances of gospel music were held primarily at religious events in churches and in public venues for African American audiences. During this time, media exposure ranged from fifteen- and twenty-minute broadcasts on general-market radio to one to three hours of daily programs on Black-formatted radio stations. Over the last two decades, gospel music experienced an explosion on many levels. Its audiences have become multiracial in composition. It is broadcast on full-time gospel-formatted stations and on religious television programs. Its performers are featured

The Roberta Martin Singers Reunion Concert Series, Smithsonian Institution, Baird Auditorium, February 1981. In the foreground: Eugene Smith, narrator.

Above: Smithsonian Institution colloquium panel on Reverend Charles Albert Tindley. Left to right: Reverend Marion Ballard, Reverend Henry Nichols, and Library of Congress music librarian Wayne Shirley. **Right:** Actor Avery Brooks as Reverend Charles Albert Tindley during Smithsonian-produced drama on Tindley's music. **Opposite top:** Fisk Jubilee Singers, 1871. (Photograph from the Fisk University Library, Fisk University, Nashville, Tennessee.) **Opposite middle:** The Sterling Jubilees of Bessemer, Jefferson County, Alabama, a community-based quartet whose history dates back to the 1930s, when they also performed as the CIO Singers. (Photograph by Cherly T. Evans, courtesy of Doug Seroff.) **Opposite bottom:** The Richard Smallwood Singers, nationally renowned contemporary gospel ensemble based in Washington, D.C. (Courtesy of Richard Smallwood.)

Above: Rosetta Tharpe was featured with Lucky Millinder and his orchestra during the late 1930s and 1940s. (Courtesy of Portia Maultsby.) **Left:** Mahalia Jackson, Newport Jazz Festival, Newport, Rhode Island, July 1956. (Frank Driggs Collection.) **Opposite above and below:** Clara Ward at the Newport Jazz Festival, Newport, Rhode Island, 1957. Duke Ellington is in the background of the photo above. (Photographs by Joe Alper, courtesy of Jackie Gibson Alper.)

Above: Dicky Freeman, phenomenal bass of the legendary Fairfield Four quartet, featured at Smithsonian Institution conference on quartet tradition, November 1982. The group dates back to the 1930s, and it built a national reputation through its 1940s live radio broadcasts. **Right:** The Orioles, a popular rhythm-and-blues vocal group that evolved its sound from the gospel jubilee quartets. (Courtesy of Portia Maultsby.)

Above left: When Aretha Franklin moved from singing gospel songs in her father's church to singing secular love songs, her sound remained gospel. (Courtesy of Portia Maultsby.) **Above right:** Dinah Washington performed with Lionel Hampton and Band. (Publicity photograph, courtesy of Portia Maultsby.) **Right:** Lavern Baker, circa 1960. (Courtesy of Portia Maultsby.)

Left: Ray Charles moved the gospel sound fully into the world of popular secular music, and this evolution became known as "soul." (Courtesy of Portia Maultsby.) **Below left**: Promotional flyer for radio station WLOU, Louisville, 1952. Schedule illustrates how gospel was juxtaposed with rhythm-and-blues programming. (Courtesy of the Department of Afro-American Studies, Indiana University–Bloomington.)

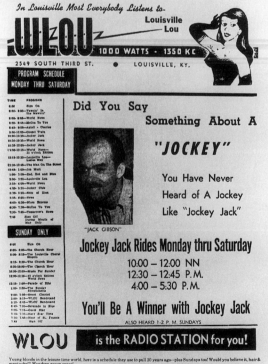

Reverend Charles Albert Tindley, United Methodist minister and gospel hymn composer. (Courtesy of Tindley Temple United Methodist Church, Philadelphia.)

Tindley Temple, 750–762 South Broad Street, Philadelphia. (Courtesy of Dr. J. Edward Hoy, Organist-Director, Tindley Temple United Methodist Church, Philadelphia.)

Top: Kenneth Goodman, organist of international acclaim and Tindley Temple member. Goodman was baptized by Reverend Tindley and on this occasion played the organ for the first time. (Courtesy of Kenneth Goodman.) **Above:** The Tindley Gospel Singers: J. B. Henry, A. G. Henry, E. J. Tindley, D. C. Wright, R. E. Hackett, N. Lockley, ca. 1920. (Courtesy of Tindley Temple United Methodist Church, Philadelphia.)

Ralph Jones, lifetime member of Tindley Temple and biographer of Reverend Charles Albert Tindley, 1980. (Courtesy of Ralph Jones.)

Reverend Marion Ballard, former pastor of Tindley Temple, at the Smithsonian conference on Tindley, 1983.

Reverend Henry Nichols, United Methodist minister who grew up in Tindley Temple, at the Smithsonian conference on Tindley, 1983.

Unidentified sculptor, left, and Reverend Charles Albert Tindley, with bust of Tindley. (Courtesy of Tindley Temple United Methodist Church, Philadelphia.)

Lucie E. Campbell, gospel music composer, national Baptist church leader, and teacher. (Courtesy of Luvenia George.)

Above: J. Robert Bradley, baritone, music director of the National Baptist Convention, began his career as student and protégé of Lucie E. Campbell. **Right:** Lucie E. Campbell's wedding picture. She married Reverend C. R. Williams in 1960 at the age of seventy-five. (Courtesy of Luvenia George.)

Top: Booker T. Washington High School, Memphis, where Lucie E. Campbell taught American history and English for over fifty years. (Courtesy of Booker T. Washington High School, Memphis.) **Above:** Lucie E. Campbell, far left, first row, as advisor to the Crown and Scepter Club, Booker T. Washington High School, Memphis, 1945. (Courtesy of Booker T. Washington High School, Memphis.)

in music festivals, with symphony orchestras, and on recordings of popular music; major concerts are jointly sponsored by record companies and national advertisers. Additionally, gospel recordings, once available only in African American "mom and pop" record shops and at performance sites, are now found in mainstream retail outlets.

Many of these trends were precipitated by the crossover appeal of the gospel song "Oh Happy Day," recorded in 1968 by the Edwin Hawkins Singers. When Hawkins recorded his gospel arrangement of the hymn "Oh Happy Day," he unwittingly opened the doors for the commercial exploitation of gospel music. The song, laced with elements from contemporary Black popular styles, was programmed as gospel and soul music on Black-oriented radio and as pop on Top 40 stations. A graduate student at the time, I remember hearing the remarks of an African American DJ when he introduced the song on WVON, a soul music radio station in Chicago: "Here's a new song climbing the charts. I don't know what to call it. It sounds like gospel and it sounds like soul. Whatever it is, the beat has a groove. I like it and I'm gonna play it." The message, aesthetic, danceable beat, and contemporary sound of "Oh Happy Day" made it accessible to a diverse audience.

Through mass-media exposure, gospel music slowly penetrated every artery of American life, linking the sacred and secular domains of the African American community, breathing life into new secular forms, and bringing flair and distinction to the American stage of entertainment.

GOSPEL MUSIC IN SECULAR CONTEXTS

Local Communities and Public Venues

The seeds for the commercialization of gospel music were planted in the 1930s when its performers were showcased in a variety of nonreligious settings. Gospel quartets were the first to garner a secular following by performing at local community events, on radio broadcasts, and on commercial records. Evolving out of jubilee quartets in the 1930s, they expanded their repertoire of Negro spirituals to include secular songs and a new body of religious music known as gospel. By the 1940s, the songs of pioneering gospel composers Thomas A. Dorsey, Theodore Frye, William Herbert Brewster, Kenneth Morris, Lucie E. Campbell, and Roberta Martin had become standard repertoire in jubilee-gospel quartet performances. Members of quartets occupied a unique position in African American community life, functioning as both evangelists and entertainers for activities sponsored by Black churches, schools, and social clubs, and by white businesses (Seroff 1980). Kerill Rubman, in his study of gospel music, comments on the widespread popularity of these quartets: "Factory and construction workers, porters, and other employees sang in company or union-affiliated quartets, performing at picnics, parties, dances, and other business or community events. Family members formed quartets. Negro colleges continued to sponsor such groups, and Baptist and Methodist churches often formed male quartets to sing sacred music at worship services and evening programs" (Lornell 1988, 18). Some local quartets developed regional and national reputations that led to a change in their status. As regional "stars" in the 1930s, they toured while maintaining full-time jobs, but by the mid–1940s, several were touring the country as full-time professional musicians (Lornell 1988, 64–78).

Gospel quartets initially performed for Black audiences. But as the gospel sound spread through radio broadcasts in the 1920s, gospel music found its way into public venues traditionally reserved for America's white bourgeoisie. Jazz critic and record producer John Hammond organized a musical extravaganza, "From Spirituals to Swing," that featured performances of blues, jazz, spirituals, and gospel music. Staged in 1938 in Carnegie Hall, Hammond selected Mitchell's Christian Singers and Sister Rosetta Tharpe to render spirituals and gospel songs, respectively. According to Hammond, "Except for one fleeting appearance at the Cotton Club, she [Tharpe] had never sung anywhere except in Negro churches. She was a surprise smash; knocked the people out. Her singing showed an affinity between gospel and jazz that all fans could recognize and appreciate" (Hammond and Townsend 1981, 203). The success of this concert and favorable reviews by music critics resulted in the staging of a second "Spirituals to Swing" concert in 1939 that featured the Golden Gate Jubilee Quartet (Hammond and Townsend 1981, 231).

During the 1950s, Hammond seized other opportunities to expose gospel singing to white America. Serving on the board of the Newport Jazz Festival, he was determined to obliterate musical and racial segregation from the nation's social fabric. To this end, Mahalia Jackson was invited to perform at the Festival. According to Hammond, "[Mahalia] gave the Festival a great boost of respectability in 1956 by her unprecedented appearance and glorious singing at a Sunday morning service in Newport's unassailably white Trinity Episcopal Church" (Hammond and Townsend 1981, 339). One year later, Clara Ward and the Ward Singers appeared on the stage of the Newport Jazz Festival, and, in 1958, Mahalia Jackson was featured again.

The cross-cultural appeal of gospel and its growing popularity across religious and social boundaries in African American communities were observed by enterprising individuals who quickly seized the opportunity to cash in on its message, musical sound, and cultural aesthetic. Facilitated by promotional strategies of the secular music industry, gospel music emerged as big business. In the 1950s, many singers became full-time performers, appearing in major concert halls, large theaters, auditoriums, and stadiums before audiences averaging twenty-five thousand or more throughout the United States and in Europe. Some performers witnessed their income rise from church free-will offerings of unpredictable amounts to actual performance fees of two to five thousand dollars. Music critic Richard Gehman noted in 1958 that "gospel singers have forged their art into a business now grossing, in the estimate of New York promoter Joe Bostic, around $15 million annually" (Gehman 1958, 113). These performances, supported by radio broadcasts and record sales, firmly entrenched gospel music in the secular fabric of Black community life. Succinctly stated by Horace Clarence Boyer, "The Black American who had never discovered gospel music, or who had simply decided to deny it for whatever reason, began to support it—not in the church, but in places outside the church" (Boyer 1979a, 9). Walter Grady, promoter for Malaco Records, which specializes in gospel and blues, further elaborates, "Most [Black] non-church goers and non-Christians can be responsive [to gospel] because of their upbringing. Once, all of us were kids and you heard gospel in the home every Sunday and maybe blues two days a week [on the radio]. . . . When you were brought up on gospel it's very hard to get away from it" (Maultsby 1990a).

For whatever reason—its spiritual message, musical sound, or cultural aesthetic—gospel music had a magnetic effect on people, especially Black people. The music industry, in recognizing the power of this music, explored various strategies to market gospel as an entertainment commodity. One approach was to showcase gospel singers in nightclubs and theaters traditionally reserved for performances of jazz, blues, and rhythm and blues music. Sister Rosetta Tharpe appears to be the first gospel singer to sing in such nontraditional public arenas. Singing and playing the electric guitar with Lucky Millinder's band in the late 1930s and 1940s, she performed Thomas Dorsey's "Hide Me in Thy Bosom" under the title "Rock Me," which she recorded in 1939 with Millinder's band (MCA 1357).

Prompted by John Hammond, during the early 1940s, the Golden Gate Jubilee Quartet and the Dixie Hummingbirds joined Tharpe as singers of gospel music performing in nightclubs (Tallmadge 1974, 14; Salvo and Salvo 1974, 62). Such performances, however, were rare among gospel performers, since the Black church considered this activity blasphemous and, therefore, inappropriate (Hentoff 1963, 46). Even so, gospel music resurfaced in nightclubs during the following decades.

In the mid–1950s and early 1960s, Clara Ward and Della Reese, who performed at various times with Mahalia Jackson, the Clara Ward Singers, and the Roberta Martin Singers, were among the few gospel singers (including Bessie Griffin, the Dixie Hummingbirds, the Nathaniel Lewis Singers, and Howard Saunders) who accepted offers to perform in nightclubs and theaters. Surrounded by criticism from gospel performers, ministers, and the Black community, both Ward and Reese defended their position. Ward maintained that her mission was to evangelize rather than entertain: "Although perhaps there are many people who would not share my feelings on the subject, I now feel that God intended for his message to be heard in song not solely by those who attend churches, but also by the outsiders who in many cases never attend a house of worship. For that reason the Ward Singers and I have taken our gospel singing into the Apollo Theater in New York . . . [and into clubs in Las Vegas]" (Ward 1956, 16). Della Reese, to the contrary, declared that her performances with the Meditation Singers at New York's Copacabana served only an entertainment purpose: "We are not presented as holy singers; we are there to show that gospel is interesting music. We don't perform in night clubs to save souls." She also acknowledged that financial considerations played a role in her decision to perform gospel in nightclubs: "I like a comfortable apartment, a healthy bank account and some good solid real estate" ("Gospel to Pop to Gospel" 1962, 107, 110).

Despite lucrative offers for nightclub appearances, many gospel singers refused. Mahalia Jackson declared, "It's not the place for my kind of singing" (Gehman 1958, 114), and James Cleveland, in agreement, revealed, "I don't feel I can do much good in a club.

I don't feel that the atmosphere is conducive, and I don't feel that the reason for bringing me there is the reason for which I am singing" (Lucas 1972, 21). Rejections from established gospel singers and the objections of African American ministers and members of the African American community, however, did not dissuade enterprising club owners from exploring alternative marketing strategies. A new twist to an old concept was the establishment of "gospel nightclubs." The May 18, 1963 and May 24, 1963 issues of *Billboard* and *Time*, respectively, reported that one such club called Sweet Chariot opened in Manhattan. Although the targeted clientele was America's white teenagers, marketing techniques proved insulting, demeaning, and contradictory to the mores of Black people. Restrooms were labeled *Brothers* and *Sisters*, and waitresses dressed as angels served alcoholic beverages during performances of gospel music. Curious patrons nevertheless filled the club to capacity, prompting the owner to announce plans to open similar clubs in Chicago, San Francisco, and Los Angeles (Hentoff 1963, 46).

Within two years, declining clientele and continued criticism from the African American community influenced the closing of some of these clubs, but not before Columbia Records recorded and repackaged gospel as a "popular" music genre. Convinced that this "new" music would rebound sagging record sales, a Columbia executive proclaimed, "It's the greatest new groove since rock 'n' roll. In a month or two, it'll be all over the charts" ("Gospel Singers: Pop up, Sweet Chariot" 1963, 48). Although Columbia's recordings did not make the charts (see Williams 1963 for a review of the recordings), its executive accurately assessed the future impact of gospel music on the pop music field. Aided by radio, gospel redefined the sound, beat, and stylings of popular music.

Gospel Music on Radio

Radio became the major source of entertainment in the 1920s. Even though its programming was targeted at middle-class white America, the gospel singing of Sanctified and Baptist storefront congregations traveled the airwaves through the Sunday morning broadcast of church services. By the late 1930s, live performances of gospel quartets, including the Southernaires, the Golden Gate Jubilee Quartet, Mitchell's Christian Singers, the Fairfield Four, the Swan Silvertones, and the Selah Jubilee Singers, had become integral to many formats. These fifteen- and twenty-minute daily or weekly broadcasts proliferated during the 1940s and 1950s in response to the growth of postwar urban African American populations (Lornell 1988, 22–26; Spaulding 1981, 101–8).

Controlling a multibillion-dollar economy, African Americans became a major consumer group at a time when the white radio audience was declining. The advent and growing popularity of television redefined the position of radio as the primary entertainment medium. Struggling to survive, radio stations experimented with programming in search of new audiences. Many expanded their Black programming, while others revamped their formats to become full-time Black-oriented stations. For example, in 1943 "only four stations throughout the country were programming specifically for blacks, [but] ten years later, 260 stations were attracting national and local sponsors to their broadcasts" (MacDonald 1979, 366). By 1961, over 310 stations "devoted some portion of their programming to black interests, about 70 of which geared at least 10 hours of air time, each week, in this area. Slightly more than half of those 70 aimed all their programming at the black [sic] community. [At the close of the decade], at least 65 outlets were geared entirely to black [sic] audiences" (Garnett 1970).

The proliferation of Black programming formats increased the exposure of gospel music. Jack Gibson, a DJ on Chicago's WJJD (a general-market station) from 1947 to 1949, recalled that gospel programs aired daily "for about an hour, 9:00–10:00 A.M. Everybody's gone to work and the woman left at home wants to settle down before she starts into housework. So she would listen to the gospel music" (Maultsby 1979).

As gospel music's audience grew by leaps and bounds during the 1950s, so did its programming on stations with an all-Black format. Birmingham's WEDR and Houston's KYOK, for example, featured two gospel music programs daily for two and three hours, respectively. On Sundays, both stations broadcast Black church services and live performances of gospel music (Maultsby 1990b, 1990c). This programming format also characterized gospel music broadcasts throughout the 1960s. The April 1962 programming schedule of Atlanta's WERD, the nation's first Black-owned and -operated radio station, for example, lists two daily gospel music programs. The first one, "Gospel Gems," aired from 6:15 to 7:30 A.M., and "The Gospel Train" from 3:05 to 4:05 P.M., the latter replaced by "Old Ship of Zion" on Saturdays and broadcast from 4:30 P.M. until the station went off the air at sunset. Sunday's format was entirely religious—church services and a variety of religious music programs.

Most radio stations targeted at African American communities were low powered (two hundred fifty to ten thousand watts) and licensed to broadcast from sunrise to sunset. Nashville's WLAC was an exception. It was a fifty-thousand-watt CBS affiliate station whose power catapulted its evening Black music programs to several regions in the United States, Canada, the Caribbean islands, and, via shortwave radio, to New Zealand, Europe, and North Africa. Before these programs were launched in 1946, the station served as the radio home from 1939 to 1951 for the gospel quartet the Fairfield Four. This group enjoyed wide exposure through their fifteen-minute morning broadcast, which was recorded and syndicated to other stations (Landes 1987, 68). When WLAC instituted its evening programs of Black music, gospel was included only in the advertising of "record specials" offered through mail-order outlets that sponsored the programs. This arrangement juxtaposed gospel with rhythm and blues and blues records, blurring the lines between sacred and secular and making gospel music available to both religious and nonreligious audiences.

Black-formatted stations began competing with general-market radio for national advertisers in the late 1960s and early 1970s. Scrambling to increase market ratings by diversifying their listening audience, these stations either rescheduled their daily broadcast of gospel music to 5:00–7:00 A.M. or discontinued the programs altogether. Black religious services and gospel music nevertheless continued to dominate Sunday programming (Maultsby 1990c). When most Black-oriented stations abated their gospel music programs, WLAC ironically instituted its first gospel show since 1951, when the Fairfield

Four went off the air. WLAC's DJ William "Hoss" Allen launched and hosted a four-hour gospel program in 1971, known as "Early Morning Gospel Time," that aired 1:00–5:00 A.M. daily. Recalling the show's rise from its humble beginnings, Allen commented, "I knew so many record companies that had gospel and didn't know what to do with it. They had no exposure. So I called four record companies and sold them two hours and forty-five minutes [of advertising time]. That's how the gospel [program] started. It got bigger, bigger and bigger until it was as big as the blues had been, because nobody was playing gospel for four hours at a time anywhere, every night, five hours on the weekend. Well, it became the biggest gospel show in the country" (Maultsby 1984a). Allen's listening audience was diverse, including night-shift employees, truck drivers, "dyed-in-the-wool gospel fans, . . . a lot of shut-ins and people who have trouble sleeping and are just laying in bed all day and they lay awake all night" (Landes 1987, 75).

Radio was instrumental in expanding the listening audience for both gospel and rhythm and blues. The early practice of juxtaposing the two forms exposed their affinity. Among the churchgoing gospel fans who once distanced themselves from "sinful" music, some demonstrated tolerance, while others became consumers of rhythm and blues without relinquishing their loyalty to gospel music. Similarly, many "sinners" came to appreciate gospel music, identifying with its aesthetic and even its spiritual message. The experiences of Walter Grady, a record promoter and former record retailer, graphically illustrate this point: "I've even seen situations when I owned a record store where 'winos' would come in with a six-pack of beer under one arm and a bottle of wine in one hand, buy two blues records and two gospel records which means they were going to party but they still were going to give a few minutes of listening to God's music which was gospel music" (Maultsby 1990a).

Throughout the 1970s, gospel music took a back seat to the hegemonic programming of Black popular music. During this decade, Black-formatted radio stations concentrated on improving market ratings, attracting crossover audiences, and courting national advertisers. But in the 1980s, gospel music resurfaced as a viable commercial product, giving rise to several full-time gospel-formatted stations. The expanding consumer market for gospel music generated by radio and live performances created a demand for gospel records.

Gospel Music on Record

During the developing years (late 1940s–50s) of full-time, Black-oriented radio stations, DJs were challenged with the task of finding records to play. The unprecedented demand for Black music exceeded the supply. Mail-order record shops that sponsored Black music radio programs frequently ran out of stock. Retailers, in an effort to replenish their supply, went "all over the country trying to buy Black records and there weren't a whole lot" (Maultsby 1984a). This shortage was triggered by government restrictions on the use of shellac during the second World War, the 1942–44 ban on recording stemming from a musicians' strike, and the small number of record companies specializing in Black music.

The first recordings of Black religious music were issued during the first decade of the twentieth century. Beginning in the 1920s, major and independent companies marketed the music of African American preachers and their congregations and jubilee quartets under the label of "race music" (Oliver 1984). Religious music represented one-third of the five hundred race records issued in 1927 and about one-fourth of those released during each of the next three years (Dixon and Godrich 1970, 57). The Depression years severely curtailed the recording of race music. Many companies folded, and the few that remained in business limited their involvement in gospel music to reissuing previously recorded material and recording jubilee-gospel quartets and such established performers as Mahalia Jackson and Rosetta Tharpe.

The recording industry resumed full-scale production after the war years, but many of the companies that once specialized in race music chose to abandon this field. The demand for Black music nevertheless persisted. Responding to this demand, local entrepreneurs formed independent record companies and became the primary producers of postwar Black music. Some of these companies, including Savoy, Apollo, Specialty, Peacock, Nashboro, and Vee-Jay, developed an impressive catalogue of gospel music that supported the programming efforts of radio. Although major companies largely ignored gospel music during the first four decades after the war, they joined the gospel bandwagon in the 1980s. Aware of the cross-cultural popularity of this music and its pervasive influence on popular styles, they teamed up with independent companies to record and distribute gospel music. Radio, in turn, became a promotional tool for these companies and the growing number of gospel music promoters. Forming a national network, record companies, radio stations, retail outlets, and promoters brought unprecedented exposure to gospel music. The demand for the gospel sound and its beat led to the appropriation of this music by purveyors of popular styles.

The Transformation of Gospel into Popular Song

Paralleling the rise of gospel music was the growth of a teenage consumer market for popular music. African American teenagers, who served their musical apprenticeship performing in church choirs and in professional gospel groups, were lured into the more lucrative field of popular music. Gospel singer Albertina Walker contends that even though gospel music became "big business," it was "a good money-making business for everybody except the singer" (Banks 1974a, 74). Gospel singer-minister Reverend Cleophus Robinson noted that crooked managers, promoters, and record companies exploited "the art and its artists for the money, then put very little money back into the art to strengthen it and make it more popular" (Banks 1974b, 65). Rather than reinvest in the form, the industry capitalized on the popularity of the gospel sound, offering gospel singers money and other perks to switch to blues, jazz, and rhythm and blues. Savoy Records, for example, offered Clara Ward ten thousand dollars to become a blues singer ("Clara Ward . . . Gospel Singer" 1953, 38). She and others declined such offers, but some defected and transformed gospel into various popular music styles—rhythm and blues, soul, funk, and other contemporary forms. Beginning in 1949, *Billboard* used the term *rhythm and blues* to identify all post–World War II forms of Black popular music. In 1969, this term was changed to *soul*. Through the 1970s, soul music was transformed into funk and disco.

Among the first gospel singers to establish successful careers as rhythm and blues artists were soloists Sister Rosetta Tharpe and Dinah Washington and quartets including the Delta Rhythm Boys (formerly the Hampton Institute Quartet); the Larks (formerly the Selah Jubilee Singers); a gospel group led by Billy Ward and renamed the Dominoes; and the Isley Brothers. They and others found the transition from gospel to rhythm and blues to be "just a matter of changing the words," as Lou Rawls notes (Shearer 1983). All of the components—sound construct, interpretative devices, and performance style—that define the gospel tradition are found in its secular counterparts.

Rhythm and blues vocal groups had a religious sound, according to Diz Russell, a vocalist with the Orioles, because they imitated instruments in a manner popularized by gospel-jubilee quartets, and they duplicated the "straight-up" harmonies heard in church. This harmonic structure places the bass on the bottom to accentuate the chord. Russell adds, "A floating tenor, which comes in and out, carries the chord up and down. The baritone remains in the middle of the chord and sings a straight part" (Maultsby 1984b). Through their immersion in African American church culture at a very young age, emerging musicians not only learn fundamental musical concepts but also master aesthetic principles essential to Black music performance.

Soul-disco performer Candi Staton, for example, recalls her first performance at a Baptist church at age five and the responses of the congregation: "I sang and those people started shouting, really getting involved in what I was doing and that frightened me more than my singing because I didn't know why they were shouting. I didn't understand the feelings that they felt" (Shearer 1981). Having a similar experience singing a solo in an AME church choir at age eight, disco performer Donna Summer reminisces, "the people started crying and it scared me that I could touch people and they were moved by something that I had that was intangible. It gave me an incredible sense of power" (Shearer 1982).

Staton and Summer were too young to comprehend why people "shouted" and "cried," but a review of a concert by soul singer Aretha Franklin provides an explanation while revealing the affinity between performances of gospel and Black popular styles:

At every show I wondered what it was—that very special thing she was always able to get going with an audience. Sometimes there were 16,000 people in a sports arena and Aretha would be working on stage, doing *Dr. Feelgood* [sic] and then *Spirit in the Dark* [sic], and it seemed that all 16,000 people would become involved in a kind of spiritual thing with her, sort of like what must have happened on the Day of Pentecost, and those people—all kinds: dudes, sisters in Afros and those in blonde wigs, even church-looking people—would start moving with the music, and as Aretha took them higher and higher some of them would scream and jump up on their seats, and even men like 50 and 60 years old would run down to the stage and try to touch her. (Sanders 1971, 126)

Aretha's performance transformed the concert hall into a type of spiritual celebration—one similar to that of an African American worship service in which the preacher and gospel singers engage in verbal and physical exchanges with the congregation. Gospel music scholar and performer Pearl Williams-Jones accurately observes that "in seeking to communicate the gospel message, there is little difference between the gospel singer and the gospel preacher in the approach to his subject. The same techniques are used by the preacher and the singer—the singer perhaps being considered the lyrical extension of the rhythmically rhetorical style of the preacher" (Williams-Jones 1975, 381).

Aretha revealed to music critic Phyl Garland that her vocal style was influenced by the preaching techniques employed by her father (Garland 1969, 199). This singer–preacher link is described by Aretha's brother, the Reverend Cecil Franklin:

You listen to her and it's just like being in church. She does with her voice exactly what a preacher does with his when he *moans* to a congregation. That moan strikes a responsive chord in the congregation and somebody answers you back with their own moan, which means I know what you're moaning about because I feel the same way. So you have something sort of like a thread spinning out and touching and tieing [*sic*] everybody together in a shared experience just like the getting happy and shouting together in church. (Sanders 1971, 126)

As Aretha moans a meaningful message to her audience,

She leans her head back, forehead gleaming with perspiration, features twisted by her intensity, and her voice—plangent and supple—pierces the hall:

> Oh baby, what you done to me . . .
> You make me feel, you make me feel,
> You make me feel like a natural woman.

"Tell it like it is," her listeners exhort, on their feet, clapping and cheering. ("Lady Soul: Singing It Like It Is" 1968, 62)

Aretha's masterful display of vocal dexterity and her down-home, foot-stomping, intense and demonstrative performance style continue a tradition popularized in the 1950s by Big Maybelle, Big Mama Thornton, James Brown, Little Richard, Jackie Wilson, and the Dominoes. In the 1960s, this style defined performances of the Isley Brothers, Wilson Pickett, Gene Chandler, Otis Redding, and Sam and Dave. While this performance style prevails in rhythm and blues and its derivative forms, it represents only one dimension of the gospel sound in Black popular music.

The gospel sound encompasses many vocal styles and timbres. It ranges from the lyrical, semiclassical, and tempered style of Roberta Martin, Alex Bradford, Inez Andrews, and Sara Jordan Powell to the percussive and shouting approach of Sallie Martin, Archie Brownlee, Albertina Walker, Clara Ward, and Norsalus McKissick. Many singers, including Mahalia Jackson, Marion Williams, and the Barrett Sisters, employ components from both styles in their performances. This range of stylistic possibilities has brought variety to the Black popular tradition.

The vocal style of many rhythm and blues and soul singers, for example, is more lyrical and tempered than that of Aretha. Among the exponents of this style are the Orioles, Little Anthony and the Imperials, the Impressions, Roy Hamilton, Sam Cooke, Jerry Butler, Brook Benton, Smokey Robinson, O. C. Smith, Isaac Hayes, Dinah Washington, Dionne Warwick, the Jones Girls, and Deniece Williams. The church roots of their lyrical and tempered style and the way it differs from the percussive and foot-stomping approach of Aretha Franklin and others are explained by Shirley Jones of the Jones Girls: "Our sound was developed primarily by singing in church with our mother. Even though we are [former] gospel singers, we are not the foot-stomping, down-home gospel type singers. We are more the subdued side of it. Very soft voices . . ." (Maultsby 1983a). Deniece Williams also acknowledges that, despite her upbringing in the Church of God in Christ, her style is not "the same deliverance as Aretha or Mahalia Jackson, [but] you feel it. I've had a lot of people say [when] you sing it, I feel it. I think that feeling comes from those experiences of church and gospel music and spirituality which play a big role in my life" (Maultsby 1983b).

That "feeling" experienced by Williams's audiences results from her subtle use of aesthetic principles associated with gospel music. Regardless of vocal style employed, singers of popular idioms use a wide range of aesthetic devices in interpreting songs: melismas, slides, bends, moans, shouts, grunts, hollers, screams, melodic and textual repetition, extreme registers, call–response structures, and so on. Dinah Washington, a protégée of Roberta Martin, was a master in the subtle manipulation of timbre, shading, time, pitch, and text. Her trademark sound echoes the vocal control, timing ("lagging behind the beat"), and phrasing of Roberta Martin. Dinah's style was imitated by a host of singers, including Lavern Baker, Etta James, Nancy Wilson, Dionne Warwick, and Diana Ross.

Vocal techniques, timbres, and delivery style were not the only components of gospel appropriated by rhythm and blues. Gospel rhythms and instrumental stylings, which originated in secular contexts, became integral to this sound. David "Panama" Francis, studio drummer for many Black artists, brought a rhythmic excitement to post–World War II popular forms when he incorporated the rhythms of the Holiness church into several rhythm and blues recordings. In Screaming Jay Hawkins's "I Put a Spell on You" (1956) and Lavern Baker's "See See Rider" (1962), for example, he employed the $\frac{12}{8}$ meter (known as common meter in the Church of God in Christ) and the triplet note pattern associated with this meter (Maultsby 1983c). These structures as well as the rhythms that accompany the "shout" (religious dance) provide the rhythmic foundation for many contemporary popular songs.

Ray Charles was another performer who drew from his church roots for musical inspiration. His performances employ every cultural aesthetic known to the Black folk church, including the movements of its congregants. Francis, who played drums on Charles's "Drown in My Own Tears" (1956), explains how he used brushes rather than sticks to capture the nuances of these movements in this song:

Ray was the one who told me to play with brushes like in the church and with a gospel feeling. All I played was straight quarter notes with brushes. If you remember, in the church, that was the way the mothers used to keep the babies quiet on their knees when they were singing; all they did was lift their foot and then drop it—just a straight ¼ . . . . And they'd be patting the baby and it would go right back to sleep. And that's what I was playing on the drums in "Drown in My Own Tears." Ray Charles suggested it and showed me how to do it, too. (Maultsby 1983c)

Ray Charles also incorporated the structures and instrumental stylings of gospel music in his songs. When he repackaged the well-known gospel version of the spiritual "This Little Light of Mine" as "This Little Girl of Mine," in 1955, he retained the underlying repeated eight-bar structure. In doing so, Charles broadened the musical parameters of rhythm and blues beyond its traditional twelve-bar blues structure.

In subsequent recordings, including "Drown in My Own Tears" (1956), "Right Right Time" (1959), and "What'd I Say" (1959), Charles employed the gospel piano style of Roberta Martin in conjunction with his gospel-rooted vocals. Martin, in developing a distinctive performance style, elevated the role of the piano from that of background for vocals to one of "an integral and integrating force in the performance, supplying accompaniment, rhythm, and effects. Her style is characterized by improvisatory fills, a rhythmic bass line and colorful and complex chord structures" (Williams-Jones 1982, 15). In the 1960s, the Roberta Martin piano style, the rhythms of the Black folk church, and the harmonic structures and vocal stylings of gospel music transformed rhythm and blues into a new popular idiom known as soul music.

The spirit and energy of soul music were so powerful that this style penetrated all arteries of the African American community and spilled over into those of mainstream America. In 1969, James Brown, a pioneer with Ray Charles in the development of soul music, "became the first black man in the 30-year history of *Cash Box* to be cited as the male vocalist on single pop records. For the uninitiated, 'pop' means sales to the whole record-buying public, not simply in the predominantly Negro rhythm 'n' blues market" (Barry 1969, 56). Brown's influence was so great that many white singers, including the Righteous Brothers, Joe Cocker, Tom Jones, and Elvis Presley, imitated his style, giving rise to the concept of "blue-eyed soul singers."

James Brown, proclaimed the "godfather of soul," along with his female counterpart, Aretha Franklin, the "queen of soul," made gospel music and its delivery style a permanent fixture in American popular music. Horace Clarence Boyer, quoted in *U.S. News & World Report*, observed that "gospel became a style of performance into which you could put any message" ("Gospel Music Rolls out of the Church, onto the Charts" 1986, 56). In other words, gospel music became more than a musical genre; it was an idiomatic style that wielded tremendous influence not only on Black popular idioms but on the entire American popular tradition. The musical trends of the 1970s and 1980s support this axiom.

When funk and other urban forms evolved from soul music during the mid–1970s and 1980s, they retained the energy, rhythms, textures, and stylings of gospel music. The funk style developed by Larry Graham of Graham Central Station, for example, employs many of the features associated with the 1950s gospel sound. In the 1977 song "Release Yourself" (Warner Bros. BS 2814), the texture produced by mixed voices, the high-energy and percussive vocal style, the instrumental stylings of the organ and piano, and the beat of the tambourine recreate the fervor of the Roberta Martin Singers and the singing of Black folk churches.

Many components of gospel music have been incorporated into popular music, where they have intermingled with new techniques and expressions and then recycled back into gospel. This cyclical process has expanded the foundation of gospel and popular forms, generating new styles in both traditions. It therefore calls into question the artificial boundaries that historically have separated religious and secular styles, their performers, and their audiences. Whereas many singers once were compelled to choose between gospel and popular, they now freely move between and juxtapose both traditions on a single album. Deniece Williams, Ashford & Simpson, Al Green, and Candi Staton are singers who consistently include gospel songs on their albums of popular music. Williams explains her commitment to gospel: "I'd grown up singing in the choir and I'd always wanted to record a gospel song. . . . I told CBS I wanted to record a gospel album some-day. They said, 'Yeah, sure, sure,' but never thought I was serious. I don't think CBS thought I'd go on to record a gospel song on every album after that [1976], either, but I did" (Gospel music column 1987). In 1986, when Williams's contract was up for renewal at CBS, she was granted permission to record a gospel album for Sparrow Records. The album, *So Glad I Know* (Sparrow SP 61121), not only received two Grammys but also appeared on four music charts: inspirational, gospel, pop, and Black music. Following Williams's lead, many singers in the popular idiom have begun to include gospel songs on their albums. The rap song "Pray" by M. C. Hammer (Capitol CDP 7928572) is an example of this trend among the 1990s generation of Black performers.

The 1980s witnessed the move of gospel music into the pop and rock corners of the music industry as its performers were featured as background singers on popular record-ings. In 1984, the British group Foreigner recorded its "I Want to Know What Love Is" on *Agent Provocateur* (Atlantic A281999) using a gospel choir. When Foreigner toured America, it employed the services of local gospel choirs in every major city. The Winans have proven to be on the cutting edge of gospel music, pioneering new but controversial trends with each album (Gospel music column 1988). Perhaps the most controversial has been the use of established vocalists, instrumentalists, and producers from various popu-lar idioms. For example, the 1987 album *Decisions* (Qwest 925510–1) features Anita Baker in the crossover hit "Ain't No Need to Worry." The Winans' first single, "It's Time" from *Return* (Qwest 261612), is a gospel rap produced by Teddy Riley, the force behind the success of Bobby Brown, Keith Sweat, and David Peaston. Other nongospel musi-cians included on the album are Stevie Wonder and Kenny G.

If other artists follow the direction of the Winans and Deniece Williams, the 1990s indeed will witness a continued wedging together of the sacred and secular spheres of

Black community life. As contemporary gospel groups attempt to reach the youth and non-Christian market, and as religious record labels adopt "secular" promotion methods, the question posed in 1979—"Is it possible that one day gospel music will no longer belong to the church?"—will continue to be pondered.

2

CHARLES ALBERT TINDLEY

(ca. 1851–1933)

~

SEARCHING FOR
TINDLEY

Bernice Johnson Reagon

*This article is based on an oral-history project conducted by the author
with members of the Tindley Temple Church in Philadelphia; Tindley
descendants in Philadelphia, Ohio, and Berlin, Maryland; and ministers in the United Methodist Church who came up under Reverend
Charles Albert Tindley.* —ED.

I came to the Reverend Charles Albert Tindley* looking for a songwriter. His name had come up a few times in the two decades I had
spent becoming more conscious of the relationship between African American people's
cultural expressions and our historical experiences. He was spoken of in relationship to
Thomas Dorsey. The line usually went, "Thomas Dorsey, often called the 'father of gospel music,' was greatly influenced by Rev. C. A. Tindley, a Black Methodist [sometimes,
erroneously, Baptist] minister from Philadelphia who during the early part of the century
wrote such hymns as 'Stand By Me.'" His name came up again when I was doing research
on "We Shall Overcome," the signature song of the Civil Rights Movement, for my
dissertational studies, for in 1901, Tindley had published a song called "I'll Overcome

---

*Tindley's birthdate has been given variously as 1851, 1856, and 1859. Tindley's son, Elbert Tindley, uses the
date 1851 in the sixth edition of the Tindley hymnal *New Songs of Paradise*.

Someday." It was Tindley the songwriter I sought when I planned the second Smithsonian Conference on the Pioneering Gospel Music Composers, devoted to the music of Charles Albert Tindley. It was the songwriter I sought when in June 1981 I attended a service at Tindley Temple.

I found much more. I found a community whose story began in Maryland's Eastern Shore Black Methodist communities. The core membership of Tindley's church came from Berlin, a small community on Maryland's Eastern Shore where Tindley was born on July 7, probably in 1851. From the early 1800s, this region had been the locus of strong proselytizing by evangelists from Wesleyan's Holiness movement which, in the United States, became the Methodist church. With its willingness to open its message to the Black community, slave and free, this movement was vigorously received, and the Methodist church remains the dominant denomination in the area. Without formal denominational training, the early Black lay ministers on the Eastern Shore drew from their observations and spiritual experiences to fashion a style of worship steeped in the African-derived culture of their communities. This rich tradition of worship impacted greatly on the cultural environment that evolved within the early Tindley Temple (Reagon 1981a).

When I entered Tindley Temple on that Sunday morning, I carried with me all of the stereotypes that a Black Georgia Baptist holds toward Black Methodists. I expected a middle-class, staid, reserved, orderly congregation. My experience that morning began a process of realigning those images. I walked into the church a few minutes before the eleven o'clock service. Several small groups of people were scattered throughout the main pews. Each group had a leader, and the members were testifying. I wanted to go outside and look to be sure I was not in a Pentecostal church. But it was Tindley Temple United Methodist Church. Built in 1924 under the leadership of Reverend Charles Albert Tindley, it had twelve doors representing Tindley's vision of twelve gates to the heavenly city, no steps so that those with physical disabilities could enter, and a massive organ with five sections of pipes that had been purchased during the Depression. Reverend Claude Edmonds, then pastor of Tindley Temple, spoke about Methodism and the kind of ministry Tindley evolved:

In the Methodist Episcopal Church at that time, he was not the traditional preacher. There could have very easily been a sign out here, Tindley Temple Baptist, Tindley Temple Pentecostal, and people would have believed that's what he was, just by the experience. So if you have an image of what a United Methodist Church is like, that is, I think the usual image is a staid, quiet, reserved, dignified, not too many amens . . . then Tindley Temple is just the opposite of that. It has all those ingredients but it's a strong worshipping church. . . .

This is my home church so I can go back as far as Tindley because I was actually three years old when he died in 1933. It seems obvious to me besides what traditionally was told to us, that the church was very Pentecostal, very Baptist. It was the preaching center in Philadelphia. Tindley packed it every Sunday morning, every Sunday night. Black folk, white folk, you name 'em. My mother used to say . . . if you didn't get to church by 9:30 or so, you just didn't get a seat in this new building which came to be in 1924. (Reagon 1981b)

As the service unfolded that June morning, I was able to witness a cultural tradition that embraced both the order and selections of well-loved "high" church literature and the practice, richness, intensity, and spontaneity found in the most traditionally based Black forms of worship. There were hymns, anthems, prayers, and creeds. There were "amens" and hand-claps and shouts of "Thank you, Jesus" and a spirit that ran throughout the service. Members talked about Tindley Temple as a church of "hot" and "high" service. They talked about a group of African American Methodist, urban churches whose core membership came from the Eastern Shore of Maryland. They talked about Reverend Charles Albert Tindley as a man who believed in Holiness, believed in tarrying services where people prayed and sang all night long, believed in involving members from all walks of life in the service in whatever way they needed to be spiritually fed.

These beliefs produced a worship form in which members would shout "holy" after "Inflammatus," and that simply did not compute for me. However, it was normal for Kenneth Goodman, who had been baptized by Tindley and who grew up in Tindley Temple Church. He described the way in which Tindley instituted the older Eastern Shore tradition of singing and praying bands in his Philadelphia church:

The Eastern Shore had weekend groups that exalted the Lord by singing and praying. They were held, as the slaves used to do, when for fear of being punished they had to steal away into the woods to hold prayer meetings. The women were in white dresses. The men were in white shirts with collars built in, singing and praying all night. At Tindley Temple, my mother was a member of the singing and praying band. They still wore white dresses, and the men were in shirt sleeves. They'd make a circle in the lower auditorium. They would sing all night. (Reagon 1981c)

There are two Tindley musical legacies. The Tindley of Tindley Temple was one of the most powerful Black Methodist preachers of his day and a great minister to the Black people who, at the turn of the century, poured into south Philadelphia and formed a culturally rich, Black urban community. He wrote songs to support his sermons. This is the first story, a songwriter born out of a great preaching tradition and a phenomenal outreach ministry. Ralph Jones, who was baptized by Tindley and is his biographer, commented on his style of leadership:

He had terrific organizing abilities. He knew how to select leadership, and his ministry was such that it was not confined to the four walls of this church building; his ministry went to the streets. At the same time South Street was for Blacks who came to Philadelphia, especially Broad and South Streets, and Tindley would walk up and down the street and all the sporting class people, and all the theatrical people who used to come to stay in the theater and what not, he would talk and preach to them. . . . There were a couple of bordellos, a couple of gambling houses, a couple of hotels "ladies of the evening" would use; but he would go and preach to those people on the street. (Reagon 1981d)

On this same subject, Reverend Henry Nichols, United Methodist Minister and pastor, who had also grown up in Tindley Temple, talked of his early impressions of a ministry that went beyond the church congregation: "All during the Depression, he would beg food to have a soup line right there at the church. Anybody who wanted could come get a bowl of soup and then he'd teach a Bible lesson. That's why all the beggars in town knew Tindley" (Reagon 1981e).

As a spiritual leader, Tindley made of his church a sort of vessel into which people were welcome to bring all their traditions. He was among those ministers who believed that the spiritual needs of the community could not be addressed without taking into consideration the practical and material needs for food, housing, and clothing. The history of his pastorage is replete with stories of his coming to the aid of his congregants and the larger community. During the 1920s, Tindley turned the church basement into a soup kitchen to feed people who were without jobs. He organized a savings unit to help church members accumulate down payments toward their first homes. He took intense interest in the training and education of the young in his congregation. He attempted to include everything he or his congregation might need, everything the world might demand. Kenneth Goodman recalled a poignant story of how Tindley's ministry touched members of his congregation and moved them to embrace the less fortunate:

But this Sunday was particular. This ragged, tattered lad, about sixteen, and he didn't have any shoes on—he had pieces of cardboard tied around his feet and rags tied with strings to protect him from the elements. It must have been really—around zero. The snow was deep. And he was among those that came to join the church. And so Rev. Tindley prayed over them, and Mr. Charlie Brown, the church secretary, took their names. When he came over and asked Francis, he said, "What is your name?" "Francis Johnson is my name," he said. "Your address?" . . . And he broke down and just shook sobs. He had no address. He had nowhere to go. He was an orphaned boy, and [had] been going from post to post, from home to home, and here he was in this church on this morning to give his heart to God, but no place to go.

Rev. Tindley—oh, you know he was a master .. . I often wonder whether Rev. Tindley was the Christ that came back . . . because he *lived* that life. . . . And Rev. Tindley asked the audience, he said, "Now, you have rejoiced in the Lord this morning. Now we have a chance to show our love for God. Here is a lad—no place to go. No relatives. I'm sure some heart in this church will open to take him in their home."

You couldn't hear a sound. Not a sighing moan. And I said, as young as I was, "Now these aren't Christian people." He asked three times—and he said, "I have a full house myself. I have a large family. But if you don't, I am going to take him in." And the stillness was just penetrating.

And we were sitting in the amen corner . . . and guess who stood up? Lucie Goodman! And William Goodman, my father, stood beside her and she spoke. My mother was a feisty little woman. She said, "Pastor Tindley" and her voice sounded stranger than I've ever heard it. I said, "What is going on, now?" She said, "I don't know why I'm standing, Pastor Tindley, because I do have a large family, and our resources are very, very minimum, but by the help of God, we'll take Francis in, we'll share a crust of bread with him, we'll see that he's clean, and we'll have a place for him to sleep. And he'll be warm." I thought, "Now that is Christianity." (Goodman 1982)

Ralph Jones talked about the members who made up the congregation and how Tindley evolved an infrastructure within the church to support the goals of the new urban community:

We never had wealthy people in our congregation, they were hard-working people . . . Tindley stated that if you wanted to be somebody . . . and if you wanted to own something you had to make provision for it. So he started the Mt. Calvary Building and Loan Society for this church. People would put in five and ten dollars until they got enough equity to pay for their row houses which were selling then for nine hundred to fifteen thousand dollars. They would get the down payment, the Building and Loan Society would take the mortgage, and they were able to buy their homes. (Reagon 1981d)

Tindley Temple became a major vehicle for shaping the urban community experience of its congregants. The experience was of spiritual and moral guidance, emotional and practical support. Members were counseled on ways to survive in an urban setting, on economic, educational, and political directions and issues. The Berliners from Eastern Shore Maryland who came into the church were helped to develop a lifestyle incorporating elements of the new, urban environment with the culture and traditions of rural Maryland. According to Reverend Marion Ballard, who himself had migrated from the Eastern Shore to Philadelphia and had pastored Tindley Temple after Tindley had passed, there was a distinct pattern to where people moved when they relocated in the cities from the rural South (Reagon 1981f). In Philadelphia, they usually moved into a particular neighborhood or section because relatives lived there or because the central membership of a church in that neighborhood was formed by former residents of specific Eastern Shore counties:

They were scattered over the city of Philadelphia. Some in the Germantown area. It's a strange thing, but people coming from certain counties tended to go to certain churches. People coming from Talbott, Caroline, [and] Dorchester [Counties] tended to go over in the Germantown area. The people coming from Somerset [County] tended to go over to Haven church here in North Philadelphia. The people from Wooster County (Wooster's the county in which Dr. Tindley was born) tended to go to Tindley Temple Church. (Reagon 1981f)

Tindley's autobiographical statement in his *Book of Sermons* (1932) implies that he was not a slave. The assertion frequently found in biographical sketches, that he came "of slave parents," seems to be drawn from his reference to "slave ancestors." He recalls that because of economic hardship after his mother, Hester Miller Tindley, died, his father, Charles Tindley, was forced to hire him out. This practice was not unusual for freed Blacks. Hired-out workers often worked alongside slaves, experiencing much of the reality of the slave plantation. The major differences were that there was some remuneration (in Tindley's case, to his father) and that hired-out workers did get the opportunity to go home. Describing his struggle to learn to read, Tindley comments on how this experience affected him:

It therefore became my lot to be "hired out," wherever father could place me. The people with whom I lived were not all good. Some of them were very cruel to me. I was not permitted to have a book or go to church. I used to find bits of newspaper on the roadside and put them in my bosom (for I had no pockets), in order to study the ABC's from them. During the day I would gather pine knots, and when the people were asleep at night I would light these pine knots, and, lying flat on my stomach to prevent being seen by any one who might still be about, would, with fire-coals, mark all the words I could make out on these bits of newspaper. I continued in this way, and without any teacher, until I could read the Bible almost without stopping to spell the words. (Tindley 1932)

In his hometown, Berlin, Maryland, a section of the community is called Tindleytown because so many Tindleys reside in this area. Among his mother's people, it is said that when Tindley's mother passed he was a young child and was raised by his mother's sister, Caroline Miller Robbins, until he was old enough to be hired out; he then returned to live with his father. The Millers were descendants of Arnold Miller, who had purchased his freedom and one by one purchased his wife and children. He was assisted in this effort by one of his daughters, Julia, who, as soon as she was free and old enough, moved to Philadelphia and sent money from her earnings back home to help pay for the freedom of other members of her family. Tindley's father was a slave owned by Joseph Bridell, but his mother was free, and when she passed, Tindley was raised by her family and thus claimed the status of his mother (Reagon 1990b).

Descendants on both Tindley's mother's and father's side of the family carry stories that say that in addition to his own efforts, Tindley received some lessons in reading from Calvin B. Taylor, the son of Arthur W. Taylor, one of the families he was hired out to work for. Calvin Taylor grew up to become the founder of the Calvin B. Taylor Bank, the local bank in Berlin (Reagon 1990b).

In 1875, when Tindley came to Philadelphia intent on a new life, he stayed with his aunt, Julia Miller (Reagon 1990b). He began working as a hod carrier, carrying mortar for bricklayers. He also served as sexton for the John Wesley Methodist Episcopal Church, which later was renamed the East Bainbridge Street Church. Studying at night and in correspondence courses, he educated himself and passed the examinations for the Methodist ministry. Throughout his life, he continued to study a wide variety of subjects including Hebrew, Greek, and Latin, and an emphasis on education was among the unique elements of his ministry (Tindley 1932).

In 1902, Tindley was called to the pastorate of the East Bainbridge Street Church, which grew rapidly under his ministry, moving to the Calvary Methodist building in 1904 and then to the present structure, Tindley Temple United Methodist Church. In 1924, the new Tindley Temple had a roll membership of approximately ten thousand, about half of whom were active. It was the center of the South Philadelphia community, and its minister, a mesmerizing figure, was known as one of the greatest preachers among Black Methodists (Reagon 1981f).

His skill as a preacher, blending profundity with simplicity, was so great that seminary students of all races came to his services to study his method. In his sermons, he seemed set upon affecting people, telling a story so that they could not miss the point, drawing material from the contemporary culture so that the various ideas and issues would seep in. Kenneth Goodman described how Tindley "made an impact on my life with his simple stories":

[In] one [story] I remember, I couldn't have been more than ten years old, he was preaching about a tree. "Has anyone ever seen a fruit tree partake of its own fruit?" The congregation said, "No." He asked a few other questions. "But I tell you what you seen. I come from the country. Of course, you've never been in the country." (This would bring laughter because all these people were rural.)

"You've never seen a peach tree eat its own peaches. You've never seen an apple tree eat its own apples. But you have seen a tree so laden with fruit that its branches reach the ground so a toddler can pick and partake. Our lives should be like that tree. Not what we maintain for ourselves but give to others, as God gave his son." I said, "I want to be like that tree, serve others, share what I can with others."

Tindley said, "Even a tree has to be nourished. To withstand, it must have a power greater than itself to lean upon." He also said, "There are three ways to get up in the world. Some people are so anxious, they blow up. You can grow up or blow up. If you blow up, you'll come down real soon, like Humpty Dumpty. You can grow up by knocking everyone else down. Sometimes you'll reach the top but you'll not stay long. If you grow up like a tree, its a long and painful process. You are victim to the elements, to winter. Then comes spring and summer. The foliage comes out. Grow up like a towering oak and you'll stay."

He didn't teach us how to die and about the hereafter. He taught us how to live. How to love each other. How to emulate Christian principles. That was the great thing about him. (Goodman 1982)

Tindley's power as a preacher is legendary. Reverend Marion Ballard spoke of the culture of Philadelphia when Tindley preached:

During the era of his preaching, there was no television. There was no radio. There was no baseball. There was no nothing. In the city of Philadelphia on a Sunday, it was a closed city. We had blue laws so you were limited to what you could do on Sunday. He had that advantage. But we recognized that we never carried crowds that he did. Nothing like it. . . .

There is one sermon that I recall he preached each year at Christmas time and that was "Heaven's Christmas Tree." That to me is a remarkable feat because as I think of preaching, to preach the same sermon to the same people year after year and for it to be acceptable to those people, that's something. That's doing something. . . .

When you remember Tindley, you remember the great crowds that came to the church constantly to hear him preach. In fact, the present edifice was built for preaching. Today you would not see a church built to seat three thousand people. No congregation today would hardly think about that unless it is an extraordinary group of people. But that church was built, I believe in 1924, and it was built to seat three thousand people. That was because of the power of this preacher. (Reagon 1981f)

Of this same magnetic power, Reverend Henry Nichols added:

Thirty-five hundred could be seated; another fifteen hundred could stand around the walls, and *every Sunday morning*, rain or shine, by twenty after ten, if you weren't in, you didn't *get* in.

Because the place would be packed—they'd even lock the doors. The fire department came down and told us to stop doing that because of the danger. The Methodists used to get so happy in the balcony . . . that's why they got that second rail around there. Folks would get so happy and start leaning on that railing, and they put the second rail so that nobody would fall. (Reagon 1981e)

It was as if Tindley were pulling people into a new time, resolving fears of the unfamiliar but at the same time validating and preserving the essence of the culture of the Eastern Shore. This approach very likely was key to Tindley's ability to build a congregation of people from different classes and with different cultural experiences.

Music of all kinds was performed at Tindley Temple, and behaviors toward music and worship service were not stratified. The church that sang Handel's *Messiah* at Christmas and Rossini's "Inflammatus" on Sunday morning also held Eastern Shore–style, all-night tarrying services and testimonials and expressed a strong belief in Holiness. Each member could receive it all in his or her own way, shouting or getting happy or being more quietly stirred.

Tindley's songs, written to enhance his ability to convey points in his sermons, were simply based on everyday life experiences so that they could be easily understood by the congregation. His songs were part of his sermonizing and often were introduced within the sermon or sung by his daughter, Emmaline, as part of the service. Reverend Henry Nichols spoke of the power of Tindley's preaching and how Tindley saw his songwriting as secondary and supportive to his sermonizing:

He did not write music; he didn't write gospel music just to write gospel music. His music came out of experience, in most instances, some type of personal experience or some scriptural experience led to his seeking to put to music—for those who would perhaps not get it in the sermon— the gospel message. . . .

Now and then he would tell us the reason behind his hymns. The one I remember best is the one on "Nothing Between." Tindley said he was sitting in his backyard one day doing some writing and a gust of wind came up and blew a piece of trash between what he was writing, between his pen and the piece of paper. He couldn't see it. He stopped and moved it and then the thought came to him, "Now, that's what sin does, comes between person and God." And he sat down and wrote:

> Nothing between my soul and my savior,
> So that his blessed face may be seen.
> Nothing preventing the least of his favor,
> Keep the way clear, let nothing between.

Now during the Depression, things really were bad, people were really starving. I remember, I was a boy then, and he wrote a hymn on the beneficence of God, "God Has Promised to Provide for Me." Very fascinating about that hymn, it was written out of the experience of how in the midst of nothing, God provides for His children. People used to sing that hymn and get happy. It's not a swinging hymn. None of his hymns are. People trying to swing them and they ruin them when they swing them, they won't make it.

> Here I may be weak and poor,
> With afflictions to endure

> All about me not a ray of light to see
> Just as He has often done
> For His helpless trusting ones,
> God has promised to provide for me.

I grew up in Tindley Temple before it was Tindley Temple, when it was East Calvary. I was converted in the old church, which was called East Calvary. The site now is a gasoline station next to the new building, which is called Tindley Temple. I too was one of those who had to sit on someone's lap as a boy, because the place was packed and jammed. People from everywhere—Black and white—before integration was supposedly popular, were there to hear Tindley preach. As a matter of fact, sometimes because of our notoriety for being late, we were the ones who didn't get the seats.

People would come to hear him preach. Sometimes he would pray aloud, then preach an hour, and nobody would leave. It was 1923; that's when Tindley was the pastor. In those days, we were raising money to build the structure that you'll see tomorrow and I think it's good to know that the building was built primarily to house the crowds that came to hear Tindley preach. . . . Some buildings are for Christian education purposes. But he was that kind of master preacher and very few buildings have ever been built by Black folks for Black preachers.

That's what makes it unique, that he was that kind of preacher, who had very little formal training but eventually received a doctorate because of his own personal studies and became a prolific writer as well as a songwriter. (Reagon 1981e, Nichols 1982)

A recurring theme in Tindley's songs and sermons is the belief that true change or release from worldly bondage can be attained only through struggle. This theme received wide acceptance within the Black oral tradition. In his sermon "The Furnace of Affliction," Tindley urged his listeners to go willingly through the furnace in order to find a space free of the heat, to find the highest grade of gold and silver within the human spirit: "I welcome this morning, all the persecutions, unkindnesses, hard sayings and whatever God allows to come upon me. I welcome the hottest fire of trials if it is needed for my purification. Oh, the things that we have in our lives that can never go in heaven are more numerous than we are apt to think. They must all be taken out before we leave this world. God's way to get them out may be the way of the furnace" (Tindley 1932). Several of his songs use the image of going through life as a storm. In each there is both the withstanding of the storm and the promise of the other side:

> "STAND BY ME" (1916)
> When the storms of life are raging
> Stand by me, stand by me
> When the world is tossing me
> Like a ship upon the sea
> Thou who rules wind and water,
> stand by me

> "THE STORM IS PASSING OVER, HALLELUJAH" (1916)
> Courage my soul and let us journey on
> Though the night is dark, it won't be very long.

Thanks be to God, the morning light appears.
And the storm is passing over, hallelujah.

Reverend Marion Ballard connected Tindley's songs to his life as a Black man:

He deals with the Black experience in the songs. There's no question about that . . . I think more
or less he had to. Coming out of the era that he did with the hardships that he experienced, the
way he came along, I think it was a simple matter for him to deal with the everyday experiences
of Black people. This is one of the reasons that Black worship, in my mind, has always been
different from white worship. Because Black people have had a hard time trying to cope and some
of the problems they have had, whites have never faced. . . . So that when a Black person goes to
church on Sunday morning, . . . a great many of them have very, very, heavy burdens that
they've had to bear and the preacher somehow has to try to say something that is going to help
that person to carry on in the next week. Something should happen to him in there. And it calls
for a different kind of preaching from what you get in the white churches. (Reagon 1981f)

According to Reverend Henry Nichols,

Tindley wrote a hymn that we used to sing with great gusto. . . . It came out of a rich personal
experience, and then it became meaningful to us who were born during or before the Depression.
When Tindley was in the ministry, we did not have minimum salaries . . . and equitable salary
funds, Social Security, or that . . . you know, whatever the congregation might try to pay him—
most of the times, they didn't want to try.

Tindley said one morning he and his family sat down . . . getting ready for breakfast, and his
wife said, "There is no food here." He said, "That's all right. Fix the table. Put the dishes on—
we'll have breakfast." And she looked at him and said, "But Dr. Tindley, didn't you hear me?
There's no food here." He said, "That's all right. Fix the table. Let's sit down and have prayer."
And so she did. The children sat down, and I'm sure the children thought he was gone. . . . And
he said, "Let's bow our heads." No food; empty plates. And then he began to pray, "Dear Lord,
we thank you for what we are about to receive." And *just then*, he said somebody *knocked on the
door*. He stopped and went to the door, and one of the officers said, "Brother Pastor, didn't know
whether y'all had anything to eat this morning. Brought you some food over." Now, we don't
know anything about that, because we got food stamps, and all of this other stuff. . . . But that's
why he wrote "God Has Promised to Provide for Me"

All my raiment and my food
All my health and all that's good
All within his own written guarantee
God is caring for the poor
Just as He has done before
He has promised to provide for me.

I remember back in '29, when the banks went out . . . Roosevelt hadn't got into office yet . . .
Tindley had soup lines. I used to go down there, try to be of a little help as a boy. There'd be
lines for blocks waiting to get a little soup. And then he'd give them soup and sit down and talk to
them about their soul. But in those days, we'd sing, "God Has Promised to Provide for Me." . . .
Tindley also said, "You know, the only way you can really become defeated on your way to
heaven is to allow life's difficulties to get inside of you, and to turn you sour." He said, "One of
the things that we have to do—we must do—is to make sure that we do not try to take ven-

geance. That if we belong to Him, then He in His own time will take care of the situation. . . . I want to read what he [Tindley] wrote about that ["Let Jesus Fix It for You"]:

If your life, in days gone by
Has not been good and true
In your way no longer try
But let Him fix it for you

Perhaps your temper is to blame
For many wrongs you do
Take it to God in Jesus' name
And He will fix it for you

If, in your home, the trouble is
The course you should pursue
Go talk with God, your hand in His
And He will fix it for you

And if some sin your soul have bound
With cords you cannot undo
At Jesus' feet, go lay it down
And He will fix it for you

Maybe to you the world is dark,
And comforts far and few
Let Jesus own and rule your heart
And He will fix it for you

Let Jesus fix it for you
He knows just what to do
Whenever you pray, let Him have His way
And He will fix it for you. (Nichols 1982)

Reverend Nichols spoke of Tindley's range in capturing the experiences of many:

As he wrote the music . . . well, brothers and sisters, he wrote from an *experience*. Not only his experience, but the experience of others . . . . Tindley was well aware of nature. As a child, he had spent time in studying nature down on the Eastern Shore—and in some parts of Philadelphia, because it wasn't quite as urbanized as it is now. He noticed certain things that happened with the changing of the seasons. He had a way of taking those things that were natural and sometimes material and translating them into that which was spiritual.

And so every year, the first Sunday in spring, he would request that each person bring with them a twig, a flower, a leaf, or something that has just come out of the ground, as a signal that spring has begun. And then his subject was the same as the hymn he wrote, entitled "Spiritual Spring Time":

Just as the winter is bleak and bare physically,
The sinner is bleak and bare when he knows not Christ.
But when Christ comes into his life,
Then the birds begin to sing;
Then the flowers burst into bloom;
Then the grass is ready for cultivation.

He translated it into a hymn, so that we not only had the sermon, but then you have the hymn that you could use, and if you couldn't remember all six stanzas, you could remember the chorus. In the text, he'd raised the same question that the scientist has just told us about; that spring was here because the sun had a certain line. So, the chorus would say to the sinner: when you accept Jesus Christ, He will then ask you:

> Has the sun crossed the line?
> Do you know?
> Has it melted all the ice and the snow?
> Have the birds begun to sing?
> Do you feel the joy of spring?
> Has the sun crossed the line?
> Do you know?

So you would not remember the verse, but you could answer the question whether the sun crossed the line. Are you still cold, hard, and indifferent? Or, have the birds begun to sing, or the flowers bursting? And let me give you just one verse:

> Like the action of the ground on the axis turns around
> 'Neath the sun of mighty powers, life and light
> So a wretched sinner whom, when he sees his awful doom,
> Turns from sin and seeks to know, and do the right

Then he goes to the chorus:

> Has the sun crossed the line?
> Do you know? . . .

Then we would shake each other's hands and ask each other:

> Has it melted all the ice and the snow?
> Have the birds begun to sing?
> Do you feel the joy of spring?
> Has the sun crossed the line?
> Do you know?

So that's how he preached; that's how he made his sermons. He didn't go way over there and get some long terms that no one understood. (Nichols 1982)

Tindley's most famous sermon was his Christmas tree sermon. Every Christmas for years he would preach the same sermon. People would reportedly come to Sunday morning service at 8:00 A.M. to get seats, then they would stay all day to hear Tindley preach about the Christmas tree. His niece, Stella Tindley, and his granddaughter-in-law, Geraldine Tindley, had strong memories of this great sermon: "Well, on Christmas he preached about 'Heaven's Christmas Tree,' which had these packages: love, charity, salvation. . . . He would take each package from this tree, which was the 'Heaven's Christmas Tree,' and he preached on love this year, hope, and charity. The next year, he would preach on a different package, salvation, forgiveness, and that's how the sermon would go. Each year it would be 'Heaven's Christmas Tree' but just different packages" (Reagon 1981g).

Tindley also composed a hymn for the sermon entitled "Heaven's Christmas Tree" (ex.

1). This song and the sermon were mentioned by everyone associated with Tindley Temple, and the song "Heaven's Christmas Tree" is included in his published collection of gospel hymns. It was not one of his compositions that found resonance outside of his personal ministry. The Tindley Temple congregation embraced a larger part of his work than is found in the oral tradition where his songs gained prominence as classic gospel songs of the twentieth century.

The other Tindley story is about the movement of his songs, often without acknowledgment of him as composer, into African American oral tradition, to become standards within the twentieth-century sacred music repertoire. The most famous titles have been sung and recorded in all the various styles of Black gospel singing—quartet, solo, duet, ensemble, and choir. Today, most Protestant hymnals include several of Tindley's compositions.

Reverend Nichols thought he understood one way Tindley's songs found their way into church communities outside of the African American Methodist congregations:

Always at Tindley Temple's services, on Sunday nights, when Tindley was living, half of the congregation was white. . . . Only because of him. It wasn't his church. It was Tindley. . . . It was him. It was the man. You go almost anywhere in Methodism and you'll find white Methodists, middle-aged, saying that they either heard Tindley or their parents heard Tindley. That's how his songs got around. Today, I get more requests from young people: Can you get me one of Tindley's songbooks? It's almost phenomenal how they just know his songs. . . . And the real funny part about it is, you go through the South [and you find] the most rabid of the Bible-belt [white] people singing "Take Your Burdens to the Lord" [and not knowing] that Tindley was Black. (Reagon 1981e)

Reverend Nichols spoke of finding Tindley wherever he traveled, going beyond the African American community:

It has been my privilege to have traveled around the world once; halfway around twice; and I've spent many a good time in Africa, Alaska, Japan, and England on missions for the church; in every one of those countries including South Africa, I've heard them sing, "Take Your Burdens to the Lord and Leave Them There." The only thing they *didn't* know was that Tindley was a Black man. He transcended race; he had a message. And it wasn't only for poor folks; for there are a lot of rich folks that have burdens that *they* take to the Lord, and leave them, too—so let's not think that the message is only for those of a certain socioeconomic group. They are for *all* who hurt. *All* who want to make heaven their home. (Nichols 1982)

In many instances, singers of such songs as "Leave It There, Some Day" (often called "Beams of Heaven"); "Nothing Between"; "We'll Understand It Better By and By"; "The Storm Is Passing Over"; and "City Called Heaven" know nothing of the author: Reverend Charles Albert Tindley, a songwriter, great preacher, publisher of songs and sermons, and pivotal force in the development of Black American composed gospel song.

When I was seven years old, I sang in my first funeral. My sister Mae Frances, who was five at the time, and I sang a song called "What Are They Doing in Heaven Today?"

Example 1. "Heaven's Christmas Tree" (Charles Albert Tindley, orig. © 1915). All of the Tindley songs reproduced here are in the public domain.

The song was taught to us by our teacher, Mrs. Mamie Daniels. I never knew anything about the song except that it was a funeral song. I do not know when I did not know the chorus to "We'll Understand It Better By and By"

> By and by, when the morning comes
> All the saints are gone to gathering home
> We will tell the story of how we overcome
> And we'll understand it better by and by

I, like others of my generation, knew the chorus, but did not know the composer, and only rarely sang all of the verses:

> We are tossed and driven on the restless sea of time
> Somber skies and howling tempest oft succeed a bright sunshine
> In the land of perfect day, when the mists have roll'd away
> We will understand it better by and by

> We are often destitute of the things that life demands
> Want of shelter and of food, thirsty hills and barren lands
> We are trusting in the Lord and according to His word
> We will understand it better by and by

> Trials dark on every hand, and we cannot understand,
> All the ways that God would lead us to that blessed Promised Land;
> But He guides us with His eye, and we'll follow till we die
> We will understand it better by and by

> Temptation's hidden snares often take us unawares,
> And our hearts are made to bleed for a thoughtless word or deed
> And we wonder why the test when we tried to do our best
> We will understand it better by and by

Tindley was, however, well known as a composer among other gospel composers. According to Horace Clarence Boyer, Lucie E. Campbell Williams, composer of "Something Within" and "He Understands; He'll Say, 'Well Done,'" served on the committee that selected Tindley's songs to appear in the 1921 publication of *Gospel Pearls*. Charles Pace, composer of "Bread of Heaven," honored Tindley by allowing the Pace Jubilee Singers to record several of his songs. Thomas Dorsey, often heralded as the "father of gospel music," used Tindley as a model in composing his own songs during the 1930s (Boyer 1982a).

The singers of Tindley's songs read like a list of who's who in African American gospel music. There are country-style singers such as Washington Phillips performing "Take Your Burden to the Lord, Leave It There" (Columbia CO 14277-D). There are the great soloists such as Rosetta Tharpe singing "Beams of Heaven" (Decca 3254) and "What Are They Doing in Heaven Today?" (Savoy MG 14214) and Marion Williams singing "The Storm Is Passing Over" (Spirit Feel SF 1003).

The songs have continued to hold up as they have moved into the present choir era, with, for example, "The Storm Is Passing Over" by Donald Vails and the Choraleers as one of the major gospel hits of the early 1970s (Savoy 14421). The list goes on; Tindley's songs appear in the recorded repertoire of the Caravans ("Stand By Me," on Exodus LP51); the Fairfield Four ("Stand By Me," on Nashboro 7232); and Sweet Honey in the Rock ("We'll Understand It Better By and By," on Flying Fish FF 375).

When a song enters the African American tradition, it operates by the principles of that tradition. Thus, even though these songs were composed by Tindley, singers create new and individual statements with them, as they often did with the older spirituals or hymns. For example, "Stand By Me" is a song found in many repertoires of choirs, quartets, soloists, and small groups of the gospel genre, and the arrangements are as varied as the groups. There is clearly enough of the original composition in text, melody, or form to trace it back to its source as a Tindley song. Consistent with the African American tradition, however, the song also belongs to the singer who operates in performance as a composer/arranger.

This phenomenon makes it possible to trace Tindley's songs as they move through the African American worship tradition. It also demonstrates that the broader African American community clearly has had favorites that continue to show up in each stage of evolution of the gospel music tradition. Donald Vails's "The Storm Is Passing Over" is an example of a Tindley composition restated in a contemporary context—the choral sound that took shape in gospel music during the 1970s.

In the same way, one can learn things about songs that did not move within the broader community's church repertoire. One example is Tindley's "I'll Overcome Someday." This composition was performed within Tindley Temple and other congregations that use the songbook as transmission source. The song that is in the oral tradition was in wide usage within Methodist and Baptist churches across the South in the same form with slight variations in melody, meter, and text (Reagon 1975). There is strong evidence that in this case Tindley borrowed from the traditional song for his composition. "The Pilgrim's Song," set to music by his son, Elbert Tindley, is another example of a Tindley composition that was based on a traditional song; one finds the older traditional song being transmitted rather than the Tindley composition. With the Tindley compositions that enter the tradition—"Stand By Me," "Nothing Between," "Someday," "We'll Understand It Better By and By," "What Are They Doing in Heaven Today?"—there is no older preceding song or composition moving through the tradition.

Reverend Charles Albert Tindley wrote at least fifty-three songs, whose themes cover much of the general Christian experience. When African Americans dip into the well of his music, we pull out those pieces that speak most strongly to our experience: change and struggle as keys to service and deliverance.

Tindley's songs became an extension of the message he felt charged to give. As the Philadelphia congregants packed his services to absorb his sermons, so the larger African American community absorbed his songs. Like water in a dry land, these new songs gave musical energy to the twentieth-century African American sacred experience.

CHARLES ALBERT TINDLEY

Progenitor of African American Gospel Music

Horace Clarence Boyer

The creation and development of that African American art called gospel music and its wide acceptance by 1950 can be attributed to fewer than one dozen composers. These pioneers, without ASCAP (American Society of Composers, Artists, and Publishers), BMI (Broadcast Music, Inc.), or any of the all-important composer protectors of the 1980s, wrote, sang, taught, and distributed their music throughout the United States because they felt it to be their calling; it was their way of making a contribution to religion and the world.

Gospel Pearls (1921) was the first hymnal published expressly for the use of Black church folk that used the term *gospel* in its title. It contained six songs written by Charles Albert Tindley (1851–1933) and thereby introduced Tindley to Black American church audiences as a composer of songs that were to have an arresting influence on all types of world music within fifty years. However, the first generation of African American gospel music composers, who would bring this music to its present state of popularity, already knew of Tindley and his compositions and had selected him as a model.

Lucie Eddie Campbell Williams (1885–1963), for example, who wrote the popular "Something Within" and "He Understands; He'll Say, 'Well Done,'" was among the persons serving on the committee that selected the songs for inclusion in *Gospel Pearls*. Another notable gospel figure who esteemed Tindley was Charles Henry Pace (1886–1963), composer of "Bread of Heaven," who paid homage to Tindley by recording several of his songs with his Pace Jubilee Singers and Hattie Parker. The Pace Singers recorded three songs on June 30, 1928: "Leave It There," "Stand By Me," and "Nothing Between" (Tyler 1980, 212).

Campbell and Pace were not the only gospel composers who admired and respected Tindley's talent. William Herbert Brewster (1899–1987), composer of "Move on up a Little Higher" and "Surely God Is Able," stated, "To my mind, he [Tindley] was one of the greatest, if not the greatest gospel songwriter I ever knew of" (Boyer 1979b), while Roberta Martin (1907–1969), who wrote "God Is Still on the Throne" and "Let It Be," paid tribute to Tindley by recording his "We'll Understand It Better By and By" (Kenwood 480). Appropriately enough, the person who called greatest attention to Tindley was the composer whom Tindley had most influenced and who would inherit his mantle— Thomas Andrew Dorsey (b. 1899). As early as 1942, only nine years after Tindley's death, Dorsey declared that Tindley "originated this style of music [gospel], and what I wanted to do was to further what Tindley started" (Bontemps [1942] 1967, 78).

These gospel songwriters, all of whom came into prominence during the 1920s–40s, paid homage to Tindley because he was the first Black composer to recognize the validity and potential of sacred songs characterized by simple—almost predictable—melodies, harmonies, and rhythms, and messages that dealt forthrightly with such subjects as the joys, trials, and tribulations of living a Christian life in the twentieth century, as well as the rewards of heaven. Tindley's songs used the musical and verbal language of the poor, struggling, often illiterate Black Christian at the turn of this century. Years after he published his last songs (1926), most concerts of traditional gospel music still include his songs, particularly such direct and ear-catching ones as "When the Storms of Life Are Raging, Stand By Me" and "We'll Understand It Better By and By."

THE METHODIST MINISTER

As a young man of about seventeen, Tindley married Daisy Henry. In 1875 they moved to Philadelphia, where there was a community from Berlin, Maryland, Tindley's birthplace. There he worked as a hod carrier and as a sexton at the John Wesley Methodist Episcopal Church (later renamed the Bainbridge Street Methodist Episcopal Church), while attending school at night. Tindley was still the church sexton when he took the examination for the ministry in 1885, little anticipating that one day he would return to this church in a vastly different position.

After passing his examination, Tindley was assigned to a church in Cape May, New Jersey, then later to a parish in Spring Hill, New Jersey. Following a series of appointments—in Odessa, Delaware, and in Pocomoke and Fairmont, Maryland—he was sent to the Ezion Methodist Episcopal Church in Wilmington, Delaware. Parenthetically, Ezion is important in the history of Black church music: It was for this church (then known as the Ezion African Union Church) that the Reverend Peter Spencer published a hymnbook in 1822. It was only the second time in history that a hymnal had been compiled expressly for a Black congregation (Southern 1977, 300). (The first hymnbook had been compiled by Richard Allen in 1801 for his newly formed African Methodist Episcopal Church in Philadelphia.) Tindley's experiences in Delaware were crowned by his appointment in 1900 as the presiding elder of the Wilmington district.

He was holding this position when he was called to pastor the Bainbridge Street Methodist Episcopal Church in Philadelphia, where he had been sexton. Beginning his pastorate in the church in 1902 with 130 members and property valued at ten thousand dollars, Tindley built the membership to over ten thousand during his tenure of thirty-one years and amassed a church property valued at half a million dollars. The new sanctuary seated thirty-two hundred (he often rented stadiums for special services at Easter and Christmas). His devoted followers tried three times to elect him bishop, but the same popularity that had attracted members to his churches alienated the voting clergy of his denomination and denied him a prize he desired greatly. However, his leadership at the annual conference, the seat of authority, advancement, and his prestige, was never disputed.

The 1930s ushered in a crucial period for Tindley, but his troubles actually had begun in the previous decade. In 1924, his wife Daisy died. This loss was benumbing as it came just as he was about to dedicate the new church by holding the Christmas service in the new sanctuary. Tindley particularly missed his wife's sharing that triumph with him. It was in 1924 that the church was renamed Tindley Temple. By the end of the 1920s the church found itself with tremendous financial problems. At the beginning of 1930 the bank holding a mortgage on the church threatened to foreclose in the next sixty days if a year's overdue interest was not paid. The church managed to raise the necessary money, but later the trustees invited Dr. G. Wilson Becton, a popular gospel minister, to conduct a crusade at Tindley Temple.

Becton attracted large crowds and made substantial financial contributions to the church, but the majority of the congregation decided he was too flamboyant for them. Thereafter they sought to relieve him of his services, which proved to be no easy matter. When Becton finally left, he took three thousand members of the church with him to start a new church in Philadelphia. Moreover, the church still faced a two hundred thousand–dollar mortgage and a balance due of fifteen thousand dollars on the new organ (Jones 1982, 129, 137). Tindley coped with the problems valiantly, despite the fact that age was affecting his strength and health.

During the early part of 1933, Tindley injured one of his feet and gangrene set in, but he continued his work. Though he was absent from services at Tindley Temple for extended periods because of his injury, he could occasionally be seen walking around Philadelphia (he never owned a car), comporting himself with dignity and spirit. For two weeks in July, he languished in the Frederick Douglass Hospital of Philadelphia. Then on July 26, 1933, Charles Albert Tindley departed this life. He was survived by his second wife, Jenny Cotton Tindley, whom he had married in 1927, and by several children.

During his lifetime, Tindley was renowned as a gospel preacher, although today he is remembered primarily as a gospel songwriter. He was helped in his musical ministry by his eight children, all of whom exhibited a fondness and talent for musical performance, though none became composers. Emmaline, called Emma, was the most talented, a fine contralto and a skilled pianist; on more than one occasion she served as accompanist to her contemporary, contralto Marian Anderson. Charles, Jr., and Elbert served as arrangers for the published versions of his music.

It was not unusual for Tindley to punctuate his sermons by singing verses or choruses of his own songs. The second or third time, the congregation would join in the singing, with Tindley as leader. Beginning in the 1950s, this kind of performance would be called a gospel songfest. His sermons as well as his songs testify to a strong person, both in conviction and in musical talent. He even had the physical image of a man of strength; he has been described as a "veritable giant, six-feet-two, and weighing 230 pounds, rugged, honest, humble, compassionate" (Jones 1982, 129, 137).

THE DEVELOPMENT OF GOSPEL

While the title "father of gospel music" goes to Thomas Andrew Dorsey, and rightly so, the seed that Dorsey nurtured and brought to maturity had been planted as early as the turn of the century. The Evangelical Movement, which swept the United States during that time, with its emphasis on glossolalia and the practice of the Act of Humility (the washing of feet at communion), inspired the organization and founding of many Holiness and fundamental sects. The Evangelical Movement, particularly as it affected Black church music, had its basis in the Azusa Street Revival of Los Angeles (1906–9), for it was there, through the preaching of Elder William J. Seymour and others, that Pentecostal churches adopted speaking in tongues and washing of feet. Black gospel music and its style came from the Pentecostal churches, particularly through the work of Charles Harrison Mason (1866–1961), founder of the Church of God in Christ, the church into which I was born (Patterson, Ross, and Atkins 1969, 14–19).

The Baptist "lining hymns," sorrow songs, and jubilee spirituals as well as Protestant hymns all had a firm place in the Black church worship service, but this music lacked the intensity heard and felt during the spirited choruses and refrains heard at street meetings, in the parlors of Black Christian homes, and in the new storefront churches. The music excited the musical taste of many Black Christians. Such refrains

Leader:	I'm a soldier
Congregation:	In the army of the Lord
Leader:	I'm a soldier
Congregation:	In the army

were heard throughout the South, and as Southerners migrated to the North, they brought this music with them. These songs differed from the camp-meeting spirituals and Negro spirituals of the nineteenth century in that they were designed to capture the essence of the urban religious experience, with its diverse elements of industry, dense population centers, and a pseudo integration of the races.

The new music of the Black composers that increasingly found acceptance in the Black church was a hymn-like composition differing little from that written by such white composers as William B. Bradbury, Robert Lowry, and William Howard Doane—that is, a song with (1) its text based on conversion, salvation, and heaven; (2) its form a two-part structure of verse and chorus, each eight bars in length; (3) its rhythms characterized by a predominance of quarter and dotted-eighth notes; and (4) its chorus performed in the antiphonal style.

Tindley moved away from this formula in several respects. In the first place, he concentrated on texts that gave attention to such important concerns of Black Christians as worldly sorrows, blessings, and woes, as well as the joys of the afterlife. Second, he placed many of his melodies in the beloved pentatonic scale and left a certain amount of space in his melodic line and harmonic scheme for interpolation of the so-called blue thirds and sevenths. He also allowed space for the inevitable improvisation of text, melody, harmony, and rhythm, so characteristic of Black American folk and popular music. Tindley, himself a cosmopolitan person, wrote songs expressly for his congregation and other Black Christians and attempted to speak directly to them. As time has proved, he spoke not only to them but to others who found this new kind of music attractive.

Gospel performance style, with all its musical and theatrical indulgences, had begun to take shape and was practiced at Tindley Temple by the Reverend Charles Albert Tindley and his congregation. Eyewitness reports and Ralph H. Jones, biographer of Tindley, often refer to the gospel songfests held on prayer-meeting nights at Tindley's church and the occasional songfest that would develop during his sermons. The famous songs of Dorsey, Brewster, Campbell, Pace, and Roberta Martin differ from those of Tindley more in performance practices than in compositional and notated style, for, as Dorsey reported, these composers simply built on what had been started by Tindley, who died just as gospel music began its climb to respectability among all peoples.

Tindley was a pioneer in encouraging the organizing of gospel groups. Seven male members from his church formed the Tindley Gospel Singers in 1922; by April 1929, they were experienced enough to serve in a five-week evangelism campaign with the Reverend F. F. Bosworth at Anderson, Indiana. The largest part of their repertoire consisted of Tindley songs. Indeed, gospel singers, rather than church choirs, were responsible for the popularity of Tindley's music—and it did become very popular.

It is significant that Tindley is represented in each of four hymnals for the Black church published since 1977: *The New National Baptist Hymnal* (1977) includes four of Tindley's songs; *Songs of Zion* (1981) of the United Methodist Church contains 11 of his songs out of a total of 250; *Lift Every Voice and Sing* (1981) of the Episcopal Church has 3 Tindley compositions out of 151 entries; and the first hymnal published for the Church of God in Christ, *Yes, Lord!* (1982), includes 7 Tindley songs in its total of 525. His position as progenitor of Black gospel music is certified by his inclusion in these hymnals along with such noted modern composers as James Cleveland, Doris Akers, Andrae Crouch, Walter Hawkins, and Elbernita "Twinkie" Clark.

PUBLICATION OF THE SONGS

There are no records to indicate when Tindley composed his music, for it appears that, like Mozart, he walked around for weeks or months with songs "in his head" and requested a scribe to notate them only when he had completed several compositions. The list of published works (see table 1) provides dates of publication only, not of composition. He published his first songs in 1901, a total of eight; among these was "I'll Overcome Some Day," first published in C. Austin Miles's *New Songs of the Gospel* (Miles and Lowdens 1901). (Miles is best remembered today for his gospel hymn "In the Garden," also known as "I Come to the Garden Alone.") During the years 1901–26, Tindley published songs on twelve different occasions. The largest number appeared in 1901 and 1905, eight in each year. After Tindley's death, his widow, Jennie Cotton Tindley, published new songs in 1934, and his son Elbert Tindley published more songs in 1941.

The eight songs published by Tindley in 1901 met with unexpected success. For example, "What Are They Doing in Heaven?" became extremely popular and even today is beloved by gospel singers and gospel music lovers. "I'll Overcome Some Day" was popular shortly after its publication, then went into a decline for a number of years. During the Civil Rights Movement of the 1960s, new attention was given to the Tindley composition because of the immensely popular "We Shall Overcome." The success of his songs undoubtedly influenced Tindley in the decision to join with three other ministers, all bishops, to form the Soul Echoes Publishing Company at 420 South Eleventh Street in Philadelphia. The company's first publication in 1905 consisted essentially of a collection of Tindley's songs, but, in the fashion of the day, it also included well-known compositions of other composers. This publication, *Soul Echoes: A Collection of Songs for Religious Meetings*, was followed four years later by a second, enlarged version (see table 2).

By 1916, Tindley, along with two of his sons and three other associates, had formed the Paradise Publishing Company, with which he remained associated until his death. The major function of this company was to publish Tindley songs. *New Songs of Paradise! No. 1* contained all Tindley compositions except for a few standard hymns, such as "Abide with Me" and "Still, Still with Thee." The first four editions of *New Songs of Paradise* (the exclamation point was dropped from the titles after No. 1) were published during the lifetime of Tindley, No. 4 from the business address 1509 Christian Street, Philadelphia. As indicated in table 2, editions of *New Songs* were published in 1934 and in 1941. *New Songs, No. 6* is significant in that it includes the entire catalogue of Tindley, as well as a few questionable entries.

Table 1   Chronology of Published Songs by Charles Albert Tindley

Year	Title*	Arranger	Year	Title*	Arranger
1901	"A Better Home"	Charles Albert Tindley	1913	"Will You Be There?"	F. A. C.
	"A Stranger Cut the Rope"	C. A. T.		"Joyous Anticipation"	F. A. C.
	"After a While"	C. A. T.	1915	"Your Faith Has Saved You"	C. A. Tindley, Jr.
	"From Youth to Old Age"	J. Chandler Wright		"Heaven's Christmas Tree"	C. A. T., Jr.
	"Go Wash in the Beautiful Stream"	C. A. T.		"Mountain Top Dwelling"	C. A. T., Jr.
	"I'll Overcome Some Day"	C. A. T.	1916	"Christ Is the Way"	C. A. T., Jr.
	"What Are They Doing in Heaven?"	C. A. T.		"Leave It There"*	C. A. T., Jr.
	"The Lord Will Make the Way"	C. A. T.		"I Believe It"	C. A. T., Jr.
1905	"Nothing Between"*	Francis Alfred Clark	1919	"The Home of the Soul"	C. A. T., Jr.
	"It May Be the Best for Me"	F. A. C.		"Spiritual Spring Time"	C. A. T., Jr.
	"Pilgrim Stranger"	F. A. C.		"I'll Be Satisfied"	C. A. T., Jr.
	"We'll Understand It Better By and By"*	F. A. C.		"He'll Take You Through"	C. A. T., Jr.
	"To-Day"*	F. A. C.		"A Better Day Is By and By"	C. A. T., Jr.
	"The Storm Is Passing Over"*	F. A. C.	1923	"Let Jesus Fix It for You"*	Frederick J. Tindley
	"Some Day (Beams of Heaven)"*	F. A. C.		"Just Today"	F. J. T.
	"Stand By Me"*	F. A. C.		"In Me"	F. J. T.
1906	"I Have Found At Last a Saviour"	F. A. C.	1926	"Saved and Satisfied"	F. J. T.
1907	"I'm Going There"	C. A. T.	1941	"The Heavenly Union" (poem published 1934)	Elbert T. Tindley
	"I Will Go, If My Father Holds My Hand"	F. A. C.		"Our Suffering Jesus" (publication date of poem unknown)	E. T. and Hazel P. Tindley
1909	"Consolation"	William D. Smith		"Have You Crossed the Line?" (poem published in 1934)	E. T. and H. P. T.
	"God Will Provide for Me"	W. D. S.			
	"My Secret of Joy"	W. D. S.		"Go Talk with Jesus About It" (publication date of poem unknown)	E. T. T.
	"Some One Is Waiting for Me"	W. D. S.			
	"Pilgrim Stranger"	W. D. S.		"Pilgrim's Song" (poem published in 1901)	E. T. T.
1911	"Here Am I, Send Me"*	F. A. C.			

*Asterisks indicate songs that are now standard in the gospel repertoire.

THE ARRANGERS OF TINDLEY'S SONGS

The term *arranger* is employed uniquely in a discussion of Black gospel music for, in most cases, such a person may not alter, subtract, or add anything to what the composer

Table 2   Collected Works of Charles Albert Tindley

Title	Edition	Year of Publication	Publisher	City
Soul Echoes	No. 1	1905	J. S. Caldwell L. J. Coppin G. L. Blackwell C. A. Tindley	Philadelphia, PA
Soul Echoes	No. 2	1909	Same as above	Philadelphia
New Songs of Paradise!	No. 1	1916	Paradise Publishing*	Philadelphia
	No. 2	?	P. P. Co.	Philadelphia
	No. 3	?	P. P. Co.	Philadelphia
	No. 4	?	C. A. Tindley	Philadelphia
	No. 5	1934	Jennie C. Tindley	Worton, MD
	No. 6	1941	Elbert T. Tindley	Philadelphia
			Elbert T. Tindley and Hazel P. Tindley	Lansing, MI

*Charles F. Brown, President; Julius C. Young, Secretary; Charles Young, Assistant Secretary; Frederick J. Tindley, Business Manager; Charles A. Tindley, Jr., Musical Critic; Charles A. Tindley, Treasurer.

gives him or her. For that reason, the arranger serves the same function as a secretary taking dictation from a speaker and typing the same. As a matter of fact, the current term for such activity is *transcriber*, a term much more accurate in this context than arranging, which suggests that another person has altered, for good or bad, the fixed composition of the original composer. We retain the term *arranger* here, however, because of tradition.

During his publishing period, Tindley, who was musically illiterate, worked with at least five arrangers. His first arranger was J. Chandler Wright, who arranged "From Youth to Old Age" and shared the copyright with Tindley. The only information available about Wright is that he was an organist who could notate music.

Tindley's second and most important arranger was Francis A. Clark, important not only because of the relatively large number of songs he arranged for Tindley but also because of the sizable number that became gospel classics or "standards." While little is known of Clark's personal life, he was a celebrated and highly respected Black musician in Philadelphia during the first two decades of this century; he was always referred to as Professor F. A. Clark. On February 17, 1913, the *Philadelphia Bulletin* carried an announcement from the Wesley AME Zion Church that "Professor F. A. Clark, our own musical composer, has been secured as chorister of Wesley. Professor Clark needs no introduction to the music-loving public for his works speak for itself [*sic*]." As late as 1943, Clark was still active, having arranged the gospel song "And He Called Me His Own" written by Ida Walker of Philadelphia and published in the 1945 edition of Martin and Morris's *The National Gospel Singer* (1945). Clark worked with Tindley on and off during the period 1905–13, arranging twelve songs, among them, "Stand By Me," "Nothing Between," and "We'll Understand It Better By and By."

The next arranger to work with Tindley was William D. Smith, who arranged five songs. The only thing we know about Smith is that at one time he "deserted sacred music long enough to write a song entitled 'I'd Love to See an Educated Frog'" (Shirley 1981).

From 1915 through 1919, Charles Albert Tindley, Jr., arranged eleven songs for his father and wrote the music for his father's text "Mountain Top Dwelling" (Boyer 1982b). Frederick J. Tindley was his father's last arranger, transcribing four songs for publication in 1923, of which the most famous arrangement is "Let Jesus Fix It for You."

After Tindley's death, Elbert T. Tindley arranged three of his father's songs, and with his wife, Hazel P. Tindley, arranged two others, which they included in the 1941 edition of *New Songs of Zion*.

For some unknown reason, Tindley himself took credit for arranging eight of his songs, among which were "Go Wash in the Beautiful Stream" and "What Are They Doing in Heaven?" Neither in interviews nor in his writings did Tindley mention that he studied music; it was generally assumed that he could neither read nor write music. Undoubtedly, these eight songs were transcribed by others in the Philadelphia area.

ANALYSIS OF THE GOSPEL HYMNS

The Texts

Tindley was thinking of a particular audience when he wrote his songs and when he sang them during sermons: African American Christians who had been freed from the bonds of slavery only thirty-six years before he published his first songs. They were the new arrivals in the North who poured in daily—most of them poor and illiterate—and who valued highly the simple, direct, and emotional style of life of which Tindley spoke. He used their language, taking a biblical passage such as Isaiah 6:8, for example, and restating it in common, everyday words:

> Also I heard the voice of the Lord, saying
> Whom shall I send, and who will go for us?
> Then said I, Here am I; send me. (Isaiah 6:8)

> "HERE AM I, SEND ME"
> If the Saviour wants somebody just to fill a humble place,
> And to show that to the lowly God will give sufficient grace,
> I am ready now to offer all I am, what-e'er it be
> And to say to Him this moment, "Here am I, send me."

Tindley was a master in calling forth through imagery and symbolism the biblical and folk heroes and heroines so dear to the hearts of his people. Even today, ministers quote his texts in the midst of their sermons as if the texts were poems, as indeed they are. Tindley also was aware of the importance of hymn meters. He seems to have made a special effort to use the meters so beloved in the Black church of yesteryear: the short meter, the common meter, and especially the long meter. Among some African American congregations, it was the practice to perform the metrical scheme 8, 7, 8, 7 as if it were long meter, with eight syllables to each line. While the line

```
1  2  3  4   5    6    7   8
Just as I am with - out one plea
```

actually has eight syllables, some congregations would take a seven-syllable line, such as:

```
1   2   3   4    5  6  7   8
And take me home to my Go - od
```

and, by adding an extra syllable to "God," create an eight-syllable line. Frequently the chorus of a song will use a variant of the verse meter, as in the example that follows from "A Stranger Cut the Rope."

Tindley's lyrics—like those of gospel songwriter Reverend William Herbert Brewster, who was to follow in his footsteps—most often recount a story or propose a situation. A story line is established in the first part of the song and continues throughout but is punctuated with the major theme or a moral as the story progresses. Tindley often begins in a contemplative manner, setting up the situation, then brings the story to an intermediate climax even in the first stanza of four, six, or eight lines. At this point, he interjects the moral or the ideal conclusion. His long-meter hymn "I'm Going There" and his short-meter double hymn "A Stranger Cut the Rope" are examples of this use of lyrics:

"I'M GOING THERE"
And often when I would do good,
And keep the promise as I should,
I miss the way, and coming short,
It makes me mourn and grieves my heart.

Chorus

Although a pilgrim here below
Where dangers are and sorrows grow,
I have a home in heav'n above,
I'm going there, I'm going there.

"A STRANGER CUT THE ROPE"
'Twas early in the day;
    The sun was shining bright,
I thought to go my way,
    And get back home by night.
But when my captor tied
    Me down and left me there,
"No hope for me," I cried,
    And sank into despair.

Chorus [6, 6, 8, 6, 6, 6, 8, 6]

A Stranger cut the rope,
    It was my only hope,
When my poor soul upon the shoal
    Of sin and death did lie,
The tide was coming in,
    The consequence of sin;
A Stranger heard my helpless cry,
    And cut the fatal string.

He relates the story or describes the situation in the verse or the "A" section, and uses the chorus, or the "B" section—which is repeated after each dramatic or narrative episode in the verse—to emphasize the theme or moral. More than almost all other gospel composers, except perhaps Thomas A. Dorsey and James Cleveland, Tindley had a penchant for writing "sing-along" choruses, choruses so exciting or moving that congregations join in the singing. Indeed, many of his songs are better known by the first line of the chorus than by the original title. A celebrated example is "We'll Understand It Better By and By," better known as "By and By When the Morning Comes" (ex. 2).

In actual performance, the song generally is introduced by its chorus and concludes with the chorus. Consequently, not only does the chorus first state the song's theme (or its moral) but it also serves as the unifying element. The chorus thus actually becomes the "A" of the song form, which takes on the following structure in performance: ABABABA, and so on. Tindley uses the verse–chorus or AB form in thirty-six of his songs and the strophic form in the remaining ten songs.

Musical Elements

Of the forty-six songs in the Tindley catalogue, fifteen, or approximately one-third, use the diatonic major scale. Fourteen songs, or somewhat fewer than one-third of the total, use a pentatonic scale. Of the several varieties of the pentatonic, the most favored in African American folk music and church music seems to be the scale composed of major seconds and a minor third, such as would result from using tones 1, 2, 3, 5, and 6 of the diatonic scale. This is the scale of such longtime favorites as "Swing Low, Sweet Chariot," "Steal Away to Jesus," and "Amazing Grace." (Although "Amazing Grace" was written by a white composer, Black churches everywhere have adopted it.) When the final tone of this scale serves as the key tone, the melody has a minor sound, as in, for example, "Sometimes I Feel Like a Motherless Child."

The remaining seventeen songs of Tindley's use gapped scales, which fall into three categories: scales with the seventh tone omitted, represented in ten songs; scales with the fourth tone omitted, as in six songs; and a four-tone scale (1, 2, 3, 5) used in one song. For the most part, however, many of these songs are essentially pentatonic. Where the seventh tone is missing, the fourth appears rarely and typically on the last beat of a measure as a passing tone; in the case of melodies with a missing fourth, the seventh tone

Example 2.   "We'll Understand It Better By and By" (Charles Albert Tindley, orig. © 1905).

1. We are tossed and driv-en on the rest-less sea of time;
2. We are of-ten des-ti-tute of the things that life de-mands,
3. Tri-als dark on ev-ery hand, and we can-not un-der-stand
4. Temp - ta-tions, hid-den snares of-ten take us un-a-wares,

som - ber skies and howl-ing tem-pests oft suc - ceed a bright sun-shine;
want of food and want of shel-ter, thirst- y hills and bar-ren lands;
all the ways that God would lead us to that bless - ed prom-ised land;
and our hearts are made to bleed for a thought-less word or deed;

in that land of per - fect day, when the mists have rolled a -way,
we are trust-ing in the Lord, and ac - cord-ing to God's word,
but he guides us with his eye, and we'll fol - low till we die,
and we won-der why the test when we try to do our best,

we will un – der-stand it bet - ter by and by.
we will un – der-stand it bet - ter by and by.
for we'll un – der-stand it bet - ter by and by.
but we'll un – der-stand it bet - ter by and by.

Example 2.   *(continued)*

By and by, when the morn - ing comes,

when the saints of God are gath - ered home,

we'll tell the sto - ry how we've o - ver-come,

for we'll un - der-stand it bet - ter by and by. (by and by)

is apt to appear rarely. The songs "Leave It There" (ex. 3), "Some Day" (ex. 4), and "The Lord Will Make the Way" (ex. 5) illustrate Tindley's use of these scales.

In regard to melodic contour, Tindley's melodies most often ascend gradually to a peak, then just as gradually descend to the final, which typically is the key tone. This melodic shape may reflect the emotional mood of the song; Tindley generally begins in a meditative manner, using the low part of the register, then becomes more intense, moving

Example 3.   "Leave It There" (Charles Albert Tindley, orig. © 1916).

1. If the world from you with-hold of its   sil – ver and its gold,
2. If your bod - y suf - fers pain, and your health you can't re-gain,
3. When your en - e - mies as - sail, and your heart be-gins to fail,
4. When your youth-ful days are done, and old   age is steal-ing on,

and   you   have   to   get   a – long   with mea - ger   fare,
and   your   soul   is   al - most sink - ing   in   de - spair,
don't   for - get   that   God   in   heav - en   an - swers prayer;
and   your   bod - y   bends   be - neath   the   weight   of   care,

just re - mem-ber in   his Word how he   feeds the lit – tle bird,
Je - sus knows the pain you feel,   he can   save and he can heal,
he   will   make a way for you,   and will   lead you safe - ly through,
he   will   nev – er leave you then, he'll go   with you to   the end,

take   your   bur – den   to   the Lord and leave   it   there.

Example 3.   *(continued)*

Refrain

Leave it there, (leave it there) leave it there, (leave it there)

take your bur-den to the Lord and leave it there.

(leave it there)

If you trust and nev-er doubt, he will sure-ly bring you out;

take your bur-den to the Lord and leave it there. (leave it there)

into the higher parts of the register in developing the song. Invariably, it is the third strain of the song that is the most exciting, in terms of both music and text. The song "Nothing Between" illustrates Tindley's melodic contours (ex. 6).

Tindley was a composer for whom the lyrics of a song constituted its major element; while melody and harmony certainly were handled with care, these elements were regarded as subservient to the text. As is true of Black folk music of the early twentieth

Example 4. "Some Day" (Charles Albert Tindley, orig. © 1905).

1. Beams of heav - en as I go, through this
2. Of - ten - times my sky is clear, joy a -
3. Hard - er yet may be the fight; right may
4. Bur - dens now may crush me down, dis - ap -

wil - der - ness be - low, guide my feet in peace-ful ways,
bounds with-out a tear; though a day so bright be - gun,
of - ten yield to might; wick - ed - ness a while may reign;
point - ments all a - round; trou - bles speak in mourn-ful sigh,

turn my mid - nights in - to days. When in the
clouds may hide to - mor-row's sun. There'll be a
Sa - tan's cause may seem to gain. There is a
sor - row through a tear-stained eye. There is a

dark - ness I would grope, faith al - ways sees a star of hope,
day that's al - ways bright, a day that nev - er yields to night,
God that rules a - bove, with hand of power and heart of love;
world where plea-sure reigns, no mourn-ing soul shall roam its plains,

Example 4.   *(continued)*

and soon from all life's grief and dan-ger I shall be
and in its light the streets of glo-ry I shall be -
if I am right, he'll fight my bat-tle, I shall have
and to that land of peace and glo-ry I want to

Refrain

free some day.
hold some day.
peace some day. I do not know how long 'twill be,
go some day.

nor what the fu – ture holds for me, but this I know:

if Je - sus leads me, I shall get home some day.

century (for example, the emerging blues), Tindley's music relies almost wholly on the primary chords of the key, I, IV, and V. The use of multiple nonharmonic tones, however, is characteristic of Tindley's harmonic style, and these are found on the beat as well as off the beat, though seldom on structural pulses.

Harmonic analysis of "Stand By Me," one of the most famous and most typical of his songs, will serve to illustrate his harmonic vocabulary (ex. 7). On structural pulses—

Example 5.   "The Lord Will Make the Way" (Charles Albert Tindley, orig. © 1901).

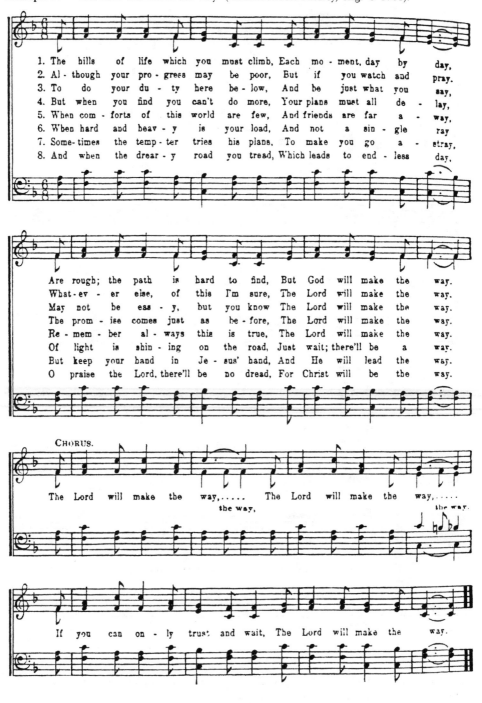

Example 6. "Nothing Between" (Charles Albert Tindley, orig. © 1905).

Example 7. Harmonic elements in "Stand By Me" (Charles Albert Tindley).

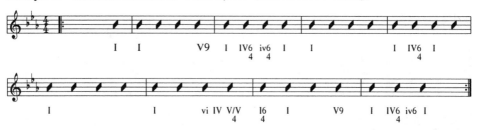

beats one and three—the tonic chord (I) has been used, except in m. 6, where the supertonic (vi) appears. The slow harmonic rhythm of this composition is typical of Tindley's writing. At times the use of passing tones, single or double, creates the effect of richer chords—as in the last chord of the anacrusis and of m. 5, or the chords on the fourth beats of mm. 1 and 7, but these chords can hardly be analyzed as ii_3^4 and V^9, respectively, in light of the general harmonic context. The use of the borrowed minor iv_4^6 in mm. 2 and 8 is a common hymn and gospel song device that results from the use of chromatic passing tones. A chromatic passing tone also accounts for the V_3^4 of V on the last chord of m. 6 (ex. 8).

When Tindley enriches his harmony, he typically uses secondary dominant or dimin-

Example 8. "Stand By Me" (Charles Albert Tindley, orig. © 1905).

1. When the storms of life are rag - ing Stand by me; (Stand by me;) When the
2. In   the midst of trib - u - la - tions, Stand by me;   In   the
3. In   the midst of faults and fail - ures, Stand by me;   In   the
4. In   the midst of per - se - cu - tion, Stand by me;   In   the
5. When I'm grow-ing old and fee - ble, Stand by me; (by   me) When I'm

storms of   life   are rag - ing, Stand by me; (stand by me;) When the
midst   of   trib - u - la - tions, Stand by me: When the
midst   of   faults and fail - ures, Stand by me;   When I
midst   of   per - se - cu - tion, Stand by me;   When my
grow - ing old and fee - ble, Stand by me; (stand by me;) When my

Example 8.   *(continued)*

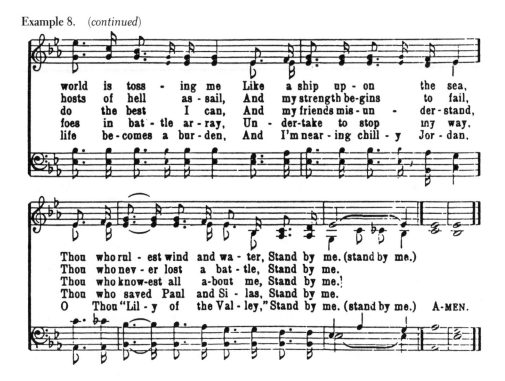

world   is   toss - ing me   Like   a ship   up - on   the   sea,
hosts   of   hell   as - sail,   And   my strength be-gins   to   fail,
do   the best   I   can,   And   my friends mis - un   -   der - stand,
foes   in   bat - tle ar - ray,   Un - der-take   to   stop   my   way,
life   be - comes a bur - den,   And   I'm near - ing chill - y   Jor - dan,

Thou   who rul - est wind   and wa - ter,   Stand   by   me. (stand by me.)
Thou   who nev - er lost   a   bat - tle,   Stand   by   me.
Thou   who know-est all   a-bout me,   Stand   by   me.!
Thou   who saved Paul   and Si - las,   Stand   by   me.
O   Thou "Lil - y   of   the Val - ley," Stand   by   me. (stand by me.)   A-MEN.

ished sevenths, often on the third beat of the measure to lead into V–I cadences but also at other points (see ex. 3, "Leave It There," mm. 1, 3, 5, 6, etc.). Generally, however, Tindley's songs are based on simple, primary harmonies that complement the texts.

Gospel arrangers and transcribers tend to place compositions in the keys in which they are performed or as close to those keys as their musicianship will permit (some transcribers of gospel music cannot *think* in all keys and, consequently, tend to avoid keys with more than four flats or sharps). Tindley appears to have followed this practice, for the melodic ranges of his songs seem to correspond to his vocal range, based on a description of his voice as "midway between light and dark, but heavier than Jesse Jackson's" (Boyer 1982b). The songs are placed in keys whose highest tones he could easily reach, D or E above middle C, while the lowest tones, second-space C (bass clef) or one or two tones below, were also in a comfortable range. The distribution of keys found in the forty-six songs is as follows: fifteen, key of F; nine, key of E♭; nine, key of G; four, key of C; three, key of A♭; three, key of D; two, key of g; and one, key of B♭.

Although Black folk music traditionally has exhibited a predilection for duple meters, the gospel meter of today is $\frac{12}{8}$ or other meters using some multiple of three. That compound meters obviously were associated with gospel music in Tindley's time is suggested by his use of such meters in twenty-three, or exactly one-half, of his songs. The other twenty-three songs have duple meters, using $\frac{4}{4}$ meters in twenty songs and $\frac{2}{4}$ meters in three songs.

The style of Black traditional church music during Tindley's compositional period called for heavy accents on the dotted-rhythm patterns, with a relatively subtle syncopation or none at all (except in the Holiness church, where rhythm was an all-important element of composition and performance). Along with observing these rhythmic conventions, Tindley also employed martial rhythms and even, occasionally, "stopped" rhythms. An example of this can be seen in Tindley's "It May Be the Best for Me" (ex. 9).

PERFORMANCE PRACTICES

Black gospel performance style as we know it was in its infancy when Tindley was writing his songs. An examination of what happens to one of his songs when it is performed in modern style indicates how songs may change character in actual performance. In 1905 Tindley used the key of E♭ major for his song "Stand By Me," but the melody essentially is pentatonic: The fourth tone of the major scale is omitted, and the seventh tone appears only twice, each time with the brief value of a sixteenth. When the Caravans, a women's gospel group, recorded this song in the 1960s, it underwent several changes (see my transcription in ex. 10).

First, the Caravans changed the key to B♭ major. Gospel songs are transposed to the most comfortable key for the singer, regardless of the original keys in which the songs were written. Most gospel singers operate on the premise that gospel music is a singer's art, not a composer's art, and in performance their wishes dominate all others. Amateur singers may begin to sing even before the keyboardist plays the introduction; the keyboardist is expected to find the key by playing a scale to reach the key the singer is using.

The change of key has little effect on the range of "Stand By Me." In the original key, the range is that of a major eleventh (from low B♭ to high E♭); while the transposed version shifts the melody down a major fourth, it also expands the range by two tones to a minor thirteenth (from low F to high D♭). Tindley placed the melodic climax of his song on the high E♭ (see m. 5 in ex. 7) in order to exploit the brilliance and intensity of a high note, but Cassietta George achieves a similar effect with her D♭ at the comparable place in the modern version. This note is high in *her* register and, moreover, she delivers it in a broad ("fat") and brassy tone. Then too, it gains brilliance by its contrast to the relatively low registers preceding it. Both the melody and the text are enhanced at this point, as Tindley might have desired.

A second change involves the scale used. In the modern version, the melody becomes minor pentatonic (the single occurrences of the second and third degrees of the parallel major must be regarded simply as brief embellishments of the pentatonic). In this performance, and in other gospel performances, the change to the minor mode of a song originally written in the major mode is not intentional. Rather, it occurs as the result of the singers "bending" and "softening" the so-called bright degrees of the scale: 3, 5, 6, 7. When this bending process is carried out to its fullest degree, tones are actually lowered a half step, which results in a change of mode for the melody. The use of the minor mode gives a darker color to the music and lends more plaintiveness to the mood.

A third change has to do with tempo. The Caravans use a tempo not traditionally

Example 9. "It May Be the Best for Me" (Charles Albert Tindley, orig. © 1905).

Example 10.   "Stand By Me" as performed by the Caravans, transcribed by Horace Clarence Boyer.

Example 10. *(continued)*

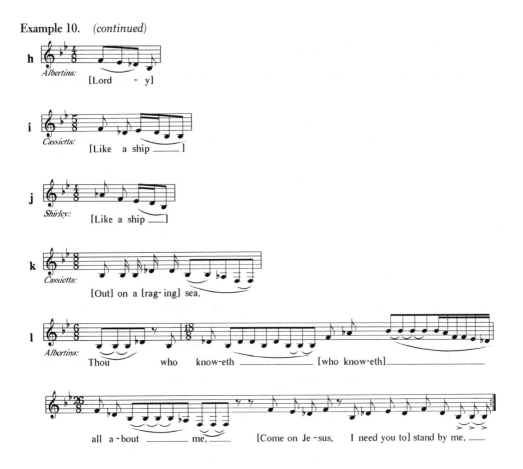

associated with the performance of "Stand By Me." This is significant, for the tempo of a gospel performance ultimately determines its classification, although any song may, at one time or another, be performed in one of three tempos: slow to moderate, fast, or "without regular pulse" or "ad lib." It is believed that Tindley intended "Stand By Me" to be performed with a regular, moderate pulse (there is no tempo indication on the score), but the Caravans render it in the slow, languorous, nineteenth-century lined-hymn style, sometimes using a single syllable of Tindley's text as the basis for a spun-out phrase. This kind of improvisation entails much embellishment of the original melody and results in a singing style reminiscent of the Baptist lining hymn. The Caravans embellish principally by singing melismas on syllables that formerly carried single tones. See, for example, the melody beginning at 10c, where Shirley Caesar sings seven articulated tones on the word *when*, then carries the melody to its melismatic peak in articulating fourteen tones on the word *storm*. Melismas appear early in this performance, the first occurring in the third word of the text, *storm*, and the next with the upward bend on the word *life*, and continuing throughout the performance.

In most gospel performances each soloist sings a single stanza and, for the sake of variety, the succeeding stanzas are given to different soloists. The Caravans, however, divide each stanza into four sections, with Albertina Walker taking the first part; Caesar, the second; George, the third; and Walker returning to close out the stanza. The device of dividing the stanza between two or more soloists is called *swing lead*, a term coined by male quartets in the 1920s to describe the practice of assigning the chorus of a song to the tenor, regardless of who sang the verses (usually a baritone or bass).

Not only is the music subjected to improvisation, the text also is treated to dramatic alteration. It is continuously interrupted to accommodate interpolations; sometimes the added words are related to the text, or the additions may simply be sounds that build up the rhythmic intensity. The text interpolations sometimes take on an independence of their own as, for example, in the passages *e–h* where call-and-response patterns develop in the reiteration of the phrase *like a ship*. None of these things, however, detract from the message of the text; on the contrary, the message is enhanced.

To summarize, in this performance, as in most gospel performances, the music has been completely altered to fit the mood and craft of the singers. At times the original melody is barely discernible, and most of the original rhythmic patterns have disappeared. But the song nevertheless retains both the message and the effect of the original hymn Tindley wrote in 1905.

Charles Albert Tindley not only was a good composer; he was unique. He knew his Bible and could translate its archaic language into the soft, picturesque, and sonorous language of his people, and ultimately of all people. He was an extraordinary storyteller; he told his stories in simple and direct melodies, using harmonies that did not overpower the simplicity of his messages. Above all, he left the spaces necessary for gospel singers to become engrossed in their singing. He knew that gospel music was the singer's art, not that of the composer. The progenitor of African American gospel music was singer and composer in one.

3

Lucie Eddie Campbell Williams (1885–1963)

LUCIE E. CAMPBELL

Composer for the National Baptist Convention

Horace Clarence Boyer

When the history of African American gospel music is written, the first period will extend from 1893 to 1921, a period of radical and successful transition in traditional Black sacred music from the beloved antebellum spiritual of the rural Black Christian to the modern-era gospel music of the urban Black Christian. This real history will propose a chronological order of great pioneers of gospel music in which Lucie Eddie Campbell stands fourth in the line of creators who followed after William Henry Sherwood. In 1893, Sherwood published a book in Petersburg, Virginia, called *Harp of Zion*, the first book to include gospel music by an African American composer.

The Reverend R. H. Boyd, then secretary of the Publishing Board of the National Baptist Convention, heard about Sherwood's book and requested a copy of the plates to ascertain if the publication would meet the Convention's musical standards. He found the book acceptable and published a copy for the Baptist Young People's Union (BYPU).

Sherwood was followed by Charles Price Jones of Jackson, Mississippi, who began publishing a kind of gospel song as early as 1899 with his songs "The Harvest Is Past" and "Jesus Has Made It All Right" and who published the popular "I'm Happy with Jesus Alone" in 1900. Jones was followed by Reverend Charles Albert Tindley of Philadelphia, who in 1901 published the first in a series of forty-five gospel hymns and songs that became the catalyst for the transition from Negro spirituals to gospel.

In 1919, the first woman to join the ranks of these performing composers, Lucie E.

Campbell, copyrighted her first songs, one of which—"The Lord Is My Shepherd"—was included in the monumental 1921 edition of *Gospel Pearls*. Campbell served as a member of the committee that chose the music for *Gospel Pearls*, and some of the new songs were included along with the standards. In addition to her composition, there were songs by Tindley, Jones, and a person about whom little is heard but who was important, Carrie Booker Person, composer of "Someone Is Hitting the Home Trail Tonight" and "Ring It out with a Shout."

Campbell's interest in music began when she started to learn piano as a child by listening to the piano lessons of her sister in Memphis during the late 1890s. She became a proficient musician and wrote out her own manuscripts by hand. She basically was self-taught, and although her college records show that she studied music, she graduated as a liberal arts major from Rust College in Holly Springs, Mississippi, with a bachelor of arts degree in 1927.

Campbell's professional career as a composer extends from 1919 to 1962, a period during which few years passed without a Lucie Campbell song (see table 3). Various sources report that she wrote over one hundred songs. Unfortunately, only forty-six of her songs are in print, forty-one of which have been used for this analysis.

From 1930 to 1962, she introduced a new song each year at the National Baptist Convention. Her songs became gospel standards, sung by all races and creeds. Campbell has the distinction of having composed the second most popular song in all Black Christendom after Thomas A. Dorsey's song "Precious Lord," which is, of course, "He Understands; He'll Say, 'Well Done.'" One can go to a Black church at the time of a funeral and find Catholics, Lutherans, Methodists, Baptists, and Holiness singing this song, and they will be singing it without the sheet music.

From the time she was elected music director of the Baptist Training Union Congress in 1916 to her last visit to the National Baptist Convention in 1962, Campbell exerted her musical influence throughout the entire African American community. Campbell was a woman of strong conviction and a person who required all others to bow to her wishes; there was no question that the National Baptist Convention, the largest denomination of African American Christians in the world, would sing what she and her colleagues preferred. Initially, Campbell worked with a mentor, E. W. D. Isaac, Sr., the organizer of the National Baptist Training Union, and later with his son, E. W. D. Isaac, Jr. What kinds of songs did Lucie E. Campbell want the National Baptist Convention to sing? The answer is simple: the songs she wrote and the songs and singing of the new pioneers of gospel who came to this music with the same conviction she possessed. *

According to Elmer Ruffner, who had been a pianist for one of the traveling groups, called the Goodwill Singers, Campbell was so important and powerful in the National

---

* The Isaac and Campbell traveling groups included people such as Dr. J. Robert Bradley; J. Earl Hines; Thomas Shelby, who has been with the church of the Reverend C. L. Franklin (great gospel preacher and father of Aretha Franklin) for forty-five years; and Reverend Charles Simms, one of the vice-presidents of Gospel Music Workshop of America.

Table 3 Selected Compositions by Lucie E. Campbell

Copyright Date	Title	Copyright Date	Title
1919	"Are They Equal in the Eyes of the Law?" "Something Within" "The Lord Is My Shepherd"	1948	"I Need Thee, Precious Lord" (arr.)
1923	"Heavenly Sunshine" "Just to Behold His Face" "The King's Highway" "Welcome Chorus"	1949	"Awake! for Thy God Reigneth" "There Is a Fountain" (arr.) "Footprints of Jesus"
		1950	"Looking to Jesus"
1931	"Nobody Else but Jesus"	1952	"A Sinner Like Me" "Even a Child Can Open the Gate" "They that Wait Upon the Lord"
1932	"My Savior"		
1933	"He Understands; He'll Say, 'Well Done'" "Is He Yours?"	1956	"His Grace Is Sufficient for Me"
		1958	"Come Ye Blessed of My Father" "The Path through the Valley Leads Home"
1936	"Is He Yours?" "Room! Room!"	1959	"God's Long Reach of Salvation"
1940	"I Want to Be Ready to Put on My Gospel Shoes" "Spiritual Medley: Tramping, Wanna Be Ready, Walk Children"	1960	"Love Not Nails Held Him There" "The Story of Salvation Must Be Told (in Africa, China and the Isles of the Sea)" "Unto Thee, Thou Holy One"
1941	"Touch Me, Lord Jesus"	1962	"Signed and Sealed with His Blood" "Sometime Soon"
1946	"Jesus Gave Me Water" "Praise Ye the Lord"	1963	"Come, Lord Jesus, Abide with Me"
1947	"Holy Three in One" "In the Upper Room" "Just As I am" (arr.) "The Lord's Prayer" "My Lord and I (On the Heavenly Road)" "Not Yours but You" "Offertory Prayer" "This Is the Day the Lord Has Made" "When I Get Home"	No Copyright Date	"Hail, Ye Baptist Leaders" "I Know I Won't Stop Singing" "I Thank Thee" "In the End" "Jesus, Keep Me Humble" "Lucie E. Campbell's Soul Stirring Songs" "No Sorrow, Too Light" "Praise the Lord, Ye Heavens"

Baptist Convention that anyone who wanted to sing on the program had to audition for her, singing the same song he or she planned to sing on the program (Boyer 1980). Campbell didn't want anything to come through that did not follow the pattern she felt was appropriate for the times. Lucie E. Campbell was blessed with great leadership and organizing ability. This asset, along with the fact that she herself was composing during the formative years of the gospel movement, gave her the opportunity to help develop the new tradition.

Lucie Campbell published her songs beginning in 1919. Among the forty-one songs used for this analysis, one was published in 1921; six in 1941; two in 1946; nine in 1947; five in 1949; one in 1951; three in 1952; one each in 1953, 1954, and 1956; three in

1958; one in 1962; and two in 1963. She died on January 3, 1963, but two songs were published that year since they were at the printers when she died. Reverend C. R. Williams, her husband, had them published. These two songs were "Sometime Soon" and "Come, Lord Jesus, Abide with Me."

Campbell's professional initiation into music publishing resulted from her membership on the committee to select music for *Gospel Pearls*. Campbell influenced a whole area of gospel music and never published through a major music house. If she didn't publish her songs through the National Baptist Convention's Sunday School Publishing Board in Nashville (one song) and the BYPU (one song), she published them herself or with her longtime partner and later husband, Reverend C. R. Williams.

When Campbell published her own songs, she included her home address on the sheet music. The compositions carrying the address of 711 Saxon Avenue bore the copyright of Campbell and Williams in Memphis. Sheet music reveals that when they moved to Nashville around 1960, they lived at two addresses: at 328 Second Avenue North they published one song, and after they moved to 4342 Enchanted Circle, they published three songs.

As a pioneer gospel composer, Campbell helped set the performance style for gospel music. One of her great loves was the lined hymn, which she perpetuated in her compositions. Her affinity for slowly paced songs can be traced to this older tradition of congregational performance. In the Baptist church of the 1920s, there was great love for songs performed in the Baptist lining-hymn tradition. A deacon or one of the members "lined out" the words of the hymn, followed by the congregation singing the words they had just been given. This tradition was very effective in congregations where literacy was rare. Even as more practitioners of the tradition learned to read, the lining style of singing a hymn continued to be one of great preference among certain congregations.

In the African American Baptist church, the process of lining was elevated. In fact, congregations did not actually line the text of the hymn. In African American churches the hymn was said to be "raised." In lining, one recites the words in an oratorical fashion in order to give text, and then the congregation sings them in time and in tune. For instance, one would recite the often-favored text by Charles Wesley, common-meter hymn:

> Oh for a thousand tongues to sing
>   My great redeemer's praise

and the congregation would sing in metrical fashion:

> Oh for a thousand tongues to sing
>   My great redeemer's praise
> The glories of My God and king
>   The triumphs of His grace.

In the Black Baptist congregation, the deacon or member raised the song by intoning— chanting—the opening line, thereby setting the mood for the tune, time, and tempo. The deacon would chant:

Example 11. Deacon's chant in Baptist lined-hymn tradition.

and then the congregation would sing:

Example 12. Congregation's response in nonpulsed meter (free form).

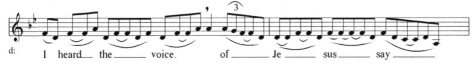

The singing has a surging, choral sound, reminiscent of a ship going over a body of water. This is the kind of song that inspired "Miss Lucie," as Campbell was called by her colleagues and students.

Of the forty-one songs I was able to find, five are of what we now call the gospel lining-hymn tradition. To ensure that her compositions would be performed in this Baptist lining tradition, she would add words at the top of the score. For example, she used such directions as "slow, with expression," the mark that she used on "Something Within"; or "reverently," as on "A Sinner Like Me." Another instruction she used was "pleadingly," as in the song she wrote in tribute to her protégé, J. Robert Bradley, "Even a Child."

As a lyricist, Campbell was an inspiring presence in the new expanding field of gospel. She was blessed with the gift of melody and lyrics that spoke for the African American Christian in such words as "Touch, touch me, Lord Jesus" or "Something within me that banishes pain."

Campbell had a passion for the gospel ballad, a slow song in which the singer thinks out loud about joy or sorrow. It might be of interest to note that these songs tend to fall in a rhythmic pulse of four pulses of four beats to the bar. One of her loveliest gospel ballads is a song called "Heavenly Sunshine," which unfortunately is not well known (ex. 13). Dr. J. Robert Bradley, who introduced the world to many of Campbell's compositions, sings it on his recording *I'll Fly Away* (Nashboro 7139). Campbell wrote gospel music, but she wanted it sung in a classical style. Bradley, who was trained as an opera singer and sang with a blend of the European operatic vocal technique and the more African-derived, emotion-filled vocal tampering with line and melody, was perfect for the performance of Campbell's compositions. Of the forty-one songs analyzed, ten fall in the gospel ballad category, including "The Lord Is My Shepherd" and "A Sinner Like Me."

Campbell's involvement in the music of the African American church came during a

Example 13. "Heavenly Sunshine" (Lucie E. Campbell, orig. © 1923). © 1951 UNICHAPPELL MUSIC INC. (Renewed).

Example 13.   *(continued)*

Example 14. "Praise Ye the Lord" (Lucie E. Campbell, orig. © 1946). © 1951 UNICHAPPELL MUSIC INC. (Renewed). All rights reserved. Used by permission.

Example 14. *(continued)*

Example 14. *(continued)*

Example 14. *(continued)*

Example 14. *(continued)*

Example 14. *(continued)*

Example 14. *(continued)*

period when European choral music was accepted as the highest form of sacred music for Black Christian churches. (The leaders of Black church music were seeking to elevate the musical standards of the congregations.) Campbell never let her affection for the anthem waiver. She wrote in the gospel style and in the Western European Protestant church tradition. In 1946, she published an anthem called "Praise Ye the Lord" (ex. 14). Nine songs analyzed are anthems, including arrangements of "There Is a Fountain Filled with Blood" and "Just As I Am, Without One Plea."

This same composer was equally at home with a gospel song. Note the four beats to the measure supplied by the bass in "Jesus Gave Me Water" (ex. 15).

Understanding the African American church and its penchant for rhythm and pulse, Campbell also wrote the sort of song that moved at a steady tempo. This kind of song, called *jubilee*, was performed in a moderately fast tempo, had a bit of syncopation, and was performed in the responsorial, call-and-response tradition. Jubilee song performed at a faster pace served as the principal music of Holiness congregations at the turn of the century. When the people in these churches performed a holy dance (a shout), they reached back into African American music history and reshaped a song form that would free them from extended text. In this style of singing, a soloist improvised the text of a song (the call), while the congregation repeated a statement after each call (the response). Such a song is "I'm a Soldier" (ex. 16). Campbell found the structural simplicity and performance range of the jubilee song attractive and wrote several songs in that style, including "When I Get Home" (ex. 17).

It would have been unusual for Campbell to compose a *shout* song, given her penchant for slow and moderate pacings and the European classical element in her music. However, some of these jubilees written at a moderate pace were performed as shout songs. A shout song is one that is performed at an extremely fast tempo, accompanied by vigorous, polyrhythmic hand-clapping, and one to which members of the congregation perform a holy dance or shout.

Reviewing some of the technical elements of Campbell's compositions, one finds that she wrote nine in the key of C; nine in Bb; eight in Ab; five in Eb; four in F; three in G; two in Db; and one in F minor. It is surprising to find that Campbell was very traditional in the use of scales. For example, out of the forty-one songs analyzed, thirty-three employ the standard diatonic scale. The standard diatonic scale is a series of tones arranged in a sequence of rising and falling pitches in accordance with any of various systems of intervals (musical steps), especially such a series contained in one octave. The diatonic is the

Example 15. "Jesus Gave Me Water" (Lucie E. Campbell, orig. © 1946). © 1950 renewed 1978 SCREEN GEMS–EMI MUSIC INC. All rights reserved. International copyright secured. Used by permission.

Example 15. *(continued)*

Example 15.   *(continued)*

Example 15. *(continued)*

Example 16.   Call and response in "I'm a Soldier" (trad.).

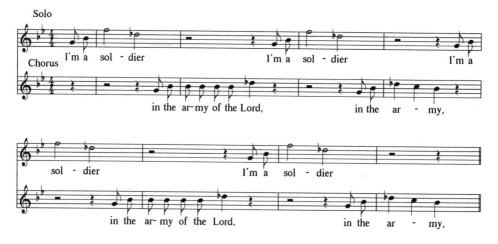

Example 17.   "When I Get Home" (Lucie E. Campbell, orig. © 1947). © 1950 renewed 1978 SCREEN GEMS–EMI MUSIC INC. All rights reserved. International copyright secured. Used by permission.

Example 17. *(continued)*

Example 17.   *(continued)*

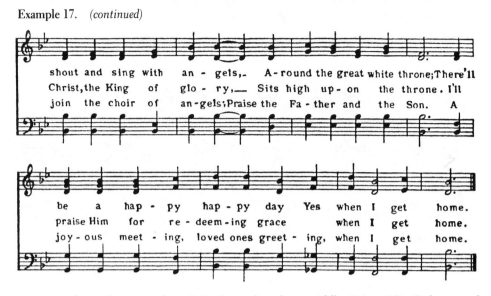

shout and sing with   an - gels,_   A - round the great white throne; There'll
Christ, the King   of   glo - ry,_   Sits high up - on   the throne. I'll
join the choir   of   an - gels; Praise the Fa - ther and   the Son.   A

be   a   hap - py   hap - py   day   Yes   when I   get   home.
praise Him   for   re - deem - ing grace   when I   get   home.
joy - ous   meet - ing,   loved ones greet - ing,   when I   get   home.

most popular scale in use; here it is shown based on middle C (ex. 18). Only one of Campbell's songs uses the pentatonic or five-tone scale, employing tones 1, 2, 3, 5, and 6 of the diatonic scale (ex. 19).

Example 18.   The standard diatonic scale, based on middle C.

1 2 3 4 5 6 7 8

Example 19.   Pentatonic scale using tones 1, 2, 3, 5, and 6 of the diatonic scale.

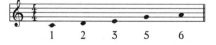

1   2   3   5   6

Seven songs are based on the so-called gapped scale, the seven-tone diatonic scale with one tone missing, creating a scale of six tones. "Jesus Gave Me Water" and "When I Get Home" appear to use the diatonic scale, though the fourth scale degree is never used, while "Look Away into Heaven" never uses the seventh scale degree.

While Lucie E. Campbell was a strong melodist, her strength as a composer was not in harmony. However, occasionally one finds interesting harmonies in her works. In her composition "Footprints of Jesus," harmonically quite daring for her, in addition to using the V^9–V in m. 6 (as part of the half-cadence), she actually uses the vii^7–V in m. 12 as part of the final cadence of each section of the song (ex. 20).

Miss Lucie's greatest contribution to gospel music is the so-called gospel waltz. This is a song that uses the waltz time. The waltz is a kind of composition in which three beats are established in the left hand, or in the bass, and then a contrasting theme is given in the treble, or in the right hand. In the hands of African Americans, this rhythm is "Africanized." The three beats given to the left hand to establish the rhythmic pulse are further divided into three beats, so that a song originally written in $\frac{3}{4}$ becomes a song in $\frac{9}{4}$, or more popularly, $\frac{9}{8}$, while a song written in $\frac{4}{4}$ becomes a song in $\frac{12}{8}$ (ex. 21).

The gospel waltz became so popular that by the 1950s this gospel rhythm, an innovation of Lucie E. Campbell, was standardized. The technique was carried on by another great composer from Memphis, Reverend W. Herbert Brewster. In fact, the gospel rhythm had become so pervasive in the 1950s that when Ray Charles decided to create a new kind of music called *soul*, he borrowed it for his rendition of "I'm a Fool for You." The song sounded just like a gospel waltz.

Example 20.   "Footprints of Jesus" (Lucie E. Campbell). © 1949 renewed 1977 SCREEN GEMS–EMI MUSIC INC. All rights reserved. International copyright secured. Used by permission.

Example 20. *(continued)*

Example 20. *(continued)*

After last stanza
Special Chorus

Foot-prints of Je-sus,____ Lead-ing the way_____ Foot prints of

Footprints of Jesus Lead-ing the way.

Je - sus,____ By night and by day;_____ Sure if I
I shall reach

Foot-prints of Je-sus By night and by day;

fol - low,____ Life will be sweet;_____ Led by the
heav en's____ Por-tals so sweet_____ Saved by the

Sure if I fol-low, Life will be sweet.
I shall reach heav-en's Por-tals so sweet.

prints of____ His wound-ed Feet!_____

Led
Saved by the prints of His wound - ed Feet.

Example 21.   Lucie E. Campbell's "gospel waltz" rhythms.

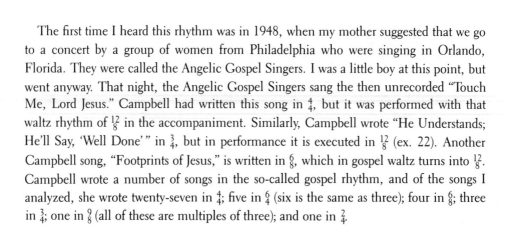

The first time I heard this rhythm was in 1948, when my mother suggested that we go to a concert by a group of women from Philadelphia who were singing in Orlando, Florida. They were called the Angelic Gospel Singers. I was a little boy at this point, but went anyway. That night, the Angelic Gospel Singers sang the then unrecorded "Touch Me, Lord Jesus." Campbell had written this song in $\frac{4}{4}$, but it was performed with that waltz rhythm of $\frac{12}{8}$ in the accompaniment. Similarly, Campbell wrote "He Understands; He'll Say, 'Well Done' " in $\frac{3}{4}$, but in performance it is executed in $\frac{9}{8}$ (ex. 22). Another Campbell song, "Footprints of Jesus," is written in $\frac{6}{8}$, which in gospel waltz turns into $\frac{12}{8}$. Campbell wrote a number of songs in the so-called gospel rhythm, and of the songs I analyzed, she wrote twenty-seven in $\frac{4}{4}$; five in $\frac{6}{4}$ (six is the same as three); four in $\frac{6}{8}$; three in $\frac{3}{4}$; one in $\frac{9}{8}$ (all of these are multiples of three); and one in $\frac{2}{4}$.

Thomas A. Dorsey is called the "father of gospel music," and with just as much justification, special significance is attached to the name Lucie E. Campbell. Long before Dorsey decided to become a full-time gospel music composer and conductor, Campbell was composing gospel music and teaching it to the entire National Baptist Convention, the largest organization of African American Christians in the world. Not only was she a teacher and composer, but she also served as a musical model for those to follow. Known as an officious leader both in and out of the church, she nevertheless taught a kind of compassion and tolerance of individual musical style; she had specific ideas about how her songs were to be performed, but she admired and accepted arrangements of her songs by such diverse singers as the Ward Singers, the Angelic Gospel Singers, the Davis Sisters, and Brother Joe May. This would be of little significance if her songs did not speak with such genuine eloquence to the very heart and soul of gospel music lovers. All who have heard her music and have understood it have said, "Well done."

Example 22. "He Understands; He'll Say, 'Well Done'" (Lucie E. Campbell, orig. © 1933). ©
1950 renewed 1978 SCREEN GEMS–EMI MUSIC INC. All rights reserved. Used by permission.

1. If when you give the best of your serv - ice,
2. Mis - un - der - stood, the Sav - ior of sin - ners,
3. If when this life of la - bor is end - ed,
4. But if you try and fail in your try - ing,

Tell - ing the world that the Sav - ior is come;
Hung on the cross; He was God's on - ly Son;
And the re - ward of the race you have run;
Hands sore and scarred from the work you've be - gun;

Be not dis - mayed when friends don't be - lieve you;
Oh! hear Him call - ing His Fa - ther in Heav'n,
Oh! the sweet rest pre - pared for the faith - ful,
Take up your cross, run quick - ly to meet Him;

He un - der - stands; He'll say, "Well done."
Not my will, but Thine be done."
Will be His blest and fi - nal "Well done."
He'll un - der - stand; He'll say, "Well done."

Example 22.   *(continued)*

~

LUCIE E. CAMPBELL

Her Nurturing and Expansion of Gospel Music in the National Baptist Convention, U.S.A., Inc.

Luvenia A. George

On the wings of the wind a melody penetrated my ears with a familiar tune
. . . and I became hypnotized. I walked to the back stage door of the Memphis, Tennessee city auditorium [where the National Baptist Convention,
U.S.A, Inc. was in session]. There I saw a brown-skinned lady, with a head
full of hair, waving her hand over 500 people in the choir [while] in the audience there were 10,000 Christians singing, "What a Fellowship!" (BRADLEY
1979–80, 30)

Lucie E. Campbell was "the brown-skinned lady" described in action by J. Robert Bradley, the great concert and gospel singer
whom she discovered and who later became her protégé. As performer, music director,
composer, and teacher, she was a dynamic leader who set the standard for the performance of religious music in Black Baptist churches of this country for over forty years.
Her songs became classics within the new music repertoire of the National Baptist Convention, U.S.A., Inc., the largest African American organization in the world, now with
a membership of over six million. Campbell was one of the best known and most influential women in this giant assemblage.

This organization, which Lucie E. Campbell helped to sustain and which provided
the platform for her life work as a composer and musician, had its genesis in the development of major African American Baptist organizations in the latter part of the nineteenth century (Dinkins 1980, 24; see table 4). In 1895, the National Baptist Convention
of the U.S.A. was formed in Atlanta, with Dr. Elias Camp Morris of Arkansas as the first
president (Jackson 1980). The formation of this national organization of Black Baptists
represented the merger of the following powerful organizations founded in the postslavery
period: (1) the Baptist Foreign Mission Convention, formed in 1880 to create a vehicle
for sending Black missionaries to Africa; (2) the American National Baptist Convention,
organized in 1886 to provide an arena for Black Baptists to get to know one another and

Table 4   Selected Timeline of the African American Baptist Church in America

Date	Event
1631	Roger Williams emigrates to Boston from England in rebellion against authority of the Anglican Church.
1750	George Lisle, slave, born in VA; later became a minister and purchased his freedom.
1772	Founding of first Black Baptist Church at Silver Bluff, SC.
1776	First Baptist Church of Williamsburg, VA, established for Negroes by local white Baptists.
1783	George Lisle leaves Savannah to become first Negro foreign missionary in Jamaica.
1791	First Baptist Church of Williamsburg admitted to membership in white Baptist association.
1792	Rev. David George established first Baptist Church on west coast of Africa in Sierra Leone.
1807	Lott Carey is baptized in Richmond; joins First Baptist Church.
1815	African Baptist Missionary Society established in Richmond; Lott Carey among organizers.
1821	Lott Carey sails to Liberia as missionary.
1836	Providence Missionary Baptist Association formed in OH, the first independent African American organization of Baptist churches in America.
1838	Wood River Baptist Association formed in IL.
1840	American Baptist Missionary Convention established; consisted of churches in New England and middle Atlantic states. During Civil War, sent Black ministers to aid slaves in South.
1845	White Baptists split over slavery.
1853	Founding of Western Colored Baptist Convention; consisted of Providence and Wood River Baptist Associations plus Negro churches in Western states.
1864	Northwestern and Southern Convention established; included Western Colored Baptist Convention and churches not formerly in either.
1866	Consolidated Convention established in Richmond; merger of the American Baptist Missionary Convention and the Northwestern Convention.
1867	Consolidated Convention holds first meeting in Nashville.
1873	Founding of the General Association of the Western States and Territories.
1874	Founding of New England Baptist Missionary Convention.
1880	Founding of the Baptist Foreign Mission Convention of the United States of America, Nov. 24, in Montgomery. Rev. William McAlpin, pres., Rev. William W. Colley, corr. secy. This would be the dominant Baptist organization for fifteen years. Aim: to send Black missionaries to Africa.
1886	The American National Baptist Convention organized Aug. 25 in St. Louis, with six hundred in attendance, to form a convention whose general aims were not foreign missions. Under impetus of Dr. Wiliam J. Simmons of KY, it was considered the most important meeting of its kind yet held in this country.
1893	The Baptist National Educational Convention organized in Washington, D.C. Aim: to secure statistical information about Baptists and help educate future ministers and other young people. Philip F. Morris, president.
1895	Founding of the National Baptist Convention of the United States of America, Sept. 28, in Atlanta. This was a merger of the three dominant Baptist organizations: The Foreign Mission Convention, The American National Baptist Convention, and the National Education Convention. Dr. Elias Camp Morris of Arkansas was elected first president. The establishment of a Publishing Board to provide Sunday School literature for Black churches was an important reason for forming the new convention.
1896	National Baptist Publishing Board established in Nashville. Rev. R. H. Boyd, publisher.
1897	The Lott Carey Missionary Convention formed when a number of VA leaders withdrew from the Convention in protest of the establishment of a Publishing Board and dissatisfaction with the organization of the Foreign Mission Board.
1906	First National Sunday School and BYPU Congress held in Nashville. This historic meeting was sponsored by the National Baptist Publishing Board and Rev. R. H. Boyd.
1915	A split in the National Baptist Convention over ownership of the Publishing Board. Rev. Boyd and his followers organize as the National Baptist Convention of America, with Rev. E. Perry Jones of MS as president. The original convention later becomes the National Baptist Convention, U.S.A., Inc.

Table 4   (*continued*)

Date	Event
1916	The National Sunday School and BYPU Congress of the National Baptist Convention, U.S.A., Inc. organized in Memphis. Rev. D. W. Cannon, president; Rev. E. W. D. Isaac, general director, and Lucie E. Campbell, music director.
1961	Progressive Baptist Convention of America organized in Cincinnati, Nov. 14–15, Rev. T. M. Chambers of Los Angeles, president. This convention split from the National Baptist Convention, U.S.A., Inc., in a dispute over tenure of officers and support of Dr. M. L. King, Jr., and the Civil Rights Movement.
1988	A split in the National Baptist Convention of America over control of the National Baptist Publishing Board. The new convention becomes the National Missionary Baptist Convention in Dallas, Nov. 14–15, with Rev. S. M. Lockridge, of San Diego, president. Rev. E. Edward Jones of Louisiana remains president of the National Baptist Convention of America.
1989	The National Baptist Congress of Christian Workers, auxiliary to the National Baptist Convention of America, Inc., holds its first annual session June 12–16 in Shreveport.

Source: Information compiled from Moses n.d., Vedder 1907, Woodson 1921, Jordan 1930, Adams and Talley 1944, Miller 1953, Pelt and Smith 1960, and Jackson 1980.

to hold discussions on and promote Baptist literature; and (3) the Baptist National Educational Convention, organized in 1893 with a focus on religious education.

The unification of Black Baptists was partly a result of tensions that had arisen between Black and white Baptist leaders. From the beginning of the nineteenth century and especially after the Civil War, whites had been interested in the religious education of African Americans. The Home Mission Society of New York and the American Baptist Publication Society of Philadelphia had furnished educational and denominational literature to African American churches. White Baptists did not think Blacks were ready to manage their own affairs in this area, but the majority of Black leaders thought differently.

At the second annual meeting of the newly established Convention, Black Baptists laid the foundation for the establishment of their own Publishing Board. For some years the white publishers had allowed them to provide the covers and backs of Sunday School literature but not the inside information (Dinkins 1980, 24). This had greatly rankled the Black leaders, many of whom had received good educations in the very schools of the church organizations that would not allow them to contribute literature. The issue had become a sore point among them.

The Publishing Board was thus established, with Reverend Richard Henry Boyd as corresponding secretary. Also, Boyd was corresponding secretary of the Home Mission Board of the Convention, and he used this office to disseminate the new literature that was to be published. At this point something occurred that was to have far-reaching consequences. Reverend Boyd incorporated the Publishing Board in the state of Tennessee without indicating affiliation with the National Baptist Convention of the U.S.A.; therefore, all publications were copyrighted in his name. This was possible because the Convention had authorized the establishment of a publishing house but had voted no capital to fund its operation ("The Baptist Controversy" 1916, 315).

In his account of the events of that time, Dr. Boyd stated, "I found the building, put in the first telephone, compiled my own list of names to get the enterprise going . . . [and] used $1,000 of my wife's inheritance as collateral" (Boyd 1915, 70). Although some officers of the Convention, including the president, Dr. E. C. Morris, were uncomfortable with Dr. Boyd's operations, there was great rejoicing throughout the denomination over the founding of the Publishing Board. Historian Lewis G. Jordan later noted, "When our Publishing [Board] issued its first series of Sunday School supplies, it became popular in a day and came nearer to receiving the united patronage of the entire brotherhood than any enterprise before or since. Fostered and supported by our constituency, hungering for it twenty years, it grew amazingly, and rapidly became the most efficient, influential department of the National Baptist Convention" (Jordan 1930, 249).

In the following year, 1897, the Publishing Board issued its first quarterly, *The Sunday School Teacher*. Shortly thereafter, churches were purchasing nearly all of their literature from their own Publishing Board. At this point, a certain wing voiced dissatisfaction about the complete break from the use of literature by the white American Baptist Publication Society. In addition, the Foreign Mission Board's headquarters moved to Louisville from Richmond, where it had been since 1880 as the Foreign Mission Convention. These dissatisfactions caused the formation in 1897 of the Lott Carey Convention. However, the new National Baptist Convention of the U.S.A. continued to grow as the majority of Baptists affiliated with it.

In 1899, on the verge of a new century, the Convention organized the Baptist Young People's Union, commonly called the BYPU. Its purpose was that of general religious education of young people. In 1900, another momentous event occurred: the Baptist Women's National Auxiliary Convention was organized in Richmond at the fifteenth annual session of the National Baptist Convention. S. Willie Layton was elected president, and the renowned Nannie Helen Burroughs was elected corresponding secretary. That same year an alliance was formed with the Southern Baptist Convention for home mission work. In 1903 the Convention authorized the Home Mission Board, under Dr. Boyd, to receive and disburse funds to help bankrupt or needy churches.

In 1905 the National Baptist Convention of the U.S.A. received international recognition among religious groups when it sent a full quota of forty delegates to the first meeting of the Baptist World Alliance in London. The 1905 reports of the Publishing Board showed that in nine years of its existence, it had an aggregate business of $2.4 million. In that same year the seeds were sown for the organization that would bring Lucie E. Campbell into prominence when the Convention held a chautauqua (an educational and recreational meeting) to promote its programs and materials (Dinkins 1980, 25).

In 1906 the National Sunday School and BYPU Congress was organized at Nashville, sponsored by a now-wealthy Publishing Board under Dr. Boyd's impetus. Also in this year the Women's Convention launched a training school for women and girls in Washington, D.C., under the auspices of Nannie Helen Burroughs.

In 1915 there occurred one of the most tragic events in the history of African Americans in this country: the split in the Baptist organization. In September, in Chicago's First

Regiment Armory, the National Baptist Convention of the U.S.A. split over the owner-ship of the Publishing Board. The Home Mission Board and the National Baptist Pub-lishing Board (NBPB) under Dr. Boyd withdrew from the parent body. He and his follow-ers organized themselves at the Salem Baptist Church in Chicago, solidifying the defection of the Convention's most powerful components.

Between 1916 and 1920, Peace Commissions attempted to reconcile the two organi-zations, but to no avail (Jackson 1980, 110–16). The National Baptist Convention of the U.S.A. became the National Baptist Convention, U.S.A., Incorporated. The "Boyd fac-tion" became known as the National Baptist Convention of America, Unincorporated, with the word *unincorporated* used rarely. The unincorporated Convention lasted seventy-three years, undergoing a split on November 15, 1988.*

In 1916, one year after the 1915 split, a call was sent out by the National Baptist Convention, U.S.A., Inc., for a meeting to be held in Memphis to organize a new Congress. Lucie E. Campbell was asked to be one of nine organizers because of her reputation as an outstanding Christian worker and singer.

1916 was a critical year in the life of both the Convention and the new Congress as there was considerable apprehension concerning the future of the two organizations and, indeed, of the entire African American Baptist denomination. The period following the split of the Convention required an atmosphere at the Congress that was stimulating and elevating. Good attendance was crucial for keeping the organization intact and preventing defection by the churches. Good music was an important part of this, as in any Black religious gathering. It was in this milieu that Lucie Campbell shone. At the annual sessions of the Congress, she used her music to set a tone and atmosphere of exuberant yet controlled joy and spiritual fervor that was stimulating and satisfying to the thousands of delegates. Sunday School and BTU teachers, young people, ministers, Christian edu-cation leaders and workers came to hear, sing, absorb, and take home to their congrega-tions songs of hope, spirit, and inspiration.

Campbell staged pre-Congress musicales, Friday night pageants and performances, and directed the singing of huge choirs and immense audiences during the daily assem-blages. Soloists and ensembles also sang in between the many speeches, reports, and demonstration classes during the Congress. She chose the music and performers care-fully, completely in charge of who sang what songs and when. Her aim was to inspire and uplift the audience and to keep things moving. The delegates bought and took back to their churches the anthems, spirituals, hymns, and gospel songs they heard, many of which had been written by Campbell and performed under her direction (George 1983a, 6).

---

*The November 15, 1988, split again involved the NBPB, this time concerning its relationship with the Sunday School and Baptist Training Union (BTU) Congress. The NBPB, under the ownership of the Boyd family, had financed and underwritten the Congress since the split of 1915 (George 1990). Dr. T. B. Boyd III, president and CEO of the NBPB, and the Sunday School and BTU Congress now form the nucleus of the new National Missionary Baptist Convention of America, with Dr. S. M. Lockridge as president. Dr. E. Edward Jones remains president of the National Baptist Convention of America, now incorporated (NBCA, Inc.). The NBCA, Inc. has organized the National Baptist Congress of Christian Workers Auxiliary.

Charles L. Dinkins notes that "E. W. D. Isaac, Jr., and Lucie E. Campbell wrote songs for the Congress and published song books which became widely used throughout the denomination. These books, together with the *Baptist Standard Hymnal*, published by the Sunday School Publishing Board, set the standard for church music. *Gospel Pearls* (1921); *Spirituals Triumphant Old and New* (1927); *Inspirational Melodies No. 2* (n.d.) and other song books were promoted in the Congress" (Dinkins 1980, 27–28).

From 1919 through the 1920s and 1930s, Campbell wrote hymns that the new Publishing Board included in their collections, such as "The Lord Is My Shepherd" (1919) in *Gospel Pearls*; "Something Within" (1919), "Heavenly Sunshine" (1923), "Room! Room!" (1923), and "The King's Highway" (1923) in *Inspirational Melodies No. 2*; and "Something Within" and "Look Away into Heaven" (1921) in *Spirituals Triumphant Old and New*. These three hymnbooks are still in print and widely used in African American churches.

Campbell frequently used *Inspirational Melodies No. 2* in general-assembly singing at the Congresses. In the book's preface, the authors called for this new literature to become an instrument of the traditional, democratic congregational style of singing:

The old and young in our religious meetings should be taught to act in concert with respect to the singing as well as to other features of the worship. We desire to see the day come when, in all our religious meetings, the admonition, "Let all the people sing," shall be heeded in the most serious manner. We *insist* [emphasis added] that Choirs, Choruses, Glee Clubs and other singing aggregations should *lead* the singing only, and that all others engaged in the worship should take active part. (*Inspirational Melodies No. 2*, preface)

The preface is signed "The Music Committee," whose members were Reverend E. W. D. Isaac, Miss L. E. Campbell, and E. W. D. Isaac, Jr.

These early hymnbooks contain a remarkable collection of original songs and arrangements of spirituals written by such talented African American composers as Edward Boatner, the Work Brothers (John Wesley and Frederick), Reverend Charles A. Tindley, Thomas A. Dorsey, J. D. Bushell, William Henry Smith, and E. C. Deas, among others. Boatner, Bushell, and Deas were also active with the Convention in other ways.

All of Campbell's early hymns were copyrighted by and dedicated to the National BYPU Board, 409 Gay Street, Nashville. It was not until the late 1930s and early 1940s that she began copyrighting songs in her own name; prior to this she had given her music freely to the Congress. According to Thomas A. Dorsey, Campbell had disapproved of composers of religious music who, like him, sold their music to the public for profit (George 1983b). It must be noted that she was a public-school teacher of English and history for over fifty years and did not rely on her music for a living. She once said, "Teaching is my vocation, music is my avocation" (Gilkey 1947, 5).

Her hymns were four-part, homophonic compositions published in shape-note notation, a system that assigns a different shape to each note of the scale. This method helped nonliterate musicians learn to read music and was preferred in the rural South from the turn of the century until the late 1930s.

Campbell's songs were popular with African American churchgoers because her lyrics related to and reflected Black experience. She was oriented to biblical narratives and used imagery vividly to interpret and bring coherence to her own life and the life of her people. "Something Within" was written for Connie M. Rosemond, a young blind Black man of Chattanooga, "because he couldn't see and he wanted to sing but refused to sing the blues" (Gilkey 1947, 5). She had encountered Rosemond one day on the famous Beale Street in Memphis. There she heard a man make a side bet of five dollars that he could make the blind youngster "get down in the alley," as Beale Streeters called singing the blues, if he offered him five dollars. As a crowd gathered, Rosemond refused to sing the requested blues, saying, "No, I can't sing the blues for you or anybody else for five dollars or fifty dollars, I'm trying to be a Christian in this dark world, and I believe I've found the way out of darkness into light, I can't explain it, but there's something within me" (*The Golden Hour Digest* 1940). To Lucie Campbell, who was in the crowd, this was a confrontation between good and evil. Rosemond's words inspired her to write "Something Within," the first gospel hymn to be composed, published, and widely disseminated by an African American woman:

> Preachers and teachers would make their appeal,
> Fighting as soldiers on great battlefields;
> When to their pleadings my poor heart did yield.
> All I could say, there is something within.
>
> Have you that something, that burning desire?
> Have you that something, that never doth tire?
> Oh, if you have it, that Heavenly Fire
> Let the world know there is something within.
>
> *Chorus*
> Something within me, that holdeth the reins;
> Something within me that banishes pain;
> Something within me, I cannot explain
> All that I know, there is something within.

The opening verse begins by citing two of the most highly respected members of the African American community in 1919, "Preachers and teachers." "Fighting as soldiers" would remind listeners of the first World War, which had ended only two years before. "Something within . . . holdeth the reins . . . banishes pain . . . I cannot explain"—this poem speaks to every African American: Life is a struggle, but we have something within us that tells us we are more than what is seen on the outside.

Campbell's introspective lyrics could speak to the experience of many; the ability to go on through a life burdened with struggle often was based on a deep belief that there was an inner source of strength to draw upon. The song was an instant favorite when introduced at the National Baptist Convention in 1919 in Atlantic City, and, being easily adaptable to the improvisational techniques of gospel singers, it remains a great favorite today. For example, the current popular group Take 6 has recorded it (Reprise 25892).

In 1919, Campbell composed four songs: "Something Within"; "The Lord Is My Shepherd" (dedicated to her mother, Isabella Wilkerson Campbell); "Please Let Your Light Shine on Me"; and "Are They Equal in the Eyes of the Law?" The latter two were the only secular songs she was associated with in her long career. The lyrics for "Please Let Your Light Shine on Me" and "Are They Equal in the Eyes of the Law?" were written by Sergeant A. R. Griggs, and Campbell supplied the music. Both songs reflect the anger of African American members of the armed forces at the prejudice and discrimination remaining in America after the war. It was not out of character for Campbell to feel strongly enough about racial injustice to write music for poems that took the form of social protest; her former students recalled that she taught African American history long before it was popular to do so. The two songs carried the copyright of the Campbell-Griggs Publishing Company of Memphis and are the only songs of her early period that were not published in hymnals. Even on a piece of secular music, however, Lucie E. Campbell affirmed her identity with the Baptist church (ex. 23).

Throughout her life, she was an active worker in the Baptist denomination at local, state, and national levels and was totally involved in the music of the Memphis African American community. According to J. Robert Bradley, she first worked at First Baptist Church in Memphis (Reverend A. M. Townsend, Pastor). She also played the organ at Central Baptist Church (Reverend Floyd Williams, Pastor), where her mother held membership. After the death of Reverend Townsend, she joined Central Baptist Church. She was later an organizing member of Bethesda Baptist Church, which had a small membership and existed about five years; Reverend C. R. Williams, her long-time friend and future husband, was pastor (George 1983c).

In the 1930s Campbell's career began to expand, and she directed her energies to more spectacular activities. In Congress and Convention sessions, one of her responsibilities had always been to lead the large audiences in the singing of the congregational music. Now, she began to "carry over" this skill into the local community. An example follows: On March 29, 1931, the city of Memphis named a city park in honor of its outstanding citizen, W. C. Handy, composer of the famous "St. Louis Blues." It was a day Handy never forgot; mounted police led a two-mile-long parade, the largest in the city's history, and outstanding Memphians of both races were seated on the dais. In his autobiography Handy noted, "We were approaching the speaker's stand where bands were blaring out 'The Memphis Blues,' and again the 'Beale Street Blues.' Then a great chorus was heard, led by Miss Lucie Campbell, in [singing] 'Lift Every Voice and Sing,' The Negro National Anthem, and then my own 'Aframerican Hymn'" (Handy 1941, 262).

In May 1932, Campbell produced a musical extravaganza, *Memphis Bound*, at the Booker T. Washington High School, performing it twice more that month for a white audience at Ellis Auditorium and for a Black audience at the Greenwood CME Church. In June of the same year, she presented the pageant *Ethiopia* to the National Baptist Congress at its annual meeting in Memphis. According to Reverend D. E. King, Campbell's script called for a large cast, including the Queen of Ethiopia, six page boys, soloists, and a large background chorus (George 1983d). She was to use the same theme

Example 23.   Cover of sheet music for "Please Let Your Light Shine" (A. R. Griggs, Lucie E. Campbell).

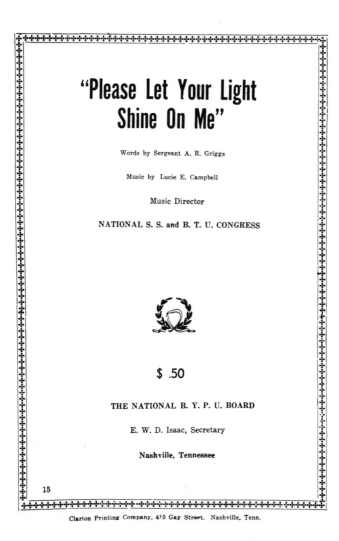

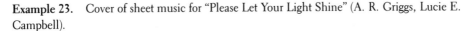

several times in later productions, as in the pageants *Ethiopia at the Bar of Justice* and *Ethiopia, Stretch Forth Your Hands unto God*.

These pageants were colorful and exciting. The costumes and scenery were striking, the dramatic readings were lively and appealing, and a wide variety of music was used, including some of Campbell's. As music director of pre-Congress events, she alternated between staging pageants and musicals for the delegates, seemingly preferring to produce large pageants when the Congress met in Memphis, where her resources were greater.

The pre-Congress and pre-Convention musicales featured thousand-voice mass choirs, made up of persons from all over the country who sang in their home church choirs. According to singer Harry Mae Simmons, Campbell was an inspiring director "who could assemble voices and make them touch your heart strings" (George 1983e). She stood only five feet, two-and-a-half inches tall and weighed between 110 and 115 pounds, but she possessed a compelling, commanding voice. Her student, Marian Speight, recalls, "When she spoke, everybody took note: Miss Lucie was a director-general who moved her forces in the classroom, in the halls, in the auditorium, as well as in the Baptist church" (George 1983f).

J. Robert Bradley and Campbell got along well from the beginning. He introduced many of her songs to the public and became the greatest interpreter of them. In 1932, she met a young organist, Thomas H. Shelby, Jr., who became another protégé, and she appointed him official organist for the Congress. With Bradley and Shelby, she had formed an alliance with two musicians whose careers would be inseparably intertwined with hers until her death.

In 1933, Campbell wrote one of her best-loved hymns, "He Understands; He'll Say, 'Well Done.'" Bradley sang it at a religious service, and one hundred persons united with the church immediately afterwards (George 1983g). At the end of the decade, in 1939, she attended the Baptist World Alliance in London. There Bradley sang the perennially popular "Something Within," which was received warmly by the huge international audience.

The national Congresses and Conventions continued to be the primary media for introducing and disseminating new songs to a national Black audience. Bradley recalls selling Campbell's songs at the Congress by the hundreds, for five and ten cents a copy; other songwriters also set up booths from which to sell their music. In a 1983 interview, the late Kenneth Morris, the Chicago composer, remembered that the selling of his music at both the Congress and the Convention was a major source of his income (George 1983h). If Campbell chose one or more of their songs to be sung at an annual session, gospel entrepreneurs had an instant success. Sallie Martin would sing and sell Dorsey's songs, and later her own Martin and Morris studio repertoire; Roberta Martin and her groups would do the same for the Roberta Martin studio.

Lucie E. Campbell was born April 30, 1885, in Duck Hill, Mississippi, the youngest of eleven children of Burrell and Isabella Wilkerson Campbell; both parents were former slaves. Her life encompassed that period of African American history that gave recognition to the beauty and originality of the spirituals and saw the demise of minstrelsy, the crystallization of ragtime, the emergence of the blues as a genre, the beginning of jazz, the impact of African Americans on Broadway, and the great migration to urban areas that ushered in the era of modern gospel music. Her songs gradually began to show the influence of the Chicago gospel songwriters and singers, such as Thomas Dorsey, Kenneth Morris, Roberta Martin, Sallie Martin, and Mahalia Jackson. Robert L. Holmes, Jr., Nashville composer and another protégé, notes that "Jesus Gave Me Water," written in 1946, was a definite break from her earlier hymn-writing format and was Campbell's way of responding to Mahalia Jackson's style of singing (George 1983i).

Developments in religious music ran parallel to developments in other music areas; indeed, there were occasional crossovers. One notable example is Dorsey, who was a pianist for blues singer Ma Rainey and later became "the father of gospel music." Campbell kept her activities in the religious community: she was a pioneer composer who "crossed over" from hymn writer to gospel song composer. She was instrumental in bringing to the national Baptist community the new gospel music through her position as music director. Robert L. Holmes, Jr., remembers a Congress of the early 1950s when the Clara Ward Singers, a flamboyant gospel group, were denied a place to sing on one of the programs. When Campbell heard of the slight, she promptly scheduled the group to appear, as she was not averse to the "new" style of singing (George 1983i). Sallie Martin said of her in a 1983 interview, "She was beautiful; she had 'grace' enough to bring Black music out of the hymn writing tradition" (George 1983j).

This was also the era of the first generation after slavery of Black college-trained men and women who shaped the future direction of African American music. Will Marion Cook, Harry T. Burleigh, and R. Nathaniel Dett are members of this group; although not a degreed musician, Lucie E. Campbell was also a member. Her music served as a model of the genre for composers and performers across the nation. She was a Black Memphis "breakthrough" in gospel music due to the appeal her songs had in the white community; Pat Boone and Lawrence Welk recorded "He Understands; He'll Say, 'Well Done.'" Her songs often are sung today at the Grand Ole Opry in Nashville and have been recorded widely; they reach beyond the local community, as does all African American music.

Campbell married Reverend C. R. Williams in 1960 at the age of seventy-five, a fitting end to a lifelong friendship; it occurred six years after her retirement as a schoolteacher in Memphis and two years before her death on January 3, 1963, in Nashville. Her large, honor-laden funeral was held in Mount Nebo Baptist Church in Memphis on January 7, 1963. At her death, she was still music director of the National Sunday School and BTU Congress of the National Baptist Convention, U.S.A., Inc. She had held the position an astounding forty-seven years. A commemorative stone was placed on her grave twenty years later, in June 1983, at a ceremony held during a meeting of her beloved Congress in Memphis.

Lucie E. Campbell's life and music reflect a woman whose songs effectively bridged the gap between hymnody and a new gospel song form. In so doing, she helped create a rich musical environment within the expanding Black Baptist denomination—an environment that became a cradle, nurturing those young composers who followed her. She therefore comes to us as a major songwriter and master organizer in the flowering of twentieth-century African American sacred music.

LUCIE E. CAMPBELL WILLIAMS

A Cultural Biography

Reverend Charles Walker

At the tender age of six years, I was introduced to the music director of the National Baptist Sunday School and Baptist Training Union Congress. She was preparing her singers for some kind of pageant. I remember that my sister was given a bit part in the pageant, and as my mother took me toward the stage to meet Lucie Campbell, I could feel the excitement in my mother's being—the kind of excitement that wells up in one when one is in the presence of greatness. My mother proudly introduced me to this great lady, and she shook my hand, which was extended as far as I could reach, because she was on the stage, and I was just in front of the stage. For me, this was an unforgettable moment. There was something about her eyes and her demeanor that captivated me. While I was too young then to appreciate all of the nuances of that moment, years later, reflecting upon it, I've culled out of it some precious impressions. Those eyes were filled with the fire of artistic temperament, and yet there was a veiled peace underneath. She was motherly in her demeanor—stern yet loving; playful, yet serious; a kind of commanding presence that made one a little fearful, and yet at the same time, one could sense a personality of extraordinary warmth, love, and gentleness.

Some years later, as a teenager, I sat in awe as the beautiful music of the Youth Rally Choir rang through the Municipal Auditorium in Shreveport. There was an inspiring pageant entitled "Youth at the Crossroads." This was followed by a consecration period in

121

which youth offered their lives for Christian service both at home and abroad. Underneath all of this pageantry and consecration was the guiding hand of Lucie Campbell. In the annals of the National Baptist history, Lucie Campbell stands out as a dedicated servant of her people and church. There is, perhaps, no area of our denominational work that has not been touched, either directly or indirectly, by the genius of this extraordinary woman.

Her commitment to the gospel mandate of service (Matt. 28:19–20) made her available in many areas of public service, and many of her devoted disciples are still serving today in religion, education, politics, the arts, sports, the legal profession, medicine, and many areas of human service and development. The expanse of her personality made her equally at home with people from all walks of life. She was indeed a grand lady possessed with unusual charm and wit.

Who, indeed, was Lucie Campbell? What were the factors that contributed to the formation of the complex yet transparent personality? What were the roots that produced this spiritual and musical genius? How did she blend those varied talents of hers in the service of her Lord? What is it that makes her music live on in spite of the tremendous evolution of sacred religious music that has taken place in the last several decades?

She burst upon the stage in a very dramatic fashion in the little town of Duck Hill in Mississippi. Perhaps I should say just out of town, because Miss Lucie, as she was called by most of the people who worked closely with her, was born in a caboose when her mother, Isabella Wilkerson Campbell, was returning from a visit with her husband, Burrell Campbell, who was a railroad worker. It was likely that Mr. Campbell worked with the Illinois Central Railroad, since Illinois Central had purchased the Mississippi Central Railroad in 1873. It was this same railroad that was to produce tragedy in Miss Lucie's life even before she could comprehend the magnitude of the tragedy. Her father, filled with excitement as he traveled home to see the newborn Lucie, was killed in a train accident just outside of Duck Hill.

Duck Hill is an interesting little town, located in Carroll County, Mississippi. Carroll County was one of the sixteen counties established by the Mississippi legislature in 1833 out of the area established by the third Choctaw session in the Treaty of Dancing Rabbit in 1830. This was the beginning of the settlement of this territory, even though this area had been claimed for Spain in 1540 by Hernando de Soto. This area was inhabited by the Ibituphos of the Muskogean tribe. According to Norman L. Izell in his *History of Duck Hill*, "The settlement was named for a Choctaw Indian chief (also known as "Doctor Duck" because of his proficiency with medicines made from roots and herbs)" (Izell n.d., 2).

In the year of Miss Lucie's birth, 1885, the town of Duck Hill experienced something of a boom when the big hill was drilled for iron. The Illinois Central Railroad purchased the big hill; lots were sold, and speculators flourished "swapping lots." One of the people who did well during this boom was John A. Binford, the first white man to settle in the Duck Hill area in the 1820s. It was his grandson, Lloyd T. Binford, who owned Miss

Lucie's grandmother as a slave. The grandfather, John A. Binford, was treasurer of the Mississippi Central Railroad at its inception. According to Izell:

Captain Binford owned most of the land that the railroad used in laying tracks from Elliot to Eskridge. When the line was completed, the railroad wanted to name the station "Binford" and had a sign put up so indicating. Captain Binford, being a Quaker, disapproved, and had them remove the sign and call the station Duck Hill. Captain Binford's grandson, Lloyd T., donated the land for the town high school and permitted it to be called Binford High School. In June 1880, the Binfords deeded some land to the local Baptist church for construction of a church building [the local white Baptist church]. Colonel Binford was a very close friend of Jefferson Davis, and when Davis died in New Orleans, Colonel Binford was one of the pallbearers. He accompanied President Davis' remains to Richmond, Virginia, where he was interred. (Izell n.d., 2–3)

It is evident that the Binford family was, indeed, a very prominent family in Duck Hill. I'm sure that old Colonel Binford never dreamed that a genius of such power and international influence as Lucie Campbell would trace her roots to the Binford plantation.

With Burrell Campbell dead, nine children to raise, Mrs. Campbell decided to move to Memphis, seeking a better life for her children. Miss Lucie was not yet two years of age when the family moved to Vance Street in Memphis. Those early years were difficult years for the Campbell family, but Mrs. Campbell was a woman who had great faith in God and extraordinary strength. She took in washing and ironing in order to provide for her children, and she wanted all of her children to have an adequate education. It was also her desire that they be exposed to the fine arts. She could not afford to provide piano lessons for all of her children; so it was decided that the oldest sister, Lora, would be given music lessons.

It appears that Mrs. Campbell took great pride in Lora but not in Lucie. However, in later years, it was Lucie who took care of her mother, and those who knew them testified to their inseparability. When the girls were young, the mother always presented the other girls with pride to the visitors in the home. According to Charles Kennedy, one of Lucie Campbell's students, Mrs. Campbell would call the other girls out for an introduction, and when one would inquire about the other daughter who had not been introduced, Isabella would reply, "Oh, that's old Lucie" (Walker 1986).

Lucie Campbell's discipline and genius helped her to teach herself music. She would listen in the next room while piano lessons were given to Lora and then she would practice the lessons on her own, devising methods of accomplishing the same results as her sister and doing the various assignments. Thus, she in effect taught herself music.

Her elementary and high school education was acquired in Memphis, and she quickly distinguished herself as a bright student. She won the penmanship award in elementary school and in high school, the top prize in the Latin class. She graduated in 1899 from Kortrecht High School, which later became Booker T. Washington High. She had the distinction of being valedictorian of her class. According to Thomas Shelby, formerly

Miss Lucie's student, on the day of her graduation, her mother, aware that it was an unusual honor, told her friends, "my daughter is going to get her 'dictory' tonight" (Walker 1982).

Miss Lucie began teaching in public schools in Memphis at the age of fourteen years. It was during the period when one could teach without a college degree or even a high school diploma. She taught at the Carnes Grammar School, and her salary was a grand forty dollars a month. Her high school teaching career began in 1911 at Booker T. Washington High School in Memphis. She presided over the classes of English and American history. She was remembered as a teacher who loved her students and demanded excellence from all of them. Many of the outstanding leaders today were taught by Miss Lucie, and to them she gave a sense of pride, achievement, dedication, and purpose. She did not tolerate inattention to duty. Excuses were not accepted for unfinished assignments, and yet she spent many hours after school tutoring those who had problems with their work.

There were only two "Negro" high schools in Memphis, and as far as Miss Campbell was concerned, Booker T. Washington was *the* high school in Memphis. It was a school of dignity and discipline. She took pride in its traditions and guarded its reputation with all of her energies.

In those days, informal and formal interactions were carefully orchestrated. Politeness, manners, decorum, and deference to elders were emphasized. Students were required to be present for morning devotion at 8:30 A.M. The faculty was required to be present at 8:15 A.M., and fines were levied against faculty members who were tardy, which was rare, indeed. Then, the church influence in the total life structure was more profound, and religion was the dominant influence in the lives of people. In the afternoon at two o'clock, each classroom had its individual devotionals, which were composed of hymns, spirituals, Scripture readings, and prayer.

Social graces were also taught in the school. For example, as part of an alumni program that took place on April 16, 1927, at Booker T. Washington High, addresses were delivered by prominent people from the business and arts community and musical selections were rendered. In the printed program only two preprogrammed items are listed: 7:00–7:30 P.M., Social Intercourse period; and 7:30–8:00 P.M., Discussion of Business Matters. This particular program also began with an invocation by Rev. L. E. Owens (*Booker T. Washington High School: Retrospective* . . . 1927, 29).

The rules for decorum were strict and vigorously enforced by Miss Lucie as well as by other members of the faculty. Each teacher had an assigned floor, and they'd watch everything that happened on their floor, which they ruled with an iron but loving hand. It is said that Miss Lucie kept her door open at all times, so that nothing would happen in the hall that did not immediately claim her attention. It was not unusual for her to call out a name of a student in the midst of her instruction. The student, no doubt on his or her way to some mischief, would be startled to hear his or her name come booming out of Miss Lucie's classroom! She kept close watch over her children. She cared. She prayed for her children. She aided them in every possible way. But she demanded excellence in every area of their lives.

During a time when pregnancy before marriage was considered the most severe mark against the social character of a young woman, Lucie Campbell reportedly had the uncanny ability to tell if a woman had become with child, sometimes before the young lady herself knew it. One of her former students, Thomas Shelby, shared with me an incident that occurred the day before graduation. The students who were to receive their diplomas were naturally excited and filled with anticipation for the next day's graduation exercises. They were in line for the rehearsal of the processional. The student pianist struck the opening chords of the processional, and the processional rehearsal began. Then, from the rear of the hall, the familiar voice of Miss Lucie boomed out, "Just a moment! Come here!" She directed this order to one of the young ladies in the line, who stood there stunned and frightened. "You'll never disgrace this school with two of you in line! Both of you can't march in this line, baby. Sit down. I'll mail you your diploma! Get out of line!" (Walker 1982). This perhaps seems rather harsh and cruel from today's vantage point; however, if one understands the milieu out of which Miss Lucie came and the sacred and spiritual climate that prevailed in that day, her actions were consistent with what was and was not tolerated.

Lucie E. Campbell was a church woman who witnessed to the presence and power of Jesus Christ in her life all during the school day, from Monday through Friday. She no doubt would be fired today for being too religious on the job. Her ideas and ideals about Christian womanhood as related to beauty, power, social standing, and behavior represented principles strongly held by Black women involved in educational and church circles during the first half of the twentieth century. These women believed that there was great work to be done in lifting the race and shaping the young.

Campbell's contributions within the Baptist church included her work through women's organizations, which usually got the pulpit only on Women's Day; through her talent as a musician and composer; and through her support of selected male leaders. She was in great demand as a Women's Day speaker and a conference speaker, and the texts of her addresses dramatically document her views on Christian womanhood.

She frequently substituted for Nannie Helen Burroughs, who was president of the Women's Auxiliary of the National Baptist Convention and probably one of the most powerful women in Black Baptist Christendom. Burroughs was a close associate of Mary McCleod Bethune, and there is a school named in her honor in Washington, D.C.

Lucie Campbell's addresses sounded the call to the women of this nation to be proud, devout, and virtuous. In one of her addresses, she said:

From whatever viewpoint you evaluate a woman, she is the most influential being in the world. She can lead a man to the highest pinnacle of beauty, of purity, nobility and usefulness; or to the lowest depths of shame and infamy. Woman was behind the fall of Adam, the first man; behind the fall of Samson, the strongest man; behind the fall of Solomon, the wisest man. Despite man's boasted strength, courage and intellect, he will follow a woman anywhere. Someone boastfully remarked that man is the head. A quick-witted woman replied, "Then woman is the neck—the head cannot turn without the neck." (Washington 1971, 20)

In another speech, Miss Lucie extolled the virtues of Christian womanhood in this manner:

Women should feel proud of their esteemed and conspicuous place accorded them in the conception of great Bible writers. When John, the revelator was banished to the Isle of Patmus to be shut off from public society, away from friends and comrades, prohibited from being able to go to the temple or synagogue for worship, he petitioned Jehovah God to parade before his gaze something or somebody by which the church could be personified. Angels were bubbling over to perform the tasks, but they were not chosen. So they drooped their wings and bowed their heads disappointedly. . . . John still pleads for something or someone by whom or which he can picture the beauty of the Church. The mighty billows of the deep, with the rays of the sun prancing and dancing upon their bosom, resembling the distant beads of pearls, offered themselves. But they were too unreal to personify the Church that must stand the storms and wiles of Satan. . . .
   "Who then?" and "Where shall I go?" said John, "to find a fit subject to personify the Church on the Isle of Patmus?" John prayed, supposedly alone, but he was close to heaven—close enough for his vision to behold a new heaven and new earth, no doubt. John had begun to despair—the darkest hour is just before day. John looked again, and said, "And I saw a woman clothed in the sun. A great wonder. A woman who walked on the moon for her silver slippers. At the crown of her head was bedecked with the stars."
   . . . Women, we are somebody—clothed in the sun. No need for costume jewelry or real diamonds, rubies or pearls. The sun is enough. You can barely look at the sun with the naked eye. It is too dazzling. A perfectly dressed woman will bear heavily on the eye. (Washington 1971, 27)

Now, this matter of femininity was a serious one for Miss Lucie. She glorified in her womanhood. She pampered herself. She dressed with modesty. Though a strong woman, she was nevertheless a proud and feminine woman. For example, one of the great experiences at the National Baptist Convention was when Miss Lucie made her grand entrance on the stage. The people would come from miles around to see Miss Lucie strut. She'd throw her shoulders back, and she would strut out on the stage. The people would break out in a frenzy just at her entrance on the stage.

This theme of modesty and femininity was a constant theme in Miss Lucie's speeches. In another speech, Miss Lucie discusses Adam and Eve. She said, "As soon as they began to know right from wrong, they began pinning on leaves. Put on your clothes, women! I know of nothing more beautiful than this array of women in white before me tonight" (Washington 1971, 30).

Miss Lucie was evangelical in her witness, and the evangelism was pronounced and strong. Although she was an intellectual of the first order and educator of profound depth and power, her heart was in evangelizing. This graduate of Rust College and Tennessee State University, this postgraduate student of Columbia and the University of Chicago, was one who, with great power and persuasion, called many to the Lord Jesus Christ. In a speech entitled "The Call to Arms," Miss Lucie sounds the evangelical call:

The record shows that when Paul and his companions went over to answer the Macedonian call, the first to accept and heed the call was a woman. Women have always been pioneers in the Great Call to Christianity. Lydia was the first convert in Europe. The crying need of the hour is evangelism or "soul-winning." No longer should the Church boast of how much money we raise during the year but how many souls have been saved. Money is a by-product and will surely come if men and women are converted. Lydia didn't have money, but she gave what she had: free room and board. I'm happy to say that the first evangel was a woman—the Samaritan woman at the well. She brought the town to Jesus, and what have you done? He is still calling.

Oh yes, sisters, we were the first at the tomb on the morning of the Resurrection, and the first to see the risen Lord, and greatest of all, the first to hear the call, "Mary." First to get the first command to tell the boys, "The Master is come and calling for thee." Or the words of Martha to her sister, Mary, "Oh, for more Marthas that might introduce Jesus to the world today." (Washington 1971, 16)

Miss Lucie, in all of her pronouncements, in all of her activities, projected a vibrant faith in the Lord Jesus Christ. Hers was a faith that would not shrink. It was as natural as breathing for her. It was the very life force which energized her. You could not long remain in her presence without being gripped with the reality of something momentous.

The mores of the period with the Black Baptist ministry prevented Lucie Campbell from making her speeches from the pulpit. However, one of her students, Charles Kennedy, told me that she could preach better than most preachers. The student said, "Miss Lucie could stand down on the floor and break up a church" (Walker 1986). *Break up a church* means that the depth and power of her speeches would send people into ecstasy. They would shout all over the place, and sinners would come running to be saved.

Not only was Miss Lucie a sought-after Women's Day speaker, but she was also a very dynamic commencement speaker, and her addresses were always filled with pointed words of wisdom. She had a love for young people and was always prodding them to virtue and great achievement. In a commencement address to the Lincoln High School graduation class in East St. Louis, she said, "Society admires its scholars; but society reveres its heroes whose intellect is clothed with goodness. The youth whose loins are girded with virtue is invincible. The inner life dominated by a worthy ideal will have its flower in a beautiful character. Get your values right and begin with yourself. In finding the goalposts, one must follow these three rules: self-reverence, self-knowledge, and self-control" (Washington 1971, 52).

Let not these gems of thought suggest for a moment that Miss Lucie was not very human herself. Let it not be suggested that she, too, was not grappling with the restrictions of her own humanity. Lucie E. Campbell did not reside in the ethereal atmosphere of some Olympian height. She grappled with the same temptation and problems of being human as we all. She was a woman with a fiery temperament and temper. That artistic fire that resided in her soul made itself apparent in her interpersonal relationships. She and her mother had strong and somewhat domineering personalities. She struck fear in many hearts. There was a strength of presence that she had that made you know it had to be done Miss Lucie's way. As long as she had her way, it was all right. It mattered not your station in life; when you met Lucie Campbell, you met a strong, dominant, confident personality.

Miss Lucie and her mother were long-standing members of the great Metropolitan Baptist Church, ministered by the renowned Dr. A. M. Townsend, for whom the Townsend Press is named. Anyway, a good friend of Dr. Townsend reported to me that Mrs. Isabella Campbell was president of the Mother's Board of Metropolitan and that the Townsends and the Campbells were close personal friends. The two families frequently rode to church and other places together, and it is reported that Mrs. Isabella Campbell would not permit Mrs. Townsend to sit in the front seat of the pastor's car because she, Mrs. Campbell, was president of the Mother's Board and must be accorded the honored seat with the pastor (Walker 1986).

It was the Metropolitan Church that nurtured Miss Lucie in the Christian faith. It was this church that encouraged her and aided her in her educational pursuits. The church members took pride in her achievements. She was their "Little Lucie." They watched her grow from childhood into womanhood. She was educated, cultured, intelligent, and creative. There weren't too many people who had achieved as much as Miss Lucie. The love was mutual. Lucie loved Metropolitan and gave her all in its service. Yet she would be deeply wounded at Metropolitan, and out of that trauma would come one of her greatest compositions. It is perhaps that flaw in her personality, a kind of possessiveness of character, that set the stage for what was to be an explosive situation in the Metropolitan Baptist Church.

In 1922, the pastor, Dr A. M. Townsend, resigned to assume the office of corresponding secretary of the Sunday School Publishing Board of the National Baptist Convention, U.S.A., Inc. The church appointed Reverend T. A. Moore as supply pastor. There was some talk of issuing a call to Reverend S. A. Owens, then president of Florida Memorial College. Miss Lucie was against the calling of Dr. Owens and used her influence to block the call.

A call was issued to Reverend J. T. Brown, who was the pastor of the famous Spruce Street Baptist Church in Nashville. After ten months at Metropolitan, Reverend Brown resigned to assume the office of secretary of the Sunday School Publishing Board. When Reverend Brown resigned, the movement to call Dr. Owens surfaced again. This is not surprising, for Dr. Owens was a man of sterling qualities. He was a Morehouse College graduate, a classmate of Mordecai Johnson, and later a member of the Morehouse faculty. In addition to serving as president of Florida Memorial College, he had served as president of Roger Williams College for a period of three years. While pastor of the Bethel Baptist Church in Daytona Beach, Florida, he had licensed the young Howard Thurman as a local preacher and participated in the ordination of Dr. Thurman into the Christian ministry in Roanoke. So he was much sought after. Despite Miss Lucie's objections, the church met and voted to issue a call to Dr. Owens.

Well, Dr. Owens accepted, and the church, by majority vote, elected him its pastor. There was much joy in the congregation as it awaited the arrival of its new pastor. Joy in all quarters except among the followers of Miss Lucie. Unofficial meetings were called at Miss Lucie's home to discuss the strategy to prevent him from assuming the pastorate, and Miss Lucie was the leader of the opposition. The tension and division increased in the congregation. Miss Lucie was a woman of considerable power and influence. She had one of the associate ministers and several deacons in her camp. It appeared as though she would succeed.

The climax came one Sunday morning shortly before Dr. Owens arrived. Reverend T. A. Moore was in charge of the pulpit, but Miss Lucie had decided that a minister of her choosing would preach. The choir was torn with division: the pro-Campbell and anti-Campbell groups. The "pro-Campbellites" took over the choir stand as the time approached for the morning worship. Reverend Moore was brushed aside, and the minister chosen by Miss Lucie began to conduct the service. The members were incensed, but they all remained calm, for no confusion was desired.

Now, Deacon Jeter, a kindly, saintly man who loved Metropolitan with every fiber of his being, stepped into the picture. It was Deacon Jeter who had mortgaged his home in order to purchase pews when Metropolitan moved into its new edifice. It was Deacon Jeter who had shown concern for the widow Isabella Campbell and her nine children. It was Deacon Jeter who had visited the Campbell home to inquire if there was enough food, clothing, and other necessities. He was sort of like a father to Miss Lucie. Deacon Jeter saw that tensions had risen to a dangerous level, and he did not want a disturbance; he did not want the police to be called into his beloved Metropolitan. The wrong man was in the pulpit. Miss Campbell was at the piano. Murmuring could be heard among the congregation, and restlessness and resentment were apparent. Something had to be done!

Members began to speak out in protest. Things were about to get out of hand. Deacon Jeter thought that if Miss Lucie left the piano, the situation would be defused. He went to the piano and gently suggested that she leave the piano. Miss Lucie exchanged words with him. She became infuriated, took her umbrella . . . the congregation exploded! People stood up and crowded the aisles. Fights broke out. It was frightening. One member who was present said, "My girlfriend and I were very frightened. We could not get down any of the aisles to the exits. So we got on the floor on our knees between the pews, and crawled all the way to the side of the church and then out the back door" (Walker 1983). Someone called the police and reported that the worship at Metropolitan was being disturbed. Plainclothes police came. By this time, Miss Campbell's preacher was again in the pulpit. The plainclothes officers merely beckoned to the preacher without uttering a word.

It was reported that the next evening the deacons met and voted to church Miss Lucie and all of her followers. When a member of a congregation is churched, he or she is brought into what is like the trial that precedes what the Catholic church calls *excommunication*. So they voted to church Miss Lucie. This recommendation was brought to the church in a subsequent church meeting, and the vote was placed before the church body. It was passed by a majority vote that the right hand of fellowship be withdrawn from those members involved in this disturbance. Miss Lucie, along with about one hundred of her followers, were put out of the Metropolitan Baptist Church.

One of the deacons who was in this group came back to the church, apologized for his behavior, and was restored. Miss Lucie never came back, never apologized, and began a kind of church "homelessness." She was shocked at the decision of the church. She was embarrassed and hurt. She loved her church. She loved the people there. It was a tragic moment. Naturally, her followers supported her. Their devotion to her bordered on worship. For them, Miss Lucie could do no wrong. Miss Lucie drew that kind of devotion, for she also gave that kind of devotion. If she loved you, you could do no wrong.

On the other hand, many others in the congregation felt that Miss Lucie deserved the treatment that she received. No doubt some were a little less friendly to her. Some, to be sure, were downright hostile towards her. There were ministers who barred her from their churches. There were other ministers who were determined that she would be blackballed throughout the state of Tennessee. All of these factors plagued her. She could not see the inevitable result of her own strength and her own will and her own charisma that drew people to her as avid disciples. She could not understand the dynamics of strong wills colliding within the Baptist structure. Her pain was intense. Her embarrassment was penetrating. Her sorrow was inexpressible. This perhaps would not have been so if she could have shaken the idea that she was misunderstood. However, out of the milieu of that awful experience, Lucie Campbell composed one of her most inspiring gospel hymns, "He Understands; He'll Say, 'Well Done' ":

> If when you give the best of your service
> Telling the world that the Savior is come
> Be not dismayed if men don't believe you
> He understands; He'll say, 'Well done.'
>
> Oh, when I come to the end of my journey
> Wearied of life and the battle is won
> Carrying the staff and the cross of redemption
> He understands; He'll say, "Well done."

Church controversy again brought another classic gospel hymn. This time, the scene was the Central Baptist Church. After the controversy of Metropolitan Baptist Church, Miss Lucie was apparently without a church home for some years. She went to Central Baptist Church after some years and began working with the choir. Her good friend, Reverend Floyd W. Williams, was the pastor. One of the members of Central related to me the beginnings of several controversies that ultimately led to her expulsion from the membership of Central Baptist:

In 1929, I was a member of the Junior Choir, directed by brother J. D. Cook. It was our responsibility to sing the second and fourth Sundays in each month. Miss Campbell directed the Adult Choir, which sang on the first and third Sundays.

One fourth Sunday, some important out-of-town guests came, and Miss Campbell wanted the Adult Choir to sing instead of the Junior Choir. The Junior Choir refused to leave the choir stand, and some strong words were exchanged. A church meeting was called to deal with the problem. All the young people of Central came to the meeting ready to express their dissatisfaction. When the meeting was opened and the matter brought to the floor, one young person asked if it was lawful for a nonmember to be present in this meeting. The reason for the question was that Miss Lucie was not a member of Central Baptist Church, even though she directed the choir.

When the young woman raised the question of membership, Miss Campbell yelled out, "I pay as much money in this church as anybody!" The young people retorted, "It doesn't matter how much money you give to the church. That does not make you a member!" (Walker 1988).

The church upheld the young people's right to sing on the appointed Sunday, and the meeting was closed without any further action. Pastor Williams and the deacons took Miss Campbell into the church office after the meeting and received her into the membership of the Central Baptist Church. However, a greater conflict was yet to come.

In the winter of 1943, the beginning of the permanent breach with Central began to form. Contrary to popular belief, the conflict was not between the pastor and Miss Lucie but between a Deacon Vesey and Miss Lucie. Reverend Roy T. Morrison was pastor of Central by this time. Deacon Vesey was a strong, outspoken personality, and so was Miss Lucie. A clash was inevitable.

Miss Lucie wrote a letter to the pastor stating that she could not work with such a man as Deacon Vesey. There had apparently been a long-standing feud between the two, and this merely added fuel to the fire. This pastor had a conference with her and asked her to apologize to the deacon. Miss Lucie refused. The pastor then held a meeting with the two protagonists and the Board of Deacons in order to resolve the matter. Miss Lucie remained firm in her rejection of the deacon. A church meeting was called, the facts were presented, and again Miss Lucie was asked to apologize to the deacon. She refused, and the church voted to withdraw the right hand of fellowship.

The very next Sunday, Miss Lucie returned and sat in the audience. After Reverend Morrison preached, he extended the invitation. Miss Lucie came down the aisle and sat in the chair to be received back into the church. Another person came forward also. Reverend Morrison received this person into the membership and left Miss Lucie sitting there. She returned to her pew, got her umbrella . . . a deacon left the sanctuary and called the police. The police came into the church and quietly escorted Miss Lucie and her cook, who had accompanied her to church, out of church.

Many followed Miss Lucie. The membership of the church dropped dramatically. Miss

Lucie and her followers filed suit against the pastor and the church. The judge threw the case out of court, saying that he would not adjudicate a church matter (Court Records 1946).

Again, Miss Lucie felt that she was mistreated and embarrassed, and for a moment she thought of leaving church work altogether. She came to realize that what was in store for her had been well worth the pain. She also began to contemplate her contributions to the problem. She came to the point where she lost sight of the earthly purview and became even more fixed on Jesus. Out of this crisis came the composition "Just to Behold His Face," a strong statement of encouragement (ex. 24).

The 1952 song "Even a Child Can Open the Gate" (ex. 25) was inspired by her meeting a young man who was to become perhaps the greatest exponent of the gospel hymn, Dr. J. Robert Bradley. This magnificent artist, who serves today as director of music for the Christian Education Department of the Congress of the National Baptist Convention, U. S. A., came to Miss Lucie's attention in 1932. The Convention was meeting in Memphis, and J. Robert Bradley was a little boy on the Mississippi River with his bucket catching crawfish. There on the river, he heard the intoxicating sounds of Baptist hymn singing. He left the river, followed the sounds that brought him right on the stage of the National Baptist Convention meeting, and Miss Lucie was leading the singing. One of the choir members saw him and said, "Get that snotty-nosed urchin off the stage! Look at him—every knot standing in a row!" Before he could be removed from the stage, Miss Lucie said, "No, let him stay." He still had the mud from the Mississippi between his toes, the smell of fish still on his hands. But in that little boy dwelled the voice of unusual power and clarity. Miss Lucie took him, took one of her nice lace handkerchiefs, wiped his face, stood him on a chair, and told him to sing. He sang, and the heavens opened. People shouted all over the auditorium, and the Bradley era began. Dr. L. K. Williams, president of the National Baptist Convention, called to Miss Lucie Campbell and said, "Lucie, where'd you get that boy?" She said, "Out the river." He said, "Well, keep him. He's going to be great" (Walker 1984).

This same Dr. Bradley broke tradition when he included Miss Lucie's composition in his London debut in 1955, which took place in Royal Festival Hall. After performing the great arias and recitatives and leider of the great European masters, Dr. Bradley sang "Touch Me, Lord Jesus" and "Something Within." The audience, which included the Queen Mother of England, was strongly moved. Dr. Bradley then turned to the royal box where the royal family sat and announced that the outstanding lady who composed the two gospel hymns and who meant so much to him was present that night in the hall. He presented her to the royal family and the audience. Thunderous applause greeted her. Miss Lucie, graceful as she was, outdid herself in her curtsey to the Queen (Walker 1984).

Miss Lucie's "Something Within" is a famous composition, as is the story behind the composition (ex. 26). The song was dedicated to a blind gospel singer named Connie Rosemond, who inspired it. Mr. Rosemond customarily played his guitar on Beale Street, and people put coins in his little cup and wished him well. Miss Lucie had come to the fish market to purchase some fish. There sat Connie Rosemond, playing hymns and

Example 24. "Just to Behold His Face" (Lucie E. Campbell, orig. © 1923). ©
1951 renewed 1979 SCREEN GEMS–EMI MUSIC INC. All rights reserved. International
copyright secured. Used by permission.

Example 24.   *(continued)*

Example 25. "Even a Child Can Open the Gate" (Lucie E. Campbell). © 1952 <small>UNICHAPPELL</small> <small>MUSIC INC.</small> (Renewed). All rights reserved. Used by permission.

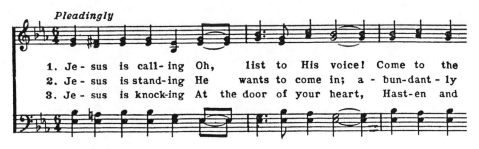

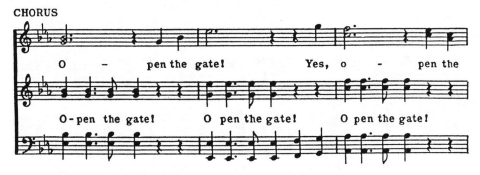

Example 25. *(continued)*

Example 26. "Something Within" (Lucie E. Campbell, C. R. Williams, orig. ©
1919). © 1950 renewed 1978 SCREEN GEMS–EMI MUSIC INC. All rights reserved. International copyright secured. Used by permission.

spirituals, as was his custom. It was winter—cold, damp, rainy. Mr. Rosemond's feet were wrapped in burlap bags as he sat and played. Some of the neighborhood men came out of the bar and listened to the musician play and sing. One of them called to Mr. Rosemond after a while and said, "Hey, Connie! I'll give you five dollars to play 'Caledonia,' or some other blues," and Mr. Rosemond replied, "Oh no, I can't do that." The man's partner taunted him.

Connie Rosemond stood his ground and responded again, "I can't do that; all that I know is that there is something within." Campbell, witnessing this scene, was taken with Rosemond's conviction and the image of having "something within." It moved her to write the hymn that brought her to national attention as a gospel hymnodist. In 1919, at the National Baptist Convention, she introduced a promising young contralto named Marian Anderson. She also presented Connie Rosemond, the blind street singer, who performed her composition "Something Within."

Indeed, Miss Lucie had "Something Within." A fire of genius, a fire of spirituality that revealed itself not only in her life but in the gospel hymns that came from her pen.

4

THOMAS ANDREW DORSEY

(b. 1899)

"TAKE MY HAND, PRECIOUS LORD, LEAD ME ON"

Horace Clarence Boyer

"For more than fifteen years I have been writing, teaching, and producing music for church worship. I have experienced music of every phase and from many categories. This wide experience has given me a great insight on the work, and now I feel I am an authority on the ministry of music in the church.

"When it comes to the ministry of music in the church, I think it should not be too stiff, too classical or too jazzy. I think every church service should have a balanced musical program with a variety of songs to coincide and fit in with the minister's sermon. Also to blend with the general trend of the service. A well-balanced worship service should consist of a processional hymn, chant of the Lord's Prayer, a hymn that can be sung by the congregation, two spirituals, one anthem, two gospel songs, a meditation hymn for the period of silence, a soul-stirring soloist, if you have a soloist.

"All music should be well rehearsed the week before. No choir or singers should get up promiscuously to sing in an intelligent service. The choir should study the songs, the music and the meaning, so when offered to the congregation, a knowledge of a well-prepared song through prayer and study will be detected.

"As I go from town to town, I find some very good choirs and then some very poor choirs. I find some who sing the music too slow and some who sing it too fast. I find some who do not possess enough spirit and others who have too many embellishments that may be mistaken for spirit. Variations on the piano or organ or swinging a song beyond its beauty is not spirit. Loud vociferous singing, uninspired gesticulations or self-incurred spasms of the body is not spirit. I believe in shouting, running, and crying out if the holy spirit comes upon one, but I don't believe in going to get the spirit before it comes."
(DORSEY 1949)

141

The full magnitude of the contributions of Thomas Andrew Dorsey to gospel music, an art form of which he has been called the father, may only now begin to be realized. As a composer, pianist, organizer, and conductor of choirs, he must be ranked with the most notable innovators of twentieth-century music. All gospel choirs and gospel music lovers owe a debt of appreciation to Mr. Dorsey for his courage, vision, musicianship, and integrity at a time when gospel music did not enjoy the popularity it does today.

Dorsey believed in his calling and has a record that quite possibly will remain unequaled in this century. Should gospel music threaten to move toward excess, as many art forms tend to do at the peak of their development, the songs, style, and spiritual temperament of Thomas Andrew Dorsey, the "father of gospel music," will serve as strong reminders of the way it ought to be.

Anyone who attempts to analyze Dorsey's compositional style takes on an awesome task, for he has made such an arresting influence on gospel music that his name is synonymous with the entire genre. In fact, his association with gospel music is so great that there were periods during the 1940s and 1950s when all new gospel songs were called "Dorseys." Within the African American oral tradition, this naming of an entire genre of songs and singing style after one of its major composers is a way of acknowledging that a composer set the standard by which all others working in that genre will be measured.

Another example of this kind of naming occurred as the eighteenth- and nineteenth-century African American Christians developed their own distinct style of lining the new Protestant hymns. They sang the hymns of Charles Wesley and John Newton, but it was the lyrics of Isaac Watts that resonated so deeply within the collective psyche of the congregation that even today, in some communities that still practice the lining-out tradition, all lining hymns are called "Dr. Watts."

Dorsey was not the first to write gospel songs, for before him there were William Henry Sherwood, whose "Mountain Top Dwelling" the National Baptist Convention published in 1893; Charles Price Jones, who published his "Where Shall I Be When the First Trumpet Sounds?" in 1899; and, of course, Reverend Charles Albert Tindley, who in 1901 published eight songs. Tindley was followed by the first major woman composer, Lucie Eddie Campbell, who attracted major attention after the premier performance of her composition "Something Within" at the National Baptist Convention in 1919.

The body of work created by Dorsey stands out because it synthesized all of the elements of the newest of African American sacred music into a twentieth-century whole and because Dorsey composed in such a captivating and inclusive style that all those who were to come after him automatically, consciously or unconsciously, borrowed from and added to the concept and practice he had established. If we, as we move toward the close of this century, listen carefully to the work of the composers of contemporary gospel, such as Edwin Hawkins, Elbernita Clark, and Andrae Crouch, we will also hear Thomas A. Dorsey.

Dorsey was a prolific composer, having composed, according to his word, over five hundred gospel songs alone (Boyer 1964a). This does not include the many blues that he wrote during the period he led the band and was the arranger for the great blues legend Gertrude "Ma" Rainey; the many jazz and blues compositions he wrote while working with Hudson Whittaker, known as Tampa Red; nor the jazz compositions he wrote for his group, Texas Tommy and Friends, with which he recorded in the 1930s.

There are more extant compositions by Thomas Andrew Dorsey than by any other gospel music composer. Much of his music was published and printed and is still available to the public. This is important, because Dorsey didn't even write down all of the music that he wrote, much less publish it. In some cases, there would be a period of years between composition and publication, as in the case of "How about You," which was written in 1932 but was not published until 1941. He published the songs almost every year from 1930, when he published "He'll Know Me over Yonder," to 1968, when he published his last song, "Sometimes My Burden's So Hard to Bear" (see table 5). Dorsey's composition "If I Don't Get There" was included in *Gospel Pearls* in 1921, but that collection was published by the National Baptist Convention.

No prolific composer writes down or publishes everything he or she creates because of the sheer exhausting work of copying and the expense of publishing the completed compositions. Dorsey's efforts were even more challenging because he was working in a culture that was primarily oral in its transmission of music, and he basically had to publish his own compositions. James Cleveland (1931–1991), for example, composed over three hundred songs, but he had copies of only seventy-five. It appears that when the choir or the group learns the song—and often this seems to be the case with the composer as well—the sheet music, used to move the music through a learning process (here only a link in a larger oral-transmission act), is often discarded. Within gospel music, the song begins to have real life when it enters the performance medium. It is thus unusual that we have at the beginning of this work in gospel music history so much of Dorsey's library.

In order to arrive at some conclusions about his gospel music style, I analyzed 158 songs. Dorsey wrote 99 percent of the lyrics for his compositions, and when we utter such catch phrases as "I'll tell it wherever I go" and "I gave my heart to Jesus, how about you?," we are simply repeating the words of Thomas A. Dorsey. Dorsey, like Tindley before him and William Herbert Brewster and James Cleveland after him, was able to take the anxieties, joys, and aspirations of the poor, rejected, and often uneducated African American population and express them in lyrics that not only captured the very essence of the Christian movement but also spoke for each Christian as if he or she were making a personal statement. For example, in uttering a prayer, one could simply say, "Take my hand, precious Lord." That's a prayer. If Dorsey wanted to express the joy of conversion and subsequent salvation, he would place the expression in the cadence of the street with "I can't forget it, can you?" If one of the sisters wanted to give thanks for living a Christian life and the rewards that she would receive from it, she'd sum it all up by saying simply, "There will be peace in the valley for me someday."

For the composer who enjoys writing lyrics, as Dorsey did, once a text has been settled upon, there is the difficult task of assigning notes to it to bring it to life—writing the melody. Dorsey is not known as a singer, although he had been a singer all his life (as he

Table 5 Selected Compositions of Thomas Andrew Dorsey

Copyright Date	Title	Copyright Date	Title
1930	"He'll Know Me over Yonder"	1939	"Hide Me in Thy Bosom"
1931	"Don't You Need My Savior Too?"		"Keep Praying All the Time"
	"Jesus, My Comforter"		"Peace, It's Wonderful"
	"Right Now"		"Remember Me"
	"Treasure in Heaven"		"Today"
1932	"Changes"		"When I've Done My Best"
	"Shake My Mother's Hand for Me"		"When the Last Mile Is Finished"
	"Take My Hand, Precious Lord"		"Wings over Jordan!"
1933	"I Can't Forget It, Can You?"	1940	"Does It Mean Anything to You?"
	"Surely My Jesus Must Be True"		"God Be with You"
	"You Can't Go through This World by Yourself"		"How Many Times"
			"I Know My Redeemer Lives"
1934	"A Crown for Me"		"If You Meet God in the Morning"
	"Did It Happen to You Like It Happened to Me?"		"Life Can Be Beautiful"
	"He Has Gone to Prepare a Place for Me"		"My Time's Not as Long as It Has Been"
	"I'm Satisfied with Jesus in My Heart"		"Singing My Way to Rest"
	"I'm Singing Every Day"		"Walking up the King's Highway"
	"It Is Real with Me"		"Wasn't That an Awful Time?"
	"It's All in the Plan of Salvation"	1941	"Come Ye That Love the Lord"
	"O Lord, Show Me the Way"		"He Is Risen for He's Living in My Soul"
1935	"I Know Jesus"		"How about You?"
	"I'm Going to Follow Jesus All the Way"		"I Claim Jesus First and That's Enough for Me"
	"Watching and Waiting"		"I Thank God for My Song"
	"What Then?"		"I'm Going to Live the Life I Sing about in My Song"
1936	"I'm Talking about Jesus"		"Jesus Remembers When Others Forget"
	"Jesus Never Does a Thing"		"Just Wait a Little While"
	"Save Me as I Am"		"Look on the Brighter Side"
1937	"My Desire"		"Meet Me at the Pearly Gates"
	"I'm Just a Sinner Saved by Grace"		"Someday Somewhere"
1938	"Forgive My Sins, Forget, and Make Me Whole"		"Somewhere"
	"Get Ready and Serve the Lord"		"The Savior's Here"
	"I'll Tell It Wherever I Go"		"There's an Empty Chair at the Table"
	"I'm Goin' to Hold on 'til Jesus Comes for Me"		"Walk Close to Me, O Lord"
	"If Jesus Bore His Cross So Can I"		"When the Gates Swing Open, Let Me In"
	"It Is Thy Servant's Prayer A-men"		"Won't You Come and Go Along?"
	"Jesus Is the Light"	1942	"I Don't Know Why I Have to Cry Sometime"
	"Make Me the Servant I Would Like to Be"		"I Want Jesus on the Road I Travel"
	"Maybe It's You and Then Maybe It's Me"		"Let Us Go Back to God"
	"O Who's Goin' to Lead Me"		"The Flag for You and Me"
	"Something New Burning in My Soul"		"The Lord Knows Just What I Need"
	"There'll Be Peace in the Valley for Me"		"There's a God Somewhere"
	"There's a Better Day Coming Right Here"		"What the World Needs Is Jesus Most of All"
	"Use My Heart, Use My Mind, Use My Hands"	1943	"Be Thou Near Me All the Way"
	"Who Is Willing to Take a Stand for the Lord?"		"God Is Good to Me"
			"If We Never Needed the Lord Before, We Sure Do Need Him Now"

Table 5 (*continued*)

Copyright Date	Title	Copyright Date	Title
	"Let Me Understand"		"Jesus Only"
	"The Lord Will Make a Way Somehow"		"Jesus Rose Again"
	"Thy Kingdom Come"		"Just One Step"
	"When I've Sung My Last Song"		"Old Ship of Zion"
1944	"He's All I Need"	1951	"I Am His and He Is Mine"
	"I'll Never Turn Back"		"I Want to Be More Like Jesus"
	"I'm Goin' to Wait until My Change Shall Come"		"I'm Goin' to Work until the Day Is Done"
	"Take Me Through, Lord"		"Lead Me to the Rock That's Higher Than I"
1945	"I Got Jesus in My Soul"		"My Soul Feels Better Right Now"
	"I'm Waiting for Jesus, He's for Me"		"Never Leave Me Alone"
	"Somebody's Knocking at Your Door"		"Someway, Somehow, Sometime, Somewhere"
	"That's All that I Can Do"		"The Lord Is My Shepherd"
1946	"Come Unto Me"		"There Is Something about the Lord Mighty Sweet"
	"It's Not a Shame to Cry Holy to the Lord"		"When They Crown Him Lord of All"
	"Someday I'm Going Home"	1952	"Count Your Blessings from the Lord Each Day"
	"Thank You All the Days of My Life"		"I'm Climbing up the Rough Side of the Mountain"
	"The Lord Has Laid His Hands on Me"		
	"There Isn't but One Way to Make It In"	1953	"In My Savior's Care"
	"Your Sins Will Find You Out"		"My Mind on Jesus"
1947	"Ev'ry Day Will Be Sunday By and By"	1954	"It's a Highway to Heaven (Walking up the King's Highway)"
	"How Much More of Life's Burden Can We Bear?"		"My Faith I Place in Thee"
	"I May Never Pass This Way Again"	1955	"Standing Here Wondering Which Way to Go"
	"When Day Is Done"		"Windows of Heaven"
1948	"Search Me, Lord"	1956	"I Thought of God"
1949	"Glory for Me"	1957	"Behold the Man of Galilee"
	"He Never Will Leave Me"		"Say a Little Prayer for Me"
	"Something Has Happened to Me"	1960	"Singing Everywhere"
	"Tell Jesus Everything"		"Troubled about My Soul"
	"That's Good News"		"We Must Work Together"
	"The Little Wooden Church on the Hill"	1962	"I Thought on My Way"
	"This Man Jesus"	1964	"While He's Passing By"
	"When You Bow in the Evening at the Altar"	1968	"Sometimes My Burden's So Hard to Bear"
1950	"Don't Forget the Name of the Lord"		
	"It's a Blessing Just to Call My Savior's Name"		

aptly proved with the singing of "Precious Lord, Take My Hand" in the 1982 film on gospel music, *Say Amen, Somebody*), but he understood the human voice extraordinarily well. In point of fact, he knew every possible aspect of the Black vocal style—it must not be forgotten that he was "born" into the Baptist church; he worked as a blues singer with Tampa Red; he accompanied Ma Rainey on piano and was her music director; and he led his own jazz band. He wrote a melodic line that was well within the average singer's range, always beginning at a comfortable pitch. He would ascend to a high note at the climax and then gradually return to the comfortable pitch of the beginning, as in "Precious Lord . . ." (ex. 27). The song begins in the comfortable or low range of the average singer, but a climax has been placed at the words

> Thru the storm, thru the night
> Lead me on to the light.
> Take my hand, precious Lord,
> Lead me on.

The word *storm* is assigned to the highest note in the composition. By the end of the song, Dorsey has returned to the middle register.

The tones employed in the melody of "Precious Lord, Take My Hand" constitute its scale. Dorsey employed a gapped scale, which in visual terms would look like a five- or six-year-old child with a tooth missing; there would be a space to leap back and forth from. He liked scales that provided the same kind of space a Black speaking style conveys when African American people all of a sudden raise their voices in pitch and then return to a more comfortable pitch.

He did, however, employ the diatonic scale, and 47 of the 158 songs analyzed use this scale. Melodies based on the diatonic scale include "When the Last Mile Is Finished" and "Walk Close to Me O Lord" (ex. 28). Of more interest, however, is his use of the diatonic scale with added *chromatic* tones—those that are not part of the scale but fall

Example 27.   Pitch changes in the melodic line of "Precious Lord, Take My Hand" (Thomas A. Dorsey, orig. © 1932). © 1948 UNICHAPPELL MUSIC INC. (Renewed). All rights reserved. Used by permission.

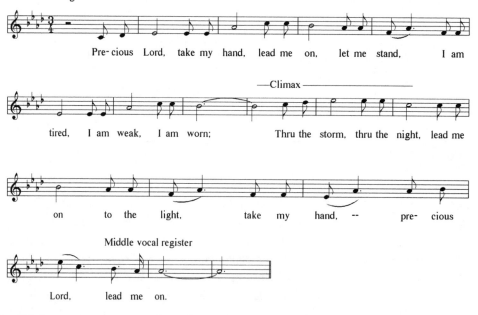

Example 28. "Walk Close to Me O Lord" (Thomas A. Dorsey, orig. © 1941). © 1948 UNICHAP-
PELL MUSIC INC. (Renewed). All rights reserved. Used by permission.

Example 29.   "Today" (Thomas A. Dorsey). © 1939 UNICHAPPELL MUSIC INC. (Renewed). All rights reserved. Used by permission.

between the notes of the scale. This scale is used in "If Jesus Bore the Cross, So Can I" and the very popular "Today" (ex. 29). "Today" is set to the diatonic scale of F, the notes of which are F, G, A, Bb, C, D, E, F; all of these tones appear in the melody of the verse. However, when Dorsey reaches the chorus, he uses the Db on the second statement of the title, employing chromaticism:

F F Bb   F   F Db
Oh to-day, Oh to-day

In one song, all of the tones of the diatonic scale are used, but the seventh degree is flatted, another example of Dorsey's understanding of the Black musical tradition. He knew that Black singers of folk music automatically flat the seventh in most cases, so he simply wrote that tone into "I'm Going to Hold on Until Jesus Comes."

The gapped scale appears to have been his favorite, for he set fifty-three of the songs analyzed to this scale, specifically the five-tone scale called *pentatonic*. Such traditional songs as "Steal Away," "Swing Low, Sweet Chariot," and "Nobody Knows the Trouble I See" are built on this scale. Those songs are based on only five tones, but the good composer uses them in such a way that the listener is unaware of the economy of pitches. In some instances, Dorsey alternates between two versions of the same pitch. For example, in "Search Me, Lord," on the first syllable of the word *straighten* he uses a flatted version of C (ex. 30). Flatted tones, sometimes called *blue notes*, actually are an African American performance practice of softening the melody by lowering a tone.

Additionally, he places a delay on the syllables one would ordinarily prolong in speaking, so that while the rhythm flows with the basic pulse in most circumstances, syncopation is employed. For example, instead of saying "Jesus," he might say:

Je- SUS; Je-SUS;
(da- DA;   da-DA)

All of a sudden, the emphasis shifts.

Dorsey also employs the triplet figure. One might get the triplet figure by saying, "I - da - ho; I - da - ho" (DA - da - da; DA - da - da). He employed the triplet figure in "Consideration" (ex. 31).

Another rhythmic trait of Dorsey is what is called *four-to-the-bar*, meaning that in $\frac{4}{4}$ time, each of the four beats gets an articulation. Historically, four-to-the-bar has been associated generally with blues, jazz, and the piano style called *boogie-woogie*. Dorsey includes this four-to-the-bar pattern in "He Never Will Leave Me" (ex. 32). He came by this through his earlier experiences in blues and jazz bands.

The individual rhythmic impulses must be grouped into small units to give the composition a rhythmic order. Gospel music has selected as its primary meter $\frac{4}{4}$—four pulses, whether or not these pulses have additional secondary beats. Since 1950, the so-called

Example 30. "Search Me Lord" (Thomas A. Dorsey). © 1948 UNICHAPPELL MUSIC INC. (Renewed). All rights reserved. Used by permission.

Example 30. (continued)

Example 31. "Consideration" (Thomas A. Dorsey). © 1953 UNICHAPPELL MUSIC INC. (Renewed).

Example 31. *(continued)*

Example 31. *(continued)*

Example 32. "He Never Will Leave Me" (Thomas A. Dorsey). © 1940 UNICHAPPELL MUSIC INC., HILL & RANGE SONGS INC., RIGHTSONG MUSIC INC. (Renewed). All rights reserved. Used by permission.

Example 32.   *(continued)*

gospel meter has been $\frac{12}{8}$, and it is interesting that $\frac{12}{8}$ is still four with two additional beats to each one. So you have: 1 2 3, 2 2 3, 3 2 3, 4 2 3. This is the basic gospel beat.

Likewise, it is interesting to note that in these 158 songs, Dorsey did not use $\frac{12}{8}$ once, even though he had helped to create it. The $\frac{12}{8}$ did not appear in published music until 1970. Earlier, there had been no need to use it; there was something in baroque music called a *note inégale,* in which a note is written one way and played another way. It's

Example 32. *(continued)*

SPECIAL CHORUS

rather like two eighth notes in jazz that are played as a triplet figure, long to short (ex. 33). This is usually written into the score. If the performer is on the *inside* of the tradition, he or she knows the tradition and automatically plays this way. So Dorsey wrote his music in $\frac{4}{4}$, but it was played in $\frac{12}{8}$. When he taught his music to the choir, although the score before them was in $\frac{4}{4}$, he would play it in $\frac{12}{8}$, and it would sound like a gospel waltz.

Of the songs I have analyzed, Dorsey published 7 songs in waltz time, or $\frac{3}{4}$; 1 song in $\frac{6}{4}$; 29 songs in $\frac{2}{4}$; and 112 songs in $\frac{4}{4}$. All of these songs—half of them fast, half of them slow—would be performed in $\frac{12}{8}$ time.

Example 33.   Notes written in $\frac{4}{4}$ time but played in $\frac{12}{8}$.

The simultaneous sounding tones, or harmony, that accompany Dorsey's melody have been called perfect by all of those students who have studied his music because it is felt that gospel, with its straightforward lyrics and melody, ought to be accompanied by harmony that in no way detracts from the lyrics or the melodic line. This is exactly what Dorsey did in his compositions. He used basically a I–IV–V type (ex. 34).

Example 34.   Harmony in I–IV–V chord pattern of Dorsey compositions.

Any of these chords could have a seventh added to it. Prior to 1969, the seventh in gospel music was a flatted seventh. Dorsey would add a seventh; therefore, all of these chords would have a seventh. Of the songs I analyzed, 95 percent use a simple harmony like that, but the other 5 percent are songs in which Dorsey investigated the entire harmonic palette. For example, in "When I've Done the Best I Can," which was published in 1939 and used in the film *Say Amen, Somebody*, Dorsey uses the key of F, and he starts with a third in the bass (ex. 35). That's fairly sophisticated for 1939. In mm. 1–8

Example 35. "When I've Done the Best I Can" (Thomas A. Dorsey). © 1939 UNICHAPPELL MUSIC INC. (Renewed). All rights reserved. Used by permission.

the tension is produced by the descending line in the bass and the chromatic inflection in the treble. When he arrives at the contrasting section, Dorsey resorts to a B♮ rather than a B♭ and therefore changes the entire complexion of the harmonic progression. He immediately moves to the minor mode—on the ii chord—G minor, before moving to the dominant chord to lead back to the opening melodic strain (see mm. 11–12).

On March 13, 1964, I arrived in Chicago as a young graduate student and called Mr. Dorsey and asked for an interview. I introduced myself as one of the Boyer Brothers, which did not seem to mean anything to him. However, he agreed to the interview, and I spent two days with him. I asked him why he used such simplified notation in his published songs. He answered, "I want you to understand that when I started writing gospel music, people had to read it in order to play it" (Boyer 1964a). That was surprising to me, because by that time no one read gospel music. The tradition was so old and so well established that it was in the air, and one simply went to the piano and picked it out. This movement from a written transmission to a dominantly oral one led to the demise of the gospel publishing business. In fact, Dorsey eventually gave up his own publishing business because people were no longer buying sheet music.

However, when Dorsey began to publish his music, the sheet music was a crucial instrument not only for lyrics but for the melody and accompaniment. Musicians used the music to teach the song; when the basic elements of the song (singing and playing) were learned, then the oral process emerged again. Dorsey stated that he wrote in keys that musicians who served Black churches during this period could understand, using the chords they could understand and play.

Out of these 158 songs, 75 of them were in the key of F major. The next largest group was in the key of G major, followed by E♭. Only three of the songs I analyzed were in the key of C, a fact that I thought was interesting, since C is an easy key.

Form or design is that aspect of composition in which a composer decides what should come first, what should come next, and how often it should be repeated. Most gospel songs are based on the verse–chorus pattern. The verse is the section where you tell a story or recount a situation. The chorus is the part where you simply give your own feelings about that situation. For example, Dorsey used this verse in "The Lord Will Make a Way Somehow" (ex. 36):

> Like a ship that's tossed and driven,
> battered by an angry sea

In the chorus part, he wrote:

> The Lord will make a way somehow
> When beneath the cross I'll bow.

This is the form that Dorsey used for 75 percent of his songs. He also used the chorus–verse and special chorus. In fact, I think he created that form. The special chorus is the

Example 36. "The Lord Will Make a Way Somehow" (Thomas A. Dorsey). © 1943 UNI-
CHAPPELL MUSIC INC. (Renewed). All rights reserved. Used by permission.

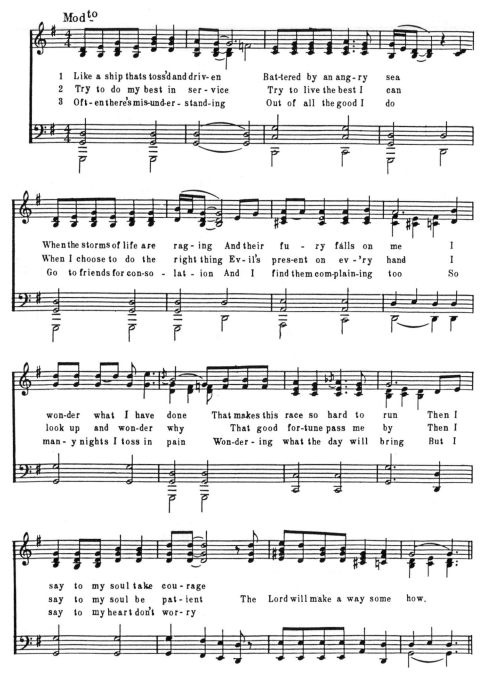

Example 37.   "There'll Be Peace in the Valley for Me" (Thomas A. Dorsey, orig. © 1938).
© 1939 UNICHAPPELL MUSIC INC. (Renewed). All rights reserved. Used by permission.

chorus, but he has added an extra part to it. In contemporary gospel, that special chorus is a vamp, in which one idea is repeated over and over. Dorsey did not like the unlimited nature of the vamp, but he did compose a special chorus.

As to categories of sacred-song forms found in the African American tradition, Dorsey wrote songs using the Baptist lining-hymn tradition, songs to be performed without a strict pulse; songs done freely, or jubilees; and songs that I call *gospel blues*. Gospel blues is a sixteen-bar song with a four-line poem: lines one, two, and four are the same, and line three is a contrasting line. He actually has two gospel blues compositions. It is interesting to me that he wrote any gospel blues at all, since this form stilts the poetic line and Dorsey was such a poet—poetry flowed from him.

Dorsey's genius as a lyricist and composer of great melodic and harmonic strength stands out in one of his most widely performed works, "There'll Be Peace in the Valley for Me" (ex. 37):

> I am tired and weary but I must toil on
> Till the Lord comes to call me away.
> Where the morning is bright and the Lamb is the light,
> And the night is as fair as the day.

Now, here's the hook:

> There'll be peace in the valley for me some day.

Then a repeat of that line:

> There'll be peace in the valley for me
> I pray, no more sorrows and sadness or trouble will be.
> There'll be peace in the valley for me.

Then a repeat of those lines:

> There'll be peace in the valley for me
> I pray, no more sorrows and sadness or trouble will be.
> There will be peace in the valley for me.

Because Dorsey was such a pioneer and such a prolific composer, the elements of the Dorsey style appear in almost all the gospel music known today. It is a style in which imagery and metaphor are brought to unusual heights in poetry that expresses Christian aspirations in the language of the people, and in which the melody is so perfectly designed that it is singable by even the most inexperienced singer. It is set to a rhythm that follows the natural flow of African American speech and is supported by a harmony that, while simple and sparse, adds to rather than detracts from the message of the song. Lastly, it has an essence that testifies to the "good news."

CONFLICT AND RESOLUTION IN THE LIFE OF THOMAS ANDREW DORSEY

Michael W. Harris

This chapter draws on interviews the author conducted with Thomas A. Dorsey in 1976 and 1977 in Chicago.—ED.

Abiographical sketch of a person serves little purpose if it consists only of a narrative of life events. The life of Thomas Andrew Dorsey, the individual most often associated with the rise of gospel blues in Black Protestant churches during the early 1930s, is no exception to this rule. From his early years in rural Georgia and then Atlanta, to his career as a blues musician in Chicago, and finally to his troublesome metamorphosis into a gospel songwriter, Dorsey looms larger than the aggregate of incidents in his life. This essay portrays both the Dorsey who progresses from event to event and the Dorsey who is greater than the sum of those events. The latter Dorsey typifies African American society at various points in its history between the 1870s when post-Emancipation Black culture began to crystallize and the 1930s when gospel blues emerged in Protestant Black churches.

This essay is mosaic in structure. Its design consists of carefully selected events that show how Dorsey became the so-called father of gospel blues. These events have been gathered into thematic images that, when viewed as a whole or pieced together, illustrate how Dorsey did not evolve in some easily perceived line, the end of which was gospel blues. Instead, they show that Dorsey was shaped by three distinct periods of personal development, the last of which yielded the Dorsey who wrote gospel blues. The three periods can be thought of as exposure, conflict, and resolution.

There are two conflictive concepts that help make the link between these periods more obvious than Dorsey as the common subject. These concepts are overarching, social and cultural in their effect. The first of these is the notion of African American duality, as described by W. E. B. Du Bois—the quest for both racial and national identities, "two strivings in one dark body" (Du Bois [1903] 1961, 17). This idea of African American duality comprises an integral part of individuals' lives. As Dorsey evolved from his period of exposure through the other periods, he never escaped this struggle of twoness; he merely became aware of it again and again in the changing context of each period. In more ways than not, this same process mirrored the development of African American society as a whole, which is why Dorsey's life may be considered so representative of that whole.

The second conflictive concept is the idea of the sacred and secular in his life. In the African American society in which Dorsey evolved, the sacred and secular were not separated into distinct spheres, each with its own recognizable ethos. The sacred and secular instead seemed almost to be opportunistic intrusions. They appeared and reappeared, most often disguised as music—sometimes even as the same music.

The Thomas A. Dorsey who emerged in the 1930s as one of the principal figures in the gospel song movement was both an individual of personal dimensions and an individual of African American dimensions. His gospels are unmistakably renderings of the two. In essence, this essay will argue how the man became his music and, to the extent that African Americanness can be individualized, how Dorsey's gospels might be said to have become the man.

The period of exposure begins with Dorsey's childhood in Villa Rica, Georgia, a town about thirty miles west of Atlanta. There, Dorsey heard two contrasting types of sacred music. The first of these was something he called *moaning*. He remembers hearing his mother, father, and old people singing this style of music on the porch at night or in church: "I've heard my mother and other folk get together, get around and get to talking and then start moaning." At church, Dorsey would hear the congregation sing a hymn or spiritual and "then they [would] moan it out." It was mysterious to him as a child how moaning evoked shouts: "There's something to it that nobody knows . . ." (Harris 1976).

The other style of sacred music to which young Dorsey was exposed was known as shape-note singing. In this music, different degrees of the scale correspond to a specific shape; for example, the tonic, or first degree of the scale, *do*, is represented by a diamond note. Dorsey first heard this music at Mount Prospect Baptist Church, where his parents worshiped from time to time. Its presence there gives us a clue to the degree this music contrasted so greatly with moaning. Shape-note singing originated in New England in the early 1700s as part of a movement to improve singing in Puritan churches. Singing masters established singing schools to train illiterate people to read not only music but words, since students had to be able to read the texts of the songs too. By 1815, the singing teachers had migrated into the South. The most well known of these instructors was Ananias Davisson, whose tune book, the *Sacred Harp*, supplied the name of the movement by which it is known to this day. As shape-note singing had been an instrument of literacy in early New England, so it was in Villa Rica among unschooled, former slaves in the last quarter of the nineteenth century. Dorsey's uncle, Corrie Hindsman, was the person who brought the music to the church; he was also the teacher at the local Black school.

Dorsey found this music fascinating. The congregation up to that time had mostly sung spirituals spontaneously—moaning being one example: "the people sang from their very hearts." This new music, however, had a different sound to it: "The shape of the note gave you the tune and the pitch. And I mean every man and every woman knew their place. It was beautiful singing. You wouldn't hear any better singing now than those folks did in those days" (Harris 1976).

The difference between soulful and book-learned music is more than the music itself: it is a difference of cultures. In one, music is a spontaneous creation—a heartfelt act—first from the individual then shared by the community. In the other, it is a communal act of learning first to read, then to sing, and then, perhaps, to feel. Its origins reach into the Puritan experience and a need to rein in expressive spirituality. The other extends back to slavery and a compelling desire for both personal and group expression. That we find both of these disparate forms present in the life of young Thomas Andrew Dorsey attests to the twoness on which this first period is so precariously balanced. African Americans in the post-Emancipation period often faced choosing between indigenous and exogenous—virtually mutually exclusive—forms of expression. To choose the former meant to align oneself with the still-vibrant and appealing slave culture and its provision for communal inspiration. It also meant not assimilating into the dominant European American culture in which African American forms of expression—especially those rooted in enslavement—were profoundly alien. To choose one meant to forsake the other, except in Dorsey's childhood setting. That the antithetical could co-reside there is a testament to a breadth of cultural exposure in Dorsey's youth that sets him apart from much of rural southern Black American culture of the time. As well, this cross-cultural awareness would mark his approach to music making throughout his life.

Religion came to Dorsey in a kind of bifurcated unity as well, except it did not imply the cross-cultural twoness Du Bois wrote about. Instead, it concerned a polarity of feelings about the place of religion in one's life. On one end is an intensely private and deeply pietistic experience; this was his mother's, Etta Plant Dorsey. Writing about the role of motherhood in the formation of religious values in a child, Dorsey makes clear his belief that maternal and religious nurturing are one: "Mother in her office holds the key of the soul, and she it is who stamps the coin of character and makes the being, who would be a savage but for her gentle cares, a Christian man" (Dorsey 1935, 59–60). Dorsey's memories of his mother's religious life make it clear that he had her in mind when he wrote this passage. Etta ran the family Bible readings and devotionals. She made it a point to feed hobos and others in need who passed by their home. Taken together, these almost inconsequential acts bespeak Etta's deep commitment to piety and to being a model of religious devotion in her family.

On the other end of the polarity stood his father's religious experience. As one of the first generation of children of former slaves and as a graduate of Atlanta Baptist College (later Morehouse College) with a Bachelor of Divinity degree, Thomas Madison Dorsey was poised to continue down this path as one of a select group of educated Blacks in the post-Emancipation period. Things seemed to work differently for him, however. For example, he never pastored a church. He spent most of his career as a guest—sometimes even itinerant—preacher: "He was known by his preaching. He was kind of an itinerant preacher. He didn't want to pastor. . . . I don't think he wanted a church. He was known all over" (Harris 1976).

The preponderance of Thomas Madison's preaching as opposed to pastoring provided an image of religion for the young Dorsey that contrasted sharply with his mother's. One of Dorsey's most poignant memories of the impact of his father's religion concerns the way he, as a four- or five-year-old, would imitate his father's preaching: "I had a church under our front porch. The porch was high and under there was my church. [My mother and father] had bought me some kind of little cane; my father had a cane too. And [I'd] go down under the house and hang my cane up and then I'd start talking to what would be my audience as if they were there. [I'd] go in and I'd hang my cane up just like he'd go in and hang his cane up" (Harris 1976). Dorsey's mimicry even included props, a sure sign of the degree to which this kind of religious behavior, in the form of pulpitry, deeply impressed him.

So stark is the disparity between these polar-opposite images that it is hard to conceive of religion to young Dorsey as being something other than a dualized entity. The melodramatics of a cane-wielding pulpiteer and the quiet piety of a gentle believer, even if they were not antithetical in young Dorsey's mind, surely supplied him with a broad range of religious sensibilities. That he acted out the former and passively "drank in" the latter would seem to indicate how he resolved whatever conflicts he saw between them. Dorsey's acceptance of polar-opposite religious attitudes, however, would not last much beyond his childhood.

Unlike religion, the sacred and secular emerge during this period with less of the conflictive character they would have in Dorsey's later years. Sacred and secular, however, are abstractions; hence, Dorsey never recalls being aware of a sacred–secular continuum in his early years. His account of his Uncle Phil's (his mother's brother) blues guitar playing can be construed, however, as his introduction to the secular dimension of African American culture. Dorsey clearly discerned a difference, particularly with respect to the individual connected to this music. Phil Plant was not the most wholesome of Dorsey's relatives. Often he was gone, roaming about mostly as a hobo. When he stayed in Villa Rica, he engaged heavily in the bootlegging business. In fact, he would enlist his young nephew to deliver the illegal liquor to his customers. Dorsey recalls well his uncle's playing: "He could really play it [the guitar]" (Harris 1976). More significantly, he remembers his uncle's popularity from being a good blues guitarist: "He was king 'round up in there" (Harris 1976). Just the setting of his uncle's performance would cause little Dorsey to associate this music—indeed, the guitar itself—with something opposite from the church settings of the other musical forms he heard. The unpredictability of his Uncle Phil's presence, the illicitness of his booze, the twanging of his guitar, and perhaps the not too savory character of his fans combined to make his uncle's music the opposite of the moaning and the shape-note singing Dorsey was accustomed to. No label was necessary.

More so than in his period of exposure, Dorsey's life during the second period—conflict—was affected by larger societal forces. Villa Rica was an isolated rural community in which the Dorseys were part of the Black elite class because Thomas Madison Dorsey was a preacher and a part-time schoolteacher. Even though neither of these careers was lucrative, Thomas Madison Dorsey still enjoyed an amount of community prestige that carried over to his family. Just being "the pastor's son," Dorsey recalls, caused people to "make over" him (Harris 1976).

This pleasant, insulated world was ruptured by some financial setbacks. In 1903, Dorsey's mother was forced to mortgage some of her land in order to pay for farming expenses. Borrowing against one's property in order to finance the coming crops was quite risky in the last decades of the nineteenth century, but it was even more since cotton and other staple commodity prices in the region had dropped precipitously. Thus, even though figures in the county land and tax records show that the actual aggregate value of Etta's land increased between 1903 and 1907, Thomas Madison Dorsey was forced to become a sharecropper for a white farmer. Even this arrangement only brought the family's income to subsistence level: "the land would not yield anything but peas and sweet potatoes," mostly for family consumption. The marketable crop, cotton, equaled yearly "just about one wagon load" (Dorsey 1961, 10). This development forced the Dorseys, along with thousands of other rural African Americans, to give up farming and to seek a better opportunity in the city. In 1908, the Dorsey family moved to Atlanta.

Contrary to their expectations, the Dorseys soon discovered that living in Atlanta actually brought about not only a further decline in their financial fortunes but a concomitant loss in their social prestige as well. Indeed, it is this sudden disorientation of his family in an urban environment that brought Dorsey face to face with many of the forces for change in African American culture and, therefore, into conflict with much of the world as he had known it up to then. Right away Thomas and Etta had to make drastic changes. Preaching became at most a sideline for Thomas. For the years 1909 through 1915, Thomas was listed in the *Atlanta City Directory* either as a porter or a laborer. Etta, who had never worked after she was married, became, according to the *Directory*, a laundress. Dorsey remembers that she worked, "taking in washing and ironing" (*Atlanta City Directory* 1909–15, 880, 716, 708, 674, 747, 823, 832).

For Dorsey the move was profoundly shocking. The family's first Christmas celebration in Atlanta almost failed to take place because Etta was sick and Thomas was only intermittently employed. The family became so desperate for food that Thomas was forced to sell the milk cow, Lily. Dorsey, who had responsibility to take care of Lily and had even walked her from Villa Rica to Atlanta, was given the task of driving her to the slaughter-house: "There I saw her killed. I never got over that" (Harris 1976; Dorsey 1961, 14). Such incidents paled in significance when Dorsey began to encounter social ostracism from his schoolmates. He was barefooted, which meant that he "was looked upon as one of the common class" (Dorsey 1961). Contrary to his days in the country where he was "made over" because he was the pastor's son, he now began to confront a virtual caste system among Atlanta Blacks: "During that time when we were about the age of ten, the boys and girls would have their birthday parties. They didn't invite me, even though they knew me very well. I guess I was not good enough, they thought, to mingle with their friends. I used to stand outside and look through the windows" (Dorsey 1961). Dorsey's immediate response to such outright rejection was to quit school. And from this time on (he was approximately eleven years old), he never had any more formal education. With his family in abject poverty and regarded as "common" people, Dorsey now felt the need to earn money and to gain self-esteem. It was the pursuit of these two ends that brought him into Atlanta's music world.

If there was any microcosm of Black America during the first decades of the twentieth century, it was Atlanta. It had its upper economic classes and its intellectual elites living in the neighborhood surrounding Morehouse, Atlanta University, Spelman, and other Black institutions of higher education. It also had its poor and uneducated classes. The sizes of the latter groups so exceeded the former that W. E. B. Du Bois worried that "the increase of the race" would come from "the hovels of the alleys" instead of the "better class homes" (Du Bois 1902, 1).

Atlanta's Black music world mirrored this larger society. Moreover, these sharp class divisions brought out the inherent conflicts in the music and religion to which Dorsey was exposed in his early life. Dorsey was first introduced to music in the 81 Theater, a nickelodeon movie house in which he was a "butch boy" selling soft drinks and popcorn during intermissions. The pianist who accompanied the film, Ed Butler, taught him a few songs on an informal basis. The movie theater can be thought of as the center point of the Atlanta music world, a place where all Black classes could converge. The presence of racial segregation and the novelty of film entertainment together guaranteed that Blacks would ignore social barriers to attend the 81 Theater. Dorsey's first exposure to the piano thus was relatively uneventful, in that while he could address one of his twin personal pursuits—the need for money—he was in no way confronting the social divisiveness of the community.

This was not to be the case when he ventured into other domains of the Atlanta Black music world, especially when he seemed so desirous of personal prestige. Sensing that formal lessons would help his cause, Dorsey began taking piano from a Mrs. Graves, who had a music studio near Morehouse and who was affiliated with the college. There he learned music in a way totally different from his sporadic sessions with Butler: he had to learn to read, and he had to learn piano technique, "how to use your fingers" (Harris 1976). This kind of fingering technique, required for Western European classical music, was strange to a young boy accustomed to learning by rote. Even more strange, however, was the westside environment into which he walked in order to visit Mrs. Graves's studio. Here was Dorsey's indoctrination into Atlanta's Black upper-class tastes, ones that had little tolerance for the more indigenous ways of Blacks on his side of town. This encounter with musical literacy should have been the analogue of the shape-note singing he heard as a child. But Dorsey was not as impressed, mostly because the rote playing he had been exposed to at the 81 Theater seemed more directly to serve his purposes: "she wasn't a jazz musician. She taught around Morehouse. The music most the folk were playing was by ear" (Harris 1976).*

This reordering of Dorsey's tastes continued as he more aggressively sought personal prestige. He quit taking piano from Mrs. Graves—"I knew about as much as I needed to know"—and began to learn the movie pianist's art in earnest. His training with Mrs. Graves did help in one aspect of picture-show accompaniment: he could read and, in a quite rudimentary sense, write music. His notational skills were useful because the theater at times booked live performances, during which the pianist would not only have to play original songs written by the entertainers but at times would have to make arrangements of music. Dorsey steadily grew into this playing, so much so that Ed Butler allowed him to substitute for him. But Butler's position was too lucrative for him to give Dorsey any more than sporadic opportunities to play. After a little over a year, Dorsey realized that he was learning a lot but not gaining a reputation or professional advancement: "I didn't have a professional job and I wasn't called professional. You see a professional, you got to be doing something up there that will at least advertise the profession. I could do all of this, but you've got to have a place to do it and you've got to have somebody to hear it. [I] could read the music" (Harris 1976).

His disillusionment with the theater pianist's world, along with his growing need for self-importance, led him to make a sharp turn toward the most exotic of Atlanta's Black music settings: bordellos and rent parties. Opportunities to perform at these sites were gained only by one's reputation; and, of course, Dorsey wanted to build a good reputation, at almost any cost. There was one aspect of making a name in these places that directly affected Dorsey's playing style: both places were under constant threat of "the law." The bordello housed prostitution and sold bootleg liquor (Atlanta was "dry" at that time); the rent party could get too noisy, and illegal alcohol flowed there, too. Thus the possibility of arrest was imminent:

Down there in Atlanta, it's warm weather most of the time. You had to throw the windows open. You could hear the piano playing a block away almost, and when the folk get in there and they get noisy, the neighbor called the law and the law come in there. Sometimes they didn't bother anybody; see what's going on. But if it was one of those places, you know, where they handle bootleg liquor, anytime they'd come, they'd pull around the wagon down there and run them in. (Harris 1976)

---

*Dorsey uses the word *jazz* here in a figurative sense. He probably meant blues or popular music, since he would readily admit that he did not even know the word *jazz* (or *jass*) until he moved to Chicago.

For Dorsey to achieve notoriety in these settings, therefore, he had to become quite pragmatic in his approach to playing. Dorsey perfected a blues style that was soft, so that the piano did not disturb the peace; melodic, so that the listener could hum or sing along; and intensely rhythmic, through a liberal use of syncopation, so that his music could be danced to easily. No other player seems to have mastered this combination of stylistic elements to the degree that Dorsey did. His party blues so carefully balanced the seemingly competing ends of being utilitarian and aesthetically pleasing that he was considered the "No. 1" party pianist in Atlanta by 1915 or 1916: "they liked my style. Some of the fellows, you know, bump, beat, you know, they played loud and folk get loud and [somebody] called the law. But I played soft and easy; you could drag it out and hug the woman at the same time. Let the lights down low and they'd have to give attention to hear the piano" (Harris 1976).

Ironically, once Dorsey achieved his long-sought success, he simultaneously arrived at a full inversion of the music preferences he had cultivated from his early years. The shape-note singing he had once listened to in awe, with its four-part harmony and strange contrast with moaning, he now rejected because of his formal piano training and the westside Atlanta milieu in which he received it. The tawdriness of Uncle Phil's blues guitar and the adulation of his listeners, fueled very likely by the alcohol little Dorsey had fetched for them, were no less present in the brothels and sweaty get-togethers attended by Dorsey's now admiring, slow-dragging listeners whose consumption of illegal liquor he musically guarded. This metamorphosis occurred in less than seven years, the years of transition from Dorsey's childhood to early adolescence. He was scarcely aware of these inversions or their scale, but they represented the prelude to his later conflicts. This fundamental change took place against the backdrop of the increasing social stratification of Black America and the effect of that on Dorsey's family. Which is the cause and which the effect are not readily ascertainable; their interrelatedness, however, is undeniable.

The first of these conflicts arose in 1921 in Chicago. Dorsey had moved there in 1916 in search of better professional opportunities and, as in Atlanta, a name for himself. He had little luck: his down-home, soft and easy blues found an audience only among recent migrants from the South like himself. He and that crowd congregated in small, out-of-the-way bars, far from the glittery nightclubs where established musicians were just beginning to thrill their listeners with the faster, up-tempo blues they called *jass*. The same intraracial social divisions that plagued Dorsey in Atlanta were present in no less virulent forms in Chicago, the bourgeois appeal and setting of jass being a typical example. Indeed, the major difference between the two social settings was that the lower economic groups in Chicago tended to be Southern migrants who had arrived after the first World War. When Dorsey saw his career advancement stymied by the condescension shown his blues, he became quite stressed. This plus the general disorientation associated with his move led to a period of depression and finally a nervous breakdown. In October 1920 he returned to Atlanta and spent the winter recuperating there.

This period of sickness set the stage for his first serious conflict. In Atlanta, his changes in tastes had concerned only music. Now religion became a factor, first through his mother's admonition that he needed to "serve the Lord, serve the Lord" (Harris 1977a). She had stood by somewhat helplessly as he, lured into Atlanta's music underworld, drifted farther away from the religious values she had taught him. Her cautioning, moreover, was more and more compromised by the financial support Dorsey provided the family—now four children—from his ever-mounting earnings as a party pianist. Now with her son in her care and his success an ever-distant memory, Etta once again began to "stamp the coin of character," to shape him into a Christian as she had so roundly in his childhood (Harris 1977a; Dorsey 1935, 59).

Even with his mother's words ringing in his ears, Dorsey ventured back to Chicago the following summer eager to return to the blues world: "I was in the . . . blues business; I *wanted* to be. I [wasn't] a member of anybody's church—there, my father's, nobody's. Didn't want to be a member" (Harris 1977a). But at the invitation of his uncle Joshua, a Chicago druggist, Dorsey attended a session of the forty-first annual meeting of the National Baptist Convention that was meeting in the city between September 7 and 12. That night Dorsey's religious emotions were rekindled by the singing of "I Do, Don't You?" by the well-known evangelist W. M. Nix: "My inner being was thrilled. My soul was a deluge of divine rapture; my emotions were aroused; my heart was inspired to become a great singer and worker in the Kingdom of the Lord—and impress people just as this great singer did that Sunday morning" (Dorsey 1941, 19–20).

Shortly after this meeting, Dorsey joined New Hope Baptist Church and began to work as its director of music. A year later he registered his first sacred composition, "If I Don't Get There," with the U.S. Copyright Office. This song appeared in the following edition of *Gospel Pearls* (published in 1921), the newest songbook of the Convention (published in 1921). Soon after, he wrote "We Will Meet Him in the Sweet By and By," which appeared in *The Baptist Standard Hymnal* in one of its early editions (Townsend 1924).

This flurry of religious activities was destined to end. Within months of joining New Hope, Dorsey quit to accept an offer to join Will Walker's group, the Whispering Syncopators. The promise of forty dollars every week compared to sporadic donations was more than enough to dampen his newly found religious fervor. But something lurked more deeply in his psyche to guarantee that his religious rededication would be short-lived. He had been persuaded to become religious not by the content of Nix's song, but by the fact that Nix could impress so many people through his singing. Dorsey's religious sensibility was awakened by a musical version of the pulpitry that had so deeply impressed him as a child, when he stood under the porch imitating his father's preaching. He was convicted by the idea of becoming a great singer, not by a need for new religious consciousness. Missing was the complement of such religious histrionics: deep religious devotion of the sort he had seen in his mother. With his quest for recognition obstructed by his quaint blues playing and his emotional state in the fragile first stages of recovery from his breakdown, Dorsey was in position to be swept away by almost anything that promised to unify two of his most powerful urgings. Once he became aware that such a unity was for now illusory—that his need for personal and professional self-esteem was as dead-ended in New Hope Baptist as it was in the second-class, migrant bars—he was fated to drop religion and begin the search elsewhere.

Ironically, Dorsey's choice of the Whispering Syncopators as his next professional step set the stage for the second conflict. That Dorsey was invited to travel with the band already indicates that he was setting his career path on a nontraditional blues trajectory. The Syncopators, one of the established bands, played jass, ragtime, vaudeville, and other popular styles in the clubs, theaters, and dance halls in Chicago and in other major cities in which Blacks owned these types of establishments and could afford to book traveling groups. This position indicates one other significant advancement for Dorsey: to be a member of a stage band, he had to have been accepted in the Musicians' Protective Union. Dorsey had tried in vain to join the Union. Just playing a few bar jobs, however, left him unqualified for membership. Now he belonged to the Union, and his salary at forty dollars per week exceeded the pay scale for theater musicians, who earned thirty to thirty-three dollars per week (*Chicago Defender* 1920; Dorsey 1961, 46).

Dorsey's sudden move into the popular music establishment obviously followed some attendant change in his performance habits. Earlier he had rejected "jass" because it was too demanding: "No, jazz is a new name on the scene. Your execution was a little faster. All the piano boys were trying to get those extra keyboard frizzles and nimbling in their fingers to make [their music] sound jassy. That's why I didn't bother much with it—took too much energy. You couldn't last an evening. Too much barnstomping. You bump, beat, be wore out" (Harris 1976, 1977a). Also, his listeners, mostly newcomers from the South, found jazz disconcerting; jazz was "pep or hot—blues was slow." "You say the name jazz in some folk['s] house, 'We don't want that; don't come in here with stuff, jazz'" (Harris 1976, 1977a).

As is usual in accounting for changes in Dorsey's career path, the answer to his switch from blatant dismissal to professional endorsement of jazz lies at least in part in developments outside of his life. The major trend prompting Dorsey to turn away from his older blues was the recording industry. Beginning in 1920 with Mamie Smith's recording of two blues songs for OKeh Record Company, blues—much like Dorsey—began to develop a split identity. Smith, a vaudeville Black singer, sang her blues in a vaudeville rather than a more down-home style. White musicians accompanied her. Her blues songs were, in essence, a creation of the white entertainment industry rather than the indigenous blues of African Americans. Even so, Black Americans, so eager for records of their music—even if the music was not genuine—bought Smith's records with pronounced enthusiasm: during the first month, over ten thousand copies were purchased. One music shop in Harlem sold over two thousand copies in the first two weeks following the record's release (Godrich and Dixon 1982, 641; Dixon and Godrich 1970, 7–8; Bradford 1965, 48–49, 118–19, 121, 123–24). Record promoters conflated the concepts of vaudeville blues and jazz by having Smith record her next disk singing "Harlem Blues" (actually recorded as "Crazy Blues"), the hit song from the blues musical *Made in Harlem*, with the accompaniment of her own group of Black musicians, Mamie Smith's Jazz Hounds (Bradford 1965, 119, 122).

Blues-jazz, jazz, vaudeville blues, whatever the terminology, became a new industry overnight. Smith made her second record on August 14, 1920, a little over a year before Dorsey attended the National Baptist Convention (Godrich and Dixon 1982, 641). Well before he had joined the Whispering Syncopators, then, Dorsey had good reason to begin "nimbling" his fingers: he was on his way to obsolescence because of jazz.

Even more telling about Dorsey's response to the newer popular Black music is the appearance of his first copyrighted blues, "If You Don't Believe I'm Leaving, You Can Count the Days I'm Gone," on October 9, 1920. For years Dorsey had played blues that he had composed or borrowed. The older blues style, being highly improvisatory and non-notated for most of its life, lent itself to a kind of public-domain, shared existence: "All blues, we didn't put them nowhere. Blues was blues. All the blues belong to you. What you gonna steal? Nothin' you could do with it if you steal it . . . all blues sounded alike for a while anyway, so we never bothered about the other fellow" (Harris 1977a).

The success of Smith's records drastically altered this attitude toward collective ownership. Someone could become rich off of a communal song. Dorsey, enjoying one benefit from his aborted formal study of music, was able to claim ownership of his songs and, for a fee, help others do the same for theirs because he could write music. By the end of 1923, he had copyrighted seven songs. As clearly as he had switched to commercialized performance practices of blues, he had as forthrightly adopted its notational conventions.

Dorsey had no reason to feel that he had made a wrong turn. By the end of 1923 he had become one of the major blues artists in the publishing and recording industries. The well-known Jack Mills music publishers put out a fox-trot arrangement of his "I Just Want a Daddy I Can Call My Own." Monette Moore, one of the leading vaudeville blues singers, recorded the song that same year. Undoubtedly his greatest popular success of that year came with Joe "King" Oliver's recording of "Riverside Blues" (Godrich and Dixon 1982, 515; Rust 1962, 467).

On the surface, such marked achievement in less than two years would indicate that this period of his life could hardly be characterized as one of conflict. But to make this steep ascent in such a short time, Dorsey sidestepped inner religious turmoil, pushed aside the blues style he preferred, and, perhaps the greatest sacrilege, took his spontaneous music and froze it in a notation not even designed to capture much of the blues player's art. If Dorsey's ego lay at the root of his drive, Dorsey also was prompted, as he had been earlier in Atlanta, by a sea of social change swirling around him. Migration, the rise of Black participation in vaudeville, the advent of the phonograph, the ever-sharpening lines between classes of African Americans all served as a tide that at some times could bring him rewards and at others could erode his most deeply held allegiances. At the end of this period of conflict Dorsey confronted blues once again, initially with devastating effects on his career, but it was the first of the resolutions he needed to make between competing musics.

Dorsey's confrontation with blues was already in the making in the beginning of 1923 as he was enjoying the first fruits of his success because of Bessie Smith's first recordings from Columbia Records. Smith sang in the older blues style instead of the vaudeville style prevalent in the recording industry. The purpose behind making her records was not to revert to the old style. Rather, it was a symptom of the increased competition among record companies to find new voices for the growing market. Indeed, Smith had been rejected by OKeh Records, the very company for which Mamie Smith had recorded. The standard was so alien to down-home singing that a voice like Smith's was considered "too rough." Her ultimate failure came when Black Swan Records, the only Black-owned company at that time, refused to invest in her. Columbia was obviously forced to gamble on a "tall and fat and scared" singer in order to keep pace with the industry. The payoff was unimaginable: within months, over 780,000 copies of Smith's first record had been sold. By the end of 1923, sales of her record approached 20 percent of all the "race" records bought that year (Albertson 1972, 27–65; Dixon and Godrich 1970, 20–22, 41, 59–60).

Without doubt, much of Smith's success was rooted in her talent. But the style through which she routed her ability was as much a factor. Black Americans, voting with their purchases of her "rough" sounding records, had given overwhelming approval to the down-home style as opposed to its "classic" counterpart crooned by the industry's ruling "queens." (For a description of classic versus down-home singers, see Titon 1977, xv–xvi.) Even more convincing proof followed Smith when Paramount Records, pressed to find not only another blues singer but one who sang like Smith, contracted with one of the most experienced of the older, original singers, Gertrude "Ma" Rainey. A veteran of years of touring throughout the South in minstrel shows, Rainey was the undisputed "Mother of the Blues" (*Chicago Defender* 1924). Rainey's popularity, though not as great as Smith's, if measured in record sales, was widespread.

To Dorsey, this sudden shift of blues preferences was perplexing: the very blues style he had found obsolete for his career goals was now popular. The most direct effect, however, concerned his role as a blues composer. Dorsey, who had copyrighted eight blues compositions in 1923 alone, no longer registered any of his music until 1928. The recording industry had little use for Tin Pan Alley blues of the sort that had given him fame. Ironically, Smith and Rainey had undercut Dorsey's career advancement with the music that Dorsey thought no longer mattered.

Dorsey's transition between his periods of conflict and resolution was not readily apparent to him. Unlike his sudden shift between the first and second periods, caused by his family's move to Atlanta and the problems attendant to urban living, this one was virtually in the making before Dorsey realized it. It was a time of fits and starts, of opportunities appearing nearby only to fade away as he tried to take advantage of them. The first concerned his attempt to ride the crest of the Smith/Rainey craze.

Although one cannot know how personally wrenching the resurgence of the older style of blues was to Dorsey, it is known that he recovered enough to return to his earlier style of music and to enjoy what would seem to him even greater success. In 1924, Ma Rainey hired Dorsey to be her accompanist because he was one of the best pianists who could play in the older style: "She was impressed with my playing and hired me as her accompanist. . . ." This joining with Rainey offered Dorsey a sense of resolution. Even more extraordinary and more indicative was his being able to compose and arrange vaudeville music for her tours in addition to accompanying her with the more traditional blues. To perform the show music, Rainey had Dorsey organize and direct her Wildcats Jazz Band (Dorsey 1961, 48).

To build his reputation with one of the most widely known down-home blues singers, not only with "lowdown" blues but with vaudeville ones too, should have been rewarding. But this apparently was not the deep musical unity Dorsey needed. Even with his playing such a major role in boosting Rainey's fame, even with his happy marriage to Nettie Harper—a woman he deeply loved—in August 1925, and even with his making an increasing number of recordings, Dorsey still fell into a deep depression similar to the one he suffered through in 1921. This one was worse, lasting over two years. During this sickness, Dorsey was unable to play piano; he spent large numbers of days in a state of profound melancholia and more than once contemplated suicide.

The clearest indication of the cause of this depression comes from what Dorsey believes to have been its cure: a religious conversion. As Dorsey describes it, he attended a church service one Sunday morning in 1928, after which he had a consultation with the minister, a Bishop H. H. Haley. Haley told Dorsey that the Lord had too "much work" for him to do to let him die. Then Haley pulled a "live serpent" out of Dorsey's throat. From that moment on, Dorsey announced that he suffered no more and pledged: "Lord, I am ready to do your work" (Dorsey 1961, 61; Harris 1977a). Shortly after this, a friend of his died after being ill for one day, leaving Dorsey to wonder why after two years of illness he was alive and his friend was dead after twenty-four hours of sickness.

This event, coming on the heels of his encounter with Haley, prompted Dorsey to make the pivotal turn toward his path to resolution. He could no longer deny that the simple pursuit of a career as a blues musician was unsatisfactory; he had only to consider his depression after beginning to work for Rainey. Even the blues he now played—the style he most ardently professed—sounded with the hollowness of his earlier jassy blues songs. Thus, by itself, musical change was a less than ample preventative against self-deprecation. Added to this reality were his brushes with religious surrealism and with the capriciousness of death. These were haunting experiences because they stirred his concern about abandoning the pious religion with which his mother had "stamped" his character in early childhood, a piety reasserted through her repeated admonition to "Serve the Lord, serve the Lord" during his 1921 bout with depression. He was utterly confounded, in essence, by the fundamental incongruities between the various musics and between the different practices of religion he had known since his childhood. This melange of indigenous and exogenous music, of pulpitry and piety, of careers made by craftily dodging one tendency to artfully exploit the other, now stood between him and his need to live a normal life.

Torn by this musical and religious fragmentation, Dorsey had every reason to seek a path that would invite the least resistance among these warring compulsions. Using his secular blues to serve the Lord—that is, composing gospel blues songs by writing sacred texts to blues songs—certainly seemed to him the logical route to some semblance of inner unity. By the evening of that long day in 1928, Dorsey had penned his first gospel song, "If You See My Savior, Tell Him That You Saw Me." Within a short time he followed this song with "How about You?"

Dorsey's personal growth had been shaped by social forces. Now firmly in the resolution period, the last of the three, Dorsey was about to feel these forces as he never had. His budding gospel career was destined to be even more formed by these forces because of a rather sudden turn in the history of African American Protestant churches in the urban North: they began to undergo changes that were similar to the ones that had so recently wracked Dorsey's life. Until these changes were completely made, however, Dorsey's new songs would cause considerable controversy.

During the late 1920s, Chicago's old-line Black Protestant churches stood as virtual mirrors of their white counterparts in terms of the worship aesthetic. No part of the Sunday morning liturgy was more illustrative of this than the music. At churches such as Olivet and Pilgrim Baptist, two of the largest congregations in Black Chicago, choirs sang the Western European–style anthems and sacred compositions of composers such as Mendelssohn, Mozart, Beethoven, Bach, and Rossini. Ministers in these churches carefully designed worship to control congregational participation, especially its more spontaneous aspects. This meant that they had to avoid the music associated with traditional Black worship. Black sacred song could be heard only in its Anglicized version, known as the concert or arranged Negro spiritual. More seriously, these ministers had to control their preaching so as not to stir emotions to the point that the congregation would erupt into the jubilation and demonstrativeness of the classic Black church. The effect of these standards of worship was to alter profoundly the ethos of upper-crust Black churches to the point that they can be considered Black only in terms of the racial, certainly not the cultural, makeup of their congregations.

These alien criteria had lengthy historic precedents. As early as the 1870s, Bishop Daniel Alexander Payne of the African Methodist Episcopal (AME) Church had tried to curtail such traditional practices as the ring shout and the singing of slave spirituals. He strongly criticized the adherents of these traditions: "Such persons are usually so because they are non-progressive, and, being illiterate, are consequently very narrow in views of men and things. A strong religious feeling, coupled with a narrow range of knowledge, often makes one a bigot" (Payne [1891] 1968, 457).

The effort to obliterate indigenous worship music grew through the late nineteenth century with the compositions of Negro spirituals by noted Black composers such as Harry T. Burleigh and John Work. Work was explicit about his concern that the slave spiritual, if not Anglicized, would serve as an impediment to racial progress: "In truth, the general adaptability of this music to a high degree of development is its hope of gaining artistic recognition. It deserves to be put into a finished form; it lends itself admirably to such a purpose; and those who would keep it as it was first reduced to writing, in their mistaken zeal would doom it to stagnation and to the contempt of highly musical people" (Work

1915, 90–99). This trend was so pronounced by the 1920s—especially among the Black elite and therefore in their churches, such as Olivet and Pilgrim Baptist in Chicago—that one exasperated observer, C. W. Hyne, labeled the music "denatured spirituals." The attempt, he said, was to "dress them up." The whole process reminded him "of the attempt of one race to remove the curl from the hair and of the other to put it in" (Johnson 1930, v–vi).

At this point the ultimate effect of this religious development on Dorsey's newly conceived career plans is clear. The old-line churches into which a self-reconstituted Thomas A. Dorsey carried his new gospel songs in 1928 comprised a virtual monolith of anti-traditionalism, especially toward indigenous Black sacred song. Dorsey, driven to the depths of inner turmoil in part for having spurned classic down-home blues, was now rededicated not only to the song style itself as a tradition worth saving but to the cause to make it the major musical medium for the gospel message in Black Protestant churches.

This vast gulf that lay between the churches' and Dorsey's goals became a virtual prison for him between 1928 and 1932. What might appear, therefore, as a time of resolution for a man consumed by inner turmoil in fact became one of frustration and vacillation. On some occasions, Dorsey "was thrown out of some of the best churches" when he performed his sacred blues. On other occasions, he was simply ignored:

> I shall never forget the embarrassment I suffered one Sunday morning when I had made arrangements with a minister to sing and introduce one of my songs in the morning service in one of the largest churches in the city. I arrived that morning about thirty minutes before service time with my singer Rebecca Talbot. The minister greeted us and gave us a seat on the front row of pews and said, "I will call for you to sing just after the morning message."
>
> Was I beaming over with joy to know my song would be sung in this church which had over two thousand people worshiping that morning! But something happened or there was a change of mind. The choir marched in, the minister preached, extended the invitation for members, lifted the offering, dismissed the congregation, and left me and my singer sitting on the front row seats without a word of explanation. (Dorsey ca. 1961, 63–64; Harris 1977a)

He mailed free copies to over one thousand ministers and had to wait for over two years before he got a reply. Even then he only received a few orders, "not enough to make a market trend or even to reimburse me for expenses" (Harris 1977a).

By August 1928, Dorsey was convinced that his blues would find no church home. It is at this point that he began to waft on his commitment. For the first time in five years he registered a new popular song at the Copyright Office on August 2, 1928, called "When You're in Love." Around the same time he began arranging music for the Brunswick Recording Company, one of the top five record companies in the peak years of the industry (Dixon and Godrich 1970, 42; Godrich and Dixon 1982, 20; Dorsey 1961, 65).

While these instances of turning back to secular blues clearly compromised Dorsey's renewed religious dedication, they did not really amount to a rejection of his faith. They were, instead, desperate attempts at remaining financially solvent and at having a sense that he was still making progress as a songwriter/performer. But he wrote and recorded one other blues song in September 1928. This piece so clearly differed from any he had composed that one would have to conclude that Dorsey had all but abandoned his new religious growth. This piece was called "It's Tight Like That." A guitarist friend, Hudson Whitaker, wrote the lyrics, which were full of sexual innuendo. Together, Dorsey and Whitaker recorded this song as the team of Georgia Tom and Tampa Red. Not only did Dorsey seem to have departed significantly from his gospel blues but, as fate would have it, he was rewarded for doing so: his first royalty check, the highest amount in his career, was written for $2,400.19. By December, the song was so popular that he and Whitaker recorded two more versions of it. The two became so notorious for their cunningly erotic blues that they coined a word for the style (*hokum*) and went on to name their duo after it, the Famous Hokum Boys. By 1932, they would make over sixty recordings of Dorsey's songs, appropriately titled, for example, "Pat that Bread" and "Somebody's Been Using that Thing" (Dorsey 1961, 36–37; Dixon and Godrich 1970, 62–63; Godrich and Dixon 1982, 199–200, 224–25, 344, 352, 574, 683–84, 748).

Just as Dorsey was basking in this fame, the kind for which he had craved during most of his career, his gospel songs seemed to attract new attention as well. A young woman sang "If You See My Savior" during the August 23, 1930, morning session of the annual meeting of the National Baptist Convention in Chicago. It was a decided hit, with "every man, woman and child . . . singing or humming the tune" (Dorsey 1961, 70; Harris 1976). This is the event that Dorsey marks as the beginning of his success as a gospel songwriter: "[I've] been in the music business ever since. . . . That was the big moment right there." Having sold over four thousand copies at that Convention, Dorsey certainly had reason to feel that he had reached the level of acceptance for which he had labored for two years (Dorsey 1961, 69–70; Harris 1976, 1977a).

This point also may be considered the final resolution of the inner conflicts that had dogged him since 1926. Even though he had decided to dedicate himself to a Christian life and his music talents to sacred music, Dorsey had to fight against the cultural obstinacy of the big churches and the economic draw of his old career. Dorsey had tried to keep his gospel music going in a small church; even that was little consolation: "I wasn't giving all my time to the church, see. I was kind of straddling the fence—making money out there on the outside, you know, in the band business and then going to church Sunday morning helping what I could do for them for they wasn't able to pay nothing. I could make money out there" (Harris 1976).

A resolution of the same sort was about to bring Chicago's major Black churches to a more inclusive worship ritual. At Ebenezer Baptist Church, where the European orientation of the worship music matched or exceeded that at Pilgrim and Olivet, the desire for a more traditional mode of worship was fueled by the call of its pastor, J. H. L. Smith, one Sunday morning in the fall of 1931, for a new group to sing the older music. As recalled by June Levell, the historian of the Ebenezer Gospel Chorus, the pastor declaimed, "I have a vision of a group singing the good old fashion songs that were born in the hearts of our forefathers down in the Southland. I want those songs that my old forefathers and mothers sing down in, way down in the Southland" (Harris 1977b).

Thomas A. Dorsey in performance, Bible Way Church, Washington, D.C., March 28, 1980. (Photograph by the *Washington Post*.)

Left: Young Thomas A. Dorsey. (Photograph from the Clayton Hannah Collection, Hogan Jazz Archives, Tulane University, New Orleans.) **Below left**: Thomas A. Dorsey recorded as "Georgia Tom." (Album jacket photograph from Riverside 8803, *Georgia Tom & Friends*, the Clayton Hannah Collection, Hogan Jazz Archives, Tulane University, New Orleans.) **Below right**: Thomas A. Dorsey at the piano, accompanying Mahalia Jackson. (Photograph from the Clayton Hannah Collection, Hogan Jazz Archives, Tulane University, New Orleans.)

Thomas Andrew Dorsey, "the father of gospel music," at Bible Way Church, Washington, D.C., May 9, 1982. (Photograph by Craig Herndon, *Washington Post*.)

Sallie Martin, singer, organizer of gospel choirs, demonstrator for Thomas Andrew Dorsey, and partner in publishing with Kenneth Morris.

William Herbert Brewster, gospel music composer and pastor of East Trigg Baptist Church, Memphis, until his death in 1987. (Courtesy of Anna L. Brooks.)

Left: Queen C. Anderson (1913–1959), gospel singer and member of East Trigg Baptist Church, Memphis, introduced many of Brewster's compositions. (Courtesy of Anna L. Brooks.) **Below**: Clara Ward and the Ward Singers performing at the Washington Jazz Festival, Washington, D.C., 1958. (Photograph by Joe Alper, courtesy of Jackie Gibson Alper.)

Reverend William Herbert Brewster, Thomas Shelby (formerly with the National Baptist Convention Goodwill Singers), Sallie Martin, Anna Lois Brooks, and Sylvia Banks of the Brewster Ensemble, 1985.

How Long Oh Lord How Long

Words and Music by
DR. WILLIAM H. BREWSTER
as sung and recorded by
The Famous Ward Singers

Published by

WARD'S HOUSE OF MUSIC
3800 North 18th Street • Philadelphia

Made in U. S. A.   PRICE 20¢

Above: Crucifixion scene from a Brewster passion play, Memphis. (Photograph by Ernest Withers.) **Left:** Cover of sheet music of "How Long Oh Lord How Long," a Brewster composition, with Ward Singers photograph. (Courtesy of Anna L. Brooks.)

Left: Alex Bradford moves into the aisles in *Black Nativity*, 1961. (Photograph by Bert Andrews.) **Below left**: Al Freeman, Jr., Cicely Tyson, Theresa Merritt, and Lex Monson at 1963 dress rehearsal of Langston Hughes's *Trumpets of the Lord*, adapted by Vinette Carroll from James Weldon Johnson's *God's Trombones* and directed by Donald McKayle. (Photograph by Bert Andrews.) **Below right**: Hilda Simms and Clara Ward play and sing in *Tambourines to Glory*. (Photograph from Schomburg Center for Research in Black Culture, New York Public Library.)

Poster for Smithsonian Institution conference on Roberta Martin, 1981. Inset: Roberta Martin, gospel music composer, singer, publisher, and creator of the Roberta Martin choral sound. (Courtesy of Eugene Smith, Norsalus McKissick.)

Top: Delois Barrett Campbell, Gloria Griffin, and Bessie Folk work on a Roberta Martin composition, Smithsonian Institution, 1981. **Above:** Romance Watson handles the microphone for Norsalus McKissick during Smithsonian Institution reunion concerts, 1981.

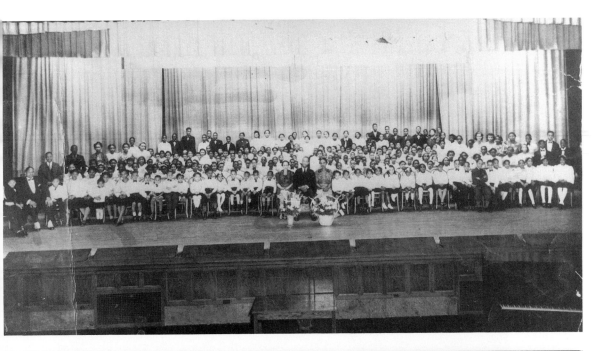

Top: Ebenezer Baptist Church junior choir, Chicago, out of which the first group of Roberta Martin Singers was formed in 1932. (Courtesy of Eugene Smith, Norsalus McKissick.) **Above:** Archie Dennis at the microphone, with Bessie Folk, Gloria Griffin, and Norsalus McKissick, Smithsonian Institution, 1981.

Top: The Roberta Martin Singers, ca. 1945. Front, left to right: Norsalus McKissick, Sadie Durrah, Bessie Folk, Eugene Smith. Rear, left to right: Roberta Martin, Willie Webb, Delois Barrett Campbell. (Courtesy of Eugene Smith, Norsalus McKissick.) **Above:** Briefly during the 1930s, a group was formed featuring Roberta Martin and Sallie Martin (no relation). Front, left to right: Roberta Martin, Sallie Martin; rear, left to right: Willie Webb, Robert Anderson, Eugene Smith. (Courtesy of Eugene Smith, Norsalus McKissick.)

"Conversations" panel, Smithsonian conference on Roberta Martin, 1981. Left to right: Pearl Williams-Jones, Eugene Smith, Leona Price, Romance Watson, Delois Barrett Campbell, Louise McCord, Bessie Folk, Norsalus McKissick, and Archie Dennis. Not shown: Gloria Griffin and Lucy Smith Collier.

Kenneth Morris, gospel music composer, arranger, and publisher. (Courtesy of Necie Morris.)

Above: Necie and Kenneth Morris and their children Kenneth, Jr., Reginald, and Raymond. (Courtesy of Necie Morris.) **Left:** Kenneth Morris as a young man. (Courtesy of Necie Morris.)

Left: Martin and Morris sheet music featuring the Sallie Martin Singers. (Courtesy of Necie Morris.) Below: The first commercially marketed Hammond organ. (Courtesy of the Smithsonian Institution, Division of Music History.)

Smith, who had assumed the Ebenezer pastorate in August of that year, had found his first months in one of the most acculturated of Chicago's Black old-line churches discomforting. Having arrived in Chicago from Birmingham, Alabama, Smith had a pronounced preference for the very Southern worship style that these Chicago old-line churches were dedicated virtually to eradicating. He was, moreover, greatly encouraged to call for such a drastic change because the congregation had been split over the sudden (and suspicious) departure of the previous pastor. Ebenezer, therefore, was demoralized; its worship, uninspiring.

Not even one so convinced of the appropriateness of the traditional African American worship ritual as Smith could have anticipated the surge to affirm his call for the older music. On the second Sunday in January 1932, a chorus of over one hundred members made its debut at Ebenezer with Dorsey as pianist and Theodore Frye as director. At the root of this surprising development was more than Smith's call for down-home, musical therapy. Most of the one hundred choristers were recent migrants from the rural South. Since the beginning of World War I, their numbers had been growing steadily. Nowhere was this increase more evident than in the large, old-line churches. The new arrivals were drawn to the large churches because these institutions had social programs that included aid for settling in Chicago and for finding employment. To a great extent, however, the newcomers' presence had little effect on operations and virtually none on worship standards, since those churches served almost exclusively as the domains of Chicago's Black old settlers, residents, in many cases, for several generations. This group was most closely tied to the effort to guide the old-line churches into their mimicry of white Protestant worship norms. If this group had a visual and auditory locus in old-line churches, it was the choir. Thus the new migrants, large in number but weak in influence, sat passively, Sunday after Sunday, listening to their counterparts espouse the virtues of white middle-class culture through the Western European choral anthem:

A lot of people here who remembered what singing was like down home, liked Smith, Lord, yes. The music the Senior Choir was singing was not what Reverend Smith nor the congregation was used to. And then them old songs that they had been used to hearing, like "This Rock I'm Standing On" or "By and By," see, the Senior Choir didn't sing them then. They sang ooh, ah, ooh, way up high and [they sang] the anthems. (Harris 1977b)

What had seemed an inexorable movement toward alien religious norms was now about to be brought to a halt by Smith's deliberate parrying of the migrants' musical sentiments off those of the old settlers: "And when he came here, of course, he'd been used to that old time singing down there and he wanted the same thing at Ebenezer" (Harris 1977b). Thus, at Smith's initiative, migrants gained a literal voice in the Sunday morning worship hour and, through them, traditional African American religious culture regained a place in old-line Protestantism.

This development is significant in that it represents the same resolution of a conflict between original and assimilated cultural experiences that Dorsey underwent. Dorsey's stumble back into down-home blues provided the correction for his earlier long slide into the commercial, Tin Pan Alley blues of his time of professional assimilation. Ebenezer's turn back to religious songs of the Southland likewise provided a counterforce to its long slide into religious assimilation. There is also a similarity to Dorsey's religious resolution: just as Dorsey experienced unrest by not being as sincere in his religious outlook as he felt he should, based on his mother's piety, so was Ebenezer deeply troubled by its attempt to separate Black Christianity from its cultural roots. In this instance the parallel situations are found in Dorsey's nervous breakdown and Ebenezer's demoralization at the loss of its preacher. In both cases, a spiritual rejuvenation was inextricably bound to music in a contextualized African American setting.

The point is more than coincidental: it portrays a delicate symbiosis between Dorsey's life and the emergence of gospel blues—indeed, between Black culture, Dorsey as an archetype of that culture, and the middle-class Black church as an institutionalization of that culture. Dorsey as an African American and the church as African American religion have complete histories only as subsets of African American culture. From the perspective of this interdependency, Dorsey's role as the "father" of gospel blues was limited in the sense of his being able to lay claim to its genesis. There was an asymmetry of old and new cultures—manifested as rural Southern and urban Northern—in Black churches. Dorsey happened to be there with an urbanized version of the rural culture's music that was powerful enough to counter the Beethoven and Mozart of the Northern culture and that was authentic enough to give status to the former Southerners. Thus, Dorsey conceived of "gospel blues," but its purpose and ultimate shape were not his to determine.

If there is a cause–effect factor in this tripartite symbiosis of (1) secular and sacred, (2) lower class and middle class, and (3) rural Southern and urban Northern, it has to be the notion of duality and its pervasiveness not just in Dorsey's life but in African American culture and religion. The similarities among exposure, conflict, and resolution between Dorsey's life and the church and the culture are traceable to the twoness that is central to the African American experience.

5

WILLIAM HERBERT BREWSTER, SR.

(ca. 1897–1987)

~

WILLIAM HERBERT BREWSTER

Rememberings

An Interview Conducted and Edited by
Bernice Johnson Reagon

*He studied theology, Shakespeare, Greek, Latin, Hebrew, and law. He
was an editor and publisher of his own newspaper, and he always
started and taught schools in the communities in which he served as
pastor. He was a believer in Christianity from a very small child. He
had a fierce commitment to work for the betterment of his people, and
he was a civil rights leader in Memphis, Tennessee, for over fifty years.
Yet, we honor Reverend William Herbert Brewster, Sr., today as one of
the major forces in the creation of new African American sacred music
literature: gospel. One of the most prolific of the pioneering gospel song
composers, Brewster wrote his compositions for his church services, his
renowned gospel-drama extravaganzas, his radio ministry, his performing groups, and the top names in gospel music. The power and lyricism
of his poetry transformed the gospel song repertoire.*

*When I interviewed him and members of his church community at
the East Trigg Baptist Church in Memphis, I encountered a tall, grand
old man in his mid-eighties, with the energy and drive of a person half
that age. Brewster was a brilliant storyteller. His speaking style was
both poetic and enthralling. It is, therefore, his own voice that should
chronicle highlights of his story.* —ED.

I was born in west Tennessee, east of Memphis. I have two birthdays on my record, and, of course, I take the first one. I was reared by my grandparents and parents together. My people were plantation dwellers. Grandmother and Grandfather were slaves. My mother and father were this side of slavery, but they endured all of the hardship of the Reconstruction period. I was born in 1897 or 1899. The way they counted dates, they counted it by certain events that occurred. The Black people didn't read at all. The white people in that area were not accurate, especially when it came to Black people. For instance, they gave me one year, that was the year of the gnats. There were swarms of gnats in that area—big gnats—and they were destructive to animals and also to people. People were hurt by them. And that was 1897. Eighteen ninety-nine was the year of the hard freeze. It was a terrifying winter. The trees were broken down under the weight of snow and ice, and the plantation houses were crushed by these terrifying winter storms. And they just figured that to be the year. But I go by the date 1897.

My people were plantation dwellers or sharecroppers. After slavery, some Black people were given so many acres and a mule. That didn't last long because they did not have education enough to keep up with their accounts and to do anything about agriculture more than they had learned as slave dwellers.

My maternal grandmother was Harriet Albertson, and her husband was Captain Albertson. After the Surrender, unfortunate things happened. The wife and husband, before that time, had been separated by the slave dealing and slave trading. My grandmother's first husband, my mother's father, was Henry Polk, a plantation slave preacher. My maternal grandparents came up from Georgia, but my paternal grandparents were Tennesseans—west Tennessee. They lived on the county line of Hardeman and Fayette Counties, the first and second counties east of Memphis. My dad's dad, Martin Brewster, was a slave preacher in slavery time. The Martin Brewster crowd were Primitive Baptists, and the Polks were Regular, what they called Missionary Baptists.

The land they worked was the old plantations. They were supposed to have gotten 50 percent, and the plantation owner, he received 50 percent. That paid for what would have been rent. They had a thing they called their "run for the year." That is, in the month of March, the plantation owner or the store [owner]—they usually had a big store, a commissary—would ask how much it would take "to run you" this year. Sometimes it was two hundred dollars for a whole family, a big family—maybe more, sometimes less. At the end of the year, after the crops were harvested, if there were ten bales of cotton, the owner of the plantation would get his five. Then all the expenses that the sharecropper had for the year, money that it took to make the crop, the food and clothing that had been furnished during the year, they would take out of his half. And they kept an account of that. Many Blacks just waited for the boss to tell them how much they'd made.

My grandparents apparently had a dream in their hearts. They knew they were not getting a fair shake, as they called it, but they were patient and they were prayerful. They had great faith in God. That was one of the things that affected my early life. They were people who had prayer, and when things went wrong and they found themselves helpless and hopeless, they resorted to prayer.

However, occasionally there were among these plantation dwellers, these sharecroppers—a man or a woman or a family—with the old Nat Turner spirit. They didn't take it easily, like people claimed they did. They had a way—they were great psychologists. They couldn't read or write then, but they could read character. They could read the difference between truth and falsehood, and a lot of times there was a riot created and some man who owned a farm would rebel and raise up and try to be a man. And that meant there was a lynching on hand.

EARLY LEARNING

My grandfather on my father's side, Martin Brewster, could read and write some, and he had a photographic memory about anything that happened. I guess I inherited a little of that because it has been greatly helpful. He could count on his fingers faster than some people could with a pencil. My father, William Herbert Brewster, was one of the studious young Blacks on a farm in Fayette County and attended the schools, such as there were.

They had the old Blueback Speller. They had two or three—they called them readers. You weren't counted by grades, there were readers. First reader, the frame of the first reader, second, third, fourth, fifth, and sixth. Yes, and that old Blueback Speller carried words, and most of the words rhymed, and at the blue margin there were sentences, poetic sentences, beautiful expressions:

> Every task once begun,
> Never leave it until it's done.
> Be the labor, great or small,
> Do it well or not at all.

That was at the bottom of that type of speller. Then the Hunt Speller came out, which was a Redback Speller. That came over in my day, that was in the early 1900s. I got a chance to start school when I was about six or seven years old.

The school terms in those days depended greatly upon the weather. By that I mean the planting season depended upon how early spring came. Sometimes the winter would have hangovers and they stayed, and the weather didn't clear until April or May. If they could start in March and get good weather, and the planting was done in time, then the month of June became the cotton-chopping and plowing month. By the fourth of July, they wanted to be through with what they called "laying by." That was, they would have the crop finished until the harvest.

During that period, between July and August and September, a boy or girl had an opportunity to go to school when they got through hoeing the cotton. If they got through in the middle of July, they could go home [and to school] until almost to the middle of

September. But when the cotton opened, the sorghum and the peas were ripe, the fodder had to be pulled, and the hay had to be cut; arrangements had to be made for winter living. Then you came out of school and went back to the fields. Many times the period would be less than two months. The whole school session, beginning in the middle of July, lasted for the big kids up to around the first of September because they had to go back to the fields.

After the gathering of the harvest, they tried to get through by Thanksgiving, but many years the weather would grow cold ahead of Thanksgiving, and if there was a rainy season, that delayed the gathering of the crops. In some seasons where the cotton sprouted in the boll, it would start raining as soon as it opened and it would rain for weeks and weeks. Then the seed of this year's cotton—that rain would fall down upon it—and it would sprout in the boll; and the corn would sprout on the cob before they could gather it. That meant everything was bad for winter. For a few years in our territory this happened.

In the winter and the fall of the year, much of the food was supplied by hunting and fishing. These were sports for other people, but it was a way of living for a lot of us. They were hunters. There were those who hunted rabbits and squirrels and quails. Fishing season would be over when the cold weather came.

In my case, my educational career started in a cabin in a cotton field with a teacher who had been fortunate to have completed the sixth and seventh grade. That was what was required because they'd say if you could master those grades you had a foundation, and that's pretty true. You get most of whatever you're going into deeply rooted in those grades.

We had a few of these schools scattered about here and yonder. When you could master two grades a year, the most you could master, they called it skipping. They would not allow a kid to be held back by the slow kids. They just put him on up and he went on through.

There was a high school in my nearest town that was established by an old Baptist preacher, by the name of David Jones. He set up my high school. He was a pretty well educated man. . . . He came into the community and yet had no relationship with the Board of Education. There was not much concern about Black education. What they wanted you to know was how to wash and iron and work in the fields, cut logs and do the things that were the chores of slaves.

That school was the best we had. We had to pay a small fee—whatever you could pay. He was a man of that type. It added up to about one or two dollars a month, if you could do it. It was a church thing. The churches would take offerings, and they had what they called subscription school. They had that method. They'd go around and you would subscribe so much. They wanted to pay the teacher fifteen dollars a week. I taught school there for twenty dollars a week.

Then there came into the community a training school fashioned after Tuskegee. A man from Tuskegee, Alabama, named Rick Straw and a couple of more people came in and they started this training school. About that time, graduation was near. They had me come to the graduation and that's all there was to that.

THE CALL TO PREACH

Then I had to acknowledge my calling to the ministry. I was about sixteen years old. Baptized one Sunday. Preached the next. The call to the ministry is a property of God's sovereignty. That's God doing what He will with His own. Everybody is not called like that.

When I went to the church during revival meeting, I had to sit on the mourner's bench that they had in those days for sinners. Most preachers preached the same thing—"you must be born again!"—and as the preacher preached, people would shout and the kids would jump and turn bottom upwards in wheelbarrow fashion and *their* conversion testimony would be accepted.

I could read the Bible before I knew my letters. They bought us picture books. And in their crude way, they explained the heroes of the Bible, such as Samson and all those fellows. They fascinated me. They just claimed my attention and I could just look at them all day long—what those old people told me and stuff.

When it came to my confession of Christ, I had to go back to the mourner's bench during revival season for several years because I wouldn't do what they required. If you got up in a sensible way, and said, "I accept Christ as my personal savior, and I believe in it with all my heart, I'll serve Him as long as I live," the response would be, "That's all you have to say boy? You go back to that mourner's bench. You ain't got nothing." That's the way they acted. They did that so much.

I tried my best to get a sensible approach that was in my heart. When I became about ten and twelve, I had gone through the Bible, I had committed chapter after chapter, verse after verse, section after section, character after character. The old preacher couldn't do that. And he was preaching to me and a lot of things he would preach, I would know different because I had read it. . . .

When I was about four years of age, my parents let me live with my mother's mother and her husband, and every night before they would retire, they would have prayer meeting between themselves. Each one would give out one of those long-metered hymns. Then they would bow and make me bow and pray. They would do that until they had both prayed and then they would get up and everybody would go to bed.

Also I adopted a prayer life at about six years old. They had, in the old Black slavery religion, a praying ground. I heard them. I heard the old people talking about a praying ground. I'd slip out and would find a place over behind the bushes and behind a log, and I would go out there three times a day and get on my knees behind that log.

And all of that time, deep in my heart, I had an abiding faith in Jesus but they wouldn't accept that. They wanted me to cut up and stand on my head and jump benches like other kids who were doing [that] and never heard from again. So when I finally reached the conclusion that the word of God is truth, that Christ is Christ and God is God, I had been on the mourner's bench so long that they thought I was a hard sinner, but I was a Christian. I had every equipment of Christianity. I believed the word as I had read it. I knew it better than the preacher did. And I believed every word of it. But they wouldn't let me by with that. They wanted me to do a lot of things that I knew I couldn't do, and I knew it wasn't necessary. Now, I believe in shouting and all that and I did my portion of it. But I didn't do it until I had a sensible seeing and hearing faith because I had a practical knowledge but not a college knowledge. I accepted the Christ and they baptized me that Sunday. I came up out of the water—and God has agencies through which he accomplishes his greatest miracles—a man who was not a preacher said, "This boy has got to be baptized! He's going to be a preacher. There is preacher all over him."

I went on by and those words struck me. I knew it was something else I had to do. God had a way of letting me know by inspiring this man to say so. I went on.

During those years, my schooling had to be very sparse. I'd go when I could. My mother became ill, she had neuralgic arthritis. It was a terrifying thing. She suffered about three years. Even with those large number of kids, I alone had to sit with her and sit by her bed to help her up like a child, day and night. I would rub her and soothe her. She was skin and bones and I couldn't leave her.

One night, I made up her bed pillows, and she smiled and fell asleep. I went to the window of the log cabin where we stayed and looked out at the stars and I said, "Am I the son of sorrow?" I had read the story of Benjamin in the Book of Genesis where they first named him Beohim, the Son of Sorrow.

I went back and looked at my mother lying there sleeping and I laid my head down on the pillow by her and heaven opened up. I'm glad I didn't know education because sometimes a lot of education makes you a poor Christian. You can't just follow blindly, with blind faith. I laid there with my head on the pillow and the heavens opened, and I saw as it were a band of angels, and it appeared they were descending, their garments, the fringes were sweeping the hilltops. They came down above me, and one came down with an open book and said, "Go ye into the world and preach the gospel."

I was awakened, it disturbed me so 'cause people didn't allow a kid to preach. For a solid week, I fasted and prayed. You asked me how it happened and this is the way it happened. I prayed on a Saturday night before the last Sunday, September 1914, and prayed and asked the Lord for a sign because that is what people went by, that is what ministers were called by and Christians were converted by. That's what Joseph in the Bible and Abraham and Isaac and Jacob and Daniel—all the major prophets and the minor ones, and even Jesus Christ himself.

I didn't know all of that then, but it affected me so until when I woke up I told the Lord, I said, "Lord, I can't stand this burden." He kept saying, "Yes, go, go. I'll be with you." I could hear that intonation. And I said, "Lord, if you want me to go, wake me up at four o'clock." Now this may sound silly, but the Lord is so gracious to us. It's God's way of showing to us in a language we can understand. I said, "If you wake me up, I'll tell my dad and see what he says."

I went on [to] sleep, and later on, something shook me and I got up out of the bed. I looked at that old grandfather clock, ticking loudly and I couldn't look at it. It was dark in the room and we didn't have lamps—like Abraham Lincoln, a lot of the time, I had to study by firelight. I had to get some paper and wrap it together and we called that a lamplighter. I lit the paper but I was afraid to raise it up, and when I did look up, it was four o'clock. It was a striking clock. You ever heard one? They strike on the hour. It was four and it struck four times.

"My God, what am I going to do?" I got up out of that bed, frightened, and went on around through one door and started in my dad's room. I had made him the end of the line to see what he said about it after heaven had bothered to talk to me. I walked in that door and there he was sitting up there waiting for me. He said, "Come on in, son. I know, the Lord has called you to preach, nothing to do but do what He said to do."

TEACHER AND PASTOR

I have studied theology, taught it, I've been a lecturer in many seminaries, such as the Baptists used to have. I've been a lecturer in some of the best white ones. It has been my role to teach the highest and the hardest subject in the field of theology, my Hebrew and my Greek. I loved it so that I went to the extreme—almost like what the other fellows did because it was so rare for young Blacks to have that language.

[When] I came to school to Memphis, . . . there were two schools, LeMoyne Normal and Howell Collegiate Institute. Mordecai Johnson was a student as I went in, and he came out and went to Morehouse; C. C. Adams, and those older men. Mordecai told me, "Herb, take my seat, boy, and do what I did, stay with it." I took that seat and went through that institution, and then [I went] from one to another, whatever the Baptists had. But when I would go to a school, I had the problem of having to teach the teachers. Now this isn't bragging, that's just the fact.

I was among the first Blacks to go to the American Baptist Theological Seminary. I left there and I started to pastoring; I was nineteen or twenty. The people didn't know I was that young or they wouldn't have let me pastor, but I was brought up by old folks and been around those old preachers, and I knew how they acted.

Then after that, it was a hop, skip, and jump affair with me for what I wanted, and I was determined to get it whatever it cost. I applied myself. Whatever, wherever it was, if it were essential to being a prepared and equipped preacher, I wanted that. I had some good, private tutorage after getting the Hebrew that they taught in the schools; I got a chance to get the heart, soul, and mind of a Jewish rabbi. There is a whole lot of difference in the Hebrew we were taught and what that rabbi taught. He was in Forrest City [Arkansas], where I had become a pastor, and he offered his service to help. It was a marvelous adventure for me.

I came to Memphis shortly thereafter, in 1924. I came back; this was my original home. At that time we had two Baptist Conventions, the Boyd Convention and the Marshall Convention [National Baptist Convention, Inc.]. They decided to merge some of the schools: Simmons in Louisville, Roger Williams in Nashville, Arkansas Baptist in Little Rock, Howell in Memphis, and four or five other schools. They made a move to establish it [the new school] here. This church [East Trigg Baptist Church] had just been built. Dr. T. O. Fuller, who was a front runner here; John Hope at Atlanta; Peter James Bryant; the founder of Wheat Street Baptist in Atlanta—they were the ones to bring me in on the scene. They had me come in to chair the Greek and Hebrew section in the new university that we were going to build across the parkway there.

Mr. Crump was the boss of Memphis, and a handful of white citizens called the Glenview Club protested it because they didn't want a school established that would attract Northern Negroes. That was the point that they made, and Mr. Crump was swallowed up by it. He decided that they were right and that they might have a race riot. I was the secretary of that movement, and when they couldn't have it, it just went out the window. I decided to open up in the basement of this church a teaching and training school for ministers and missionary and Christian workers in every department of the church.

Another man had finished his training and had a medical school about seven or eight blocks from here. He had attended the University of West Tennessee. He joined this church. He opened up a medical clinic in the basement. . . . I opened up a theological clinic in the basement of this church in 1925–26 and on up until 1930 when it began to flourish. I have a school here now that is the result of what we started because we were beaten down by the segregationists, who did not believe we would have been an asset rather than a liability to the community by attracting students from all over. They were coming here from all over anyway, over there at Howell. Men came from everywhere, from every section of the nation, because we had some of the best teachers.

FIRST SONGS

The first spiritual that I heard was as a three-year-old in a log cabin in the middle of a cotton patch. For in those days when I was born, the Black people lived close to the crops—right at the end of the cotton rows, right in your front yard among the most beautiful bloom.

So one morning, when I was about three years old, they had all gone to the fields to begin their chores. Early in the morning, they had gotten up at four o'clock, during plow time, they called it. If the cows had been put up at night in their cow pen and the calves let out, the chores for the boys who were not big enough to harness the mules and the horses and farm animals would be to go get up the calves. Sometimes, in the fall of the year, when you are finding those calves, you would be barefooted and your feet would be so cold. When you got back up to the milking place, you would race to put your feet in that warm soil. That's the truth. It seems incredible, but that's the truth.

But before I got to that age, my grandmother was the last to go to the fields. After they had eaten breakfast about four o'clock, she remained to clean up the dishes, such as they had. Those were crude old plates, so thick that if you dropped one, it wouldn't break hardly unless it fell on a brick. They had eating pans, the pie pans they used for plates.

On this morning, the elders had gone to the field to begin their early morning chores.

I was awakened. The room was filled with melody and music, and it looked like the angels were singing or something. I heard my grandmother Doris's voice. She was on the dirt floor of the kitchen that was built against that one-room shanty. I was at the foot of the bed and I leaned over first and I heard my grandmother singing. I got up and crept to the door. When I came to the kitchen door, she was moving about, doing her chores, singing. The song was "Pilgrim of Sorrow." When I saw that old lady—she was tall and what they called "raw-boned." She had long hair she would wrap with string so she wouldn't have to comb it but once a week. She wouldn't have to lose the time to comb her hair to go to the field. So there she was and had put a bonnet on her head, ready to go out the door. And she was singing a song. I never shall forget the words:

> I am a poor pilgrim of sorrow
> left out in this world alone

The first lines that caught me were:

> Go and tell Hezekiah
> Go and tell him just so
> There is a lifetime journey
> Everywhere we go

She was singing and laughing out loud almost hysterically—that "Holy Ghost laugh," they used to call it. And then she would be crying. The tears were meeting under her chin. It touched my heart so deeply.

My musical background was two-sided. First, out on the farm there were only two kinds of entertainment, and all of it was musical. The old people on the farm used to call it "reals." That was Godless songs, they thought. Songs they sang at the square dances in my community.

Then there was the great natural music. I hope this won't seem too strange and foreign, but in my day there were two songbooks. One was written by man and the other was written by God Himself. I would wake up in the early morning time and listen to the mockingbird. The mockingbird was pretty soon joined in the serenade by the meadowlarks, the field larks, the bobolinks, everything. It amazed me! The old cockadoodledo started early, flapped his wings, picked himself up, and then he'd crow and wake up those that didn't have an alarm clock.

If you were a country boy, you knew as you listened to the mockingbird that he was an impressive kind of a bird. You could listen to them all and you'd know which one was singing. You could decipher their songs; you'd learn the birds by their feathers, by their habits. Now, not all the kids went this way. Some of them wondered what was the matter with me. Here was all of the music in the world. I would sometimes climb up in a tree, and get out on a limb and take my book and rest there against the tree and listen to the various birds. Then in the evening as the twilight came on, the night birds would tune up their hearts and you're talking about something! You would get a cooing of the doves, the chirping of the crickets, and you would hear the hooting of the owl. And all of those things came together; somehow or another, they blended. That was music! In the evening times, you could stand on one hill and say hello and somebody way over, an echo, would say hello back. Oh, that was a thrill! What kind of world was this? It was exciting. Every moment, never a dull moment in the childhood as I stood there and listened to that music.

In my case, I had an obsession to analyze things. I would spend long hours away from home. I had an analytical mind. I would go through the field and would find a peculiar plant. I would dissect it. Take it to pieces. The barks of the trees, the blades of grass, wildflowers, every kind of plant. They became my friends, they became my companions. I thought I could talk to them. I hear people say they can do it now; flowers and plants do speak a language of their own. If you are studious of them, if there is some kind of innate quality that you have within yourself, your botanical learning begins as soon as you step on the first blade of grass. This was the kind of thing that affected me.

Then when we went home at night after a day's work, particularly in the fall of the year when the harvest was full bloom, our pastime was singing. My father was a teacher of that shape-note singing. It was something that even the people who couldn't read letters could read those notes and understand them perfectly. We would assemble around a big fireplace, all fourteen of us. My daddy could read that stuff, that *do re me fa sol la ti do*. For about an hour or two we would sing songs, and the type of songs that they sang were what they called plantation songs—"My Old Kentucky Home" and "Old Black Joe," which were really ridiculing the Blacks and the old spirituals. My brothers bought a guitar, and against the will of all the grownups, they learned to play it and taught me to play, too.

We bought the Methodist songbooks that had no notes, just a printed songbook. We would sing these songs they called Sunday school songs, and then they had old songs that they called the long-meter, the common-meter, and the short-meter hymns. If somebody would give it out, everybody would sing that out. They sang it twice in those days, because giving it out was singing it. Those songs embedded themselves on my heart.

I learned the lyrics and in all my music career I've been just sold on lyrics. I loved those songs that tell me something. That's the kind of music they had. Then there were some songs out—I never knew exactly what they were. People used to call them "jump-up songs," about Daniel in the lion's den. They had the sounds about the same as in the spirituals. Only they'd change it from the original spiritual, and then they would wrap that beat on it and that was the way they made time.

They would be singing songs and sometimes the words that they said in the song didn't make good sense to me. So I would go off to myself and write some words. I was about ten years old or younger when I first started. I would sing them to myself, and if I thought it was something else, I'd get my brothers and sisters and we'd play church and I would make them learn my lyrics.

There was a great singer named John Henry Jacobs who sang a song about Jonah. I had an uncle, Nelson Brewster, who was a champion singer. He could sing hootenannies. He was tall and skinny, thin as a cracker but had a most harmonious voice. When he would come to church, the people would rave about Nelson Brewster, before he would show up on the grounds. The folks would say, "Nelson is out there, go get him." And they would just beg for Nelson to come in. He was a great inspiration to me. That song usually revolved around certain prophets, then another about Samson. They sang this song which you had read in the Bible to understand, about Methuselah was the oldest man and Samson was the strongest man. Then that gave me a good field to play in. I could get lyrics, get together on those, and I got the idea of rhyming.

Uncle Nelson would come in and one of his songs was "I'm a Soldier in the Army." He would sing:

> I'm a soldier in the army of the Lord,
> I believe I'll die, in the army of the Lord.

And I said, "why do you want to die for?" I would just go get a pencil and say, "I am going to change that because I don't want to die. I'm going to march with the soldiers, in the army of the Lord." I would read the history books and find some kind of soldier and then I would write:

> I'm gonna win this battle, in the army of the Lord.

I did some beautiful things . . . like:

> Way out on the mountain,
> the battle on the mountain,
> the mountain above the clouds,
> out on Calvary's mountain.

It made sense to me eventually.

Music invaded my very being. It just naturally became a part of me. As I grew up, I began to sing even more and a little more. I got into the habit of going to church to sing. They would send me as a delegate to the Sunday School to the district conventions. I started to write little songs that nobody had heard before and decided to put tunes to them and sing them. I would try them out on the kids.

I also wrote some poetry. The first published poem that I wrote was "Give the Negro a Chance." That was in 1918, World War I. I wasn't old enough to go to the war, but I wrote that poem, started it off:

> If America would her hopes enhance,
> Tell the General and President
> Give the Negro a chance
> If the battle is hard and the war is long

> The Negro will win it with a dance and a song
> Mr. President, please give the Negro a chance

And that's where I started it all. They published it in a magazine, *Ever Ready Magazine.*

Now as for my music, I held it back for many years; I did not want to get on the market with it. My young days were so concentrated and the Lord knew I had various talents—a lot of things I could do. I started to study law, to pre-med studies and all that. I thought I would like to be something besides a minister. When they ordained me, they gave me as a symbol of my work what they called the tools of the ministry. That was a Bible and a hymnbook. The first preachers I knew were using those.

In 1930, I had been a pastor here for about five years and I had developed choirs and groups that I had under my direction and guidance and instruction. The first song that I wrote for publication was a song that came out of some experiences that I had in my early ministry. I had depended upon some people that I thought would help me. My parents did not have money. My mother had just died, and my dad was still trying to make it for a good number of us kids. I had no money with which to go to school. I couldn't borrow any.

One Saturday, there came almost an eclipse of the sun. I got on the train without money. In those days there was just an accommodation train—you could flag it down anywhere they had stops. That train was operated by Mike Brady. He had a way of sounding that whistle. Everybody knew Mike's train. It started in Memphis and went on to Summerville. It would go up in the morning and come back in the evening, or vice versa.

That day I didn't have anybody to depend upon to help me. I didn't know how I was going to make it to the first stop and I asked the Lord, I said, "You are going to have to let me ride this train. I've got to go to school." As the train pulled into the first little stop, they usually checked the passengers' ticket, and I didn't have one. I went to the window of that train; they had windows raised and let people out of the window. I looked out without a dime, and as I looked out I told the Lord I needed money. And, the first thing I saw was my brother standing a few paces away. He didn't have any business there. Black people in those days didn't have much to do for fun so they'd meet all the trains to see who got on and off. So when I saw my brother, we called him Son, I leaned out of that window. I said, "Son, Son, come here!" And he came up to me and said, "What in the world are you doing on this train?" I said, "Have you got any money? I'm going to school. I don't have money. I've got to go to school. Can you give me some money?" He said, "Here," and he ran and handed the money up in that window just before the conductor got there to pick up my ticket. My fare wasn't but twenty cents.

He gave me enough for my fare into the next station and enough over it to come on down to Memphis and get a room in the dormitory for a week until I could get a schoolboy job. I depended on the Lord instead of people. Now, a lot of neighbors laughed at me. They could have helped me. My home church didn't give me any money. So I wrote my first song, "I Am Leaning and Depending on the Lord" (ex. 38). I made that a first.

Example 38. "I Am Leaning and Depending on the Lord" (William Herbert Brewster, orig. © 1939). Used by permission of Anna L. Brooks.

VERSE

1. I am on my way to glo-ry I am trav'-ling day by day; I
2. Some-time I stand and won-der why I must suf-fer wrong, I
3. Some-time my friends de-ceive me, it knocks me to my knees, They
4. When I come down to Jor-dan there I shall feel no fear, I

sing and tell the sto-ry in this old fash-ion way, this world is not my home, Some-
raise my eyes up yon-der then I sing this hap-py song, if Je-sus leads the way, I'll
hurt me so they grieve me, Oh Lord, have mer-cy please, no mat-ter what they do, I
know He'll take my bur-den and I shall feel Him near, right by my Sav-ior's side, On

day I'll o-ver-come, I am lean-ing and de-pend-ing on the Lord (on the Lord).
make it home some day, For I'm lean-ing and de-pend-ing on the Lord (on the Lord).
know He'll bring me thru, For I'm lean-ing and de-pend-ing on the Lord (on the Lord).
thru the swell-ing tide, I'll be lean-ing and de-pend-ing on the Lord (on the Lord).

CHORUS

I am lean-ing and de-pend-ing on the Lord (on the Lord), I am

lean-ing and de-pend-ing on the Lord (on the Lord),He has brought me safe this far and He

will not leave me now, I am lean-ing and de-pend-ing on the Lord (on the Lord).

Kenneth Morris published it for me. Roberta Martin published it later as "God Hears a Prayer."

One of the songs that I love most, the one that was the greatest to me that came out of the experiences that I had, was "Lord, I Tried." That little word *try*—I wrote a little sketch of my life and I named that little booklet *My Try*, my little autobiography.

My church had been foreclosed. I had opened a school in north Memphis. Times were tight and the church owed a little over two thousand dollars, plus what I had would settle it. So I went to the man that held the mortgage and tried to pay what I had. He said, "Now, Brewster, you are a good, young man." He was one of these people who was hard on people. He said, "Now I haven't had a young colored fellow come in here with your kind of education. These people that you are pastoring don't deserve you. I am not going to take this as no payment. I tell you what I'm going to do, Brewster. I am going to put it in this envelope and seal it. I am going to lock it up. Here, see where I am putting it. I'm writing your name on it. I am going to keep this money here to give you a chance to bring me the other sixteen hundred dollars. Now, don't you be long doing it because I am doing this only for you. I have no sympathy in the world for your officers and your members because I know they could do better than this. With a young man like you, there is not another young man in this whole town that can equal to you. Why can't your people see that?"

I walked out of that office. I went to another man. The man said, "Well, Brewster, I just lent out all that I have for the time being—in the next thirty days. . . ." I said, "But I have only a week." He said, "I'm sorry, I can't help you."

Then a lady told me, "I tell you what you do. My lawyer is downtown, you go down there and tell him to stop that foreclosure and call me and I will be responsible." I went on down there but a parade stopped me. I couldn't even get to the lawyer's office. I didn't know what to do. I went on and parked and walked. But when I did get there, the lawyer was gone. So, I just continued walking and praying. "Lord, I have tried. This is your church. You take it and do what you want to do with it because I am finished. I don't know anything else to do or where to go."

That time another preacher that pastored in Mississippi saw me. He said, "Say Herbert, I'm trying to go to my church and I need twelve dollars. I don't have a dime. Can you let me have it?" His name was Patton; I called him Pat. "Pat, I don't have any money. Man, I'm in all kinds of trouble." At that moment, I looked up and saw a sign of a real estate place. I had been there before and paid money for the church's mortgage when we were buying a place I was trying to get established for a school building that had been an old folks' home. I wanted to use it to set up a Baptist school. I had said then, "Mr. Vandrust, I am going to need a little money. I will be back up some time and see if you can let me have some."

I went up to that office having forgotten that I had put in that request. "Come on, let's go. There is a man that I know will let you have the money." I told Mr. Vandrust, "Here's Reverend Patton. He wants to go to his church. Let him have twelve dollars for his fare there and back and he will pay your money when he comes back." "All right, Brewster, if you say so," responded Mr. Vandrust. He handed him a ten-dollar bill and two ones.

We turned to leave. He said, "Oh, Brewster, wait a minute. Come here." And he unlocked his safe and pulled out more. "You remember you were in here a month ago saying that you may need money for your church?" "Yes, I remember." "Well, I have some here I can let you have." I owed sixteen hundred dollars. I asked, "Well, how much is it, Mr. Vandrust?" My name was already on it. It said, "sixteen hundred dollars, Brewster." You ever been in tight spots? Do you know what it is to have both hands tied and your ankles shackled? And your eyes blinded and you couldn't see?

He said, "sixteen hundred dollars if you need it, you can have it." I said, "Excuse me." I wanted to get out of there. I didn't want to stand up there and make a spectacle like a crybaby. I was so overwhelmed, the exact amount that I needed!

I got my clear receipt, my church didn't know what happened. The deacons [had] said they wouldn't sign, and my assistant pastor [had] said, "No, I can't trust them [the membership]." I went back there and brought them that clear receipt and the deed and put them out there. They wondered [but] they don't know to this day what happened. I couldn't make them see it that if you try, you come through. God helps those who help themselves. And if you try, you can make it.

I got the song "Our God Is Able" (ex. 39) this way. I went out one night to hear a man preach. I didn't think so much of him because although he had what we would call a pretty good following, his diction was so bad. He was just rusty. He got up to preach and announced his text, "God Is Able." Oh, my God, I listened to him, I wanted to get out, but he just kept on talking about "God is able." He began to talk about Daniel, coming out of that lion's den. He said, "God is able" and mentioned Jonah, and he named others. He got about halfway through, I got my pencil and started making notes on the tune he was using. I came back to my organist, I got the lyrics right away. The whole story that he based his sermon on is in that song.

That song, the way Marion Williams sang it, made it for Clara [Ward]. She had to get out from under Clara's shadow before she shone so brightly. She was the heart of that group at that time. I wrote that and they use to come to me to write for them a song a month—all of their music. They'd keep me in here for three or four days in rehearsal. That girl came in there, and I gave her that song just like the preacher had preached it, "God is able, able. . . ."

When she [Clara Ward] first started singing, I gave her a break. Now, the Ward Singers hadn't gotten anywhere. They came to a passion play that I had in what is now Cook Convention Center. Once a year, I would go there—it wasn't a center then, it was the City Auditorium, it was big. We would pack it and jam it. She came to the Cook Convention Center and I let her sing at the intermission. She was a good one. She sang "Just a Moment in God's Presence." Everyone in there could sing. Clara could play. She didn't stop. She had more energy than any worm in an apple somewhere. She could do that.

"Pay Day" (ex. 40), I took that from a white preacher. He was a South Carolinian, Dr. Robert G. Lee, one of the truly great preachers in the community. He and I came in from Memphis about 1924. He took the big Belview Church, I took the Pilgrim Black

Example 39. Verse of originally published version of "Our God Is Able" (William Herbert Brewster, orig. © 1949). Used by permission of Anna L. Brooks. For complete score, see ex. 49.

Church. He treated me with the greatest respect. My handicap with him was, I never would read his sermons and his literature because I had a natural inclination toward oratory. I was trained like that. I still can't drop it all. I would divide my sermon up to include the practical side. But when I got ready to glorify God, everything from alpha to omega could be thrown in. If it's a flower, then let it bloom.

You had to do it. They used to make us stand up and study elocution. There was a certain way to do things. You just couldn't use your hands and just walk about. Anybody could be on the pulpit and beat on the Bible. They called them Bible beaters. They taught me to stand up there and say my thing just like I was reading Caesar and Gaul, orations of the crown and the Shakespearean plays that I loved so much. . . . All of that

I wove into my ministry and Christianized it. I reached down and got the "dis," "dat," and "udder" crowd, and I put something in it for everyone.

So he preached that sermon, "Payday Someday," and it became a legend. I didn't care about the way he preached it but I liked that topic, so I wrote a song about it. When he retired, the music director of his church, one of the biggest churches in the Southern Convention, heard that I had written the song and asked me to let them use it to surprise him. I hadn't thought about letting it out. I let the girl come and make a tape and even the lyrics, and they surprised Dr. Lee by giving him the song based on the theme of his famous sermon.

The fight for rights here in Memphis was pretty rough on the Black church. The lily white, the black, and the tan were locking horns; and the idea struck me and I wrote that song "Move on up a Little Higher" (ex. 41). We'll have to move in the field of education. Move into the professions and move into politics. Move in anything that any other race has to have to survive. That was a protest idea and inspiration. I was trying to inspire Black people to move up higher. Don't be satisfied with the mediocre. Don't be satisfied. That was my doctrine. Before the freedom fights started, before the Martin Luther King days, I had to lead a lot of protest meetings. In order to get my message over, there were things that were almost dangerous to say, but you could sing it.

"Move on up a Little Higher" was not only a Christian climbing the ladder to heaven, but it was an exaltation of Black people to keep moving. You come out of slavery, you have an opportunity to get on your ladder and keep on climbing. Don't stop when you make one; make another. That was a general idea that became popular because that had a lot of bounce in it. Mahalia [Jackson] knew what to do with it. She could throw the verse out there.

Then one of the best ones, "How Far Am I from Canaan?," the boy from the Soul Stirrers, Sam Cooke, made popular. He came here and I taught it to him and I lectured to him. They used to come here from all over. From down in Georgia, the Statesman Brothers Quartet—I wrote for them their biggest hit, "I'm Climbing Higher and Higher" (ex. 42). . . . That song made the Statesman Quartet.

It was a follow-up to "Move on up a Little Higher," because Mahalia had taken it. They tried to get me to do something about it, but I said, "I can't do that to Mahalia; if she wants it, let her take it, I can write a thousand." I wrote "I'm Climbing Higher and Higher." In it, I started at regeneration and every round going higher and higher. And it had a bounce in it. I named the planets:

> Then I'm going to climb until I pass the sun, moon and stars
> Jupiter, Venus, Neptune and Mars.

Those white boys used to get out sometimes—they were emotional and they got out on the road sometimes . . . the Happy Goodman Brothers, I wrote for them, too, and several other white groups. They took the songs and they didn't do much changing. Elvis Presley came here, a truck driver, and now he is the greatest thing.

Example 40.   "Pay Day" (William Herbert Brewster, orig. © 1958). Used by permission of Anna L. Brooks.

All the groups came here, the Golden Gate Jubilee Quartet and the Silvertones from Pittsburgh—those boys there were members of my son's church. He pastored in Pittsburgh and Philadelphia. They came from all over. These people came and got the songs. I specialized and made them different.

Example 40.   *(continued)*

name._____ There a waits a great re-
day._____ In a land_____ where all
blest._____ Where the wick - ed cease from

ward_____ More_ pre - cious than world wide fame.
sigh - ing And_ sor - row shall flee a - way.
troub - ling, And the wea - ry shall be at rest.

CHORUS

Pay_____ day. Pay_____ day_____ to the
Pay_____ day. Pay_____ day. For all my

wick - ed 'twill be an aw - ful day. Pay____ day,
trou - bles here__ be - low Pay____ day,

Pay_ day. To the ran - somed twill be a joy - ful day.
Pay_ day. In that land. Hap-py land to which I go.

Example 41. "Move on up a Little Higher" (William Herbert Brewster, orig. © 1946). Used by permission of Anna L. Brooks.

Example 41. *(continued)*

Example 41.   *(continued)*

Example 42. "I'm Climbing Higher and Higher" (William Herbert Brewster). Used by permission of Anna L. Brooks.

Example 42. *(continued)*

A young girl named Queen C. Anderson joined the church. I think she had about an eighth- or ninth-grade education. She had a memory as she read, that kind of photographic thing that if she read a song over, she could recite it. It was the most amazing thing. She had the most beautiful voice you ever heard. She could make a high voice, and with her low soprano she would louden it and widen it and deepen it. It was just amazing to anybody that heard it.

"How I Got Over," I didn't like the title of that song so much. It wasn't my idea; I never could change it. Clara did that. Clara came in here. The way I became interested in "How I Got Over," it was back in the administration of Dr. L. K. Williams, who was a Texan. There came up three brothers to the Convention. He allowed them to sing and they sang a song of that type of "How I Got Over." They had a big, tall boy and they called him Baby. And they came to see me and I worked with them, and when they left here, the song died.

Later on, I had a group that worked with the songs, and I gave "How I Got Over" to them. I discovered in order to make it Bible based, it would have been better to say, "I don't know how I will get over," because after you have gotten over, you are bound to know it was by the grace of God. I criticized myself on that. Clara came down and I gave her the lyrics. She took this number and she ran with it.

I write these songs for these common people who could not understand political language, common people who didn't know anything about economics, I had to write song after song. As long as the Lord would bring the inspiration to me, I am going to keep on doing that.

~

WILLIAM HERBERT BREWSTER

The Eloquent Poet

Horace Clarence Boyer

The biographical information in the text is based on an interview the author conducted with Reverend William Herbert Brewster in 1979. —ED.

One of the innovative giants who worked during the opening decades of the development of gospel music was Reverend William Herbert Brewster. From his music, his sermons, or even his speaking, it was clear that he was a learned person. He received a bachelor of arts degree from Roger Williams College in Nashville, which is no longer in existence but has a very strong history of productive leaders for the early Baptist church. He was awarded an honorary doctorate from Bennett College in Greensboro, North Carolina. Brewster had an extraordinary knowledge of the Bible, on which he drew heavily in writing his song lyrics. Much of what African Americans know about the Old Testament might very well come from Dr. Brewster's compositions. He would not hesitate to include biblical data that some might have called dull, boring, and uninteresting in his songs; as a result of this, gospel music lovers know things about Judea that they wouldn't have known from reading the Bible, for the information he provided was placed in an interesting musical setting.

Brewster's only formal training in music was in the church. He grew up during a period when shape-note singing was in style. By learning the scale tones by shape, a group could become musically literate and sing all parts in harmony. This was Brewster's introduction

211

to music as literature, and he actually learned to write in that style in the early days. He also played piano a little, which he taught himself; as a preacher, he also was expected to sing. Thus, with his shape-note education, his elemental facility at the piano, and his ability to sing, he wrote over two hundred songs, many of which are in the standard repertoire today.

Many of Brewster's compositions were composed to be used in his pageants or passion plays. His two most famous compositions, "Move on up a Little Higher" and "Our God Is Able," were written as set songs—songs designed to be performed in his pageants. Brewster is unique in that, in most cases, as he stated, the lyrics, melody, and harmony came to him all at once. Such was the case with his composing "Move on up a Little Higher." He was involved in writing a pageant, and he thought about a sermon he had heard a minister preach. Early in the morning, the song "Move on up a Little Higher" came to him and just flowed forth. He went over to the house of Queen C. Anderson (1913–1959), his principal soloist in the pageant, who did not read music but had a fantastic ear, and within twenty minutes, he taught Queen C. Anderson the song.

Brewster began composing as early as the 1930s, but it was approximately fifteen more years before gospel music companies would publish his songs. His first song was "I'm Leaning and Depending on the Lord." The date of the composition is unknown, for Brewster wrote many of his songs for his congregation and the local community. A year or two might separate the composition and copyright dates. In the case of "I Am Leaning and Depending on the Lord," with the sheet music out of stock, a copyright date of 1941 is the only date available. In an interview with Brewster in 1979, he informed me that all his songs since 1958 had been copyrighted and published by his own music house (Boyer 1979b). These dates give us a range of well over forty years of composing and publishing gospel music (see table 6).

The largest group of Brewster's songs was published by Ward's House of Music in Philadelphia, which came into existence in 1954 specifically for the purpose of publishing Clara Ward's and Brewster's music. By this time, almost every Ward Singers recording was also a Brewster song. In addition to Ward's House of Music, Brewster's works were published by Bowles Music House, Theodore R. Frye Publishers, Martin and Morris Music, Inc., and Roberta Martin Studio of Music, all of Chicago. Bowles is important because, with the exception of Ward, it was the major publishing house for Brewster's music. The chief arranger at Bowles was Virginia Davis.

In gospel music, an arranger is simply a scribe who writes down the music received orally from someone else and is not to be confused with the music industry's definition of arranger as someone who rearranges the melody, harmony, and rhythm in a work that he or she did not originally create. The use of the term *arranger* for the gospel scribe has often contributed to a lack of proper respect and acknowledgment of the actual composer. By the time Brewster began to publish his works on a regular basis, he was no longer writing down music. He would create the composition, teach it to his group, and they

Table 6 Selected Compositions of William Herbert Brewster

Copyright Date	Title	Copyright Date	Title
1941	"I'm Leaning and Depending on the Lord"	1952	"Have Faith in God"
1945	"I Thank You, Lord" "Lord I've Tried"	1954	"Faith That Moves Mountains" "God's Amazing Love" "I've Never Heard of a City Like the New Jerusalem" "The Wonderful Counselor Is Pleading for Me" "Weeping May Endure for a Night"
1946	"How Far Am I from Canaan?" "Move on up a Little Higher"		
1949	"I'm Getting Nearer to My Home" "Jesus Is All" "Just over the Hill" "Let Us Go Back to the Old Land Mark" "Our God Is Able" "Peace Be Still" "These Are They"	1955	"Treading the Wine Press Alone"
		1957	"Packing Up"*
		1958	"Pay Day"

*Clara Ward (1924–1973) also claims authorship of the composition.

would sing it for someone, a music scribe, who in a kind of shorthand system would transcribe the music and Brewster would have it published. Theodore R. Frye published "God Is Able," Martin and Morris published "How Far Am I From Heaven?" and "Lord, I've Tried," and Roberta Martin published "I Thank You, Lord." Today, the Brewster church organization, East Trigg Baptist Church in Memphis, Tennessee, operates a publishing house, and much of the music is published by his own company.

Brewster's works reveal a distinctive style when one analyzes their poetic form, harmony, and number of bars. Some compositions are written in what I call the *gospel blues* form. The "composed" blues or the so-called classic blues is a three-line poem with a poetic structure of AAB. An excellent example is Aaron "T-Bone" Walker's "Call It Stormy Monday" blues:

> They call it stormy Monday,
> but Tuesday's just as bad.

That's the first "A."

> They call it stormy Monday,
> but Tuesday's just as bad.

That's the second "A.";

> Wednesday's worse,
>   and Thursday's oh so sad.

That's "B." It takes four bars to sing each one of those lines, and all classic blues use basically the same harmonic progression.

In gospel blues, a song is normally composed of four lines:

> I know the Lord will make a way;
>   Oh, yes He will.
> I know the Lord will make a way;
>   Oh, yes He will.
> He'll make a way for you;
>   He will lead you safely through.
> I know the Lord will make a way;
>   Oh, yes He will.

This song has a poetic structure of AABA, and each line requires four measures of music to perform. This results in a poem of AABA structure, set to sixteen bars of music. Each gospel blues employs the same harmonic scheme, although one different from that of secular blues.

While there is clearly no real relationship between secular classic blues and gospel blues, the latter acquired its name because of the similarities of the two song forms:

1. Secular blues is based on a constant harmonic scheme, as is gospel blues.
2. Secular blues is composed of a three-line poem with the rhyme scheme of AAB, while gospel blues is composed of a four-line poem with a rhyme scheme of AABA.
3. Secular blues requires three units (three four-bar phrases) of musical time to express its poetry, while gospel blues requires four units of musical time (a different middle and closing section are incorporated into gospel blues).

One of the first gospel blues to make a wide impression on gospel music was, indeed, the verse in a composition by Brewster called "Lord I've Tried" (ex. 43). That melody and that sort of harmony cover a great number of songs in the standard gospel repertoire. Four of Brewster's songs are in that style: "Lord I've Tried"; "Thank You, Lord"; "I Am Leaning and Depending on the Lord"; and "Just over the Hill."

Without a doubt, the most popular Brewster-type song is a song I call the *vamp* or *cumulative* song. Vamp, in this instance, denotes a melodic, harmonic, and rhythmic section in which the music remains the same, but the words begin to pile on one another

Example 43. "Lord I've Tried" (William Herbert Brewster, orig. © 1945). Used by permission of Anna L. Brooks.

Example 43. *(continued)*

and the element of repetition becomes the strength of the performance. When Brewster found something good, he'd stay right there and drive it home. For example, in "Move on up a Little Higher" (see ex. 41), he creates this text:

> Move on up a little higher
>> Meet Abraham and Isaac
> Move on up a little higher
>> Meet the prophet Daniel
> Move on up a little higher
>> Meet the Hebrew children
> Move on up a little higher
>> Meet brother Paul and Silas
> Move on up a little higher
>> Meet my friends and kindred
> Move on up a little higher
>> Meet the lily of the valley
> Move on up a little higher
>> Sweet, sweet Rose of Sharon

This is the same technique used by the late Dr. Martin Luther King, Jr., in his 1963 March on Washington speech, in which he says, "I have a dream" fifteen times. The vamp is an old technique used throughout African cultural expressions in song, dance, drumming, and storytelling; repetition is used to get the message across and to fire collective intensity.

Clara Ward particularly liked songs with vamp sections and included those in most of her performances. In her rendition of Brewster's "Let Us Go Back to the Old Land Mark" (ex. 44), she sings:

> He'll be near us, He will hear us,
> We'll be given, bread from heaven
>
> Tell the story,
>> Of his glory
> It will warn men,
>> It will turn men,
> Common meter,
>> Yes, they're sweeter
> When you stop singing,
>> They'll keep ringing

These couplets file in over and over and over. Most gospel songs written today use the vamp but not as creatively, for few composers use Brewster's technique for continuous development of the message through the lyric.

We have two early songs from the folk tradition that use this cumulative form that are classics, and Brewster's lyric style may owe something to these older pieces. One is "Children Go Where I Send Thee":

Example 44. "Let Us Go Back to the Old Land Mark" (William Herbert Brewster, orig. ©
1949). Used by permission of Anna L. Brooks.

Example 44. *(continued)*

> One for the little bitty baby
> Two for Paul and Silas
> Three for the Hebrew children
> Four for the four that stood at the door
> Five for the Gospel writers. . . .

The other is the song "The Valley of Dry Bones":

> Them bones, them bones, them dry bones
> The foot bone connected to the ankle bone,
> And the ankle bone connected to the leg bone,
> And the leg bone connected to the. . . .

Brewster's compositions include another type of song called *jubilee*. Songs in this category tend to be upbeat, but they do not, in the main, have the repeated element. They are composed straight through, with a chorus and a verse. For example, in "Jesus Is All," another song recorded by the Ward Singers (Savoy 4013), he wrote this verse:

> When I went out to seek the Lord
> I walked out on His blessed word
> I remember when I prayed that last prayer
> The Holy Ghost came to me right there
> I stepped on the rock, the rock was sound
> The love of God came streaming down.
> The reason I know He saved my soul,
> I dug down deep and found pure gold.
> He's my all, my all, my all,
>   my all and all.
>
> Jesus is all; my all and all
> I know He'll answer when I call
> Walking by His side, I'm satisfied.
> Yes, Jesus is all. . . .

That is an example of the jubilee song, in which the story or situation is unveiled in the verse and celebrated in the chorus.

Brewster also composes in the *gospel ballad* tradition. A gospel ballad is basically a slow song, though with a regular beat, in which one literally thinks out loud. The tempo is slow, and the song is organized around a verse and a chorus. The song "Faith That Moves Mountains" is one of Brewster's gospel ballads (ex. 45).

The song style for which Brewster is singularly known is called the *recitative and aria*. The recitative, or the slow part of the song, carries the very serious part of the situation, for it tells the story. The aria is generally of a lighter vein—*except* in Brewster's songs, where it is still of a very serious nature, sometimes continuing the story described in the recitative. Recitative-and-aria songs always come in two or three different tempos. Nor-

Example 45. "Faith That Moves Mountains" (William Herbert Brewster, orig. © 1954). Used by permission of Anna L. Brooks.

Example 45. *(continued)*

knock, and knock by faith, Or ring the bell at Mer - cys door, The

Lord will give you grace that will make the heart glow.

Chorus II

1. Young Ab - el, the first man, died, But His in - no - cent blood from the
2. Bro - ther No - ah built the ark and deep in his heart God had placed

By | faith:

ground to God cried Bro - ther Enoch, wal - ked with God, On
a lit - tle spark Old Josh - u - a marched around till the

By | faith

Example 45.   *(continued)*

((Back to Chorus I)

mally, the first part is in a very slow, nonpulsed tempo. Unlike gospel ballads, which have a slow but rhythmic pulse, these songs are rendered in a chanted reciting style, and in Brewster's compositions, there are remnants of the old Baptist lining hymns.

Brewster loves this pacing and uses this element to open these songs. Here the singer has the opportunity to decorate the tones, alter the rhythm, and *hold* tones to reveal the true meaning of the lyric. The composition moves to the next section and to another tempo—the joyous part. "Faith That Moves Mountains," "God's Amazing Love," "Have Faith in God," "How Far Am I from Canaan?," "I've Never Heard of a City Like the New Jerusalem," "Weeping May Endure for the Night," "Treading the Wine Press Alone," "Pay Day," and "Peace Be Still" are all stunning examples of the Brewster recitative-and-aria form. "Just over the Hill" is an excellent example of a song with just two sections (ex. 46). The recitative is:

> There is a land of fateless day
>   Just over the hill
> Beyond the rainbow and the sky
>   Just over the hill.
> It's a land beyond compare, free from sorrow, pain or care
> And they tell me there's no night there
>   Just over the hill.

In singing this section, the singer would elaborate and embellish as much as he or she desired. At the completion of this section, the tempo quickens for the aria:

> Just over the hill,
> Just over the hill. . . .

In some cases these songs employ as many as three different tempos by adding a special chorus. In the special chorus, the tempo will be double that of the second section, and a vamp will be added.

Brewster does not specialize in what is called the *shout* song, a song that is performed at an increasingly fast pace. "Let Us Go Back to the Old Land Mark," as performed by Clara Ward and the Ward Singers, is an example of his shout song.

The most common scale found in Brewster's music is the major scale. The next most frequently used scale is the diatonic scale with a flatted seventh, called Mixolydian (ex. 47). When I heard the Ward Singers sing "Jesus Is All," I heard that flatted seventh and was anxious to look at the sheet music to see if he had, in fact, written the flatted seventh or if the singers had put it in, and I was delighted to find in the sheet music that he had written exactly that. It is a very wonderful combination of this major scale with a minor inflection.

There are a few songs in which Brewster uses fewer than seven tones. For example, in "Let Us Go Back to the Old Land Mark," he uses only five tones in the melody. The G♯ alternates with the G♭, and the F is used only once, in the final measure.

Example 46.   "Just over the Hill" (William Herbert Brewster, orig. © 1949). Used by permission of Anna L. Brooks.

Example 46. *(continued)*

Example 47. The Mixolydian scale.

Brewster, like Tindley before him, does not employ a very rich harmonic language. The principal reason for this was that he is first and foremost a lyricist and melodist and does not wish to have harmony detract from the words. He therefore bathes the text in a very simple, direct kind of melody and harmony. Often, composers have a special interval or a special curve or line they like to use, and it will be found in various ways throughout their work. The *triadic* melody is one of Brewster's compositional mannerisms. It is a melody built on the first, third, and fifth scale degrees of any diatonic scale (ex. 48). The "Blue Danube Waltz" by Strauss is an example of a triadic melody. Though with a different distribution of the tones, triadic melodies appear in such Brewster songs as "How I Got Over," "Move on up a Little Higher," and "Let Us Go Back to the Old Land Mark."

Example 48. Triadic melody.

Regarding the keys of his compositions, Brewster was particularly fortunate in that people were waiting for his songs as soon as he completed the compositions, and therefore he could write for their voices. Very often, a song was published in the key of the group to whom he had taught it. For example, many of the songs that the Ward Singers sang were published in the keys that were good for the Ward Singers—Clara Ward, Marion Williams, Willa Ward, and Henrietta Waddy. However, among the works that I have analyzed, I found that he published his songs only in the keys of C, E♭, F, A♭, and B♭.

Regarding Brewster's use of rhythm, like Lucie E. Campbell before him, Brewster favored the Baptist lining-hymn and gospel blues traditions. The slow, free, and surging singing style of his grandmother informed his sense of rhythm, but he was also in the forefront of establishing $\frac{12}{8}$ as the gospel rhythm. When he published "Our God Is Able" in 1949, he published it in $\frac{4}{4}$ (see ex. 39), but it is actually sung in $\frac{12}{8}$. This is consistent with the development of gospel music literature. Composers created manuscripts that were "user-friendly," and these were further guided by oral-transmission practices. "Surely God Is Able" (ex. 49), the Ward Singers' arrangement of Brewster's original composition, was published in $\frac{6}{4}$ by Frye and Brewster in 1950 and is performed in $\frac{12}{8}$, with a feeling of three; it emerged as the first recorded song to take advantage of what is now known as gospel rhythm (see discussion of gospel waltz rhythm on p. 106).

Brewster's study of Latin, Greek, and homiletics manifested itself in his tremendous ability to put words together to make biblical sense. On the one hand, he is very simple and direct, speaking in the language we know best. For example:

Example 49.   "Surely God Is Able" (William Herbert Brewster). Used by permission of Anna L. Brooks.

Example 49.   *(continued)*

1st Refrain

Example 49.   *(continued)*

"I THANK YOU, LORD"
I have so much that I can thank my Jesus for
Since I've been a soldier in this holy war.
I count my blessings one by one
Just to see what my Lord has done.
Then I say, "I thank you, Jesus."

And to make sure that he is understood, he completes this section with

I thank you, Lord.

On the other hand, he is also prone to using sophisticated prose, such as that in his "I'm Climbing Higher and Higher" (see ex. 42):

First round was regeneration,
   The second justification.
The third a happy confession
   Then the Holy Ghost took possession,
The next round great tribulation,
   That leads us on to glorification.
Well I'm climbing higher and higher
   And I won't come down.

When all of these elements are put together, we have a song that is unique; poetry and lyrics that combine folk images—subjects that friends can discuss, using the most noble poetry from the Bible and from ancient history; a melody that is diatonic and easily singable; harmonies that are simple yet beautiful; and rhythms that make the soul want to rock. Those are the elements of a W. Herbert Brewster song.

"IF I FAIL, YOU TELL THE WORLD I TRIED"

William Herbert Brewster on Records

Anthony Heilbut

If gospel music's golden era ran from 1945 to 1960, then Reverend William Herbert Brewster may be the key architect of the modern gospel sound. During that period, no other composer matched his popular success, rate of production, or spiritual influence. Brewster's achievement derived from his command of all the distinctive gospel traits and his capacity to explore them with more depth and vision than had previous composers. His lyrics draw from Black idioms and folklore—a fountain that never runs dry—and comprise the best examples of twentieth-century spirituals. They also clearly evolve from the earlier work of two inspired Methodists—the white Englishman Isaac Watts and the Black Philadelphian Charles Albert Tindley.

Brewster's music was even more audacious in its range of influences and ambitions. Without being facetious, I would like to argue that the most salient musical qualities of gospel are its rhythm and its blues—by which I mean both the moans, slurs, and melismatic patterns that adorn African American hymn singing and the ubiquitous use of the sixteen-bar blues form, what I call the Baptist blues. (To me, the archetypal example of Baptist blues is Dorsey's minor-key arrangement of the eighteenth-century hymn "The Day Is Passed and Gone.") Brewster was fortunately situated in Memphis. Not only did he have the city's musical heritage to work from (as a young man, he learned from W. C. Handy), but he was also in immediate proximity to that powerhouse of gospel rhythms, the Church of God in Christ (Heilbut 1970). To discuss Memphis gospel without citing Mason Temple is a bit like discussing sacred music in Rome without naming the Vatican.

Many Methodist and Baptist preachers have become entangled in sectarian squabbles with the various Holiness sects, but Reverend Brewster's songs are a seamless blend of Baptist and Methodist decorum and Sanctified ecstasy.

Brewster's innovations and his willingness to incorporate all manner of music and lyrical influences bespeak a generous intelligence. It is also a political one, and if there is any one reason why we honor Brewster today, it is because of the social and political message implicit in his music. Brewster's songs were often composed for inclusion in gospel dramas, and frequently these had a political subtext. During a period when civil rights became the dominant national issue, Brewster managed to insinuate themes of social progress and political struggle into his songs without turning them into watered-down propaganda, or gospel agitprop. Compare the energy of his propulsive encouragements in "I'm climbing higher and higher and I won't come down" (from "I'm Climbing Higher and Higher"—see ex. 42) and the reiterated "surely's" in "Surely God Is Able" (see ex. 49) with the diaphanous musings of "We Shall Overcome"–type anthems.

Any way you observe him, Brewster stands alone. Other pioneer gospel writers could call on substantial institutional support. Lucie E. Campbell, another Memphian, was a music director of the National Baptist Convention and was able to distribute her sheet music at church conferences. Thomas A. Dorsey, Brewster's only rival, was always a skilled promoter of his music. Aided by the organizational skills of his leading vocalist, Sallie Martin, Dorsey created a national network for his music. Its incarnation was the National Association of Gospel Choirs and Choruses that Dorsey and Martin founded in 1932. In recent years, James Cleveland's Gospel Music Workshop has been a similarly institutional setting in which to introduce new material and propagate its performance. Other gospel pioneers like Lillian Bowles, Kenneth Morris, and Roberta Martin ran small publishing studios, mom-and-pop store operations by comparison to Tin Pan Alley, but were giant forces in the new field of Black church music.

Brewster had no church convention, singers' association, or publishing company behind him. As a result he has been the least protected of major gospel composers. Mahalia Jackson's career was established after she recorded his composition "Move on up a Little Higher," and Clara Ward's biggest hit was Brewster's new version of the spiritual "How I Got Over" (ex. 50). Both women claimed authorship of these Brewster songs, although they did acknowledge his authorship of some of their other big hits. Brewster once said that such piracy hurt his feelings but didn't compel more disputatious responses. "With the racial situation getting so acute" (Heilbut 1985, 101), he had more pressing concerns than plagiarism by the world's greatest gospel singers!

Of course, while he lacked institutional support, he had something better: phonograph recordings. Between 1945 and 1960 over fifty Brewster compositions were recorded by dozens of soloists, groups, and quartets. While in 1938 Rosetta Tharpe had scored a national hit with Dorsey's "Rock Me" (Decca 2243), the first million-copy sellers of gospel compositions were Brewster tunes: Jackson's "Move on up a Little Higher" in 1947 (Apollo 164) and the Ward Singers' "Surely God Is Able" in 1950 (Savoy 4017). Gospel music's increasing sophistication of styles and techniques was reflected in his work—work

Example 50. "How I Got Over" (William Herbert Brewster). Used by permission of Anna L. Brooks.

Example 50.   *(continued)*

Example 50.   *(continued)*

Example 50. *(continued)*

Example 50.   *(continued)*

west   on the way to the land   of   rest.   Well, I'm goin' to

Oh, yes   Oh, yes

join   the heav-en-ly   choir,___   goin' to   sing and nev-er get

Oh, yes

tired.   I'm goin' to sing,   yes,___ I'm goin' to shout,

Oh, yes   Hal-le-lu-jah!   trou-bles

Oh,___ I'm goin' to thank Him   for   all_____ He's   done for

o - ver

Example 50.   *(continued)*

that also kept calling gospel back to its ancestral sources. Thus one of his most invigorating beats was set to the lyric "let us all go back to the old landmark." Sixteen-bar or Baptist blues had been a staple of spirituals like "Poor Pilgrim of Sorrow." Brewster improved and elaborated on the genre. The lined-meter hymn was a favorite musical form. Brewster appropriated it for the slow, stately verses that began his longer tunes; such compositions invariably concluded with up-tempo choruses. Slow hymns often inspired frenetic shouts. Brewster's inspiration was to combine the two in an organic entity.

Brewster's sense of the song as production extended to the interaction between lead singer and background. When submitted to the arranging skills of a Clara Ward, this led to a remarkable opening up of melodic possibilities. Not that Brewster or any other pioneer gospel composer was a spectacular melodist; most gospel tunes were either hymn melodies or sixteen-bar blues, truly public domain. But the frequently startling lyrics and the demands of phrasing, timing, and enunciation helped loosen the form, pointing in the direction of the newer "contemporary gospel" composers. These younger composers may share Brewster's musical ambition, but alas, so far none of them has matched his strengths as a lyricist.

It is as a lyricist that Brewster made his greatest mark. R. H. Harris, the originator of gospel quartet singing, once said, "With all the other writers, you need to work to bring out the message; with Old Man Brewster, the message's already there, a singer can really go to town" (Heilbut 1978). One thinks of those Brewster lyrics that spring from Black folklore or flow toward it. Consider, from "Move on up a Little Higher":

> I'm going out sight-seeing in Beulah,
> March around the altar,
> Walk and never get tired,
> Fly and never falter. ("Tribute" n.d., 23–25)

These are, most likely, original Brewster lyrics, but they would not be out of place in a spiritual. Brewster addresses this musical heritage in "Let Us Go Back to the Old Land Mark":

> Common meter, they're much sweeter,
> When they start singing, they'll be ringing,
> They'll be lingering way down in your soul. (Brewster 1949)

Or, in the same song, this evocation of ritual with a casual reference to a hymn that familiarly ushers in baptismal services:

> Sons and daughters, buried in the water,
> Coming up shouting, nobody doubting,
> Singing "On Jordan's Stormy Banks I Stand." (Brewster 1949)

To a literary critic (and Brewster is the rare gospel writer whose body of work can withstand much critical inspection), some of his most intriguing lyrics are derived from the Bible. Like Walt Whitman exulting in his congeries of categories, Brewster names the biblical cities in "The New Jerusalem":

> There are many important cities where the great Apostles went,
> Rome, Athens, Thessalonica, Antioch and Corinth,
> Then John in revelation when called to come up higher,
> Wrote to Ephesus and Smyrna, Pergamus and Thyatira,
> Sardis, Philadelphia, Laodicea, a letter around,
> But none of these was like the city John saw coming down.
> (*Special Songs* 1956, 26–28)

One has to go back to Renaissance poetry or the wild sprung rhythms of Gerard Manley Hopkins to find parallels to Brewster's apocalyptic vision in "The Book of the Seven Seals":

> When the lamb had opened seal number two,
> A blood-red horse came galloping through,
> It was to make the earth tremble beneath his tread,
> With ten thousand battle-fields strewn with the dead.
>
> He was a war horse born in the valley,
> He was a war horse born in the valley,
> He was a war horse born in the valley,
> A war horse, a war horse born in the valley.
>   (*Bless My Bones* P-Vine PLP–9051)

This is truly a syncopation of both poetic image and text!

Other Brewster lyrics, such as those in "I'm Holding On," relate more personally to the singer:

> Sometimes I'm reeled and rocked from side to side,
> But if I fail, you tell the world I tried.
>   (*Special Songs* 1953, 38–40)

The first major recording of a Brewster composition was in October 1946, when the Soul Stirrers released "Lord I've Tried" (Aladdin 203). Not only was this the quartet's first hit, but it also set the pace for the many sixteen-bar gospel blues subsequently recorded by them and by their numerous disciples, particularly the Pilgrim Travelers and the Five Blind Boys of Mississippi (whose first recording happened to be their version of "Lord I've Tried," on Excelsior 185).

In the Soul Stirrers' recording, R. H. Harris's sweetly assured vocal is a model of restraint, and the brooding chorus helped introduce a blues pattern to quartet backgrounds: previously verbal refrains exhibited a less bluesy, melodic cast. The Swan Silvertones, led by Claude Jeter, also scored a year later with "Lord I've Tried" (King 4282). Other quartets, notably the Spirit of Memphis and the Dixie Hummingbirds (not to mention the Memphis-based Southern Wonders and East Trigg's house quartets, the Brewsteraires and the Pattersonaires), have also wrecked churches with Brewster's compositions. These could be as lightweight as the neojubilee "Make More Room for Jesus in Your Life" or as substantial as "I Thank You, Lord" and "As an Eagle Stirreth Her Nest."

But Brewster's major impact occurred through the efforts of female soloists and groups. There are several possible explanations. His songs were composed for and introduced by Queen C. Anderson, a soloist who recorded a mere handful of sides but had an incalculable influence. Gospel music—by which I mean the choir-robed, largely female version—because it is more church related, less indebted to secular forms than is male-quartet music, may well be more suitable to the profundity of Brewster's messages. And finally, Brewster's lyrics are usually more verbose and complex than the average gospel song. His genius was to intuit that such elaborate lyrics, with their call for metric shifts and bravura interpretation combined with their bluesy or hymnal melodies, would force singers to call upon all their resources. The three greatest postwar female singers—Mahalia Jackson, Marion Williams, and Clara Ward—were all gifted stylists before Brewster, but because he produced their signature numbers it can be argued that they discovered their true musical selves through his guidance.

Take, for example, Mahalia Jackson's "Move on up a Little Higher" (Apollo 164). In 1937 the Golden Gate Jubilee Quartet's recording of "Won't That Be a Happy Time" (Bluebird 7340) contained a brief chorus around "moving up a little bit further," and the jubilee verses of such quartets were often highly prolix and poetic. But because of Brewster's torrid, bluesy tempos, Mahalia Jackson had to find another way. Notice the manner in which she reads the lyrics "I'm going out sight-seeing in Beulah" or "Soon as these feet strike Zion." The tempo and spirit feel are perfectly matched.

Jackson's biggest house-wreckers remained Brewster songs, such as "Just over the Hill" (Apollo 221). Here we find another transcendent release allowed a great singer by a great composer. Another thrilling moment comes in Jackson's chorus of Brewster's "These Are They" (Apollo 234). When Brewster's ensemble would perform the song, Queen C. Anderson would enumerate the "These" in the "they" by listing tribes of Israel, countries of origin, and finally—making it plain—"these are they who've been crying, who've been sighing, who've been scorned, talked about sure as you're born," and plainest of all, she would add, "that's my crowd" (Heilbut n.d.).

One of Mahalia Jackson's vocal inspirations was Mary Johnson Davis, a gifted Pittsburgh soprano who made only three professional recordings, one of them the Brewster tune "I'll Wait on the Lord" (Atlantic 890). Clearly Davis has another vision of what to do with a Brewster lyric, though hers is equally bluesy and equally imbued with the strength of a testimony.

Another musical breakthrough occurred in 1950 with the first recording of the Brewster Ensemble. This was Brewster's arrangement of the hymn "I'll Go," sung in duet form by Queen C. Anderson and her cousin Gurice Malone (Gotham 644). This may be the first recording to feature a form of cutting contests between vocalists. There had been duets before, notably those of Rosetta Tharpe and Marie Knight, but this was the first recorded performance in which two singers seemed to spur each other on and make musical comments on the other's performance. Something similar has long been a part of the interaction between minister and congregation; it took Brewster to incorporate the ad lib rite into a professional recording.

Brewster's name is identified most strongly with the Ward Singers. Clara Ward's love of hymns alerted her to the singular qualities of Brewster's slower tunes, while Marion Williams's (the Wards' other lead) aggressive, Sanctified rhythms and bluesy feel made her the top interpreter of the "harder" Brewster songs. Ward and Brewster were both fascinated by the gospel waltz, as illustrated in her version of his arrangement of "At the Cross" (Gotham 724, Spirit Feel SF 1002). Ward's delicious slur on the word *down*, with which she introduces the song's final chorus, suggests a quality of blues waltz, an idiom often employed in later soul-jazz records. The most famous Brewster gospel waltz is "Surely God Is Able" (Savoy 4017), in which Ward and Williams share solo responsibilities.

Much as Brewster's songs allowed Williams's preacher strengths to assert themselves, his lines lent themselves to Clara Ward's more clipped, abbreviated phrasing, as illustrated on "The Old Land Mark" (Savoy 4033). By the mid-fifties the Brewster–Ward team had achieved an unparalleled musical sophistication, as exemplified in "God's Amazing Love" (Savoy MG 14026). Ward's lead blends with the wordy choral background, allowing for a longer melodic line than usual, while her cunning shifts in tempo suggest a superimposition of $\frac{4}{4}$ on $\frac{3}{4}$ time. This was precisely the musical freedom later gospel composers would take for granted. Marion Williams delivered one of her bluesiest vocal leads on "I'm Climbing Higher and Higher" (Savoy 4055). Note the sly way Williams reads the word *running*. In person she would syncopate "run/run/run run/run," and so on, in a way that immediately influenced Little Richard; and Richard's pupils, James Brown and Otis Redding, would work further changes on Williams's syncopations. Her contribution is evident, but it was Brewster's lyric that endowed her virtuoso performance with its validity and logic.

During the golden era, many other gospel groups featured Brewster material. The Davis Sisters recorded five of his compositions; the Original Gospel Harmonettes, only one. But Brewster's influence on Dorothy Love Coates, the Harmonettes' lead singer and composer, is transparent. Note the echoes of his "I'm Holding On" in her "I'm Holding on and I Won't Let Go of My Faith" and of his "That's Enough for Me" in her "That's Enough" (Specialty SPS 2134). Brewster's most devoted acolyte was his son, W. H. Brewster, Jr. The son's songs closely resemble the father's: his "Tell the Angels I'm on My Way" is a gospel blues in the great tradition. Originally recorded by the Ward Singers (Savoy 4023), the song was popularized by Albertina Walker and the Caravans in their first professional recording (States 103); once again, a major career was inaugurated with Brewster's benediction. In 1980, Marion Williams recorded one of W. H. Brewster Jr.'s last compositions, "Pure Gold" (John Hammond FW 37598), with its great line

> I'll let heaven know, so proud and bold
> So glad I've come forth as pure gold.

Since 1986, Williams has recorded new versions of Brewster Sr.'s "Farther on up the Road" (Spirit Feel SF 1002), "Jesus Is All" (Spirit Feel SF 1007), "Move on up a Little Higher" (Spirit Feel SF 1011), "Surely God Is Able" (Spirit Feel SF 1011), and "I Thank You, Lord" (Spirit Feel SF 1013).

Long before the concept of Black pride was codified, Brewster's songs and sermons exemplified racial dignity. His historical sense is evidenced by the fact that in the 1930s he named Queen C. Anderson after Queen Candice of Ethiopia (Heilbut 1970). As for boldness, Brewster was never embarrassed by any of gospel's elements. Grammatical errors meshed with pedantic and often archaic diction; a stately waltz rhythm would cede to a figure out of boogie-woogie or honky-tonk piano.

Brewster put an unprecedented pressure on gospel music and lyrics, and the form proved more flexible than even he might have anticipated. There has been none since with his vision of gospel, particularly as a vehicle of social and political expression. His work comprises some of American music's purest gold.

WILLIAM HERBERT BREWSTER

Pioneer of the Sacred Pageant

William H. Wiggins, Jr.

Reverend William Herbert Brewster rightfully can lay claim to being a major gospel music figure in two ways. First, he wrote many of the songs that helped propel a distinguished group of gospel singers to national prominence. For example, his "Move on up a Little Higher" increased the fame of Mahalia Jackson; Clara Ward increased her following with her recording of Brewster's "How I Got Over"; and Marion Williams's gospel career received a tremendous boost from her recording of his "Surely God Is Able."

Second, his gospel drama *From Auction Block to Glory* (1941) crowns him as the father of this little-studied genre of Black religious expression. There were certainly Black religious dramas before Brewster's 1941 production. For example, Mahalia Jackson recalls performing in some of these pageants in her autobiography, which is entitled, appropriately enough, *Movin' on Up*:

It came about because at the Greater Salem Baptist Church the Johnson boys had formed a little singing and entertainment group. There were three brothers, Prince, Robert and Wilbur, a girl named Louis Barry, and myself.

Robert was only eighteen years old, but he was a spirited young man. He was like Sammy Davis, Jr.—just full of pep and energy all the time. He loved to sing and act. He was good at writing skits and directing them, and he had us putting on little plays for the church socials. One was called *Hellbound*; another was *From Earth to Glory* and another was *The Fatal Wedding*. He would play the husband, and I would play the wife and the others would play old folks and young folks. We cut up and had wonderful times and everybody enjoyed watching us. (Jackson 1966, 56–57)

However, what distinguished Brewster from such past Black religious dramatists as Reverend J. McCoo, who wrote *Ethiopia at the Bar of Justice*, and Mrs. Nannie Helen Burroughs, who wrote *Slabtown Convention*, is that he also composed the musical score for his plays. McCoo, Burroughs, and most other earlier playwrights fashioned their storylines to fit existing spirituals, gospel songs, and hymns. Brewster's compositional efforts in this regard sometimes met with startling success. For example, "Move on up a Little Higher" was a part of the musical score for his *From Auction Block to Glory.* "These Are They" and "How Far Am I from Canaan?," two other popular Brewster compositions, were also originally composed to be sung in one of his gospel dramas, *The Garden of Prayer.*

Brewster's genius of wedding gospel music to drama has been transferred to the American stage with memorable results by such Black American playwrights as Ossie Davis *(Purlie Victorious)*, Langston Hughes *(Tambourines to Glory)*, and Micki Grant *(Don't Bother Me, I Can't Cope)*. Dramas of this mold are all the creative offspring of Brewster's 1941 production of *From Auction Block to Glory.* This is further underscored by the fact that the Porter Singers recorded the soundtrack of Langston Hughes's *Tambourines to Glory*, with songs by Langston Hughes and Jobe Huntley, at Harlem's Second Canaan Baptist Church (Folkways FG 3538). In short, this highly successful Broadway musical was not out of place in the sanctuary of the Black church, which was also the original theater for all of Brewster's plays.

Another direct link between Brewster and this vibrant branch of the American theater is that Langston Hughes chose two gospel singers whose careers had benefited greatly from their singing some of Reverend Brewster's compositions. Marion Williams, who rose to fame in part on her recording of Brewster's "Surely God Is Able," was cast in the star role of Langston Hughes's gospel musical *Black Nativity*; and Clara Ward, whose recording of Brewster's "How I Got Over" had become a gospel classic, was the star in Hughes's gospel drama *Tambourines to Glory.*

The gospel dramas of Reverend William Herbert Brewster and Langston Hughes both spring from the common source of a much older Black religious tradition of fashioning folk pageants out of religious songs. Spirituals provided the plots and action for these earliest of Black religious dramas, which one folklorist aptly defined as "episodic performances which: (a) employ a variety of techniques to focus attention; (b) exist as public action of a small, community level group, sharing a system of understood motives and symbols; (c) have a foreknown resolution; and (d) are related to game, play, and ritual" (Bowman 1978). Black religious dramas that fit into this mold include *The Womanless Wedding, The Devil Play, The Old Ship of Zion, A Pageant of Birds, The Brideless Wedding, Noah's Ark, The Devil's Funeral,* and *Heaven Bound* (Wiggins 1976). These pageants, with one notable exception, traditionally were performed in Black churches.

Homemade props and handpainted backdrops were employed to turn the sanctuaries of Black churches into the dramas' sets. Sheets, old clothes, and other abandoned materials were refashioned into costumes for the characters.

There is some disagreement as to what these dramas' primary functions were. Fund-raising and social indoctrination have been two objectives of these productions. But most consistent with Brewster and the other Black religious-drama playwrights and their audiences has been the idea that these pageants functioned primarily as rituals of worship to save the souls of lost sinners. The following note, attached to an *Old Ship of Zion* program that I collected, underscores this fact. It reads in part: "We ask you to prayerfully observe and listen to the pageant for someday this will convert from drama to reality. If at anytime one of these songs touches you to the extent you would want a church home, . . . [we] will gladly accept you at Trinity or send you to a church of your choice" (Wiggins 1976). Mary A. Twining argues that these dramas served the twin functions of "airing certain social behaviors with an eye to controlling them" and providing "a socially acceptable outlet for people's opinions of each other's actions" (Twining 1976, 347–51). Debbie Bowman contends that these dramas produced "a collective spiritual expression" that is at the heart of the African American cultural notion of "community orientation" (Bowman 1978).

In 1931, *Heaven Bound* became the first of these religious pageants to be taken from its original church setting and performed on a professional stage before a racially mixed audience: *Heaven Bound* was staged in the Savannah Municipal Auditorium (Popkin 1931, 14–17). Six years later, the Federal Theater Project of Atlanta produced two productions of *Heaven Bound* on the Atlanta Theater's stage. The Project staff was under the direction of Sol Miroff, the technical advisor, and Julian Harris, who was responsible for the "costumes, set, and adaptation" (Sugg 1963, 251–61). The first three-day engagement opened on August 10, 1937; the second two-week run began on January 3, 1938.

Since the dawn of the twentieth century, American theater audiences had been entertained by numerous Black American "folk dramas" or dramas of "self-celebration," which had been described as being "the fusion of a sketchy plot, song, and dance" (Hay 1973, 5–8). Marshall and Jean Stearns trace Bert Williams's cakewalk routine in the play *In Dahomey* (1902) back to the ring shout, a Black religious dance with heavy African influences (Stearns and Stearns 1966, 251). It was performed at such religious services as the "watch meetings" where African American Christians gathered to observe the passage of an old year and the beginning of a new one. The ring shout dance ritual performed during these celebrations has been described thusly: "a little before midnight, someone starts shuffling and singing 'Tear Down the Walls of Zion, Goin' to see My Lord' and everybody puts his hands on the hips of the person in front of him and inches forward in a circle with a rocking motion" (Stearns and Stearns 1966, 251). One of the more popular of these spiritual-based dramas was Hall Johnson's *Run, Little Chillun* (1933).

The second year of the next decade, Brewster initiated a dramatic change in the African American religious drama tradition with his pioneering production of *From Auction Block to Glory* at the 1941 annual meeting of the National Baptist Convention. On the surface, little would suggest that this production would turn out to be a watershed event in African American religious culture. In fact, the officers and members of the Convention were so impressed with the play that they named Brewster as head of its drama department.

Brewster talked about his early work in gospel drama and some of the motivation behind his interest in this form of ritual worship:

I was a young preacher and called to pastor a church that had been split. In order to do something different that would impress more people, or more different categories, I started dramatizing my sermons. I improvised a Garden of Eden scene. I had the members go to the country and bring me some trees. I got one tree and went down to get a couple of automobile inner tubes. I took those inner tubes and cut them in two and because they were naturally round I had to cut them in sections. We had to straighten them out and put the curve in them for snakes. I put it together, got me some beads and made their eyes. I put their tongues in their mouths, and I was able to inflate that tire and wrap it around that tree. They helped me to make a stream of water. Then after I had put that snake in that tree, I had apples all over it, and I had different fruits on the other trees. That was in the church background.

It was unorthodox, but I never did go much for the orthodox anyhow. Putting these plays on was a great help to me. It came near the time of the Depression, and people could not go anywhere. We would hold these plays for churches and give them half of the proceeds, and people would give those dimes and quarters and be there. A dime went a long way, you know.

That was the real beginning of my musical career so far as writing is concerned. I started writing those songs for the plays. If I couldn't find a song, I wrote one. (Reagon 1982)

The African American community in general was very receptive to these religious pageants. National recognition was achieved through nationally based religious organizations. In 1924 Reverend James McCoo, an African Methodist Episcopal (AME) minister, presented his pageant *Ethiopia at the Bar of Justice* at the General Conference of his AME denomination. McCoo's pageant proved so successful it was later performed during Negro History Week celebrations around the country for several years after its debut. It was also anthologized in a collection of Negro plays and pageants (Richardson 1930). As late as 1971, William Walker, a Baptist minister in Chicago, copyrighted *Heaven Bound* and sold copies of his drama, just as McCoo had done several decades earlier (Richards 1982, 79–81). However, McCoo's and Walker's productions were not innovative; they did not expand the creative horizons of the traditional Black religious drama. Like many other playwrights before and since them, they borrowed the music in their pageants from the Black American song chest. McCoo used patriotic songs, Protestant hymns, and slave spirituals to fashion his pageant, while Walker's version of *Heaven Bound* relied solely upon the spirituals.

Brewster's religious pageant *From Auction Block to Glory*, however, shattered all of these old dramatic molds; his play placed the old wine of salvation through Christ in an attractive new wineskin. *From Auction Block to Glory* was the first nationally staged Black religious drama that featured gospel songs written to be sung during that production. The composing of gospel songs for a specific occasion was not new when Reverend Brewster wrote his play. For example, Reverend Charles Albert Tindley, the prolific gospel song-ster, wrote songs to enhance specific sermons he preached during the first quarter of this century in his Philadelphia church. Brewster was the first Black religious playwright to apply this principle to playwrighting.

To be sure, earlier Black religious pageant playwrights may have attempted to integrate urban gospel music into the older spiritual dramas. During the late 1920s, Mahalia Jack-son, the queen of gospel music, toured the Midwestern states with the Chicago-based Johnson Gospel Singers. The troupe put on religious plays such as *Hellbound, From Earth to Glory,* and *The Fatal Wedding,* which were written by the director, Robert Johnson, and featured him and Miss Jackson in the leading roles (Heilbut 1985, 60). With all of this creative smoke, it seems not too much to assume that the spiritual fire of gospel songs flamed bright in Black religious dramas.

However, it is Brewster, more than any other gospel composer-playwright, who was able to fashion a new Black religious drama tradition that used the individually written gospel song instead of the group-composed spiritual for the plot, symbols, and action of a church drama. Brewster's East Trigg Baptist Church was his experimental gospel drama theater; until his death, he regularly put on gospel dramas for his congregation and the larger Black Memphis community (Heilbut 1985, 99). *The Rejected Stone*, a passion play; *Deep Dark Waters*, whose theme was the destructive nature of drugs; and *These Our Children*, a gospel drama of parental thanksgiving, are just three of the numerous gospel dramas that Brewster staged one Sunday out of the month in his church (Wiggins 1981).

In talking about his passion play, Brewster revealed strong opinion about another pro-duction he had seen:

. . . a Black Hill group came here and had the passion play in the auditorium. . . . I didn't like what the Black Hill passion play showed because it wasn't authentic. It was not biblical enough. So I wrote one and made it a musical dramatization. . . .

I wrote the play called *Via Dolorosa*. I wrote a description of Jesus coming down on a cobble-stone street. It means the street of pain. The way of pain and the way of sorrow. That's the Latin name for it. I do the chorus on it. I quote it; I dramatize it. . . .

I had a chant that swelled into great crescendos until it became "anthematic" and it told a story. Then behind it, I had "Out on a Hill." "Some man led like a sheep, with a heavy cross and wounded deep." It describes them, "Out on a hill like a sheep, enough to make the angels weep." Then the next thing was the same description of what happened on Calvary. That is when I had my passion play. (Reagon 1982)

Perhaps the most impressive evidence of Brewster's stature as a pioneer in the writing of Black religious pageants is the impact of his songs and plays upon Langston Hughes and other major African American playwrights. Hughes's *Black Nativity* (1961) proved to be just as seminal a work for Black gospel-based drama on the American stage as Brew-ster's *From Auction Block to Glory* (1941) had proven to be for Black religious drama. Once again it must be noted that Hughes was not the only American playwright who wrote dramas for the American stage that drew heavily upon the Black church's gospel tradition. The same year that he produced his seminal drama, Ossie Davis's *Purlie Victorious* opened on Broadway to critical acclaim that resulted in its being filmed, duplicating the earlier success of Marc Connelly's *The Green Pastures* (1930).

Like Brewster, Hughes was a prolific writer of this dramatic form. In addition to the works mentioned earlier, Hughes also wrote these other gospel-based dramas: *Adam and Eve and the Apple* (n.d.), *Christmas with Christ* (1962; Hatch and Abdullah 1977, 116–17); *Gospel Glow* (1962); *Jericho-Jim Crow* (1963); and *The Prodigal Son* (1965; O'Daniel 1971, 218). And, like Brewster, Hughes has had a lasting creative influence upon his fellow playwrights. Hughes's greatest impact on the American theater can be observed in the works of Vinnette Carroll, the director of *Black Nativity*, and Micki Grant, the actress who played the role of Marietta Johnson in *Tambourines to Glory*. This latter-day Mary and Martha playwrighting tandem did not have much success as individual playwrights. Micki Grant's *The Prodigal Sister* (1974), an upbeat parody of the traditional Black folk character, the Prodigal Son, and Vinnette Carroll's *Trumpets of the Lord* (n.d.), an adaptation from James Weldon Johnson's *God's Trombones*, were received with very little acclaim. Their gospel song play collaborations, however, have been another story. *Don't Bother Me, I Can't Cope* (1970) and *Your Arms Too Short to Box With God* (1976) both enjoyed successful Broadway runs and extended national tours. Grant and Carroll have truly proven themselves to be gospel song playwright disciples worthy of their pioneering mentor.

What is the common denominator that William Herbert Brewster, the Baptist minister from Memphis, and Langston Hughes, the New York writer, share? I conclude that both playwrights share an appreciation for the storytelling dimension of African American verbal expression. Furthermore, both seemed able to divine that this type of expression best exhibits itself in traditional Black religious songs and narratives. As Mary A. Twining notes, "The West African story telling sessions are found in the New World as folk sermons complete with the responses from the audience, dramatic reenactment, singing interpolated into the body of the recitation, etc." (Twining 1970, 59). Twining also contends that the individual Blacks who make up the congregation for these folk sermons are not passive receivers of the biblical story. She notes that they tell stories, too: "In the church, the stories, biblical and religious, told by the preacher are admired and imitated in the Tarry services, testimonials and prayers echoed by members of the congregation. Each person tells his own story in a combination of personally generated vocabulary and formulaic phrase" (Twining 1970, 57).

Hughes's full-length musical drama *The Sun Do Move* (1942) and Brewster's gospel song "As the Eagle Stirreth Her Nest" both take their titles from popular Black folk sermons. Proper delivery of these two narrations requires that the preacher be able to describe the scene and act out the plot in body movement and dialogue. The former trait has long been observed as a part of the Black preacher's narrative style. W. E. B. Du Bois wrote that the plantation "Negro priest . . . expressed, rudely but picturesquely, the longings and disappointment and resentment of a stolen people" (McGhee 1969, 51). Hortense Spillers expressed similar sentiments in her description of Martin Luther King, Jr.'s preaching style: "Modification (adjectiveness) and nominality in King combine to create a picturesqueness and grandness of speech that were his hallmark" (Spillers 1971, 17). A hearer of one of John Jasper's sermons wrote that this legendary Black Baptist preacher described the ascension of Elijah in a way "so thrilling that everything was as plain as open day." And Jasper, ever the actor, became Elijah as the old prophet reaches the outskirts of heaven: "In the fraction of a second Jasper was transmuted into Elijah and was actually in the chariot and singing with extraordinary power the old chorus: 'Going up to heaven in a chariot of fire.' The scene was overmastering!" (McGhee 1969, 60).

Hughes and Brewster clearly saw Black gospel music as a viable transmitter of the Black traditional sermon's dramatic qualities. Brewster, the pioneer of the Black sacred pageant, defined the music that he composed for his dramas thusly: "A gospel song is a sermon set to music" (Heilbut 1985, 98). Hughes cited "gospel singing" as the genesis of *Tambourines to Glory* and expressed a desire to produce his play "before gospel singing gets so commercial Mitch [Miller] will have it" (Nichols 1963, X3). Brewster's *From Auction Block to Glory* and Hughes's *Black Nativity* are filled with original gospel songs that Pearl Williams-Jones defines as "a colorful kaleidoscope of black oratory, poetry, drama and dance" whose characters gave life to her description of the Black gospel singer as "the lyrical extension of the gospel preacher" (Williams-Jones 1975, 382). Brewster's gospel drama and Hughes's gospel song play may have reached different audiences, but they are both pioneers of the Black sacred-pageant tradition.

6

ROBERTA MARTIN
(1907–1969)

~

ROBERTA MARTIN

Spirit of an Era

Pearl Williams-Jones

Roberta Martin was the spiritual and artistic embodiment of Black American gospel music and one of its most articulate and influential exponents. Among the gospel pioneers of the 1930s, most of whom were her senior contemporaries, Miss Martin stands out as a major innovator. Her rare combination of skills soon set her apart from other gospel musicians of her era. Not only did she excel as a singer, pianist, composer, arranger, and organizer of groups and choirs, but she went on to found and operate what became the largest gospel music publishing house in Chicago. As gospel historian Clayton L. Hannah wrote in his liner notes to the 1979 Savoy album *The Best of the Roberta Martin Singers* (Savoy SGL 7018), "Although Thomas A. Dorsey is credited as the originator of gospel music, and Mahalia Jackson received the highest acclaim, Roberta Martin unequivocally made the greatest contribution. She created and left a dynasty of gospel singers and a portfolio of unduplicated gospel music" (Hannah 1979).

The Roberta Martin sound defined an entire musical era. Inspired by Thomas A. Dorsey and Sallie Martin, Martin began composing and arranging songs that author Anthony Heilbut has described as combining "the Baptist moan of her Arkansas childhood with the Dorsey bounce, the sanctified churches' syncopation, and a smidgeon of semiclassical pretension" (Heilbut 1973). This unique combination of musical elements standardized what became known as classic gospel music.

According to her younger brother, the late Fontaine Winston, Roberta Martin, born on February 12, 1907, in Helena, Arkansas, was one of six children of Anna and William Winston. When she was ten, her family migrated to Chicago. Martin graduated from Wendell Phillips High School, where she was encouraged in her musical studies by her piano teacher, Mildred Bryant Jones (Jackson 1979, 89). Martin's first church position was as pianist for the Young People's Choir of Ebenezer Baptist Church. There she worked with Thomas A. Dorsey and Theodore Frye, both of whom helped guide her early career. In 1933, with the help of Dorsey and Frye, Roberta Martin organized the Martin-Frye Quartet with Eugene Smith, James Lawrence, Robert Anderson, Willie Webb, and Norsalus McKissick. This group became the Roberta Martin Singers in 1936. In the mid–1940s, the group was expanded to include two female singers, Bessie Folk and Delois Barrett Campbell. Until the late 1940s, Miss Martin sang, played, and traveled with the group. She then devoted her energies to writing, arranging, and managing her publishing business. She also served from 1956 until 1968 as music director of Mount Pisgah Baptist Church (Boyer 1964b, 13). When she died on January 18, 1969, after a long illness, more than fifty thousand Black Americans participated in her memorial service, giving testimony to the *Chicago Courier*'s declaration of Roberta Martin as "an institution in her own time" (Jackson 1979, 122).

THE RECONSTRUCTION CONCERTS

In the summer of 1980, Bernice Johnson Reagon asked me to serve as director of a reconstruction concert series that would explore the musical legacy of Roberta Martin and the Roberta Martin Singers. Our aim was to describe an era in gospel music and the place of Roberta Martin within that era.

Much of the patterns and customs of Black America's culture remains in oral tradition. The concerts and rehearsals would offer a rare opportunity to view the inner workings of the oral-transmission process. They would present a visual synthesis of Black American gospel performance practices and enable us to observe the symbols of continuity in the Black gospel music tradition. The concerts would highlight the generative force and creative energy that gospel music has brought to American music. We also decided that a colloquium that brought the singers together with gospel music researchers and scholars would increase the ways in which the audience could observe and participate in this important cultural experience.

The progeny of Roberta Martin—the Singers—would perform, and other gospel artists and music lovers who came under the Martin influence would share remembrances and techniques of classic gospel performance. This weekend would honor the pioneering musical contributions of Roberta Martin and would provide an introduction to the gospel music idiom as well as an opportunity to conduct primary research in the performance practices, aesthetic norms, and song styles of Black American gospel music.

The practical aspects of this venture began around the piano of the Martin Luther King Center, which adjoins Chicago's Mount Pisgah Baptist Church. On a wintry November afternoon in 1980, six musical disciples of Roberta Martin whose combined skills had defined an entire musical era gathered for their first rehearsal and reassembly from semi-retirement in many years.

Lucy ("Little Lucy") Smith Collier no longer played the piano but supervised the repertoire selection and rehearsal procedures. Eugene Smith maintained his varied roles as business manager, tenor soloist, and the most incomparable of all gospel narrators. They were joined by Delois Barrett Campbell, Bessie Folk, Gloria Griffin, and Archie Dennis. The years had not diminished the spirit and enthusiasm of the Singers. Their voices easily adjusted to the familiar repertoire they had sung for more than thirty years across the United States and Europe as they pioneered the unique and magnificent Roberta Martin songs and style. At this rehearsal, the Singers were accompanied by gospel pianist Richard Smallwood of Washington, D.C. As a child, the first piano style Smallwood learned to play was the Martin/Collier style. This made him a natural choice as accompanist, and he was quickly able to recreate the sound and style of the Roberta Martin Singers' piano. It was astonishing to watch the ideas and techniques come into place again and to sense history in the remaking.

Because Roberta Martin had attracted and maintained a consistent roster of excellent musicians, recapturing the authenticity of her style was never problematical. Stylistic innovations have come into gospel music since the Martin era, but the Martin Singers who gathered for this rehearsal quickly reestablished the boundaries that framed the Martin sound. They had, after all, been the first all-star gospel ensemble in which each member of the group was both soloist and stylist. Every concert featured each singer's special repertoire performed with a collective resonance, a vocal sheen, a professionalism, and, above all, a spiritual intensity that reflected the mentor, Roberta Martin.

THE ROBERTA MARTIN SOUND

"That's the Roberta Martin sound, as only they can do it: rich, restful, and righteous," commented gospel announcer and promoter Joe Bostic (Williams-Jones 1980). And indeed, Roberta Martin and the Roberta Martin Singers have seldom been equaled and never surpassed in their development and mastery of classic gospel group singing. Their rhythmic and passionate performances reflected a rare degree of professionalism and control. As Horace Clarence Boyer noted, Martin's style was one of refinement (Boyer 1979a, 32). In a philosophical sense, the musical style served the spiritual message by the superior musical offering. Irene Jackson-Brown stated that "Miss Martin created a school—a way of playing, singing, and arranging the then-new music called gospel" (Jackson 1979, 140).

The Roberta Martin sound was achieved through Martin's original combination of male and female vocal timbres. This was in marked contrast to other gospel groups of the late 1930s and early 1940s, which tended to be all-male, such as the quartets, or all female, such as the Sallie Martin Singers or the Clara Ward Singers. Omitting the bass line identified with quartet singing and older forms of Black choral music, Miss Martin successfully integrated the vocal texture of the female high soprano, second soprano, and alto with the male first and second tenors and the baritone.

The unique harmonic sound created by this particular voicing was mellow and smooth, with dynamic nuances that ebbed and flowed and a timing that was almost imperceptibly "behind" the beat. Martin's own misty contralto quality, described by Anthony Heilbut as "refined, subdued, achieving its greatest effects through timing and phrasing" (Heilbut 1985, 10), colored the group's sound. There was a power reserve that could surge forth when needed for the more up-tempo shout songs. The blending of male and female voices in complementary fashion was accomplished by the superior musicianship each singer brought to the group. The Singers listened to one another and assimilated their individual parts in a semi-improvised freedom that belied the strong part-singing that actually took place.

The unifying element of the Martin piano style was the rhythmic and harmonically colorful chord progressions of Martin and, later, Lucy Smith Collier. In analyzing her piano style, Boyer paid particular attention to Martin's percussive octaves in the left hand and her less rigid, more complex use of chords (Boyer 1979a, 32). The piano playing was the foundation of the vocal parts, underscoring the group's rich harmonies. The piano did not merely provide background; it was an integral and integrating force in the performance, supplying accompaniment, rhythm, and effects. The pianist could propel the momentum of a song, heightening the drama by tremolos in the bass line or by responding to a call from a singer. Piano introductions, usually played while the narrator introduced or "talked up" the songs, set the mood for the singer.

THE ROBERTA MARTIN SONGS AND THE GOSPEL MUSIC PUBLISHING INDUSTRY

Roberta Martin composed approximately seventy songs. Many more bear her distinctive style of arrangement. Her lyrics are of personal witnessing or testimonies offering reassurance and consolation. The poetry of the gospel classic "Try Jesus," published by Martin in 1943, is an example of the personalization and right to individual interpretation conveyed by the new gospel songwriters (ex. 51):

> Come unto Jesus all ye that labor
> All that are weary worn and defiled
> Bring Him your burdens seek now His favor
> Tell Him your sorrows in Him confide
>
> Come unto Jesus don't waste a moment
> Your time so precious is fleeting by
> All your transgressions freely confessing
> He in His mercy He safely will hide

Chorus
He satisfies, He satisfies
Oh, if you let Him in your heart abide. . . .
Won't you try Jesus
He satisfies

While the verses stay within the bounds of nineteenth-century gospel hymnody, the basic theme, "Won't you try Jesus for He satisfies," humanizes the relationship between Savior and believer. The concept of Jesus giving satisfaction expresses the "everydayness" of the message the new songwriters and singers felt they were carrying.

The chorus to "God Is Still on the Throne," another Martin standard, published in 1959, takes the point further (ex. 52):

When in distress, just call Him
If you're oppressed, just call Him
When storms assail you and others have failed you
Yes, God is still on the throne.

Chorus
God is still on the throne
Within your bosom you have the phone
Where e're you walk you're not walking alone
Remember God is still on the throne

Roberta Martin and her contemporaries snatched the Christian message into an age of technology—of telephone, wire services, record players, and radios. With imagery like "Within your bosom you have the phone," songwriters urged believers not only to use religion for anything they needed but to bring the equipment of modern technology into the process.

Gospel music singing had its beginning in the same period as the recording industry. In the 1920s, when the industry began to give attention to Black American music, it focused in the religious field on gospel quartets and a few gospel soloists (Arizona Dranes and Blind Mamie Forehand) and Black preachers and congregations such as Rev. J. M. Gates, Elder McGhee, Elder Charles Beck, and Elder Michaux. It was not until the late 1930s that recordings of the new gospel singers/songwriters began to appear. Hymnals such as the *Gospel Pearls*, first issued by the National Baptist Convention in 1921, were the main vehicle for getting out new songs. The harmonies were traditional with standard four-part voicings. In the 1940s, gospel sheet music began to replace the *Gospel Pearls*, offering a way to supplement an essentially oral musical tradition. In addition to the words, sheet music provided more elaborate chords and arrangements than found in the *Gospel Pearls*.

Thomas A. Dorsey pioneered the concept of selling gospel sheet music. He found that performances of his music at the National Baptist Convention, then the major vehicle for spreading Black sacred music repertoire, triggered demand for copies of his songs. For

Example 51.   "Try Jesus" (Roberta Martin). Used by permission of Leonard Austin.

Example 51. *(continued)*

Example 51.   *(continued)*

Example 52. "God Is Still on the Throne" (Roberta Martin). Used by permission of Leonard Austin.

Example 52.   *(continued)*

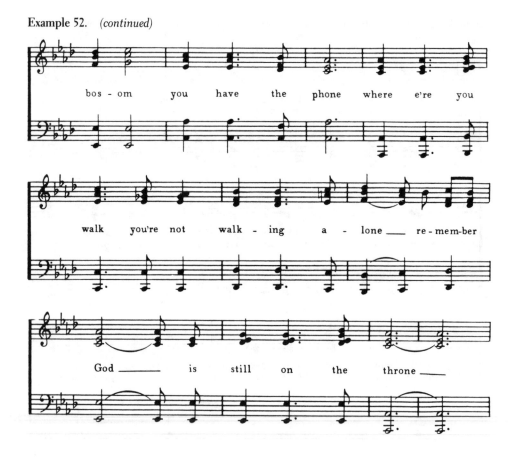

bos - om   you   have   the   phone   where   e're   you

walk   you're not   walk - ing   a - lone ___ re - mem-ber

God ___   is   still   on   the   throne ___

many years after, Dorsey and other gospel songwriters traveled extensively, promoting their song sales through the performances of gospel singers. Eugene Smith, as business manager of the Roberta Martin Singers, made annual trips to the major conventions of various denominations to meet the growing demand for gospel sheet music (Williams-Jones 1980).

The gospel literature, while capturing the basic structure of the songwriter's or arranger's compositional style, did not capture or document the performance style of the singers. A gospel song cannot be realized from the written page. It is only in performance that it has a life. When a songwriter such as Dorsey wrote a song and committed it to paper, one could see the relationship between Dorsey's compositional style and the hymn structure. One could see the influence of the call-and-response tradition. Since gospel music is primarily an oral experience, Dorsey used a special technique to sell his songs. He always brought along a demonstrator (usually Sallie Martin and later Mahalia Jackson) so that the buyer would have the sheet music providing lyrics, basic compositional structure, chords, and rhythmic suggestions and a memory of the live performance.

Roberta Martin took this union of written and oral forms to its highest level. The Roberta Martin Singers represented a performance sound, colors, vocal textures, principles of harmonic blendings, dynamics, relationships between soloists and background that could not be perceived from the literature. Gospel music literature took an element that is the antithesis of the oral tradition—written musical notation—and made it an instrument of that tradition, using it to help carry out the oral process. Often the oral process—recreating the music by ear—won out over purchasing sheet music. Dorsey bemoaned the fact that Black gospel choirs often would buy only one copy of his music and teach an entire choir by rote, while white groups would buy individual copies for each member of the choir (Dorsey 1980). For a proper reading of gospel sheet music, one needed to hear and, preferably, see a live performance. In performance, the songs were expanded into extensive improvisations not indicated on the sheet music. The singers' interpretations would actually create the song.

The Roberta Martin Singers' repertoire, Martin's compositions, and her arrangements of other songwriters' works represented a catalogue of gospel sheet music literature. Songs of James Cleveland, Alex Bradford, Willie Webb, Robert Anderson, and Lucy Smith Collier invariably had the Roberta Martin sound for which the Singers were noted. These songs were usually assured of wide distribution and good sales because they were sung by the Robert Martin Singers. When the Singers arrived in town for a concert or revival, they sold hundreds of copies of their music. Martin's arrangement of the spiritual "Didn't It Rain" was one of their best sellers. During the 1940s and 1950s, the popular gospel song sheets were modestly priced at fifteen, twenty, or thirty cents a song, with books of sixty-four pages usually selling for a dollar or a dollar and one-half. In Washington, D.C., the most memorable seller of gospel sheet music was an elderly street vendor, Noble Wiley. During the 1940s, Wiley would arrive in front of a church where gospel music was to be performed and spread his music over the sidewalks so that people could view the songs by gasoline lantern.

By the mid–1940s, Chicago was the home of several gospel music publishing houses. The best known—those owned by Lillian Bowles and Theodore Frye; Thomas A. Dorsey, Sallie Martin and Kenneth Morris; and Roberta Martin—were able to create a thriving market from the sale of sheet music of songs performed by traveling gospel singers. Begun in 1939 by Martin, who gained her knowledge of the music publishing business from her association with Dorsey and Frye, the studio prospered and was expanded from its original quarters on Sixty-fourth and East Forty-third Street to East Forty-seventh Street. In 1979, following the retirement of manager Leona Price, James Austin, Martin's widower, consolidated and relocated the business to Forty-sixth and King Drive (Jackson 1979, 100–102).

Through her prominence in the field of gospel music publishing, Roberta Martin ensured that her songs reached the thousands of gospel performers in churches throughout the United States. The proliferation of her music provided a continuous supply of fresh musical ideas that singers were expected to interpret in the classic Martin gospel style. "God Specializes" (ex. 53) is an example of Martin's sheet music design and layout, using one of the most famous songs performed by the Roberta Martin Singers. Virtually every Black church copied the choral style set by the Roberta Martin Singers, utilizing their sheet music, recordings, and live performances.

THE ROBERTA MARTIN RECORDINGS

The Roberta Martin Singers began their recording career during the 1940s on the Apollo label. Much of this early material appears as a 1979 Kenwood Records reissue, *The Roberta Martin Singers: The Old Ship of Zion* (Kenwood 507). The group's most prolific recording period was from the mid–1950s to the mid–1960s, when they recorded for Savoy Records. These albums contain Martin's best-known compositions and arrangements and capture, to the best ability of the technology of the time, her voice and pianistic artistry and the classic performances of each of the superb soloists. Along with the sheet music and live performances, the recordings helped spread the Roberta Martin sound.

Example 53. "God Specializes" (Gloria Griffin), one of the most famous songs performed by the Roberta Martin Singers. Used by permission of Leonard Austin.

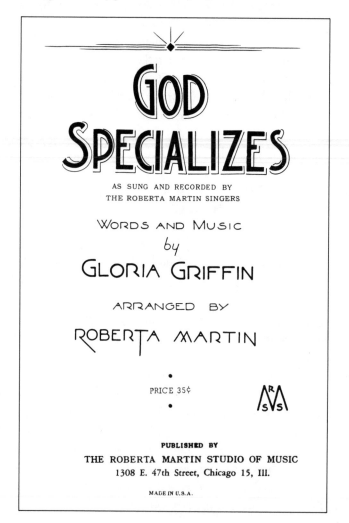

Example 53. *(continued)*

Example 53. *(continued)*

Example 53. *(continued)*

Go back to sign, sing all three
verses before ending

1. Body filled with de-sease and your medicine Don't give you ease If there's
2. Troubles in your home and your enemies Won't leave you alone If you're
3. Friendless and in dis - pair when nobody seem to care I know

God specializes God specializes God specializes God specializes

Ending

God God I tell you God

God spe-ci-al-iz-es God spe-ci-al-iz-es God spe-ci-al-iz-es

God And He will do what no

God spe-ci-al-iz-es And He will do

oth-er pow'r can do.

what no oth-er pow'r no oth-er pow'r can do.

When the Roberta Martin Singers began to record on Savoy, their strong concert and revival appearances had already secured their position within the African American community as the finest gospel singers of the day. The recordings served primarily to document that preeminence. The severe time limitation on recordings and the lack of an audience hampered the recorded performances. The industry's technology required a standard recording time of two and one-half to three minutes per selection. This precluded the stretching out and ritualization, the going beyond an initial statement with extended improvisations and solos that are basic components of live gospel performance. Despite these limitations, the Roberta Martin Singers were more successful than most artists of their era, and their recordings have both musical and historical value. While one often misses the interaction with congregations and concert audiences, the group's style, artistry, and spiritual fervor are captured.

A hint of the glory that could be revealed when congregation and Singers interacted occurred in the live recording *From out of Nowhere* (Savoy MG 14066), made at the First Baptist Church of Nutley, New Jersey, pastored by Reverend Lawrence Roberts. "I'm So Grateful," performed by Gloria Griffin and "Little Lucy," brought ten to twelve minutes of gospel exuberance, unbridled, unmuffled, and unstifled by time considerations and artificial distractions. Here was gospel performance at its best, with the singers turning loose. This live recording also vividly documents the sermonette-style introductions of Eugene Smith, introductions as riveting as the songs that followed.

THE ROBERTA MARTIN SINGERS

The Roberta Martin Singers were among the most widely traveled of all the major gospel singing groups of the 1940s and 1950s. They were a major part of the gospel music tide that spread across the United States, from Chicago to the East and then to the West. Prior to their retirement in the mid–1960s, the Singers had sung to unanimous critical acclaim in major concert halls, stadiums, churches, and festivals, and on radio and television here and in Europe.

In 1945, the Singers could earn over three thousand dollars a week for a revival in California (Heilbut 1985, xxix). In Washington, D.C., they were headliners at the old Griffith Stadium, singing before audiences of over five thousand. In 1959, the Roberta Martin Singers were the featured artists of "The World's Greatest Gospel Caravan," a cavalcade of music held at Los Angeles's Shrine Auditorium. In 1962, they topped the gospel headline of Joe Bostic's gospel music festival held at Randall's Island, New York. There they received the prestigious Thomas A. Dorsey award, presented each year to honor outstanding contributions to gospel music. In 1963, the group was featured before thousands at the New York Coliseum, appearing with other gospel luminaries such as Mahalia Jackson, Reverend James Cleveland, and the Caravans. For two consecutive years in the 1960s, the Singers appeared before an audience drawn primarily from the world of classical music as the only gospel performing ensemble at Italy's Spoleto Festival of Two Worlds. With mounting international recognition, the Roberta Martin Singers returned to Chicago to fill Wrigley Field for their anniversary celebration. In 1974, they were headliners at Detroit's Cobo Arena (Williams-Jones 1980). Theirs is an impressive account of gospel singers who maintained in every situation the dignity and the integrity of their art and the Christian principles from which it developed.

The Roberta Martin concerts were always professional, polished, and spirited. It was in their revival services, however, that the essential measure of their performing greatness was revealed. The song revivals functioned in the same manner as revival services conducted by evangelists. In fact, long before gospel singing became a performance medium for the concert stage, the basic function of the gospel singer was evangelistic. According to Thomas A. Dorsey, the term *evangelistic song* originally described the musical function of the songs now called gospel music (Dorsey 1980). The singers were "singing evangelists" whose purpose was to save souls by declaring the gospel in a song. The creator and shapers of this music said clearly that theirs was much more than a new music form. They saw themselves as ministers, as carriers of the gospel message through the singing of songs. Anthony Heilbut quotes a member of the Roberta Martin Singers as having said, "I heard somebody say the minister's the man because nobody ever got saved off singing. That's not so; singing has saved many souls" (Heilbut 1985, xxxi). Martin herself had strong feelings about the meaning of her musical ministry. In an interview with Irene Jackson-Brown, James Austin recalled Martin's words to her group: "I'm not entertaining the world. I'm singing the gospel just like they preach the gospel and people don't have to go to the theater to hear the gospel" (Jackson 1979, 126).

Throughout the 1950s, the Roberta Martin Singers came to Washington, D.C.'s Bible Way Church for an annual two-week revival. Their coming was anticipated by rituals, and the procedure for the revival service seldom deviated. The pianist would declaim the first chords, an evocation of the mood and spirit, in a slow, dramatic, speechlike manner (ex. 54):

> Only a look at Jesus
> O soul bowed down with care
> He has promised to defend thee
> He will all your burdens share

In a moderately slow, deliberately paced performance, the first stirrings and promise of the spirit to come were announced by six male and female voices:

> Only a look
> Only a look

When Eugene Smith interpolated the rhetorical question "Then why not," and the group responded with "Turn ye away from sin," the saints were ready to rejoice, and many of the sinners were ready to repent!

Example 54. "Only a Look" (Anna Shepherd), a classic opening song for the Roberta Martin Singers. Used by permission of Leonard Austin.

Example 54. *(continued)*

Following the theme song, the piano immediately went into the introduction of a rhythmic, up-tempo song that would be sung by the entire group led by any one of the six soloists. The tempo of the service increased with hand-clapping, foot-patting, and a few souls standing up to continue expressing themselves in the spirit. The entire group would then be seated while Eugene Smith, with preacher-style narration, explicated the theme and meaning of the next song. He recounted the common experiences of all the saints of God—trials, tribulations, joys, sorrows—and thematically related his remarks to the next song, which would feature another soloist backed up by the Singers. Smith, unequaled in his spirited gospel rhetoric and expressive energy, moved the church into spiritual ecstasy. With a voice of unusual amplitude and vibrancy, he talked until he made the church "happy" and himself too. He would run in the aisles, stomp his feet, or, as gospel people say, "Let the spirit have its way." Each song in the service carried a message of inspiration, a call to Christian discipleship, hope, and love. Each singer led one of the carefully arranged Martin songs that was especially suited to his or her voice and temperament. At the conclusion of these evangelistic song services, the pastor would make an altar call, and converts would come forward in response to the singing ministry of the Roberta Martin Singers.

Night after night during the revivals, the Singers would bring fresh music, new spirit, and enthusiasm that was matched by a responding congregation who had come to hear the "sermon in song." No further preaching was necessary. The singing revivalists had invoked every element of the religious service that was needed for revival and salvation. Other groups of gospel singers would offer a one-night program or service, but the Roberta Martin Singers were the undisputed masters of the gospel revival.

The life and work of Roberta Martin and the Roberta Martin Singers exemplify African American creativity and originality enriching world culture. Roberta Martin was the spirit of an era. It is an era that has not passed. Today, within African American communities where gospel music is nurtured and practiced as a way of life, hundreds of groups and choirs continue to maintain the repertoire and performing style created by Roberta Martin.

ROBERTA MARTIN

Innovator of Modern Gospel Music

Horace Clarence Boyer

In 1933, Roberta Martin organized a pioneering gospel group whose mark on the evolution of gospel music has been so great that it is necessary to look at the Roberta Martin choral style to understand classic gospel singing. The Roberta Martin Singers had a sound that was clearly a unique marriage of African elements—energy, intricate yet organized rhythms, spontaneous melodic investigation, that perennial need for tribal participation (we call it an ensemble)—and Western European elements—harmony, form, and order. They accomplished what the Western world sought to do in the classical period: they effectively combined emotion with style.

Unlike many gospel singers of today, Roberta Evelyn Winston, who began life in the first decade of this century in the little town of Helena, Arkansas, was not familiar with that new kind of music in the Holiness churches that was called gospel music. As a toddler, she sat at the piano and picked out tunes. Shortly thereafter, she became a piano student of her oldest brother's wife and concentrated on standard piano literature including Bach, Beethoven, and Brahms. She continued in this direction after the family moved from Arkansas to Cairo, Illinois, and then to Chicago. She was destined for a career as a concert pianist or a professional accompanist.

It was not until 1933 that Roberta Martin heard gospel music for the first time and decided she liked it:

275

I've been playing in churches nearly all my life, ever since I was so high. I started down at Pilgrim [Baptist Church] where I was the pianist for the Sunday School. At that time I was just interested in church hymns, anthems, choir music and secular songs. The first time I heard gospel singing, as such, was this lady and these men—Bertha Wise and her singers. Miss Wise played the piano for them. They came to our church, and oh, did we enjoy them. Actually, they were very famous—they would go around to the National Baptist Convention and sing. They were not exactly singing gospel songs but spirituals like gospel songs and the one that interested me most was "I Can Tell The World about This." This was in 1933. (Boyer 1964b)

Theodore R. Frye (1899–1963) and Thomas A. Dorsey (b. 1899) were directing a junior choir, and they asked Martin to serve as accompanist. In recalling that audition, she said that she knew only one gospel song, which she sang and played. They loved it, and she got the job at five dollars a Sunday. She said that if they had asked for another song, she would have had to play "Without a Song" (Boyer 1964b).

When she was finally persuaded by Frye and Dorsey to adopt gospel music, she brought with her a love, knowledge, and performance skill in standard hymns, anthems, spirituals, secular songs, and, of course, the master works of Western Europe she had studied for fifteen years. This knowledge and skill were reflected in the sources from which she compiled her repertoire. Standard hymns are represented by "Standing on the Promises" and "Be Still My Soul," the latter being a paraphrase of Jean Sibelius's tone poem "Finlandia." Though she did not record anthems, the group sang them. She even persuaded Delois Barrett Campbell (b. 1926) and the Barrett Sisters to record "God So Loved the World" from Sir John Stainer's oratorio "The Crucifixion." Spirituals figured prominently in her repertoire, including "Certainly Lord," her own rendition of "Ride on, King Jesus," and her adaptation of "Is There Anybody Here Who Loves My Jesus?"

Though I have had the pleasure of hearing the Roberta Martin Singers several times, I did not want to trust my memory for an analysis of the music but chose to analyze fifty-two songs recorded by the group (see table 7). These fifty-two songs constitute 65 percent of Martin's recorded music and include the most notable Martin songs.

All of the songs were not written by Roberta Martin but were selected by her and represent her taste. Eleven of these songs were written by James Cleveland (1931–1991), nine by Roberta Martin, six by Alex Bradford (1927–1978), four by Lucy Matthews (b. 1928), and two each by Jessye Dixon (b. 1938) and Myrtle Jackson (b. 1926). Eighteen other composers are represented by one song each, including "Old Ship of Zion" by Thomas A. Dorsey and "We'll Understand It Better By and By" by Charles Albert Tindley (1851–1933). This is very impressive because Tindley influenced Dorsey, Dorsey influenced Martin, Martin influenced Cleveland, and the genealogy goes on and on.

These fifty-two songs reveal that Martin's combination of the West African and the Western European traditions permeates all of her music. The African melodic tradition favors few tones, small intervals, and revolutions around a principal tone. Her composition "God Is Still on the Throne," which is now a gospel standard, is based on six tones: Ab, Bb, C, Db, Eb, and G (ex. 55). The first five tones are employed many times. The

Table 7   Selected Songs of Roberta Martin

Title	Composer	Key	Scale	Meter
"After It's All Over"	A. Bradford	F	Diatonic	$\frac{4}{4}$
"Be Still, My Soul"*	J. Sibelius	D♭	Diatonic	$\frac{4}{4}$
"Certainly Lord"	L. McDonald	G	Pentatonic	$\frac{4}{4}$
"Come in the Room"	A. Bradford	F	Diatonic	$\frac{4}{4}$
"Come into My Heart"	J. Cleveland	A♭	Diatonic	$\frac{12}{8}$
"Do You Know Him?"	M. Parker	G	Pentatonic	$\frac{4}{4}$
"Every Now and Then"	J. Cleveland	G	Mixolydian	$\frac{6}{8}$
"From out of Nowhere"	D. Allen	C	Diatonic	$\frac{4}{4}$
"God Is Still on the Throne"	R. Martin	A♭	Pentatonic	$\frac{9}{8}$
"God Specializes"	G. Griffin	E♭	Diatonic	nonmetric $+\frac{12}{8}$
"Grace"	J. Cleveland	G	Diatonic	$\frac{6}{8}$
"Had It Not Been for Him"	J. Cleveland	F	Diatonic	$\frac{6}{8}$
"Have You Found a Friend"	R. Martin	G	Diatonic	$\frac{12}{8}$
"He Didn't Mind Dying"	M. Jackson	F	Diatonic	$\frac{4}{4}$
"He Has Done Great Things"	L. Matthews*	A♭	Diatonic	nonmetric
"He Knows How Much We Can Bear"	P. Hall	C	Diatonic	$\frac{12}{8}$
"He's Always Right There"	R. Martin	B♭	Diatonic	$\frac{9}{8}$
"He's My Light"	L. Smith*	B♭	Diatonic	$\frac{12}{8}$
"He's Using Me"	J. Cleveland	G	Diatonic	$\frac{4}{4}$
"Hold the Light"	S. Lewis	F	Diatonic	$\frac{12}{8}$
"I Don't Mind"	R. Martin	F	Diatonic	$\frac{12}{8}$
"I'll Do What You Want Me to Do"	K. Woods	B♭	Diatonic	$\frac{12}{8}$
"I'm Determined"*	J. Cleveland	A♭	Diatonic	$\frac{12}{8}$
"I'm Gonna Praise His Name"	A. Bradford	E♭	Diatonic	$\frac{4}{4}$
"I'm Grateful"	G. Griffin	A♭	Diatonic	nonmetric
"I'm Just Waiting on the Lord"	R. Martin	F	Diatonic	$\frac{6}{8}$
"I'm Saved"*	J. Cleveland	B♭	Diatonic	$\frac{6}{8}$

Table 7 (*continued*)

Title	Composer	Key	Scale	Meter
"I'm Sealed"	W. Cook	G	Diatonic	$\frac{12}{8}$
"Is There Anybody Here?"	R. Martin	F	Diatonic	$\frac{4}{4}$
"Let It Be"	R. Martin	E♭	Pentatonic	$\frac{9}{8}$
"No Other Help I Know"	R. Martin	B♭	Diatonic	$\frac{6}{8}$
"Nothing But a God"	J. Cleveland	G	Diatonic	$\frac{6}{8}$
"Only a Look"	A. Shepherd	F	Diatonic	$\frac{9}{8}$
"Out of the Depths"	T. Gross	F	Diatonic	$\frac{9}{8}$
"Ride on, King Jesus"	D. Norwood	F	Pentatonic	$\frac{4}{4}$
"Satisfied"	M. McGee	A♭	Pentatonic	$\frac{4}{4}$
"Since I Met Him"	J. Cleveland	E♭	Diatonic	$\frac{6}{8}$
"Since I Met Jesus"	A. Bradford	C	Diatonic	$\frac{12}{8}$
"Standing on the Promises"	R. Carter	E♭	Diatonic	$\frac{6}{8}$
"Teach Me Lord"*	R. Martin	F	Diatonic	$\frac{6}{8}$
"The Failure's Not in God, It's in Me"	J. Dixon	F	Diatonic	$\frac{9}{8}$ + nonmetric
"The Old Account"	F. Graham	A♭	Diatonic	$\frac{12}{8}$
"The Old Ship of Zion"	T. Dorsey	A♭	Pentatonic	$\frac{12}{8}$
"There Is No Failure in God"	J. Dixon	A♭	Diatonic	$\frac{9}{8}$
"There's a Man on the Other Side of Jordan"	J. Cleveland	G	Mixolydian	$\frac{4}{4}$
"Too Close to Heaven"	A. Bradford	F	Diatonic	$\frac{12}{8}$
"Walk on by Faith"	J. Cleveland	B♭	Diatonic	$\frac{9}{8}$
"We're Marching to Zion"	arr. Bradford	A♭	Mixolydian	$\frac{4}{4}$
"What a Blessing"	L. Smith**	B♭	Diatonic	$\frac{9}{8}$
"What a Friend We Have in Jesus"	C. Converse	A♭	Diatonic	nonmetric
"Where Can I Go?"	M. Jackson	G	Pentatonic	$\frac{4}{4}$
"You'll Understand It Better By and By"	C. Tindley	G	Pentatonic	$\frac{4}{4}$

*Asterisk indicates songs in strophic form. All others are AB form.

**L. Matthews and L. Smith are the same person.

Example 55.   Melody of "God Is Still on the Throne" (Roberta Martin). Used by permission of Leonard Austin.

G is used only once. I would call this a pentatonic-scale song, since the G is actually a substitution for the Bb in the V chord. There is no interval larger than a third. When the soloist comes in, she enters on an Ab (though she will later descend to G below the Ab) and ascends to the Eb, a range of five tones. That is very much in the African tradition.

Let us now consider the European influence in her music. In the song "From out of Nowhere," intervals of a fifth, ninth, and octave are present. Under normal circumstances, these intervals might be considered Western European. But when emotion forces the singer to seek great melodic variation, the melodic leaps are African.

In these fifty-two selections, emotion has forced the range of the soloists up to two octaves. The outstanding example is that of Roberta Martin Singer Delois Barrett Campbell who, in her recorded performance of ""What a Blessing in Jesus I've Found" (Apollo 218), opens a phrase on Bb (the Bb below middle C) and then bridges the phrase with the Bb directly below high C.

Barrett Campbell was not the only singer employing a wide range, for on the song "From out of Nowhere," when Martin sings the words *from out of nowhere*, she skips up four tones to sing *Jesus found me*, but when she gets to the words *I can look back and wonder*, she skips up nine tones to illustrate the text (ex. 56):

> From out of nowhere [a fourth], Jesus found me
> I'm glad, so glad, that He did
> I look back and wonder [a ninth]
> How I could get along so long
> Without the Lord

Example 56.   Note the leap of a ninth in m. 4 of "From out of Nowhere" (Roberta Martin).

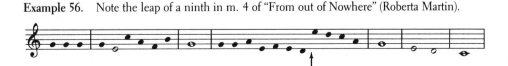

The scales employed by the Martin Singers on their recordings are the seven-tone diatonic scale; the pentatonic scale, a five-tone scale, the most popular of which uses tones 1, 2, 3, 5, and 6 of the diatonic scale; and the Mixolydian, a diatonic scale with the seventh degree flatted. The pentatonic scale is found in such songs as "Certainly Lord," led by Gloria Griffin; "Do You Know Him?," led by Eugene Smith; "Let It Be," led by Delois Barrett Campbell; "Ride on, King Jesus," led by Roberta Martin; "Satisfied," led by Eugene Smith; "The Old Ship of Zion," led by Norsalus McKissick; and "Where Can I Go?," led by Roberta Martin.

As mentioned earlier, "God Is Still On the Throne" employs a pentatonic scale of the 1–2–3–4–5 variety. The Mixolydian scale was found only in the singing of Eugene Smith. Smith enjoyed singing the flatted seventh, as in "Every Now and Then" and "There's a Man on the Other Side of Jordan." His use of the flatted seventh is partially related to the African and African American tradition of bending bright edges. The third is also bent. These are often called blue and minor tones. They should not be called minor, for any great folk singer, especially a gospel singer, will alternately brighten or darken a third or seventh, for color or timbre is more important than pitch when emotion becomes the major element.

How a song is organized determines its impression on the performer and the listener. When gospel began as a prepared (that is, rehearsed) kind of music in the Holiness church, the performers borrowed a great deal from the spirituals popular during the third quarter of the nineteenth century. Spirituals that were purely refrains or choruses (four, eight, or sixteen bars of music with no contrasting section or verse, such as "This Little Light of Mine" and "Glory, Glory, Hallelujah") were borrowed.

Roberta Martin preferred the tension and release of at least two distinct musical ideas in each song: the verse, with its complex melodic line—as in "He's My Light" and "I'll Do What You Want Me to Do"—and the chorus, a genuine sing-along refrain that the marginally sophisticated gospel ear can pick up after one hearing, as in "I Am Sealed" and "Satisfied."

Of the fifty-two songs analyzed, forty-eight songs are of the verse-and-chorus or AB variety, while only four are of the strophe or exclusive-refrain type. None of the songs that are of the gospel blues type were recorded, including the popular "I Know the Lord Will Make a Way," composed by Eugene Smith. (The gospel blues is a sixteen-bar composition of four phrases with a half-cadence right in the middle.) This is easily understood when it is remembered that very few gospel blues have contrasting sections. Martin needed tension. To ensure the presence of tension on her recordings as well as in performance, she developed a special tradition. Gospel music usually begins with the known element. The chorus is sung several times, and only then is a contrasting section offered. However, 99 percent of Roberta Martin songs begin with one or several verses before arriving at the chorus. Only after the singers have set up the verse do they give the release.

In the 1960s, I witnessed a concert by the Roberta Martin Singers during which Eugene Smith sang five verses of "I'm Sealed" (though there are only three published stanzas of lyrics) before he sang the chorus. By the time he reached the chorus, the audience was so primed that they "tore the church up."

Example 57.   "He Knows How Much We Can Bear" (Phyllis Hall, Roberta Martin). Used by permission of Leonard Austin.

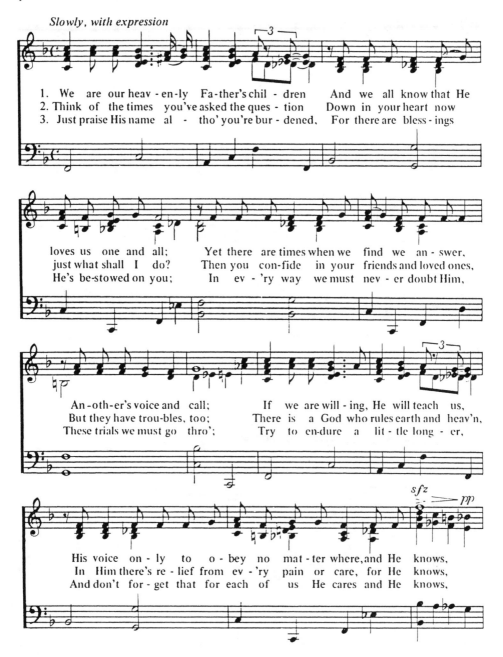

Slowly, with expression

1. We are our heav-en-ly Fa-ther's chil-dren   And we all know that He
2. Think of the times you've asked the ques - tion   Down in your heart now
3. Just praise His name al - tho' you're bur - dened,   For there are bless - ings

loves us one and all;   Yet there are times when we find we an - swer,
just what shall I   do?   Then you con-fide in your friends and loved ones,
He's be-stowed on you;   In   ev - 'ry way we must nev - er doubt Him,

An - oth-er's voice and call;   If   we are will - ing, He will teach us,
But they have trou-bles, too;   There is   a God who rules earth and heav'n,
These trials we must go thro';   Try to en-dure a lit - tle long - er,

His voice on - ly to o - bey no   mat - ter where, and He knows,
In Him there's re - lief from ev - 'ry pain or care, for He knows,
And don't for - get that for each of   us He cares and He knows,

Example 57.   *(continued)*

Form is directly related to harmony. Martin had a penchant for songs with sections divided equally by an open half-cadence, using the dominant or V chord. In "He Knows How Much We Can Bear" (ex. 57), a song brought to Martin by Phyllis Hall, a young woman who had just left an orphanage and who later worked for a number of years for Martin, the following text opens the song:

> We are our Heavenly Father's children
> And we all know He loves us one and all
> Yet there are times we find He'll answer
> Another's voice and call.

The dominant chord appears on the word *call,* exactly at the middle of this verse. This type of division is followed by the closed or V–I cadence at the midpoint, as in "Only a Look" (ex. 58):

> Only a look at Jesus,
> Oh, so bowed down with care.

Example 58.   V–I cadence in "Only a Look."

While this is also the middle of this verse, the words *with care* are sung to the chords V–I, sounding almost like the end of the song.

Because of her attention to the marriage of form and harmony, Martin was instrumental in developing the gospel cadence formula of I^6_4–V^7/ii–V^7/V–V^7–I, which brought a section or a song to its end (ex. 59). This formula may be heard in "Do You Know Him?," "Old Ship of Zion," and "Where Can I Go?" In studying piano, one learns that in the baroque period, the music was very formulaic. If one wanted to end a song, he or she

Example 59.   Gospel cadence formula developed by Roberta Martin.

simply played I^6–ii^6–I^6_4–V–I, with some tension supplied by a 4–3 suspension, maybe a passing seventh, an anticipation, and then the final chord. When Martin wanted to be a little fancy, she would add a plagal cadence IV with ornamentation and then proceed to I. Roberta Martin helped to identify gospel formulaic cadence.

Roberta Martin's most important contribution in form and harmony was the introduction of substitution chords. Before the Martin era, a pianist would reach the V chord with this progression:

| I | V | I |
1   2   3

For a richer harmonic vocabulary, Martin would substitute other chords for the I and V:

| I–V/ii | V^7/V–V^7 | I |
    1   2   3

Substitution chords were used in her rendition of Jean Sibelius's "Finlandia," known in gospel as "Be Still, My Soul":

	Be	Still	My	Soul
Sibelius	I	V	I	V
Martin	I	ii^6	V/vi^6	ii

This progression became a fixture of the Martin style and can be heard in "Come into My Heart," "Grace," "The Failure's Not in God," and "What a Blessing in Jesus I've Found." The progression is now a classic in both traditional and contemporary gospel music.

Meter was most important to the Martin style and was linked with tempo. The ideal Roberta Martin song was slow, with a foreground beat of four pulses per unit, or measure, and a background beat of three pulsations for each foreground pulse, usually with the eighth note at a metronomic marking of 92, in which gospel singers are known to be able to "work." Examples of this meter and tempo may be observed in "Come into My Heart," "He Knows How Much We Can Bear," "He's My Light," "I'm Determined," and "I'm Sealed." These songs are in the favorite gospel meter, $\frac{12}{8}$, which Martin loved. She would insinuate it into any song.

Other meters with multiples of three are $\frac{6}{8}$, as in "Standing on the Promises," "Teach Me Lord," and "Grace"; and, of course, $\frac{9}{8}$, as in "What a Blessing in Jesus I've Found," "Let It Be," "God Is Still on the Throne," and "Walk on by Faith."

Martin's fast songs were never very fast. When I asked her why, she said, "I can't understand the words" (Boyer 1964b). Her fast songs were in $\frac{4}{4}$, at a moderately fast tempo. "He's Using Me" has a metronomic marking of 92 for the quarter note, "I'm

Going to Praise His Name" is at 152, "After It's All Over" is at 168, and "Satisfied" is marked at 200, perhaps the fastest song she ever recorded. Fast songs in the Martin style employed simple harmonies such as that of her rendition of "We'll Understand It Better By and By." This song is composed of "changes" (that is, the simplest harmonies available in gospel) and is typical of Martin's treatment of harmony, meter, and form in her fast songs: I–IV–I–V/V–IV–IV–I.

Martin realized that while there is a certain emotional value in performing a song in the lining-hymn tradition, unmetered or without a regularly felt pulse, the style works best with soloists. Groups and choirs tend to adopt extraneous musical and physical properties that, while entertaining, contribute nothing musically. It is perhaps because of this reasoning that, of all the songs analyzed here, only five were performed in unpulsed meter. The most outstanding of these are Martin's own rendition of the Willie Mae Ford Smith arrangement of "What a Friend We Have in Jesus" (Apollo 238) and Gloria Griffin's performance of her composition "I'm So Grateful" (Savoy 7095).

In performance practice, Martin preferred a responsorial or call-and-response treatment of a song. On such songs as "Where Can I Go?" and "Come in the Room," the response is of the older perpetual-motion style with an articulation in every beat, reminiscent of the response to "Die with the Staff in My Hand"; while on "What a Friend We Have in Jesus," the group hums during the main part of the song and simply provides a textual punctuation at the end of phrases. The most common Martin response, however, is an "oh yes" or "ooh whoo" at the middle of the verse, adding a few more punctuations during the chorus, as in "After It's All Over."

The vamp, a short musical phrase of two, four, or eight measures that is repeated over and over, is the most important stylistic element in contemporary gospel. Purely African reiteration, it is a wonderful device and appears to contribute little to substance but a great deal to style. Although popular during her time, the vamp was not attractive to Roberta Martin, and of the songs analyzed here, only "God Specializes," "Hold the Light," "I'm Just Waiting on the Lord," "Since I Met Jesus," and "The Old Account" are given that treatment. When there is no vamp, melody and harmony must be strong.

Regarding key color, the Roberta Martin Singers sound "just right" in certain keys. Only seven keys were employed in the fifty-two songs analyzed. F major was used fourteen times and G major and A major only once. Needless to say, key selection was often related to the soloist. For example, of the thirteen songs analyzed that were led by Eugene Smith, the key distribution is as follows:

F	G	Bb	Ab	Eb
4	4	2	2	1

Roberta Martin was concerned with every aspect of the performance of a song, even the final cadence, which received very special treatment. The V–I cadence, generally recognized as "ti-do" or, with the pentatonic scale, "la-do," is standard in gospel music. However, in the Roberta Martin style, the move to the I chord is not the end of the song.

While most singers settled for the plagal or "Amen" cadence of IV–I, Martin insisted upon a chord substitution and an ornamentation:

Tradition IV   I
Martin   ii   iii   ii   I
                          I

Even this was not the end. The last sound heard was Roberta Martin or "Little Lucy" playing an arpeggio of the tonic or "home-key" chord in thirds or sixths from the middle register of the piano all the way to the top.

Little needs to be said about Roberta Martin's contribution to the gospel piano style. When she started playing the piano, she had no real model. The great pianists were Arizona Dranes and Thomas A. Dorsey. Arizona Dranes's piano style was a combination of ragtime and early jazz, and Dorsey's playing had very little relationship to that of Roberta Martin. Pianists for the Martin Singers have included Willie Webb, Lucy Smith, James Cleveland, Alex Bradford, and Louise Overall Weaver. Some played for one concert; others moved to the organ to accompany Martin's piano. Roberta Martin played gospel with the nuances of a Horowitz, the inventions of an Ellington, and the power of an Erroll Garner, all the while playing "straight from the church."

In the 1940s, when the Roberta Martin Singers were traveling to California, New York, and Texas, I was growing up in Florida and, like many all over the world, was listening to such recordings as "Old Ship of Zion" and "Only a Look" that illustrate all the elements discussed above. When these elements are put together, they create the Roberta Martin sound. That music created a tradition of which I am happy to be a part. What an honor it is to have lived during the reign of Roberta Martin.

CONVERSATIONS

Roberta Martin Singers Roundtable

*Edited by Pearl Williams-Jones and
Bernice Johnson Reagon*

*During the 1981 Smithsonian Conference on Roberta Martin, Pearl
Williams-Jones conceptualized a session in which, in a large semicircle,
singers and others who had worked professionally with Roberta Martin
shared brief statements about their experiences. Most of the people in
this session grew up in the organization Roberta Martin created. Their
remarks reveal the inner workings of an extended spiritual, cultural,
communal family.* —ED.

PEARL WILLIAMS-JONES

I had the privilege as a child born into the Black gospel church here in Washington,
D.C., to have grown up seeing, hearing, and knowing Roberta Martin and her fantastic
singers for more than twenty years.

Eugene [Smith] and I have been talking constantly since he came here. We just had
to go back and review things the way they used to be. So much of what I have found
helpful in my life of growing up in the Black gospel church, playing and singing gospel
music and, in more recent years, talking, writing, and endeavoring to share information
about gospel music with people throughout the United States, came from Roberta Martin
and the Roberta Martin Singers.

When I talk to a person like Eugene Smith, I begin to remember the late 1940s and the 1950s when the Roberta Martin Singers came every November to my father's church on New Jersey Avenue, Northwest, Washington, D.C., for a two-week revival. It would be like Santa Claus was coming to town because when the Martin Singers came, you knew that several things were going to happen. First of all, as with Santa Claus, you were going to get a lot of musical goodies. You knew you were going to get a lot of new music that you had never heard. You knew that you were going to get a lesson in how to perform that music. You were going to sit on that bench and watch Lucy Smith Collier play those changes on the piano. You watched her hands and tried to find out what key she was playing in and wondered if you could go home and do what Lucy did.

Then you watched Eugene Smith. You listened to his narration because you knew when you had your little gospel choir, in order to get the audience ready for the Roberta Martin songs that your choir was going to sing, you had to know how to narrate like Eugene, to talk it up. You'd listen to Eugene and his analogies and the things that he said, and then all over this country people were trying to narrate like Eugene Smith.

You listened to the notes that Delois Barrett Campbell sang because, if you had a high soprano voice, you then knew what that soprano voice could do in terms of highlighting the background. If you listened to Norsalus or Archie, you knew what to do with a baritone voice, how one could highlight that. We learned many, many, many unforgettable lessons.

LEONA PRICE

Leona Price lived and worked closely with Roberta Martin for fifty years. Mrs. Price became the business manager of the Roberta Martin publishing house in Chicago in the year of 1939. She worked religiously from 1939 to 1979. —ED.

I first met Miss Martin when I was a teenager attending my home church, Shiloh Baptist, formerly of 6201 South Race Street in the community of Englewood, Chicago, Illinois, currently located at 7058 South Racine Avenue, Rev. C. J. Brooks, Pastor.

During that time Miss Martin's brother-in-law, the late Reverend L. W. Hall, was pastor of Shiloh. Miss Martin became the directress of our gospel chorus and junior and youth choirs. I was president of the junior and youth choirs. As directress, Miss Martin sponsored monthly musicals every fourth Sunday. I recall many gospel greats who appeared on the music programs, such as Professor Thomas A. Dorsey, Sallie Martin, and the late Professor Theodore Frye. At that time, the Martin Singers were known as the Martin and Frye Singers. The original group consisted of young men: Eugene Smith, Norsalus McKissick, Robert Anderson, Willie Webb, James Lawrence, and W. C. Herman, who lost his life in World War II. The first young lady in the group was Bessie Folk. The second young lady was Delois Barrett Campbell, followed by Myrtle Scott, the late

Sadie Durrah, Mrytle Jackson, Gloria Griffin, Romance Watson, Archie Dennis, Louise McCord, and so many others.

Being the great spiritual lady that she was, Miss Martin won wide acclaim throughout the Englewood community with her winning smile and magnetic personality. She attracted throngs of people of all ages. The crowds that attended the Shiloh musicals! I have fond recollections of all the young people being hustled to the balcony against their wishes, so that the adults could have the best seats.

There were many gospel greats who appeared in the Shiloh musical programs, such as the late Mahalia Jackson, Myrtle Jackson, Sadie Durrah, Amelia Anderson, R. L. Knowles, now deceased, and the Atkins Singers from the Ebenezer Baptist Church. By utilizing proceeds from those musicals, Miss Martin was able to help her brother-in-law, Reverend L. W. Hall, to greatly reduce the mortgage on our church.

I became more closely acquainted with Miss Martin during the interval when she was directress of the choirs at Shiloh. She sponsored a contest with the junior and youth choirs to help defray expenses for the National Gospel Choral Union Convention in East St. Louis at the Lincoln Memorial High School. The first prize was an all-expense trip to the convention. I won the first prize and was ecstatic. This was the National Convention of Gospel Choirs and Choruses founded by Lewis Butts, Sallie Martin, and Theodore Frye.

A problem developed, however. My family decided that I could not attend a convention of that magnitude due to my wardrobe. Miss Martin was always going about helping and giving to everyone. Her ministry was giving and helping those that were less fortunate. This time I was the recipient. Miss Martin and her sister owned a boutique shop; so Miss Martin went to the shop and completely furnished my wardrobe with the things that she felt I needed. With this gesture, my parents weren't able to refuse. When they finally gave their consent, [you can] imagine my excitement with the thought of being able to travel with the one and only Miss Roberta Martin and her cavalcade of singers. This exceeded my wildest dreams. In the true generous spirit of Roberta Martin, she also assumed full financial responsibility for three other youth choir members to attend. This was typical of Miss Martin.

After the convention, I developed a fast friendship with Martin's niece, Caulyne Hall, whose father was pastor of Shiloh Baptist Church. Caulyne and I would go over to the studio to sort and classify sheet music and books. I was completely overwhelmed by the stacks of sheet music and books. I was told Miss Martin had just opened the studio a few months before I met her. Business was extremely slow. When her secretary, Mrs. Clara Blanks, had to leave her duties because of the illness of her aged parents in Cairo, Illinois, I was hired part time to work under the supervision of Miss Martin's mother, fondly referred to as Big Mama.

Big Mama liked the way I handled the affairs of the studio and suggested to Miss Martin that I be allowed to manage the business while she was on her frequent trips. In 1940, I became a permanent employee with a starting salary of eight dollars per week. One must appreciate the fact that at that time sheet music was ten cents per single copy, fifteen, twenty, or twenty-five cents for the double sheet. Songbooks were thirty-five cents. Choirs were given discounts of so much per dozen. There was even a greater discount with mail-order dealers.

It was some time before we recognized a small profit. Of course, Miss Martin's travels with the group advertised the business tremendously. She was always happy to return home and check the business receipts and complimented me on my managerial ability. Very slowly the business began to prosper.

Throughout the city of Chicago, no church was too small for her to help. She attended as many small storefront churches as large ones (probably more) with her singers, the great Roberta Martin Singers. She was a meek and humble and fully dedicated Christian woman. She was freehearted and giving and sharing with others. We had wonderful times together through our struggles. When she and her singers returned from tours and she felt their share of the proceeds was not adequate, she would give them her share and try to make ends meet from the proceeds of the studio. On the other hand, if their tour had been a financial success, she would give an extra bonus to me from her share.

Miss Martin was admired for her style of playing piano, singing, composing, and arranging. She trained her group with emphasis on melodious harmony and the gospel beat, which was uniquely hers. Many have attempted to imitate her but with little success. Miss Martin selected her singers for their individual style: Eugene Smith for his delivery; Norsalus McKissick, his marvelous tone; Delois Barrett Campbell, her voice range; Lucy Collier, her organ and piano style.

Miss Martin was a devout Christian who dedicated her life to the Lord. I recall when she started Bible class in the music studio once a week after working hours. Her singers, employees, and friends attended. Bible class was taught by Miss Martin and the late Amelia Anderson.

From Miss Martin's vast renditions of solos, her favorite was "What a Friend We Have in Jesus," which her audience repeatedly clamored for. I remember another shining hour in her life when she directed the thousand-voice choir for the National Baptist Convention at the Coliseum in Chicago in 1960. They featured the song "Grace Is Sufficient," arrangement by Roberta Martin; words and music by James Cleveland; soloist, Delois Barrett Campbell (ex. 60).

The Roberta Martin Singers received three gold records, the first from the Apollo Record Company in 1960 for the rendition of "The Old Ship of Zion," Norsalus McKissick, soloist. Two other gold records were received from the Savoy Record Company.

I also recall Miss Martin's gift as an orator, a dynamic women's day speaker who spoke throughout the country. I had the opportunity to present her annually for at least five years in my in-laws' church where I was a member and church clerk.

To perceive the genius that was Roberta Martin, one must consider all aspects of the Protestant religious spectrum at that time. During the Depression years, many sought solace in church attendance. There was little or no money in the church coffers. The

Example 60. "Grace Is Sufficient" (James Cleveland), arranged by Roberta Martin. Used by permission of Leonard Austin.

Example 60.   *(continued)*

Example 60. *(continued)*

nation was continuously being told that prosperity was just around the corner. Many ministers or employees either did not receive salaries or payments were in arrears. A mood of depression prevailed. Suddenly on the horizon appeared gospel music. The word *gospel* means good news.

Most Protestant churches were singing hymns and anthems which were basically songs to God, for example, "Nearer My God to Thee." Gospel music was sung by people to each other for spiritual uplifting and contained spiritual fervor, for example, "Come on, Children, Let's Sing." Initially there was light resistance to the gospel beat in some very staid, pompous churches. But ministers recognized the emotional release involved and encouraged the trend of having the gospel choir sing just before the sermon, invitation for new members, or offertory period. Gospel music was more fully utilized at funerals, where emotions sometimes were uncontrollable.

Roberta Martin was unlike any others of her kind. Because of her unique ability to compose, arrange, play, and sing, there was a great clamor for her personal appearance all over the country. Many artists could play, sing, compose, or arrange, but few could do all of these with competence that matched Roberta Martin. One must also realize that the Civil Rights Movement had not begun; hotel accommodations were limited for our group and sometimes nonexistent. It therefore became Miss Martin's practice to scout

out accommodations when she and her singers were invited on a tour. Since railroad accommodations, for example, eating in dining cars, were also nonexistent, much of the Martin Singers' early travel was by car. Miss Martin would advise the church committee of the number of singers in her group. When they arrived, she personally checked accommodations and, in her self-effacing manner, gave the best accommodations to her group, while she accepted the modest ones. Many humorous tales have been told of these incidents. Sometimes the singers slept in tiers in one room; however, this was overcome by their pleasant experiences.

Miss Martin could be called a pioneer in her field because she was so devoutly spiritual in her total approach to gospel music. She had a tremendous sense of harmony and would stress chording to her students. Since the bass provided the beat, many of Miss Martin's first printed gospel songs merely indicated an initial bass chord in a measure. The rest was left to the feeling of the pianist. When listening to Miss Martin play, one could detect a sustained bass chord and, at frequent intervals, an additional root note an octave lower. There was no legato dragging in gospel music. The beat made it gospel. Some musicians have argued that Miss Martin's techniques reflected a progressive bass. Since she rarely discussed her techniques, one must conclude that it was definitely what we currently refer to as soul. Without a doubt she played and sang what she felt, and one could detect many approaches to the same melody in one of her renditions.

Some of her critics said she didn't sing as frequently as they would have liked. Because of her deep spirituality, she sang most beautifully and freely when consumed with a spiritual conviction. Her apparent preoccupation with composing often gave one an impression that she was introverted. In a larger sense perhaps she was, because she was so deeply committed to her "good-news gospel." Many mornings she would enter the studio, barely speaking. She would go directly to the piano and after long intervals of playing and editing a tune, she would finally enthusiastically say, "I've got it! I've got it! Listen, listen!" Those of us in the studio would gather around her as she played and sang and encouraged us to join her by harmonizing. I feel a deep sense of having been especially blessed to have been present when such songs as "My Friend," "My Eternal Home," "Try Jesus," "God Is Still on the Throne," "They That Wait," "I Hear God," and so many others were conceived.

Many have said Miss Martin was wealthy. Unfortunately this was not true, as is evidenced by the financial condition of our group during the times in which she performed. Incidentally, if she had been wealthy, she would have been a philanthropist, for she loved giving to others more than any public figure I know. There are countless untold stories of her giving. A young man in Gary, Indiana, who was studying and working on his master's degree and suffering because of inadequate funds approached Miss Martin. She immediately planned a benefit performance with her singers to assist him financially with his tuition. The performance was a huge financial success, and Miss Martin insisted on giving the entire proceeds to the student, who became Dr. Clayton Hannah, now deceased.

Once when Miss Martin and her group were touring the South, they visited a small church in Bessemer, Alabama. The young choir director impressed her with his singing style and intense interest in gospel music. Miss Martin took him under her wing and encouraged him to such heights that he became world renowned. His name: the late Professor Alex Bradford.

Miss Martin was forever besieged by individuals who thought they could sing or who had composed a song. Most of the material in its raw form was not noteworthy. I can recall many such individuals visiting the studio and singing these tunes. Because we were so young and because some of the tunes were so strange, we often could barely suppress our laughter. Miss Martin, being the Christian that she was and recognizing the sincerity of the would-be composer, would mildly reprimand us and say, "Don't laugh; after all, this is my business," whereupon we would immediately stop snickering.

On the other hand, Miss Martin had tremendous wit and extremely subtle humor. In her introduction of the Martin Singers she often lovingly, yet jokingly, referred to the members of her group as "Old Man Reverend Eugene Smith" or "Old Man McKissick," although they were mere teenagers. It was generally known among us close to Miss Martin that when something upset her, it appeared that one of her eyes would cross. When this happened we would lovingly say, "Look out! Bert's mad."

It must also be pointed out that during the formative years of gospel music, very little was known of legislation to protect composers and arrangers. Competition was keen. Often when Miss Martin arranged an old tune such as "What a Friend We Have in Jesus" or "Amazing Grace," many other publishers released their arrangements of the same tune. Ironically, some critics accused Miss Martin of plagiarism. This was neither true nor necessary, as she carefully checked existing copyright laws and adhered to the law of public domain.

Miss Martin married James Austin in 1947. After a few years on the road, she decided to turn the travel aspect of the group over to Mr. Eugene Smith as manager of the Roberta Martin Singers. They then continued and expanded to European tours. The greatest of these tours was in Spoleto, Italy.

Meanwhile Miss Martin settled down to the serious rearing of her son—Sonny, Leonard Austin. Miss Martin was a devoted wife and mother. Her husband, Mr. James Austin, devoted full time to the financial operation of the studio while I managed the mail order and sales department. She registered Sonny in a private school, seeking the best educational opportunities for him, for even then the Chicago school system was in turmoil. Despite the fact that Sonny attended an interracial school and many of his classmates were from middle-class families, she instilled in him a sense of awareness and identity. He was never allowed to be a social climber.

Miss Martin was a woman of good taste in quality clothing and in furnishing her home. She was always down to earth. When I told her I was engaged to get married, she insisted that I hold my wedding reception in her lovely home. I did.

Because of the heavy long-distance traveling, Miss Martin always had large cars. A friend of mine vividly recalled Miss Martin helping an elderly woman to the county hospital clinic. Despite the fact that Miss Martin was driving her late-model Cadillac, when she entered the hospital trying to find where she was to take this little, elderly lady, she was wearing sneakers and a baseball cap. She was so preoccupied with her music that many times she would just wear anything that she could get around in.

During her lifetime, Roberta Martin published 280 gospel songs. Fifty-five of that number were composed by James Cleveland, fifty-one composed by Roberta Martin. The rest of the songs were composed by such artists as the late Alex Bradford, so many others. All of the songs were arranged by Roberta Martin with the exception of twenty-one which were arranged by an arranger for hire.

My Marty, as I so affectionately called her, expired at six o'clock Monday morning, January 13, 1969, in the manner of the song, "Ride on, King Jesus, I Want to Go to Heaven in the Morning." A gospel giant closed the book of life; . . . her songwriting's ended, but the melodies linger on.

ARCHIE DENNIS

As a little boy, I heard the recordings of the Roberta Martin Singers. One song in particular, I could hear it, and I'd get so blessed, I'd cry. It was Norsalus's "I've Got a Home Prepared for You." Little did I realize that one day I would stand beside Mr. McKissick and sing gospel songs.

The first time I saw them, I didn't hear them. I was at Howard University's homecoming game some years ago, and I was told too late that the Martin Singers were at Bible Way. I rushed over and they were just finishing the last song. I remember seeing Eugene and Myrtle Jackson and Robert Anderson and some others.

Later on I began to sing with the Maceo Woods Singers in Chicago, and the Reverend Billy Kyles, who now lives in Memphis, took me to the Liberty Baptist Church one night. Somehow I was called upon to sing, and the lady that played for me happened to have been Roberta Martin. That night she invited me to come the next day to her home. She said, "I'd like to hear you sing some other things." So I went and sang everything I knew.

Eugene came downstairs, and he too listened. There was no place in the Martin Singers for me at that time, but now that I look back, God was laying the groundwork. About a year and a half later, Eugene called me and said, "There's a place available in the group; would you like to come to Chicago?" That was in 1958. I went to Chicago and rehearsed with them for a week. I'll never forget the first trip out that we had was accompanying the Reverend C. L. Franklin in a week's revival at the Music Hall in Houston, Texas, and if you didn't get there by seven o'clock, there was no need to bother because the hall was jammed.

I thank God for allowing my life to be touched by the life of Miss Martin and each of my former co-workers. I thank God, for in a very special way my life has been enriched by knowing and working with Miss Martin and the Roberta Martin Singers. Thank you.

My first trip abroad was in 1963 with the Roberta Martin Singers. I was single when the group disbanded, but most of the rest were married and they had children and families, and their children were growing up, and they saw that there was a need to be at home. You can't raise your children on the road, you know, and they saw the need to go home and support their families.

When we disbanded and I thought, "Well, this is it. Lord, thanks for allowing me the eight-year period with the Martin Singers, and I guess I'll just go on home." But God is ever moving, and His plan is ever changing, and as we move with God, He takes us on and on.

In my case, I went home and started back to school and started working for United States Steel Corporation and was two steps from a sales rep when I received a word that turned out to be prophetic, that I would go around the world and to sing to nations. When I received that word, I thought, "Lord, how do you go around the world and sing to nations on weekends and get back to U.S. Steel? You know, the Martin Singers are no longer singing." I thought that this was the end, that I would work for U.S. Steel, sing on weekends, and this was it. But the Lord took me another step further, and as of this year I've been privileged to go abroad some thirty-one times with the Billy Graham Association and with World Evangelism and Language Institute for Evangelization and other things. I began to expand my horizons because I saw that the master plan of God was much bigger than I could even ask or think. We're not finished yet because He isn't finished.

The difference is commitment. We [the Roberta Martin Singers] were committed to a ministry; dollars and cents had nothing to do with it. We rode for hundreds of miles in cars, had money in our pockets, but we couldn't go in the restaurants, so we went in grocery stores. We'd buy a loaf of bread and some baloney and some Miracle Whip and get an ice-cream stick to spread it on the bread. It was like a marriage. We had no other alternative, because the message was greater than we are. Any way the thing went, we were committed to it, the lean weeks and the weeks when we got above what we expected.

One of the things Miss Martin taught us, aside from the Roberta Martin sound, was a style of living to be a Roberta Martin Singer. She taught us that God will endeavor to make the song and the singer one, and that you could sing a lie as well as tell one. I, at the time, was the youngest member of the group. They taught me and loved me and showed me that it's not just a song, but it's a life to be lived, and it's carried me all of these years.

NORSALUS McKISSICK

I'm not much of a talker. At that time [1932], she [Roberta Martin] was at the Ebenezer Baptist Church there in Chicago. She was the directress of the junior chorus and she just happened to pick us out at random. She used to call us the organizing group at that time. I first met her before then, sitting on a curb, singing "Stormy Weather." I was seven years old. She went to my father and invited me to go to Ebenezer to sing a song, "Old Ship of Zion." Ever since then we have traveled all over the country together, and I enjoyed every moment being with Miss Martin. She was more or less my mother. My mother died when I was very young, and Miss Martin took me under her wing, and I thank God today that there was a Roberta Martin.

BESSIE FOLK

I can agree with McKissick; I'm not much of a talker, either. But I would like to say that back in 1939, Roberta Martin walked into the Liberty Baptist Church. At that particular time I was a member of the Stepney Five, five little girls, and I was the shortest and the fattest in the group. They used to call me Little Miss Five by Five. I used to get kind of peeved, you know, but then I got used to it. Miss Martin, Eugene, Norsalus, Robert Anderson, Willie Webb, they marched down on the side of the aisle in Liberty Baptist Church, rushing to hear the Stepney Five. We had a young one there [who] could bass, and I was one of the main leaders.

After Miss Martin heard me, she said, "Can you come by the studio tomorrow?" I said, "Yes, ma'am, I can." So after I got out of school, went over there with my little white boots on with little dangling bells, and Miss Martin said, "I want to hear you sing "Precious Lord." So I did a little bit of it. She said, "I want to see your mama."

So Miss Martin met my mother, and then each evening from school, I was at Miss Martin's studio. This happened for about a month. Then she said, "I want you to go to Baltimore with me." The men were in Baltimore, Eugene and all of them. Miss Martin drove to Baltimore with me, and Eugene, Willie Webb, Robert and Norsalus like to have died! "Miss Martin, we don't want no girl! We don't want no girl! We don't want no girl in this group! I'm just not going to sing!" Miss Martin said, "I tell you this. If Bessie doesn't sing tonight, then I'm going home." Just like that. So that's how I became the first girl of the Roberta Martin Singers.

It went on and on and on, and they began to fall in love with me, and I fell in love with them. We were like sisters and brothers. Miss Martin taught me how to not be stage frightened, how to deliver a message in song. She was definitely my inspiration, and I love her, and I will never forget her. To me, she lives now.

LOUISE McCORD

My mind goes back to the time when I was a very little girl. My mother would take me to church and leave me. She could not attend because she had to go and work. She would always make sure that I was there, and I'd always love singing. I remember trying to sing in the choir. Something wasn't there that I felt should have been there. Prior to this time I had traveled around the world with the Voices of Tabernacle. When I came back, Eugene called and asked me to be a part of the Martin Singers.

I remember hearing songs by the Martin Singers: "Only a Look," "God Specializes." When I hear "He Is So Divine," I fell in love with Delois Barrett Campbell's voice. She became my idol. (She did not know this until I told her.) But you know you never know who is looking at you. Every run Delois made, I tried to make it. Every move, I tried to make it. Between Delois and Gloria and Lucy, just about everything I know about singing was gotten from them, the encouragement. You want to sing and you think that you can just stand up and sing, but you must be convicted. You must know the Lord. There has to be something there. You have to know what you're singing about in order to deliver a song. I tried to make those runs like Delois, but I couldn't make them until I really began to know the Lord, until I made God a part of my life and He made me a part of His. I never thought that this dream would come true, that I would be able to go around the world with the Martin Singers. But I think all that I did, it has been an experience I know that most young people—and I am young—would love to have. I thank God for that.

For those that are here that are caught and would like to get into gospel singing, let the Lord lead you. Let the Lord guide you. You'll find your true place in life. I've been so inspired working with the Martin Singers. When I went into the Martin Singers, Miss Martin was ill, and I believe "Just Jesus and Me" was the last song she wrote:

> Hand in hand along the road
> we walked together, just Jesus and me;
> heart to heart we'll always have
> a talk together, just Jesus and me.

DELOIS BARRETT CAMPBELL

In every gospel song there is a message. In order to deliver it, give it to someone else, you must know the story yourself. That's my policy. Just open up. That's all. That's all I can say. Never had a lesson. I watch a lot of singers. I find that it's from here [abdomen] and not from here [throat]. That's the secret.

I have so many precious memories today. I must really give credit for my beginning to Old Man McKissick. When just a young girl in my early teens, my aunt was the senior directress of the gospel chorus at Central Baptist Church on State Street on Chicago's South side. Norsalus was the junior director.

I was in the choir. Norsalus asked me to sing "He Will Remember Me." He invited Miss Martin to be our special guest for our annual monthly musical. Of course Miss Martin came, and she was just thrilled to have heard me sing, and from that she invited me to come to the studio like she did Bessie. I started rehearsing, and during the summer vacation period I traveled with the Roberta Martin Singers. I couldn't stay long because

I had to get back to school. Most of the time I went with them, I would leave my books; that meant I would get behind in my classes. I failed to come out in the year that I was scheduled to come out because of falling behind, singing with the famous Roberta Martin Singers. From that, it just grew.

Miss Martin certainly has played a very important part in my life. I was so green; I didn't know nothing about nothing when I came out on the road. I thank God for her and for Eugene and for all of these members of the group who have schooled me well. I love Miss Martin's arrangements. She used to make me think I could really, really sing. Even when I'd make so many mistakes, she was quite encouraging to me. She expected so much out of me. I guess, because I was the youngest among most of them. She was a friend; she was my sister; she was my mother; and we were just pals. I would consult Miss Martin about most anything; anything that was going along, Miss Martin had an answer for it.

My dad was a strict old Baptist deacon. He really didn't want me to go on the road so I had to follow behind Miss Martin. Most everywhere she went, I went. We stayed in the same room, slept in the same bed most of the time. I thank God for her.

She certainly inspired me into praying. I remember one night we were singing at Abyssinia. Each one of the singers had to take a turn leading prayer. She said, "Delois, tonight's your night; you pray." I'd say, "Who, me?" She'd say, "Yeah, you." I'd say, "I can't pray out loud. I pray, but I don't pray out loud." She said, "You must pray tonight out loud." So I started my prayer with "Our Father, in the beginning God created Heaven and earth." There went Miss Martin's cross eyes. You know that broke up the service. The rest of the night, the service, everyone was laughing.

My first airplane flight, I took it without Miss Martin. She had never flown anywhere. She always went by bus, car, or train. (We traveled quite a bit by train. We'd get berths and one drawing room, and we'd share beds.) The first time I went to Town Hall in New York City, I flew. Her husband went along with us. Miss Martin said, "Delois, I thought you had good sense. Why are you flying?" She wanted me to stay on so I could ride on the train with her. All the other members of the group were flying, and I wanted to fly. She said, "I thought you loved me. You going on the plane?" And I said, "Yes, I'm going on the plane. I'm taking my first flight this night."

We had prayer. We prayed every day. She taught classes from the Bible, so many precious memories of her. I even liked the way she smiled. I tried to smile like her. I used to stand in the mirror and try to turn my lips like she turned hers. She was such a beautiful person, and I just thank God for the privilege of letting us have her as long as we did have her. She even taught me to talk just a little bit, used to tell me, "You can do it; you can do it." She said, "You get home and learn those words."

When I married, they were at my wedding. Miss Martin was the first one, she and Gene. Gene was in my wedding. Miss Martin was on the front row and even saw that I had the most gorgeous dress when I came down the aisle. I was really streamlined and looking good, thanks to Roberta Martin.

ROMANCE WATSON

When I was just a little boy many years ago, I was living at 430 East Forty-second Street in Chicago, Illinois. Miss Martin lived directly behind my father's house at, I think, 428 or 430 or 432 Bowen Avenue. I used to stand on my father's back porch, waiting to see this big 1937 Cadillac come by and park in front of her door and for her to get out of the car. I would yell from half a block away, "Hi, Miss, Martin," and she would hear me, see me, and wave. At that time I was singing in Chicago on the broadcast of the All Nations Pentecostal Church. That was little Lucy's grandmother's church. We were all in the choir there. We all grew up with gospel singing.

In 1949 I was traveling with my family singers, the Watson Singers, and I got a call from Eugene Smith saying that Miss Roberta Martin wanted to see me and speak with me. I came by the house, and he presented me to her. We chatted for a little while, and she asked me how I would like to join the Roberta Martin Singers. For this opportunity to hit me squarely in the face, it was unbelievable. I accepted, and I was a Martin Singer from 1949. They took me to Philadelphia, Pennsylvania, which is presently my home, and we were singing at Reverend D. W. Hoggard's church, Mount Carmel Baptist Church, Fiftieth and Race Streets. I immediately fell in love with the pastor's youngest daughter, and she's my wife today.

I just have so many beautiful memories of these singers. We've had ups. We've had downs. We've had good days. We've had bad days. We've had some good experiences. We've had some bad experiences.

We used to have to ride coach going down to Florida. We've had our experiences with the back of the coal cars, wearing your best on the train to be presentable and getting to where you're going all sooty and whatnot. We like to think more of the good experiences than we do the bad ones because really they overshadow all the bad things. Through it all we've kept Christ in our lives. It was because of that, because of that church upbringing, because of knowing the Lord, that we all survived.

There were many, many times when we said, "You know, hey, I can't take it anymore. This is it." But Roberta Martin, in knowing the Lord the way she knew Him, would persevere and keep us right on the right track. I remember one incident in particular. I'd just learned to smoke, [I was] twenty-one years old, and we were at the Theresa Hotel in New York. Nobody told me that Roberta was coming in, and I'm up in the room just puffing away, puffing away, and lo and behold, Miss Martin walked in the door. Have you ever seen anybody eat a cigarette? Well, I ate my cigarette.

First of all, Roberta taught us that each song carries a message. There are songs for different people. Each one of us maybe has a favorite. One song that somebody might sing might not hit you the way this person does it, might not touch you the way it touched this person here. She taught us to present the song as though you were experiencing it yourself. First, know what you're singing about. Then you can get your song over. I'm sure all of us, being gospel minded, and those of you who are studying music have seen a lot of singers who have wanted to come in and incite an audience. They have a set routine whereby they go in and "We're going to do this; we're going to do this; and on such and such a beat, we'll all jump up. We'll shout." But, thank God, we're not that way. Roberta wanted you to be yourself. If the spirit so moves you, good. If not, do the best you can.

First, learn phrasing: each note, each word, stress it. Then get your songs across. Then if the Lord comes down and visits, all well and good. You've done your job.

We've had, as Delois said, so many pleasant memories, and I thank God for Roberta Martin. I thank God for letting her touch my life because, believe me, it has been an experience that I will hold dear for the rest of my life.

GLORIA GRIFFIN

The woman herself endowed a spiritual being in me from just going around with her. I never had any idea that the Lord would have this in store for me. One Sunday Eugene Smith came up to me and he said—my stomach is way out here—"I want you to be a Roberta Martin Singer." Well, I looked at him at first like he was crazy because I know he sees my condition. So I said, "Okay." You know, in Chicago you have a thing, you just go on. You don't believe them. You just go, "Okay." Say, "What's your number, what's your telephone number," talking real fast. I gave it to him, not expecting to hear anything.

Bessie was in the group at the time, and there was no room for me. By the time I had the baby and was ready to go, I had gone to St. Louis to work with Prophet Jones. During that time, Bessie was in a terrible car accident. I got a telegram from Chicago from Roberta Martin stating, "Here is your fare. Would you please come home so you can go with the Roberta Martin Singers next week?" I called her. I said, "I can't come, Miss Martin." She talked and talked. So two nights, I think it was, before they were supposed to go on their tour, they were at Mount Pisgah. It was around Forty-first and Bowen. I came in from St. Louis, not thinking that they were still there. When I got there, I heard that they would be right around the corner from my house. So I went, and Bert herself came up to me, "Girl, you got to get ready and leave. You've got to go with Eugene." I didn't know what to say. They told me to come to the studio as usual and start rehearsal.

Believe it or not, at that time, I'm Eugene's product. By the time he'd gotten me in the group, I got by the grapevine that Miss Martin didn't want me. "She can't sing." It didn't bother me one way or the other. What she meant to me, she still meant to me. Even though she may not have wanted me and maybe didn't think that I could sing, after I got in the group—it wasn't way later on, it was right then—something clicked between Roberta and the Martin Singers and myself. All of the other groups, Ward Singers and the Caravans. . . . God had given me a gift and the Martin Singers kept it dominant. Miss Martin pushed me. She pushed me with praise. She pushed me with spirit. Her smile meant: Just go ahead; God is with you; you can do it.

Messages in song, I learned that from her: how to deliver them, to make a sentence more profound, to end a song for a sinner or someone who is brokenhearted. Her phrasing was so terrific. When the woman was sick and I went to see her, I used to love to talk about the Bible with her. I've always been a person that loved to listen to people who had more experience than I because from them I can learn, and we never get too old to learn.

To me she's still here. She was here last night. She's been with us when we were rehearsing in Chicago. It would be utterly impossible for God's and Roberta's spirit, after fourteen or fifteen years, not to have united. Usually to gather up two people from across the world is a problem because somebody is put on. When every one of the members were contacted, it was just like our blood had been drawn together, and we were eager. We are enjoying being together. We all wish secretly in our hearts today that from here we could go to another university and another university and all over the world, just one year, and tell them that Roberta is still not dead. She's yet alive.

EUGENE SMITH

Now, there's no need in me starting. See, I start, and I go to crying. And that's something I don't want to do, so the only thing I can say is Roberta Martin and Eugene Smith went together like bacon and eggs.

Roberta Martin was sick really about three years. But she did not give down. She only went to the hospital twice. Once she came back and she stayed, oh, five or six months, and then she went back again, and, of course, that's when she went to be with the Lord.

Why did Roberta pick four males in the organizing of this group? My mind goes back to a lady who lived in Macon, Georgia, who was quite a principal character in the music field in the National Baptist Convention. Her name was Bertha Wise.

Bertha Wise later moved to Philadelphia, and she had a group of men called the Wise Singers. I don't know whether anybody in here would know anything about it. They were dynamic. I think that group inspired Miss Martin. I think Bertha Wise inspired her like she inspired so many others. Bertha Wise was a great contralto, great big woman who could play a piano and sing. That's where [the song] "I Can Tell the World about This" came from. She had a tenor who could just hold that note, "I," and then the group would come in. At the end of it, Bertha would grab it, and she would hold it. They were dynamic. They came to Ebenezer, and the people were in the streets.

After starting the group with four men, the Lord told Miss Martin something that He wanted her to do. And that was to add on. Bessie came and Delois came and they've been coming ever since. They're still coming.

The Martin Singers used to leave Chicago right after New Year's. We had many, many engagements that started New Year's Eve night. We didn't get back to Chicago until June. In the winter we would go to California or Florida. We would work from Jacksonville all the way down to Key West. By the time we would come out of Florida, the weather would be nice in this area, and we would go into Philadelphia, where for a number of years we sang at Mount Carmel Baptist Church from Palm Sunday to Easter Sunday, over thirty years.

The money wasn't always plentiful. There were times people would invite you and tell you one thing, and when you got there, it would be something different. I never will forget, we were at a church in New York City. We had been there a week and were closing out that Sunday afternoon. While we were singing in the church, somebody was in the office stealing the money. But the Lord is always taking care of us. We've never been any place that we couldn't get back home. And, we're grateful for that.

Lucy did the teaching as we went along. Roberta might have put out something. She'd mail it to me, I would give it to Lucy, and Lucy would train us. As we traveled, we would learn the song. If we were going to have a recording session, Roberta would meet us, and we would have maybe three or four days' rehearsal with her. Then we'd turn it over to Lawrence Roberts, who for years produced the Roberta Martin Singers for Savoy Records.

LAWRENCE ROBERTS

If I was to summarize the experience of Roberta Martin and the Singers with the recording industry, I would say: what she originated, others imitated but never duplicated. Roberta Martin and the Martin Singers' name and style will never die because Miss Martin's style was not geared, under any circumstances, to deal with just the feet and the hands of an audience. It was lyrics, not just music, that touched the hearts and minds of the listeners. Then the hands and feet.

Roberta had charisma and charm like no other artist. And she was intelligent. Much of what you may have heard and researched about the recording industry ripping off artists is the result of singers rushing headlong into recording, anticipating hearing themselves on the local radio station, and never really knowing what they were doing when they signed their contracts. They signed just to be heard.

If you check the catalog of Savoy Records until 1966, you'll find that Miss Martin was the first and only individual on that label—and our roster of artists reads like a "Who's Who" of American gospel—who maintained her own publishing rights. She was the only artist to receive a general advance worth anything. We were dealing with the owner, a man named Herman Lubinsky, who was the Taras Bulba of the gospel record industry. Miss Martin was the only artist who could go into his office, along with Mr. Fred Mendelsohn and myself, say a very few words, flash her famous smile, and get Lubinsky to pull out the checkbook and begin to write. Sometimes two days later, he would say affectionately, "Roberts, how much did I give her?" She was referred to by Mr. Lubinsky as the "Helen Hayes of gospel."

Now the technical end of our recordings. Back then, we did what was known as two-track sessions. For those of you who have eight tracks at home, the tape size in that encasing is equivalent to the tape we used to record the Roberta Martin Singers and all the rest of our artists. Those two tracks allowed us to control the balance between music and singers. Roberta or whoever was leading, drums, and piano would be on one track. The group, organ, and bass would be on the other. With those two tracks, we got the product that you heard last night. What we produced equals any of the records that are supposed to be so magnificently done today. We did a great job for what we had to work with. We got so much out of Roberta Martin sessions because emphasis was primarily on the lyrics. The lyric had to dominate.

Roberta Martin was, in many ways, such a genius that recording sessions went smoothly, not quickly all the time, but smoothly. When she came to the studio, she was prepared. There were no last-minute changes. Some groups were unrehearsed, over-excited, overanxious. After the producer has to call for take six of any gospel song, the enthusiasm and that part which we now call *soul* is gone. The Roberta Martin Singers' soul sound reached me. It touched me and filled me with a good feeling. What is soul? It's that part of you that reaches that part of me and let's me know where you are coming from. Her music will never die because it reached the soul. It troubled the mind with thought about God.

There were two or three major companies during those years that specialized in gospel: Savoy, Peacock, and Nashboro. As I remember, they had a pact with one another. Savoy dealt primarily with gospel groups like the Martin Singers, the Clara Ward Singers, the Gay Sisters, the Davis Sisters, and the Banks Brothers. Peacock and Nashboro were dealing with the male group sound, accompanied by guitar or *a cappella*. This included groups like the Dixie Hummingbirds and the Fairfield Four.

There are terms connected to gospel music today that were developed by disk jockeys and record companies: *traditional, inspirational, contemporary, easy listening,* and *raucous.* None of these were around when the Martins were making records. These terms came about to separate white gospel from Black gospel and to let a DJ have some idea as to the contents of the record without playing it. It was also done for the sake of making awards. Even now, white stations will not play you unless you are easy listening. You've got to be smooth, cool, calm, collected, refined, dot your Is, cross your Ts, and put every S where it belongs; and for God's sake, don't get loud. When your record is classed by the other terms, then it goes to the station where the Black DJ is in charge. No logging. Play one record seven times a day and never write it down so that you can never get what you are entitled to from BMI, ASCAP, or some of the other organizations like that. Even at the Grammy Awards, we are just beginning to get a share of what we deserve. Why couldn't "God Specializes" have been the recipient of a Grammy Award? It is shameful to say they waited until Mahalia died to give her a Grammy. I wonder who picked it up!

Roberta Martin was in many ways ahead of her time. She came to our company with a knowledge of the business. She came with a following throughout the country. She came with the backing of the National Baptist Convention of the U.S.A. In other words, she had it on arrival.

What was the key to the success of their records, other than what we heard lyrically and musically? Roberta Martin and her singers were consistent. Their identities were made with one company, and they stayed with that company until her death. Today, you hear a group on one label and because they don't hear themselves while passing through Wiswatch, Georgia, they tell the company they are unhappy and want a release. They're from one company to another, never being groomed and made with one company.

Roberta Martin and her group were consistent to company and to each other. She knew what her values were, and she got what she wanted. She knew that being a part of gospeldom and being on recordings take you where you may never actually go yourself. A lot of singers were not aware that the major companies have subsidiary companies overseas which pick up a record, put another label on it, and sell it. This is why the copyright has to be international. Roberta Martin knew all these things.

Gospel singing, the style that the Roberta Martin Singers have, will never die.

7

KENNETH MORRIS
(1917–1988)

〜

KENNETH MORRIS

Composer and Dean of Black Gospel Music Publishers

Horace Clarence Boyer

Much of the autobiographical aspect of this article is based on interviews the author conducted with Kenneth Morris in 1964. —ED.

It was a fascinatingly circuitous route that brought New York–born pianist Kenneth Morris to the position of pioneering gospel music scribe, arranger, pianist, organist, composer, conductor, and dean of Black American gospel music publishers. He was born August 28, 1917, the only child of Ettuila (White) and John Morris. While attending grammar school he began piano lessons, which he continued throughout high school. He served as substitute accompanist for the Sunday school and youth programs of his church, and by age thirteen, he and other teenage boys from his neighborhood had begun playing impromptu popular music concerts. These jam sessions resulted in paying engagements and launched Kenneth Morris's professional career.

Jazz was the rage in New York City, and by age sixteen Morris, then newly graduated from high school, had chosen to become a jazz musician. The band with which he played changed personnel often and never had an official name. It was most often billed as the Jazz Band or the Kenneth Morris Band.

For a time, Morris spent his days studying piano, composition, arranging, and orchestration at the Manhattan Conservatory of Music. He spent his nights playing the new jazz music for enthusiastic audiences in hotels, restaurants, and lounges. Though he did not study jazz at the conservatory, he developed this skill on his own and reaped early rewards for his investment. His first long-distance trip outside of New York City was in 1934. His jazz band was engaged to perform in Chicago's centennial. This trip changed the course of his life and set him on the path for which he is celebrated in the world of music.

The elaborate celebration, called the Century of Progress (dubbed *World's Fair* by much of the press and the citizenry), sought several jazz bands for day and evening concerts and performances of dance music, Morris's band among them. He remembers the experience as one of the most pleasant of his life, but the memory is marred by the fact that his playing both day and night, often in the open air, aggravated his delicate health. Illness forced him to relinquish his position in the band. Rather than return to New York, he decided to stay in Chicago and recuperate.

During his recuperation he often spent his afternoons in the warm comfort of friends and occasionally participated in jam sessions with Chicago musicians. Morris not only could read and play music scores but also could notate music. This news reached Lillian M. Bowles (ca. 1884–1949), a Chicago publisher and amateur composer who had begun publishing gospel music arrangements by Charles Henry Pace (1886–1963) in the early 1930s. Pace, an unheralded pioneer in gospel music, had organized the Pace Jubilee Singers with Hattie Parker in the mid-1920s and persuaded them to record two songs by Charles Albert Tindley (1856–1933) in 1928.

Pace had printed and published "If You See My Savior" and "How about You?" in the late 1920s for Thomas A. Dorsey (b. 1899) before Dorsey opened his own publishing house. Pace is remembered today for his gospel composition "Bread of Heaven" (Tyler 1980). In an appraisal of Pace, Morris states:

Pace . . . never got the same note that Dorsey got, but he certainly was by far the better musician of the two. And he was the first one [who] made records even of gospel songs with his group. . . . He, at that time, was working with Miss Bowles. But they had a falling out so that left her without any one to do the writing of her music. So that's how I got there. Somebody told her about me, and I started arranging music for her. That was back in 1934. And that was when we started off with Mahalia Jackson and all of them. [The] first song [I arranged then was] "God Shall Wipe All Tears Away." (Boyer 1964c)

Morris was thrust into the Chicago gospel movement, and those activities replaced his work in jazz music. He was an arranger at the Bowles House of Music for the next six years, and there he arranged three songs that broke ground in the field and became gospel music standards: Antonio Haskell's (flourished 1930–1960) "God Shall Wipe All Tears Away" in 1935; "I Am Sending My Timber up to Heaven" by Theodore R. Frye (1899–1963) in 1939; and, in the same year, "God's Gonna Separate the Wheat from the Tare," the first song that Mahalia Jackson had recorded, in 1937, and credited to Bowles (Decca 7341).

In 1937, while on a visit to the Bowles Music House, Morris met Reverend Clarence

H. Cobb, pastor of First Church of Deliverance and one of the most popular ministers in Chicago. Cobb, known for fifty years as "Preacher," heard Morris play and secured his services as choir director at his church. The church's large following of local and traveling musicians helped Cobb become a national celebrity. It was in association with Reverend Clarence Cobb that Morris published his first songs, which he had been writing on the side, or in secret.

"Heaven Bells" was published in 1937, not by the Bowles House of Music but by Cobb, and it was distributed through First Church (ex. 61). This song is clearly only one step away from a Negro spiritual of the jubilee variety, one of the principal sources of gospel music. The lyrics are monoaffectual (only one thought or mood is contained in the entire song), and there are very few words. Like the jubilee spiritual, there is no simultaneity of text between soloist and chorus. Morris uses the call-and-response pattern of so many of the jubilee spirituals. In this pattern, the soloist will sing or give the call, "Have you got good religion?" and the choir will say, "Certainly, Lord." In gospel, often as soon as the soloist begins to sing, the choir begins to accompany him or her with some sort of response. In Morris's "Heaven Bells," one finds the older lead-and-response pattern. For example, the soloist sings, "I hear those heaven bells ringing," and the choir responds, "ring, ring, ringing." The soloist comes back and says, "I hear those heaven bells ringing," and the choir sings, "ring, ring, ringing." The choir returns with "I hear those heaven bells ringing," and both the soloist and choir close out with, "Oh, Lord, I know that my time ain't long."

Morris contributed substantially to Cobb's reputation, for in addition to his choir arranging and directing, he introduced the most important innovation in gospel music up to the 1960s: the Hammond organ, which he began playing at First Church in 1939. Morris would later introduce the Hammond organ on recordings in 1947 when he accompanied Mahalia Jackson on her recording of "Move on up a Little Higher" (Apollo 164).

One person who attended First Church and occasionally sang in the choir with Morris was Sallie Martin (1896–1988), who through her pioneering work with Thomas A. Dorsey is acclaimed as the "mother of gospel music." Martin had often talked to Reverend Cobb about her desire to open a music publishing house in Chicago since there were more requests for gospel sheet music than the existing houses—those of Bowles, Dorsey, and Roberta Martin (1907–1969)—could provide. Since Sallie Martin was not a trained musician, she not only needed a scribe to notate the songs, she also needed the money to begin the business. "Preacher," Reverend Clarence Cobb, advanced her the money to open the publishing house, and she persuaded Morris to become her partner and handle the music.

The next stage of Kenneth Morris's career began in 1940 when the Martin and Morris Music Company opened in Chicago. The company, which changed its name to the Martin and Morris Studio of Music in the 1950s, is the oldest continuously operating Black gospel music publishing firm in the nation. It is still the largest supplier of Black

Example 61. "Heaven Bells" (Kenneth Morris, orig. © 1937). Used by permission of Necie Morris.

gospel music. In addition, the Martin and Morris firm was the only publishing house to solicit and publish songs of most of the established and new composers during gospel music's golden age, 1945–65.

Dorsey published only his own compositions, and although Roberta Martin published a number of different composers' works, all of her publications formed the repertoire of her own singing group, which was her principal method of advertising. Martin and Morris's publications were not performed solely by their ensemble, the Sallie Martin Singers. They published music by all the important gospel composers, including James Cleveland, Alex Bradford, Dorothy Love Coates, William Herbert Brewster, Lucie Campbell, and Sam Cooke. All of Martin and Morris's songs were arranged by Morris. Additionally, he transcribed, arranged, and published songs that were not composed by African American gospel musicians but were associated with African American gospel singers, such as "Oh Happy Day," "Peace Be Still," and "At the Cross," as well as songs for which there is no known author, such as "There's a Leak in This Old Building" and "Mary, Don't You Weep." In addition to notating and arranging the music of other composers, Morris was also responsible for demonstrating and selling music at the studio, while Martin's principal task was to travel with the Sallie Martin Singers and advertise the inventory of the publishing firm.

Morris still found time to compose his own songs, beginning a course that would lead to his composing more than three hundred gospel songs. His first year of prolific composition, 1940, proved to be one of his most fruitful.

By 1940, three years after the publication of "Heaven Bells," Morris wrote "My Life Will Be Sweeter Someday." In this work, repetition is used sparingly, and he ends the chorus with a new, non-spiritual-style line. The chorus is as follows:

> My life will be sweeter someday   A
> My life will be sweeter someday   A
> Jesus promised to reward me on that great judgment day   B
>   And my life will be sweeter someday.   A

Here we have a sixteen-measure chorus, the first, second, and last lines of which employ the element of repetition. The song is designed to be sung in concert, all at the same time, without the usual call-and-response treatment. The gospel chorus, less than ten years old in 1940, was the kind of song performed during the early part of that decade.

His first composition to attract wide attention was "I'll Be a Servant for the Lord," performed by the Wings over Jordan Choir (Barber 1978). Morris composed several other gospel music standards in 1940, among them "I'll Let Nothing Separate Me from His Love," and "My Life Will Be Sweeter Someday." It was also in 1940 that he heard a song that would not leave his mind for several weeks. He located the singer, William Hurse, and was so impressed with his rendition of the song that as he sang, Morris notated the melody. Later he added additional verses and a harmonic foundation. He arranged and

published the song that year, and within six months it had swept the nation. Everyone
was singing:

> Just a closer walk with Thee;
> Grant it Jesus if You please,
> Daily walking close with Thee
> Let it be, dear Lord, let it be.

Morris had been composing music while he was working for Bowles, and he published
a couple of songs with her; as was not unusual at the time, Reverend Cobb paid for the
publishing of his songs. However, Morris saved the majority of them, and when he and
Sallie Martin opened their publishing house in 1940, he had all of this music ready to
be published. The result is that about seventy of Morris's songs have the copyright of
1940, although only about thirty of them were actually written in that year.

Looking at fifty-seven songs from the decade of the forties and "Heaven Bells" from
1937 gives us a strong body of material by which we can analyze the early development
of Kenneth Morris's gospel compositional style (see table 8). Morris's models were William Henry Sherwood, Charles Price Jones, Charles Albert Tindley, and Thomas A.
Dorsey, and, like them, he carried on the tradition of writing both the lyrics and the tunes
for his gospel songs.

African American gospel song lyrics usually come in three varieties. First, there is the
use of scriptural quotes or paraphrases of the Scriptures, exemplified in Morris's "I've
Never Seen the Righteous Forsaken" (Psalms 37:25):

> Sometimes we wonder why our test seems so hard to bear,
> And even tho' we do our best,
> We're filled with gloom and despair;
> But thru' the gloom we see a light,
>   for old Man David said:
> I've never seen the righteous forsaken,
>   nor his seed begging bread.

This use of Scriptures also appears in Morris's "Eyes Hath Not Seen" (ex. 62), which uses
the lyrics "eyes hath not seen and ears hath not heard what the Lord hath in store for
you" (Ezek. 12:2):

> When folk around you prosper,
>   even though they're in the wrong,
> Why should you feel downhearted,
>   why should you feel alone?
> You don't have to worry, just remain
>   steadfast and true,
> Eyes hath not seen and ears hath not heard
>   what the Lord has in store for you.

Table 8 Selected Compositions of Kenneth Morris

Copyright Date	Title	Copyright Date	Title
1937	"Heaven Bells"		"If I Can Just Make It In"
1940	"Be Sure You Know for Yourself"		"I've Got an Interest Over There"
	"Does Jesus Care?"		"Must Be Jesus Love Divine"
	"Have You Made Your Reservation?"	1944	"I Know He Has Prepared a Place"
	"He Is My Savior"		"I Thank the Lord"
	"I Know Him and He Knows Me"		"I Want to Be Ready, Dear Lord"
	"I Want to See King Jesus First"		"Is It Well with Your Soul?"
	"I'll Let Nothing Separate Me"		"Jesus Is the Ruler of My Life"
	"I'm Not Ashamed to Be a Witness"		"Jesus Prayed for You and I"
	"I'm Overshadowed by His Love"		"Jesus Will Be with Me in My Dying Hour"
	"Just a Closer Walk with Thee"		"Yes, God Is Real"
	"My Life Will Be Sweeter"	1945	"Eyes Hath Not Seen"
1941	"I Can Put My Trust in Jesus"		"I'm Going to Bury Myself"
	"I Know What He's Done for Me"		"Jesus Steps Right In"
	"I Will See My Savior Some Sweet Day"	1946	"Christ Is All"
	"I'm Waiting on the Lord"		"He Answers Me"
	"Is There Anyone Who Will Help Me?"		"He Will Give Me Rest"
	"I've Never Seen the Righteous Forsaken"		"I Won't Have to Cross the River"
	"Sometimes"		"I'll Keep Moving Along"
	"Yes I Know I Love my Jesus"		"I'm Ready to Do Thy Will"
1942	"Fix My Heart"		"Just Like Jesus"
	"God's Wonderful Grace Is Sufficient"	1947	"Dig a Little Deeper in God's Love"
	"He's a Burden Bearer"		"I Know that I'll Overcome"
	"I Want to Live for Jesus"		"King Jesus Will Roll All Burdens Away"
	"I'll Be the One"	1948	"Jesus Has Traveled on This Road"
	"I'm Going Home on the Morning Train"	1949	"I'm Going to Follow Jesus"
	"Power of the Holy Ghost"		"Jesus Is the Only One"
1943	"He's a Friend of Mine"	1953	"I Can't Turn Around"
	"I Can't Forget"		
	"I Want to Go Where Jesus Is"		

His favorite composition, "Eyes Hath Not Seen" (1945), is the most ambitious, progressive, and sophisticated song in the Morris catalogue. It was made famous by Cora Martin's 1952 recording with her mother's group, the Sallie Martin Singers (Specialty 808); and by Robert Anderson's 1953 recording (Apollo 300). Morris abandoned the quatrain (four lines of verse), which by 1945 had become required in gospel music composition, thus introducing a fresh, heretofore untried approach. The lyrics "eyes hath not seen, ears hath not heard just what the Lord hath in store for you" are quite sophisticated for 1945. This song put the gospel music world on notice that sophisticated poetic text and expressive harmony would be necessary parts of contemporary gospel song.

Second, there is the song of praise or adoration of the Savior, found in both the spiritual and the gospel song, in which praises are offered to God, the Father, Jesus Christ, the Savior, Son, and the Spirit, the Holy Ghost. A representative song of this type from the Morris catalogue is "Jesus Steps Right in When I Need Him Most":

Jesus is with me
Just when I need Him most
Jesus is with me
Just when I need Him most
When I've gone to my extremes, and
All I've done in vain it seems,
Then my Jesus steps right in;
Yes, just when I need Him most.

Also of this second type is the popular "King Jesus Will Roll All Burdens Away":

Why should I feel so sad,
Why should my heart feel glad?
Why should my soul feel so happy and gay?
When all 'round me burdens fall,
Yet I'm not worried at all,
For if I pray,
King Jesus will roll all burdens away.

Third, there is the request or pleading song, in which the singer asks in a straight-forward manner for healing, happiness, assistance in paying bills, or any number of other gifts. A Morris song in this category is "Fix My Heart":

Fix my heart, oh Lord,
    so I'll treat my neighbor right,
Fix my heart, oh Lord,
    so temptation I may fight;
Fix my heart, oh Lord,
    so I'll never go astray,
Fix my heart, dear Lord,
so I'll be ready for Judgment day.

"If I Can Just Make It In" promises the Lord that for entrance into heaven, the singer would not mind the load he or she is bearing nor even the clothes he or she is wearing:

I won't mind the load I'm bearing
I won't mind the clothes I'm wearing.
I won't mind the way I'm faring,
If I can just make it in.
I won't mind the work I've done,
I won't mind the race I've run,
All of my trials will count as one,
If I can just make it in.

The decade of the 1940s proved to be Morris's most fertile as a composer. The Morris catalogue for that period includes such gospel standards as "I Can Put My Trust in Jesus"

Example 62.   "Eyes Hath Not Seen" (Kenneth Morris, orig. © 1945). Used by permission of Necie Morris.

Example 62.   *(continued)*

(1941); "He's a Burden Bearer, Yes I Know" (1942); "Jesus Steps Right in When I Need Him Most" (1945), made popular by a 1952 recording by the Davis Sisters (Gotham G 736); and "He's a Friend of Mine" (1948), one of the first songs made famous by a recording gospel choir, the Saint Paul Baptist Church Choir of Los Angeles (Capitol 70002).

Another spectacular year for Morris was 1944. Almost all of his compositions of 1944 became gospel standards. These include "Is It Well with Your Soul?"; the popular "King Jesus Will Roll All Burdens Away"; and "Does Jesus Care," which provides a lyrical solo over the perpetual-motion response "yes, my Jesus cares" (ex. 63).

In that same year, Morris produced the most popular of his compositions, "Yes, God Is Real" (ex. 64). African American church congregations know this song so well that

Example 63. "Does Jesus Care" (Kenneth Morris, orig. © 1940). Used by permission of Necie Morris.

Example 63.   *(continued)*

Example 64. "Yes, God Is Real" (Kenneth Morris, orig. © 1944). Used by permission of Necie Morris.

they need neither the score nor the text to sing it. It opens with a declaration of the inability of the mortal person to understand the universe and to survey all of its wonders:

> There are some things I may not know,
> There are some places I can't go

However, it quickly shifts to a statement of confidence proclaiming that which the person can understand and his or her joy in such knowledge:

Example 64.   *(continued)*

> But I am sure of this one thing
> That God is real
> For I can feel Him deep within.

According to Morris, "Yes, God Is Real" was his most commercially successful composition. It has been translated into twenty-four languages and is sung all over the world. Although "Just a Closer Walk" has been translated into eleven languages, "Yes, God Is Real" is the only song to reach this stature.

Morris had a particular fondness for the so-called gospel blues type of lyrics, although he was not the first to use them. Morris's most famous gospel blues is "I'll Let Nothing Separate Me from His Love." Most of these songs are divided into two parts: the verse, which paints a situation as it is—pretty horrible—and the contrasting chorus, which describes what it will be like in heaven. An example of Morris's use of this two-part form is his song "Christ Is All" (ex. 65). This song, published in 1946, is the second most popular Kenneth Morris composition:

> I don't possess houses or lands,
>   fine clothes or jewelry,
> Sorrows and cares in this old world
>   my lot seems to be.
>
> But I have a Christ who paid the price
>   way back on Calv'ry;
> And Christ is all, all and all
>   this world to me.

In the verse, the poetic form of ABCB is used, but in the chorus, it shifts to AAAA and uses rhyming words:

> Christ is all, He's ev'rything to me,
> Christ is all, He rules the land and sea
> Christ is all, without Him nothing would be,
> Christ is all, all and all this world to me.

Another example of Morris's use of this two-part form is "Yes, God Is Real."

On occasion, Morris would not wait until the last line to declare the rewards of salvation but would create an "internal refrain," intermittently emphasizing the knowledge of salvation, as in "Does Jesus Care":

> Does Jesus care when I'm oppressed?
> *Internal refrain*:
> I know my Jesus sees and cares.
> Does Jesus care when I'm distressed?
> I know my Jesus cares.

Example 65.   "Christ Is All" (Kenneth Morris, orig. © 1946). Used by permission of
Necie Morris.

Example 65.   *(continued)*

In "Jesus Is the Only One," the internal refrain is

> Who heals my wounds
> I go to Jesus
> When all my burdens and my hardships bare,
> I go to Jesus, He's the one.

Horrible situations are spoken of, but there is some reconciliation at the same time.

Then there are the straightforward songs of thanks and praise. This is the essence even when no mention of the word thanks is present, as in Morris's 1943 composition "How Sweet It Is":

> How sweet it is to trust Him
> How sweet it is to love Him
> How sweet it is to know Him
> Jesus Christ divine
>
> How sweet it is in knowing
> Someday with Him I'm going
> For thee, His love is showing
> He's a friend of mine.

"How Sweet It Is" was recorded by the Saint Paul Baptist Church Choir of Los Angeles in 1948 (Capitol 70002) and became the third recording by a choir to reach renown within the gospel field. The first was a 1947 recording of the Saint Paul Choir, conducted by J. Earl Hines, singing "God Be with You" (Capitol 40018); the second was its recording of "If We Never Needed the Lord Before" (Capitol 40033).

Morris gave equal poetic attention to request or pleading songs, as noted earlier in reference to "Fix My Heart" and "If I Can Just Make It In." The melody to which Morris set these lyrics can be characterized as one that spreads over a range of eight to ten notes, almost entirely within the range of most gospel singers. In this study of fifty-eight songs, five are built on only five tones (pentatonic), three are built on six tones (sextuple), and forty-seven are based on the seven-note scale. The tones of a Morris song are melodically distributed so that the singer has very few leaps—and those leaps can be easily executed, such as in "Does Jesus Care," which opens with a fifth.

These scale tones are shaped to create the valleys, hills, and peaks of a melody, while the melody, if performed expertly, sounds good and brings honor to the composition. It must be remembered that singers have no key to strike or button to push to assure delivery of the correct note. Rather, they have to hear the note in their inner and outer ear and program their vocal computer so that what they think is uttered when they sing. (Singers must always approach their music with the emotion that makes the lyrics come alive, but this cannot be accomplished without the intellect to think exactly of the tone to be produced.) The task is made easier if the notes of the song are not too far apart and proceed to predictable intervals or steps; Kenneth Morris understood this.

Morris's harmony is rather simple. For example, a close analysis of "Power of the Holy Ghost" reveals that Morris uses only three chords: F (F⁷), Bb, and C (ex. 66). Morris overlays these three chords with a rather active melody in such a way that the listener thinks that each time the melody changes, the harmony changes.

During the 1950s, Kenneth Morris directed most of his energies to gospel music publishing. It was during this period that requests began coming to the Martin and Morris Music Company for materials other than songs. To meet this demand, he began publishing a series of guidebooks and pamphlets that covered almost every area of lay activity in religious services. These publications included *The Universal Church Usher Instructor's Handbook* by George T. Grier, which covered such areas as ushering, conducting an usher meeting, and parliamentary law; *New and Best Selling Sermons for the Busy Minister*; and Morris's *Book of Poems with Welcome Addresses and Responses* (Books 1 and 2). Two of Morris's most popular guidebooks were *The Choir Director's Guide*, in which he covered qualifications, duties, choir training, and rudiments of music; and *The Choir Manual and Officers Guide*, with chapters dedicated to organization, election of officers, the duties of officers, committees, and the organization of a business meeting.

In the 1970s, in addition to being the first, Morris became the sole Black music distributor for all publishers of gospel music. He began distributing the music of such artists as Andrae Crouch, Edwin and Walter Hawkins, Sandi Patti, Amy Grant, and Bill Gaither. There was no gospel music that the Morris Music Company was unable to provide.

Example 66.   "Power of the Holy Ghost" (Kenneth Morris, orig. © 1942). Used by permission of Necie Morris.

Example 66.   (continued)

The route that led Kenneth Morris from a musical career in jazz to one in gospel music leaves him with a record of unparalleled contributions in the field. In 1949, at the seventeenth annual session of the National Convention of Gospel Choirs and Choruses, Inc., he summed up his own philosophy toward gospel music—a philosophy that was the basis for his accomplishments and his renown as gospel music's Renaissance man and dean of Black American gospel music publishers: "Before the leader of church music can attain the art of choosing the right song at the right time, he must know how to select songs of worth and value from which he may make a choice; then test the songs for religious content, words, literary quality, tune and trust" (National Convention of Gospel Choirs and Choruses, Inc. 1949).

༄

KENNETH MORRIS

"I'll Be a Servant for the Lord"

A 1987 Interview Conducted and Edited by
Bernice Johnson Reagon

Music is the one form of expression known to humans which is understood by
every tribe and nation. Every human, no matter what his race, religion or
creed, can be brought into mutual understanding with every other human
through the medium of music. No matter how divergent a man's speech or
way of life may be, music can bring him into mutual association and understanding with all other men. Truly, music is the universal language. We may
not understand a foreigner's speech, philosophy or habits but we can readily
grasp his sentiments and moods through his music. Thus, to say that music
speaks is not an exaggeration for music speaks to the soul of a man. Since this
is the case, we should be very particular in our church music for we are not
merely entertaining but speaking to the souls of men and women and therefore should be very careful what we "say." (MORRIS 1949, 1)

Gospel music has been fulfilling for me as a musician, a composer,
an arranger, and a Christian. I enjoy it; I have been successful
with it as a business. I am a Christian, and this music in all its connotations fulfills
something that I had been yearning for all the time and didn't know it. It satisfies my
soul. That's why I stay with it. It is something that nurtures and feeds me personally.

FORMATIVE YEARS

I was born in New York City, August 28, 1917. I started taking piano lessons when I was
a young lad; I imagine I must have been eight or nine years old. I was raised by an older
aunt. She was a Hollingworth, and she believed in musical training, so she secured a
tutor for me. She saw to it that I took the lessons. It wasn't an issue of whether I liked it;
it was something I had to do. I didn't mind it, but I never thought at that particular time
that that was going to be my life's avocation.

I was always in church. My aunt was a church person, my uncle also. My aunt was strictly a Baptist, and my uncle was a Methodist. So I played for both churches. I came up in both. My first piano job was at the Shiloh Baptist Church, [where] I played for Sunday School and BTU [Baptist Training Union]. I was about ten or eleven years old.

I was well advanced in music when I entered college. I had been taking piano lessons ever since the age of eight. In fact I was giving some lessons on my own. I attended CCNY [City College of New York] for three years and at the same time for two years I was getting music training at the Manhattan Conservatory [*sic*].

I left school for economic reasons. I started working for myself in the music field, playing piano in music bands on the side—jazz bands, pickup bands. We played for dances and things of that nature, and I couldn't maintain school and work too. Tuition was free, but [there were] books you had to buy, and of course the upkeep, maintaining yourself. . . . I worked as a musician the whole time I was there, and it caught on with me when I found out that I was able to support myself sufficiently doing that.

INTRODUCTION TO GOSPEL MUSIC

When I came here [Chicago] in 1934, I was a band musician. While in Chicago, I took deathly ill. My nerves gave way, and I was told by the doctor that I could never go back to playing night life again. Someone knew that I arranged music and could play, and they introduced me to Mrs. Lillian Bowles, a music publisher who was looking for an arranger. That's how I got into church music.

There wasn't any gospel music in Chicago per se in 1937. Most churches had the established choirs. The senior choirs would do anthems, spirituals, things of that nature. Mostly, people were singing out of songbooks, hymnbooks. Mr. [Thomas A.] Dorsey was just getting into it. When I was getting started, Mr. Dorsey was the only one in what we really call gospel now. In 1937, Mr. Dorsey was already publishing his music; he had his own publishing house and was independent. The gospel choir tradition had been started with the Baptists, with Mr. Dorsey and Mr. [Theodore] Frye.

I began to work with Mrs. Bowles in 1937. She knew music, but she was not a musician. She was a printer and got interested in printing gospel music. She was a wonderful woman but was strictly a businesswoman. She came here from Memphis, Tennessee, and set up a printing press.

Mrs. Bowles started off with a letterpress. It got too heavy, so she started to subletting, going to a bigger press because we couldn't do it on a letterpress. When you do it on a letterpress, you can run a hundred copies at a time. That was about all you would need. Like I said, it wasn't a big thing, it was a small operation. Nobody thought in terms of money. Nobody thought in terms of making a living with it. Nobody, but nobody. It was no living. You had to have an outside living. . . .

I worked for Bowles from 1937 to 1940. If someone approached her with a song and wanted her to publish it, she, not having any particular knowledge of music, would refer that person to me. Somehow or other I'd have to get the song out of their head and onto paper. This person would have to transfer this song that they had in their mind to me, and I would have to arrange it and put it on paper the way that I thought it would be commercial.

They would have their own words and most of the time they would have their own melody, but that was as far as that would go. A lot of quartets, [for example], would have their own [harmony] arrangements. But most of the time, I would always rearrange them to be suitable to be sung in church by a choir.

A quartet arrangement was usually where a person would lead the song and it would be followed by a background, but I would arrange the song so that it could be sung by a choir or a chorus. Sometimes I would arrange it so that all the parts would be sung together; that was my function as an arranger, [putting together] whichever I thought would sound the best with a group singing it rather than a quartet. A choir sound and a choir arrangement are different from a quartet arrangement, vastly different. Most quartets only deal in three chords to start off with: the I, the IV, the V; that's all, while I would be dealing maybe in five or six different chords. So the harmony was uniquely different.

Mr. Dorsey was only interested in arranging his own music, so he didn't work with anybody else's music. His harmony system was mostly the quartet harmonies. He basically stayed with the one, four, and five, and a certain country rhythm. He had a set rhythm. You could always tell a Dorsey song from the time it started to the time it ended because it was his way. He was the first one to make extensive use of minor and sevenths chords. He introduced those into gospel music.

I had a much different style. I didn't have any set patterns or rhythms. I introduced more and different chords and rhythms. I was using chords that were mostly used by the "outside." I don't think there was that much difference between Roberta Martin and myself as instrumentalists. We were all out of the same school. Our type of beat was different than what anyone else was using at that particular time. Everybody doesn't want four-part harmony. A trio sounds very good if they are well rounded. Of course, you could tell, generally speaking, if you had any kind of musical training idea at all, you could tell what the bass would be. I mean, you don't have to have four-part harmony. I wrote with the triad.

In my group, when I had all lady singers, I didn't have a good bass till Ms. Sallie Martin came along. With her, and her good bass voice, we could write in bass parts. That was what her voice was. She was a very deep soprano. We could write a bass line for her because she could sing it. [Clara Ward, the Caravans, the Davis Sisters, had low voices, but no bass line in the chord] because there were never any bass singers. They had no bass singers in these groups. And they never sang bass. They were not taught to sing bass. That is the next thing. They could have sung bass if they had been taught or made to sing bass. However, the person who was head of the group didn't [seem to] need that.

BECOMING INDEPENDENT

About . . . 1939 and 1940, I found out I wasn't getting anywhere. Mrs. Bowles was using my material and my work, and I wasn't getting paid for it proportionately. If it had not been for me, there would not have been Bowles Music. I was the only arranger and the main writer. I was the one presenting all of the ideas. The first songbook that was published was my idea; *Bowles Songbook No. 1* was my idea; I am the one who introduced her to the idea of it. We were producing so many songs that weren't selling, so I said, why not put a cover over them and you could continue to sell them. They are easier to handle, and a whole lot of things can be done with a book that you cannot do with a sheet.

I started my own business. I had a partner, Sallie Martin. She was working with Dorsey, and I was working with Bowles, so that made it a natural partnership. She was thinking that she was not getting her just due from Mr. Dorsey like I was not getting my just due from Bowles. So we decided to combine our efforts and our talents. She was a singer and I was a composer; she stuck to what she knew best and I stuck to what I knew best. I would teach the group and she would take the group on the road. In her concerts, she would introduce our material. When Mr. Dorsey started traveling around, he had to have a singer. He wasn't a singer, so he had to have a singer or a group of singers. You know he started with a trio until Sallie Martin became his main singer.

Mrs. Bowles did not have a singing group and that was her handicap. People who were out there on the road would come to her for new material. A lot of them would take the music with them. It was a gold mine. . . . The only way to produce a market was to have someone to introduce the songs to the people.

We began Martin and Morris Music Studio in 1940. She moved to California in 1948, so we set up a West Coast branch which she took care of. There was a store, and everything we did here was done out there. When Sallie Martin went out to the West Coast, there was a young lady out there who was writing songs, Doris Akers. She started working with Miss Martin on the West Coast and became a member of Miss Martin's group. We published her first songs. When she pulled out, she took one of our singers that was in the group. They pulled out.

She was a Methodist and worked mostly in the Methodist connection. We were Baptists. The songs that we sang and most of the churches we went to were through our connection with the Baptists. The Baptists were really the ones who pushed this music— at that particular time, it was. If you didn't go to the National Baptist Convention, you could just forget it. There were different singers to come up at different times to sing their songs. Professor Isaac and Lucie Campbell were in charge of the music there at the Convention.

The Pentecostal church had been using gospel from the get go; it just wasn't written. A lot of songs we later got came from them. They just used [them] ordinarily in their services.

When I started out here, the name was Martin and Morris Music Studio Teaching

School. I had to make a living. I gave lessons. We were not looking forward to the sale of music to make a living. "Just a Closer Walk with Thee" [performed at the National Baptist Convention] in 1944 put us on the map (ex. 67). Right behind that, for four or five years straight, I had hits at the Convention. "Jesus I Love You," "Just a Closer Walk with Thee," "Yes, God Is Real," "Christ Is All," and "Don't You Care"—five in a row. That is what put us on the map, in what I would call the big time.

Most of our songs were sent through the mail, or I would go out to get them. The lead sheets I received were according to the scoring ability of the person. Sometimes there were no time values, just round notes over the text on a staff. I had to make up the songs out of what I was sent. I [also] worked with William Herbert Brewster. We were friends. I would go to his house in Tennessee and we would set up an appointment. Then he would have one of his singers to come over and sing his songs, and I would take them down and bring them back to Chicago.

In the first years, we fluctuated between seventy and one hundred thousand dollars a year—in the first years, 1944–54, around a hundred thousand; for the next ten years, between one hundred sixty and two hundred thousand dollars a year. Then it leveled off.

Two things hurt us as far as music publishers were concerned. The records hurt us tremendously, and then the Xerox secondly. The records came in the 1950s, they got real popular in the 1960s, and they cut us out of business almost completely in the 1970s. So business now is only a trickle to what it was. We were hiring as many as twenty-four people at one time; now I am down to three. Of course, I've retired too, you see.

That's right, prior to the record era there were various groups on the road who would feature our music. There were other composers/publishers in the field. You had Roberta Martin, Frye, other publishers had entered the field at that time, but there was enough for everybody because they were still dependent upon the publishers to get the music. Without the records, in order for anybody to learn the songs, they had to play them. They had to hire a musician who could play it, and the musician had to have a copy of the music. You had to have the sheet music. . . . You had to have the sheet music for everybody, rather than to sit down and try to copy [it for each singer]. . . .

Also, during that particular time, even all down through the South, nowhere was Black music sold in stores. The stores would not order from us. All the stores were white stores and they would only order from white publishers. They would not order from us. So our music could not be bought in any store in the South. That's why we set up what we called agents. Everywhere we went we would [hire] agents, and you bought the music from the agents who handled the music, and they sent [the money] back [to] us. All this was in the beginning of the business. It is not until after, after 1946, that the white stores would start to even handle the music. There was such a demand for it that they could no longer ignore it.

We worked ourselves up until at one time . . . we had 326 agents all over the country and in the West Indies and England. They were handling the music. During the 1940s and the 1950s, when the demand was the heaviest, we would print five to ten thousand [copies] depending upon the nature of the song.

Example 67.   "Just a Closer Walk with Thee" (Kenneth Morris, orig. © 1940). Used by permission of Necie Morris.

Example 67. *(continued)*

SONGWRITING

In 1939, I wrote "I'll Be a Servant for the Lord," and it became a national hit. It was sung by the Wings over Jordan Choir. My "Does Jesus Care" and the old one in *Gospel Pearls* are two different songs completely, other than the title. . . . It is absolutely a brand-new song. I knew the old one, all right, same as "Christ Is All," I knew the old "Christ Is All" very well, but when I wrote "Christ Is All," it was an entirely different song completely.

Take "Just a Closer Walk with Thee"; now there's been so much controversy about that song—that is not my original song. It was an arrangement that I made on an old spiritual. It was a plantation song, and I heard it and liked it so well that I came and made an arrangement of it. I went to Kansas City, to a conference of some kind, and one of the choirs there sang it. I asked them where they heard it, and they asked their choir director, Mr. William R. Hurse, where they had gotten it from. He didn't know; he had heard it all of his life. I had never heard it before. I am the one who made the arrangement; the first one that was put in print was mine. I took it to the National Baptist Convention in 1944 and presented it with my group, the Martin and Morris Singers, and it simply clicked. After we left there, everybody was using it.

[However], at that particular time, we weren't too careful about getting copyrights so it was stolen from me. After I made my arrangement, it became very popular. . . . I don't know if I should say this or not, but there was a Southern white publisher named Winsett, and he wanted to put it in his book. When he found out that the song had not been copyrighted, he was free to take out a copyright on it. He did not change the arrangement—not too much. He put it in shape notes, that's the only thing he did. We didn't know too much about copyright during those days. I have a copyright on my arrangement, now. You have to remember that we didn't have any business sense at all. We knew nothing about business. We knew nothing about copyrighting or any of that end of it.

In the first place, Black music was a very, very limited thing. It was only for a few people. [There was] a very small number of people interested in Black music at that particular time. Sales were negligible. It was no big thing. In terms of money, it was very little thought about it—very little thought about it. . . . If we could sell a thousand copies of a song, it was considered successful. At ten cents a copy, there was no money involved. You didn't think in [today's terms]. At that time, it was simply nothing to it.

As far as the copyright was concerned, the expense of copyrighting was about two dollars, so it wasn't even worthwhile. . . . And really, we didn't even know too much about how to go about getting a copyright. We just put the copyright notice on the song, just put it on there. It wasn't until we found out from the white man how popular the songs were, how necessary it was for us to get our own copyright. He started to come in and want our music. This woke us up. When they took my song, "Just a Closer Walk with Thee," that woke me up. From that time on, we started to copyright our material. Before that, we never did. Nobody did, including Mr. Dorsey. He didn't start until he found out that it was money "in them there hills."

Of course the white companies, the big, big publishing companies, started coming in and wanting our music. They wanted to pay for permission to put our songs in sheet music and all these different things. What they had to have was proof of copyright. So this is when that happened. After 1944, we started copyrighting all our music.

REVEREND CLARENCE COBB, FIRST CHURCH OF DELIVERANCE, AND THE HAMMOND ORGAN

Reverend Clarence Cobb was one of the leading ministers in Chicago at one time. He was a most unusual man. He and his church, First Church of Deliverance, had the leading radio ministry in Chicago at one time. First Church of Deliverance is a Spiritualist church. Most people call it a sect. They won't even dignify it with the name of a denomination.

They [Spiritualists] believe everything Baptists and other Protestants believe except for the return of souls. They believe there is an active spirit world. The active spirit world is made up of the souls of those who have gone on before. This is the only difference that keeps them from being Protestant and otherwise. They practice baptism and the other traditional rites. Reverend Clarence Cobb was the leading exponent of this. He became very popular and very famous.

The Baptists believe that you go somewhere and sleep until the general resurrection day. They don't believe that. They believe that when you die, you go to some kind of spiritual world and you still remain wide awake, active, and available to the people. If you can go through a medium who has an affinity for such action, you can contact your loved ones, and your loved ones will tell you something. Or there are others over there who can tell you something or will speak to you.

Reverend Clarence Cobb was one of the first to push gospel music. His style . . . [on] the radio was so people could hear it, and it was so well accepted that people couldn't ignore it. It was a success, and you can't ignore success. The church was so successful, and he used chiefly gospel music. There were two or three good singers, and they pushed gospel music. When I came along, they had a radio choir, but I changed it around to a gospel choir. I worked for four years, from 1938 to 1942, as the director and the organist of the choir.

I introduced the Hammond organ to Chicago and to the world. I knew the organ and I played it for churches. I was the first organist for First Church of Deliverance, and Reverend Clarence Cobb was looking for a new organ for his church. The church had gotten very popular, and he was a lover of music. He had two grand pianos and was looking for an organ. He, of course, didn't have any musical knowledge, but he loved music so [much that] he took me downtown to our largest music store to see about getting an organ. . . .

One of our large stores here, Lyon and Healy, was selling the Hammond organ. They [the Hammond Clark Company] had just come out with what they called an electric organ, a Hammond organ, which was entirely different in concept in every way from the Wurlitzer organ.*

In those days, if the church had an organ at all it would mostly be a pipe or a Wurlitzer. [The Wurlitzer] was the only other electric organ there was, very much on the idea of a pipe organ. It had the same stops as a pipe but it was electric. The Hammond was different from a Wurlitzer because the stops and the action were different. The possibilities were vastly different because you could do so much with a Hammond; you could produce your own tones.

On a Wurlitzer, you had the ordinary tones, solo, vox humana [stops that imitate pipe organ sounds, although the tone actually is produced by reeds]. There was also the slowness of the action [speech, typical of reed sounds]. It was preset, and you could do nothing with it but use the preset keys [stops]. With the Hammond, of course, you had preset keys, but you also had the whole range of your imagination you could play with—you could play a dog whistle if you knew how to do it. The action was precipitous, instantaneous, just like a staccato is on the piano, and you could make it as legato as you wanted. It's endless what can be done with a Hammond organ.

I wanted nothing else. It sold itself. Reverend Clarence Cobb was only too happy to get it because it did what he wanted [since] he wanted to use it for gospel purposes. I think it was something like eight hundred dollars, and that was a whole lot of money at that particular time. . . . It was the most unusual thing you ever heard. People came from all over just to hear me play that organ. Oh yes, it swept! It swept! Instantaneously! I kept experimenting with it, and I was getting all kinds of [sounds] out of it that had never been heard by anyone else before—so much so that Lyon and Healy hired me to exhibit the organ.

At first, like everything else, from the old-line musicians there was a lot of criticisms: That it was jazz, it was nothing but the world stuff, [it was] bringing the devil's instruments into the church. [There were] . . . the usual complaints from the old-line people, some of them didn't want organs in the church. They didn't want pianos in the church; anytime instruments were brought into the church there was some kind of resentment. They didn't want gospel music, period.

NONACCEPTANCE IN THE ESTABLISHMENT MUSICAL COMMUNITY

Well, with all my songs, with all the acclaim I have received, I was not able to join the Association for Negro Musicians because [to them], I was not a musician. It was sheet music, [and it] was gospel music, which was not considered as music. Gospel was not

---

*The Hammond organ was invented by Laurens Hammond and company engineer John Marshall Hanert of the Hammond Clark Company, founded in Chicago in 1928, and it was patented in 1934 (Davis 1986, 315).

considered music until here lately. Before that time, you were not considered a musician. Just like a lot of people used to say about the Holiness church when they use tambourines, "a lot of mess!" I laughed every time I went to the bank. I was making a living doing what I was doing. Half of them were starving to death. I didn't care what they were saying. It didn't hurt me none. I was making a living, a very good one at what I was doing. I wouldn't have it no other way.

I wrote [for] . . . the level of the ability of the people who I knew was going to buy it. . . . You are talking about people not over third grade as far as ability is concerned. As a general rule, most church musicians never get past the third grade, most of them. And if they get past that, most of the time they don't play for churches because churches don't want to pay.

As a music teacher, I tried to bring forth certain musical principles, not sitting down with a pen to write out a lesson, but . . . writing it [the sheet music] in such a way it can be used as a lesson. Not only is this a music studio, but our first name was Martin and Morris Music Studio Teaching School. We gave lessons.

Another criticism was that I would have to write the music in easy keys, not too many florid passages, and within the ability of a pianist of not over a third-grade level. A lot of runs, a lot of sixteenth notes and thirty-second notes; I had to cut them down. You would have to change the time values and a lot of different chords that they are looking for and want now. We couldn't use them then. It was too foreign for their ears and they couldn't play them anyway.

If I wanted them [complex or dissonant chords] in there, naturally, when I played, I could always add and interpolate. So the sheet music was a basic structure. The only thing limiting [the musician] was his ability.

The majority of them [critics] said that it was not real music. It means that it ought to have been written up there what you are going to do. Whatever the composer intended for the person to do should be written on the paper.

There was another way we were criticized. So many people would say, unless they could point out what note to use, they didn't know what note to use—and where is the tenor note? They saw three notes; which to use for the alto, and which to use for the tenor, and there is no bass? They wanted to teach four parts, but they couldn't very well.

To write SATB [soprano–alto–tenor–bass] meant a different type of score. You had a clef for each part and you would have a piano score independently at the bottom. So all this meant space and paper. You were using up a whole lot of paper. From my angle, it wasn't necessary. . . . Most of our score was written for the pianist, incidentally. That is all that was necessary. We would try to incorporate as much of that into the piano score. It was not written for the choir director unless she was efficient in music. . . .

Today, we have the same complaint. They come here [to the studio], and they are willing to take lessons because, well, "I can only play what I can see, and when I get through playing, it is not what these other people [gospel musicians] are doing." When you reduce yourself to playing cold notes, it sounds just like I said, cold. That's what you've got, cold. I don't care how well placed they are, how accurate they are, you are getting cold notes. So you are only repeating what someone else has done basically, but you don't get the gospel feel because gospel, soul, is what we are talking about, is what you put into it and not into the notes. I can play . . . the same song twenty times and never repeat myself, or twenty times I'll play it in a different way because I feel differently twenty times. That's soul. That's gospel. . . . It's soul, and gospel has come to mean soul.

THE FUTURE

I am the only one left [Kenneth Morris died in 1988]. Everybody either passed or they are no longer interested because they can't sell the stuff. Lucie Campbell was publishing her own music. When she passed, her company passed and her music passed. I don't see anything in the future. I have some grandchildren coming along who might be interested in carrying it on. I have four sons; one of them is working with me now to handle the business, but he is not interested in the publishing end of it. This is a mail order house. We ship music all over the world.

We no longer do any publishing per se. I don't publish any new work. I hate to tell you this, but new songwriters have nowhere to go unless they are able to make records. If they are able to make records, some of the record companies have their own publishing house. That is how Andrae Crouch and some of the others are doing it.

There are no sheets anymore. There are mostly books now. We are the only ones left, and we don't publish now. I bought out my former partner [Sallie Martin] in 1973. I got Theodore Frye and the Roberta Martin catalogue around 1978; we also have the Bowles catalogue and with it we got Beatrice Brown, who wrote some of our best sellers.

Choirs and soloists throughout the world still order our music. We also distribute editions that belong to other gospel music publishers. The white companies are still going, you know. They haven't closed up. We carry everybody's catalogue—if it is religious. That's one of our logos, "If it's in music, we have it."

CLASSIC AND CONTEMPORARY COMPOSERS

So what we have now is the modern beat, the modern gospel song. The melodies are almost all the same. The harmonies are not that much different. It is a new beat that has been put to this. So that now you can turn on the radio and unless someone tells you what the name of the song is, you can't tell whether it is country, western, rock and roll, or whatever the modern terms. You can't tell any difference now because the sound is the same. I am not able to differentiate when anybody starts; I cannot tell you offhand what it is going to turn out to be. You turn on your radio today—the fact is that they have stations here in Chicago which are devoted to nothing but religious music—and you would not be able to tell whether you are listening to a rock and roll station or a religious station.

It does for the contemporaneous people of today exactly what our music did for the contemporaneous people in the 1940s, 1950s, and 1960s. Music evolves exactly like everything else. These are facts. So, they were upset when I came along. A lot of people said I was playing the devil's music. They didn't want to hear it in the church. Our biggest fight, when we came along, was from church people. They are the ones who fought us, not the other people in the world. They were the ones who said it was the music of the devil, Satan. It was not church music. They wanted songs that were in the traditional hymnbooks. [Gospel] was not church music. The music with rhythm, they didn't want that. That was not church music.

Well, our generation is saying the same thing of the young people of today. That is nothing but the world's music. We are saying the same thing our people told us. We are telling the children of today exactly the same thing our parents told us. And in the same words. So it is no difference. The people today are just as gospel minded as we were. Some of these songs, I can't even play them. It is hard to play them. I confess the difficulty. These children don't have any difficulty. They don't stop because they are being criticized. They are enjoying what they are doing. People are still being saved and coming to Christ. So who are we to argue? Music goes on.

REFERENCES CITED

Adams, C. C., and Marshall A. Talley. 1944. *Negro Baptists and Foreign Missions*. Philadelphia: Foreign Missions Board of the National Baptist Convention, U.S.A., Inc.

Albertson, Chris. 1972. *Bessie*. New York: Stein and Day.

Atlanta City Directory. Listings for 1909–15.

Banks, Lacy. 1974a. "Albertina the Mirror." *Black Stars* (Aug.): 68–74.

———. 1974b. "The Double-Barreled Gospel of Rev. Cleophus Robinson." *Black Stars* (Apr.): 64–69.

"The Baptist Controversy." 1916. *Crisis* II (Apr.): 314–16.

Barber, Samuel. 1978. "The Choral Style of the Wings over Jordan Choir." DMA diss., University of Cincinnati.

Barry, Thomas. 1969. "The Importance of Being Mr. James Brown." *Look* (Feb. 18): 56–62.

"Black Gospel: Rocketing to Higher Prominence." 1987. *Billboard* (Oct. 10): G–6.

Bontemps, Arna. [1942] 1967. "Rock, Church! Rock!" Reprinted in *International Library of Negro Life and History: The Negro in Music and Art*, ed. Lindsay Patterson, 74–81. New York: Publishers Co.

Booker T. Washington High School Retrospective Prospective from 1889 to 1927 (G. P. Hamilton, Principal 1892–). 1927. Memphis: Henderson Business College.

Bowman, Debbie. 1978. "'Do You Have Your Ticket Tonight?': A Presentation of the Black Folk Drama, *The Old Ship Of Zion*." Paper presented at the annual meeting of the American Folklore Society, Detroit.

Boyd, R. H. 1915. *A Story of the National Baptist Publishing Board: The Why, How, Where and by Whom It Was Established*. Nashville: National Baptist Publishing House.

Boyer, Horace Clarence. 1964a. Interview with Thomas A. Dorsey, Chicago, Mar. 24.
———. 1964b. Interview with Roberta Martin, Chicago, Mar. 24.
———. 1964c. Interview with Kenneth Morris, Chicago, Mar. 24.
———. 1979a. "Contemporary Gospel." *The Black Perspective in Music* 7 (Spring): 5–11, 22–58.
———. 1979b. Interview with William Herbert Brewster, Memphis, Aug. 20.
———. 1980. Interview with Elmer Ruffner, Savannah.
———. 1982a. *The Compositional Style of Rev. Charles Albert Tindley.* Washington, DC: Smithsonian Institution, National Museum of American History, Program in African American Culture.
———. 1982b. Interview with William D. Horner.
Bradford, Perry. 1965. *Born with the Blues: Perry Bradford's Own Story: The True Story of the Pioneering Blues Singers and Musicians in the Early Days of Jazz.* New York: Oak Publications.
Bradley, J. Robert. 1979–80. "Miss Lucy: The Legacy of the Woman and Her Music." *National Baptist Voice* (April): 30–31.
Brewster, W. Herbert. 1949. *The Old Landmark.* Memphis: Bowles Music House and Rev. W. Herbert Brewster.
Burnim, Mellonee. 1988. "Functional Dimensions of Gospel Music Performance." *Western Journal of Black Studies* (Summer): 112–20.
"Clara Ward . . . Gospel Singer." 1953. *Our World* (Dec.): 38–41.
Chicago Defender. 1920, 1923, 1924 (Feb. 2), and 1932.
Court Records, Chancery Court of Shelby County, TN. 1946. No. 48063, Joe Johnson, A. J. Polk, Marie Sturtyvant vs. Rev. Roy P. Morrison, *et al.*, Final Decree of Dismissal issued Jan. 7, 1946.
Dargan, William. 1983. "Congregational Gospels." Ph.D. diss., Wesleyan University, Middletown, CT.
Davies, Hugh. 1986. "Hammond Organ." In *The New Grove Dictionary of American Music* vol. 2. London: Macmillan Press Ltd.
Dinkins, Charles L. 1980. "The Saga of the National Baptist Congress/Christian Education in the National Baptist Convention: Historical, the Present Situation, Projects." In *Utilizing Resources for Christian Education: 1980.* Nashville: Townsend Press.
Dixon, Robert M. W., and John Godrich. 1970. *Recording the Blues.* New York: Stein and Day.
Dorsey, Thomas A. 1935. *Inspirational Thoughts.* Chicago: Thomas A. Dorsey.
———. 1941. *Songs with a Message: With My Ups and Downs.* Chicago: Thomas A. Dorsey.
———. 1949. "Ministry of Music in the Church." In Kenneth Morris, *Improving the Music in the Church,* 42–45. Chicago: Martin and Morris.
———. ca. 1961. "The Thomas Andrew Dorsey Story: From Blues-Jazz to Gospel Song." Unpublished typescript, Dorsey collection.
———. 1980. Remarks during performance at Bible Way Church, Washington, DC, Mar. 28.
Douglass, Frederick. [1855] 1962. *The Life and Times of Frederick Douglass.* Reprint. New York: Collier Books.
Du Bois, William E. B. 1902. "The Work of Negro Women in Society." *The Spelman Messenger* (Feb.): 1–3.
———. [1903] 1961. *The Souls of Black Folk.* Reprint. Greenwich, CT: Fawcett Publications, Inc.
Fenner, Thomas P. [1874] 1901. *Cabin and Plantation Songs.* New York and London: G. P. Putnam's Sons, the Knickerbocker Press.
Freeman, Edward Anderson. 1953. *The Epoch of Negro Baptists and the Foreign Mission Board.* Kansas City: Central Seminary Press.

Garland, Phyl. 1969. *The Sound of Soul*. Chicago: Henry Regnery Company.

Garnett, Bernard E. 1970. "How Soulful Is 'Soul' Radio?" Unpublished paper produced for Race Relations Information Center, Nashville.

Gehman, Richard. 1958. "God's Singing Messengers." *Coronet* (Jul.): 113–16.

George, Luvenia A. 1983a. *Lucie E. Campbell and the Enduring Tradition of Gospel Hymnody*. Washington, DC: Smithsonian Institution, National Museum of American History, Program in African American Culture.

———. 1983b. Interview with Thomas A. Dorsey, Chicago.

———. 1983c. Interview with J. Robert Bradley.

———. 1983d. Interview with Reverend D. E. King, Chicago.

———. 1983e. Telephone interview with Harry Mae Simmons.

———. 1983f. Correspondence with Marian Speight, Jul.

———. 1983g. Telephone interview with Thomas Shelby.

———. 1983h. Interview with Kenneth Morris, Chicago, Aug.

———. 1983i. Interview with Robert L. Holmes, Jr., Nashville, June 13.

———. 1983j. Interview with Sallie Martin, Chicago, Aug. 19.

———. 1990. Telephone interview with T. B. Boyd III, Sept.

Gilkey, Ada. 1947. "Music Just Came Naturally but She Had to Eavesdrop to Nurture that Talent." Memphis *Press-Scimitar*, Mar. 5.

Godrich, John, and Robert M. W. Dixon, comp. 1982. *Blues and Gospel Records: 1902–1942*. London: Storyville Publications and Co.

The Golden Hour Digest 3, vol. 1. Apr 1940.

Goodman, Kenneth. 1982. "Rev. Tindley's Ministry: A Musical History." Paper presented at the Smithsonian Institution conference on Charles Albert Tindley, Washington, DC, May 8.

Gospel music column. 1987. *Billboard* (Aug.).

Gospel music column. 1988. *Billboard* (Jul.).

"Gospel Music Rolls out of the Church, onto the Charts." 1986. *U.S. News & World Report* (Aug.): 56.

Gospel Pearls. 1921. Nashville: Sunday School Publishing Board, National Baptist Convention, U.S.A.

"Gospel to Pop to Gospel." 1962. *Ebony* (Jul.): 107–12.

"Gospel Singers: Pop up, Sweet Chariot." 1963. *Time* (May): 48.

Hammond, John, and Irving Townsend. 1981. *John Hammond on Record*. New York: Penguin Books.

Handy, W. C. 1941. *Father of the Blues: An Autobiography by W. C. Handy*. Edited by Arna Bontemps. New York: Macmillan Company.

Hannah, Clayton L. 1979. Record album notes to *The Best of the Roberta Martin Singers* (Savoy SGL 7018).

Harris, Michael W. 1976, 1977a. Interviews with Thomas A. Dorsey, Chicago.

———. 1977b. Interview with June Levell, Chicago, Dec. 8.

Hatch, James V., and Omanii Abdullah. 1977. *Black Playwrights, 1923–1977: An Annotated Bibliography of Plays*. New York: R. R. Bowker Company.

Hay, Samuel A. 1973. "African-American Drama, 1950–1970." *Negro History Bulletin* 36 (Jan.): 5–8.

Hayes, Roland. 1948. *My Songs: Aframerican Religious Folk Songs Arranged and Interpreted*. Boston: Little Brown and Co.

Heilbut, Anthony. 1970. Interview with William Herbert Brewster, Memphis, June.

———. 1973. Record album notes for *The Roberta Martin Singers "The Old Ship of Zion"* (Kenwood 507).

———. 1978. Telephone interview with R. H. Harris, Nov. 22.

———. n.d. Transcription of live performance, aired on radio, by Queen C. Anderson.

———. 1985. *The Gospel Sound: Good News and Bad Times.* New York: Limelight Editions.

Hentoff, Nat. 1963. "Gospel Gimmick." *The Reporter* (Aug.): 46–47.

Inspirational Melodies No. 2: A Choice Collection of Gospel Songs. n.d. Nashville: The National Baptist Training Union Board, National Baptist Convention, U.S.A., Inc.

Izell, Norman L. n.d. *History of Duck Hill.* Unpublished manuscript, Duck Hill Public Library, Duck Hill, MS.

Jackson, Irene. 1979. "Afro-American Gospel Music and Its Social Setting with Special Attention to Roberta Martin." Ph.D. diss., Wesleyan University.

Jackson, J. H. 1980. *A Story of Christian Activism: The History of the National Baptist Convention, U.S.A., Inc.* Nashville: Townsend Press.

Jackson, Mahalia, with Evan McLeod Wylie. 1966. *Movin' on Up.* New York: Hawthorne Books.

Johnson, J. Rosamond, transc. 1930. *Utica Jubilee Singers Spirituals: As Sung at the Utica Normal and Industrial Institute of Mississippi.* Boston: Oliver Ditson Company.

Jones, Ralph H. 1982. *Charles Albert Tindley: Prince of Preachers.* Nashville: Abingdon Press.

Jordan, Lewis G. 1930. *Negro Baptist History, U.S.A.: 1750–1930.* Nashville: Sunday School Publishing Board.

"Lady Soul: Singing It Like It Is." 1968. *Time* (June): 62–66.

Landes, John. 1987. "WLAC, the Hossman, and Their Influence on Black Gospel." *Black Music Research Journal* 7:67–81.

Levine, Lawrence W. 1977. *Black Culture and Black Consciousness: Afro-American Folk Thought from Slavery to Freedom.* New York: Oxford University Press.

Lift Every Voice and Sing. 1981. New York: The Church Hymnal Corporation.

Lornell, Kip. 1988. *"Happy in the Service of the Lord": Afro-American Gospel Quartets in Memphis.* Urbana: University of Illinois Press.

Lucas, Bob. 1972. "Gospel Superstar." *Sepia* (May): 21–26.

MacDonald, J. Fred. 1979. *Don't Touch That Dial!* Chicago: Nelson-Hall.

McGhee, Nancy. 1969. "The Folk Sermon: A Facet of the Black Literary Heritage." *CLA Journal* 13 (Sept.): 51–60.

Marsh, J. B. T. 1892. *The Story of the Jubilee Singers.* Cleveland: Cleveland Printing and Publishing Co.

Martin, Sallie. 1986. *Oral Testimony.* Washington, DC: Smithsonian Institution, National Museum of American History, Program in African American Culture.

Maultsby, Portia. 1979. Interview with Jack Gibson, Orlando, Feb. 28.

———. 1983a. Interview with Shirley Jones, Los Angeles, Mar. 9.

———. 1983b. Interview with Deniece Williams, Los Angeles, Apr. 22.

———. 1983c. Interview with David "Panama" Francis, Orlando, Dec. 31.

———. 1984a. Interview with Hoss Allen, Nashville, Sept. 7.

———. 1984b. Interview with Albert "Diz" Russell, Washington, DC, Sept. 27.

———. 1990a. Interview with Walter Grady, Atlanta, Aug. 17.

———. 1990b. Interview with Eddie Castleberry, Atlanta, Aug. 17.

———. 1990c. Interview with George Nelson, Atlanta, Aug. 17.

Miles, C. Austin, and C. Harold Lowdens. 1901. *New Songs of the Gospel.* Philadelphia: Hall-Mack Co.

Miller, Perry. 1953. *Roger Williams: His Contribution to the American Tradition.* Indianapolis: Bobbs-Merrill.

Morris, Kenneth. 1949. *Improving the Music in the Church.* Chicago: Martin and Morris.

Moses, W. H. n.d. *The Colored Baptists Family Tree: A Compendium of Organized Negro Baptists Church History*. Nashville: The Sunday School Publishing Board of the National Baptist Convention of the U.S.A., Inc.

National Baptist Convention: Proceedings of the 41st Annual Meeting. 1921. Nashville: National Baptist Convention.

National Convention of Gospel Choirs and Choruses, Inc. 1949. Program booklet for meeting in Los Angeles.

The New National Baptist Hymnal. 1977. Nashville: National Baptist Publishing Board.

Nichols, Reverend Henry. 1982. "The Songs and Sermons of Rev. Tindley." Paper presented at the Smithsonian Institution conference on Charles Albert Tindley, Washington, DC, May 8.

Nichols, Lewis. 1963. "Poems to Play: Langston Hughes Describes the Genesis of His 'Tambourines to Glory.'" *New York Times* (Oct.): X3.

O'Daniel, Therman B. 1971. *Langston Hughes, Black Genius: A Critical Evaluation*. New York: William Morrow and Company, Inc.

Oliver, Paul. 1984. *Songsters and Saints: Vocal Traditions on Race Records*. New York: Cambridge University Press.

Patterson, J. O., German R. Ross, and Julia Atkins Mason. 1969. *History and Formative Years of the Church of God in Christ with Excerpts from the Life and Works of Its Founder—Bishop C. H. Mason*. Memphis: Church of God in Christ Publishers.

Payne, Bishop Daniel E. [1891] 1968. *History of the African Methodist Episcopal Church*. Edited by C. S. Smith. Reprint. New York: Johnson Reprint Corporation.

Pelt, Owen D., and Ralph Lee Smith. 1960. *The Story of the National Baptists*. New York: Vantage Press.

Philadelphia Bulletin. Feb. 17, 1913.

Popkin, Zelda F. 1931. "'Heaven Bound': An Authentic Negro Folk Drama out of Old Savannah." *Theatre Guild Magazine* 8 (Aug.): 14–17.

Reagon, Bernice Johnson. 1975. "Songs of the Civil Rights Movement 1955–1965: A Study in Culture History." Ph.D. diss., Howard University.

———. 1981a. Interview with William Jason, Philadelphia, Sept. 12.

———. 1981b. Interview with Reverend Claude Edmonds, Philadelphia, Sept. 12.

———. 1981c. Telephone interview with Kenneth Goodman, May 28.

———. 1981d. Interview with Ralph H. Jones, Philadelphia, June 14.

———. 1981e. Interview with Reverend Henry Nichols, Philadelphia, June 13.

———. 1981f. Interview with Reverend Marion Ballard, Philadelphia, June 12.

———. 1981g. Interview with Stella Tindley, Philadelphia, Sept. 12.

———. 1982. Interview with W. Herbert Brewster, Nashville, Aug. 16–17.

———. 1983. *Rememberings: William Herbert Brewster*. Washington, DC: Smithsonian Institution, National Museum of American History, Program in African American Culture.

———. 1987. Interview with Kenneth Morris, Sept. 30.

———. 1990a. "We'll Understand It Better By and By." *Topic* 187: 51–53.

———. 1990b. Interview with William L. Robbins, Sr., Berlin, MD, Sept. 12.

Richards, Deborah Bowman. 1982. "A Bibliographic Essay on Afro-American Folk Drama." *Ohio Folklife: Journal of the Ohio Folklore Society* (Spring): 79–81.

Richardson, William. 1930. *Plays and Pageants from the Life of the Negro*. Washington, DC: The Associated Publishers.

Rust, Brian, comp. 1978. *Jazz Records: A–Z: 1897–1942* 4th ed. 2 vols. New Rochelle, N.Y.: Arlington House.

Salvo, Patrick, and Barbara Salvo. 1974. "45 Years of Gospel Music." *Sepia* (Apr.): 60–64.

Sanders, Charles. 1971. "Aretha." *Ebony* (Dec.): 124–34.

Seroff, Doug. 1980. Record album notes for *Birmingham Quartet Anthology* (Clanka Lanka Records CL 144, 001–14, 002).

Seward, Theodore F. 1872. *Jubilee Songs: As Sung By the Jubilee Singers of Fisk University*. New York: Taylor and Barwood.

Shearer, Karen. 1981. Interview with Candi Staton on radio program "Special Edition," Westwood One, Culver City, CA, Oct. 10.

———. 1982. Interview with Donna Summer, Westwood One, Culver City, CA, June 21.

———. 1983. Interview with Lou Rawls, Westwood One, Culver City, CA, Apr. 12.

Sherwood, William Henry. 1893. *Harp of Zion*. Petersburg, VA: Sherwood.

Shirley, Wayne. 1981. "Tindley Record Notes." Record album notes for unreleased Library of Congress recording.

Songs of Zion. 1981. Nashville: Abingdon Press.

Southern, Eileen. 1977. "Musical Practices in Black Churches of Philadelphia and New York, ca. 1800–1844." *Journal of the American Musicological Society* 30, no. 2 (Summer): 296–312.

Spaulding, Norman. 1981. "History of Black Oriented Radio in Chicago 1929–1963." Ph.D. diss., University of Illinois.

Special Songs of Clara Ward and the Famous Ward Singers Vol. I. 1953. Philadelphia: Ward's House of Music.

Special Songs of Clara Ward and the Famous Ward Singers Vol. III. 1956. Philadelphia: Ward's House of Music.

Spillers, Hortense. 1971. "Martin Luther King and the Style of the Black Sermon." *The Black Scholar* 3 (Sept.): 17.

Spirituals Triumphant Old and New. 1927. Nashville: National Baptist Training Union Publishing Board, National Baptist Convention, U.S.A.

Stearns, Marshall, and Jean Stearns. 1966. "Vernacular Dance in Musical Comedy: Harlem Takes the Lead." *New York Folklore Quarterly* 22 (Dec.): 251.

Sugg, Redding S., Jr. 1963. "Heaven Bound." *Southern Folklore Quarterly* 27 (Dec.): 251–61.

Tallmadge, William H. 1974. Record album notes for *Jubilee to Gospel: A Selection of Commercially Recorded Black Religious Music, 1921–1953* (JEMF–108).

Tindley, Charles Albert. 1916. *New Songs of Paradise*. Philadelphia: Paradise Publishing Co.

———. 1932. *Book of Sermons*. Philadelphia: Paradise Publishing Co.

Titon, Jeff T. 1977. *Early Downhome Blues: A Musical Analysis*. Urbana: University of Illinois Press.

Townsend, A. M., ed. 1924. *The Baptist Standard Hymnal with Responsive Readings: A New Book for All Services*. Nashville: Sunday School Publishing Board, National Baptist Convention, U.S.A.

"Tribute: The Life of Dr. W. Herbert Brewster." n.d. Memphis: n.p.

Twining, Mary A. 1970. "An Anthropological Look at Afro-American Folk Narrative." *CLA Journal* 14 (Sept.): 57–59.

———. 1976. "'Heaven Bound' or 'The Devil Play': A Note on Dichotomous Predicates." *CLA Journal* 14 (Mar.): 347–51.

Tyler, Mary Ann Lancaster. 1980. "The Music of Charles Henry Pace and Its Relationship to the Afro-American Church Experience." Ph.D. diss., University of Pittsburgh.

Vedder, Henry C. 1907. *A Short History of the Baptists*. Philadelphia: American Baptist Publication Society.

Walker, Reverend Charles. 1982. Interview with Thomas Shelby, Detroit.

———. 1983. Interview with member, Metropolitan Baptist Church, Memphis.

———. n.d. Interview with Deacon Jeter, Metropolitan Baptist Church, Memphis.

———. 1984. Interview with J. Robert Bradley.

———. 1986. Interview with Charles Kennedy, Romeoville, IL, Feb. 6.

———. 1988. Interview with members, Central Baptist Church, Memphis.

Ward, Clara. 1956. "How a Visit to the Holy Land Changed My Life." *Color* (May): 15–17.

Washington, William M., comp. and ed. 1971. *Miss Lucie Speaks: Addresses of Miss Lucie E. Campbell.* Nashville: C. R. Williams (exclusively distributed by the National Baptist Training Union Board).

Wiggins, William H., Jr. 1976. "In the Rapture." In *Festival of American Folklife*, program booklet, Smithsonian Institution and the National Park Service, Washington, DC.

———. 1981. Interview with W. Herbert Brewster, Memphis, Oct. 6

Williams, Joe. 1985. *Reflections on Mr. Thomas A. Dorsey.* Washington, DC: Smithsonian Institution, National Museum of American History, Program in African American Culture.

Williams, Martin. 1963. "Gospel at the Box Office." *Saturday Review* (Aug.): 41.

Williams-Jones, Pearl. 1975. "Afro-American Gospel: A Crystallization of the Black Aesthetic." *Ethnomusicology* 19 (Sept.): 373–84.

———. 1976. "Performance Style in Black Gospel Music." In *Black People and Their Culture: Selected Writings from the African Diaspora*, 115–19. Washington, DC: Smithsonian Institution, National Museum of American History, Program in African American Culture.

———. 1980. Interview with Eugene Smith, Chicago, June.

———. 1981. Interview with W. Herbert Brewster, Memphis, Oct. 6.

———. 1982. "Roberta Martin: Spirit of an Era." In *Roberta Martin and the Roberta Martin Singers: The Legacy and the Music*, ed. Bernice Johnson Reagon and Linn Shapiro, 12–21. Washington, DC: Smithsonian Institution, National Museum of American History, Program in African American Culture.

Woodson, Carter G. [1921] 1945. *The History of the Negro Church.* 2nd ed. Washington, DC: The Associated Publishers.

Work, John. 1915. *Folk Songs of the American Negro.* Reprint. New York: Negro Universities Press, 1969.

Yes, Lord! 1982. Memphis: COGIC Publishing Board; Nashville: Benson Company.

DISCOGRAPHY

GOSPEL

All of My Appointed Time: Forty Years of Acapella Gospel (Stash St 114).

Anderson, Queen C. *I'll Go* (Gotham 644).

Anderson, Robert. *Eyes Hath Not Seen* (Apollo 300).

Andrews, Inez. *Lord I've Tried* (Spirit Feel SF 1006).

Angelic Gospel Singers. *Touch Me Lord Jesus* (Mal 4381).

Baylor, Helen. *Highly Recommended* (Word WC 8463).

Benton, Brook. *The Gospel Truth* (Cotillion SD 058).

Birmingham Quartet Anthology: Jefferson County Alabama (1926–1956) (Clanka Lanka CL 144, 001).

Bless My Bones (P-Vine PLP–9051).

Boyer Brothers. *Step by Step* (Savoy MG 14155).

Bradford, Alex. *Alex Bradford* (Everest Records GS 67).

————. *The Best of Alex Bradford* (Specialty SPS 52133).

————. *A Lifetime of Believing* (Cotillion SD 057).

Bradley, J. Robert. *I'll Fly Away* (Nashboro 7139).

Brighten the Corner Where You Are: Black and White Hymnody (New World NW 224).

Brownlee, Archie. *Precious Memories* (PLP 102).

The Caravans. *Let's Break Bread Together* (Exodus LP 51).

The Clark Sisters. *Conqueror* (Word/A & M WC8400).

──────. *You Brought the Sunshine* (Nine/Sound of Gospel SOG 1132).

Davis, Mary Johnson. *I'll Wait on the Lord* (Atlantic 890).

Davis Sisters. *The Best of the Davis Sisters* (Savoy DBL 7017).

──────. *Jesus Steps Right in When I Need Him Most* (Gotham G 736).

Fairfield Four. *The Angels Watching over Me* (AVI Gospel 50023).

──────. *One World, One People, One God, One Religion* (Nashboro 7232).

Five Blind Boys of Alabama. *The Best of the Five Blind Boys of Alabama* (Hob HGS 17003).

Five Blind Boys of Mississippi. *Lord I've Tried* (Excelsior 185).

Franklin, Aretha. *The Gospel Sound of Aretha Franklin* (Checker CK 10009).

Golden Gate Jubilee Quartet. *Won't That Be a Happy Time* (Bluebird 7340).

Gospel Harmonettes. *The Best of Dorothy Love Coates and the Original Gospel Harmonettes Vol. 2* (Specialty SPS 2141).

──────. *That's Enough* (Specialty SPS 2134).

The Gospel Sound Vol. II (Columbia CG 31595).

Gospel Warriors (Spirit Feel SF 1003).

Greatest Gospel Hits (Gusto K–5023Y, King Records reissues).

Green, Al. *Soul Survivor* (A & M CS5150).

Griffin, Gloria. *I'm So Grateful* (Savoy 7095).

The Harmonizing Four. *Golden Jubilee* (Jewel 0148).

Heavenly Gospel Singers. *Heavenly Gospel Singers* (Heritage HT 305, reissue of NuGrape CBR–003).

Jackson, Mahalia. *God's Gonna Separate the Wheat from the Tare* (Decca 7341).

──────. *How I Got Over* (Columbia C34073).

──────. *Just over the Hill* (Apollo 221).

──────. *Mahalia Jackson 1911–1972* (Nashboro/Kenwood 506).

──────. *Mahalia Jackson's Greatest Hits* (Columbia C 58804).

──────. *Move on up a Little Higher* (Apollo 164).

──────. *These Are They* (Apollo 234).

Jordan, Vernon. *Live* (Glori ReBorn JC 1052).

Jubilee to Gospel: A Selection of Commercially Recorded Black Religious Music, 1921–1953 (JEMF 108).

Ladies and Gentlemen of the Gospel (Nashboro 7157).

The Little Wonders. *The Little Wonders of Havre de Grace, Maryland* (Kaleidophone KS 801).

Martin, Roberta. *The Unforgettable Voice of Roberta Martin* (Savoy MG 14221).

──────. *What a Friend We Have in Jesus* (Apollo 238).

The Roberta Martin Singers. *The Best of the Roberta Martin Singers* (Savoy SGL 7018).

──────. *From out of Nowhere: The Roberta Martin Singers "Live"* (Savoy MG 14066).

──────. *God Is Still on the Throne* (Savoy 14031).

──────. *Grace* (Savoy 14022).

──────. *Old Ship of Zion* (Kenwood 507).

──────. *The Original Roberta Martin Singers: Here This Sunday* (Kenwood 480).

──────. *Prayer Meeting* (Kenwood 487).

──────. *Try Jesus* (Savoy 14039).

──────. *What a Blessing in Jesus I've Found* (Apollo 218).

Martin, Sallie. *Sallie Martin* (Savoy MG–14242).

The Sallie Martin Singers. *Precious Lord* (Trip TLP 7021).

──────. *Eyes Hath Not Seen* (Specialty 808).

May, Brother Joe. *The Best of Brother Joe May Vol. 1* (Nashboro 7050).

———. *The Best of Brother Joe May Vol. 2* (Nashboro 7101).

———. *Search Me Lord* (Specialty SPS 2132).

Phillips, Washington. *Take Your Burden to the Lord and Leave It There* (Columbia CO 14277-D).

Pilgrim Travelers. *The Best of the Pilgrim Travelers Vol. 1* (Specialty SPS 2121).

———. *The Best of the Pilgrim Travelers Vol. 2* (Specialty SPS 2140).

Saint Paul Baptist Church Choir (Los Angeles). *He's a Friend of Mine* (Capitol 70002).

———. *God Be with You* (Capitol 40018).

———. *If We Never Needed the Lord Before* (Capitol 40033).

Smallwood, Richard. *The Richard Smallwood Singers* (Onyx Records).

Soul Stirrers. *The Gospel Sound of Sam Cooke with the Soul Stirrers Vol. I* (Specialty SPS 2116).

———. *The Gospel Sound of Sam Cooke with the Soul Stirrers Vol. II* (Specialty SPS 2128).

———. *Jesus Gave Me Water* (Specialty 802).

———. *Lord I've Tried* (Aladdin 203).

———. *The Soul Stirrers Featuring Sam Cooke* (Specialty SPS 2106).

Staple Singers. *Pray On* (Up Front UPF 133).

———. *Will the Circle Be Unbroken* (Buddah BDS 7508).

Swan Silvertones. *Get Right with the Swan Silvertones* (Archives Alive 8122–70081, reissue of Veejay releases).

———. *Lord I've Tried* (King 4282).

———. *Love Lifted Me* (Specialty SPS 2122).

Sweet Honey in the Rock. *Feel Something Drawing Me On* (Flying Fish FF 375).

Staton, Candi. *Sing a Song* (Beracah BRI-C2001).

———. *Stand up And Be a Witness* (Beracah BRI-C2020).

Take 6. *So Much 2 Say* (Reprise 25892).

———. *Take 6* (Reprise 25670).

Tharpe, Sister Rosetta. *Beams of Heaven* (Decca 3254).

———. *Gospel Train Vol. II* (Lexion/Polygram 841391–4).

———. *Rock Me* (Decca 2243).

———. *Singing in My Soul* (Savoy MG–14224).

———. *The One and Only Sister Rosetta Tharpe: Precious Memories* (Savoy MG 14214).

Vails, Donald, and the Choraleers. *In Deep Water* (Savoy SL 14421).

Walker, Albertina. *You Believed in Me* (Benson C02673).

———, and the Caravans. *Tell the Angels I'm on My Way* (States 103).

Ward, Clara, and the Ward Singers. *At the Cross* (Gotham 724 and Spirit Feel SF 1002).

———. *The Best of the Ward Singers of Philadelphia, Pa.* (Savoy 7015).

———. *God's Amazing Love* (Savoy MG 14026).

———. *How I Got Over* (Hob HBX 2137).

———. *I'm Climbing Higher and Higher* (Savoy 4055).

———. *My Jesus Is All and All* (Savoy 4013).

———. *The Old Land Mark* (Savoy 4033).

———. *Surely God Is Able* (Savoy 4017).

———. *Tell the Angels I'm on My Way* (Savoy 4023).

Williams, Deniece. *So Glad I Know* (Sparrow SP 61121).

Williams, Marion. *Farther on up the Road* (Spirit Feel SF 1002).

———. *Gospel Warriors* (Spirit Feel SF 1003).

———. *I Thank You Lord* (Spirit Feel SF 1013).

———. *Jesus Is All* (Spirit Feel SF 1007).

———. *Move on up a Little Higher* (Spirit Feel SF 1011).

———. *Pure Gold* (John Hammond FW 37598).

————. *Surely God Is Able* (Spirit Feel SF 1011).
The Winans. *Return* (Qwest 261612).

POPULAR MUSIC

Baker, Anita. *Decisions* (Qwest 925510–1).
Benton, Brook. *Golden Hits Vol. II* (Mercury MG 20774).
————. *The Incomparable Brook Benton: 20 of His Greatest Hits* (TVP 1008).
Big Maybelle. *Big Maybelle Sings* (Savoy 14005).
Brown, James. *Live at the Apollo: Vol. II* (King 11022).
Butler, Jerry. *Ice 'n' Hot* (Foundation FR 2821).
Chandler, Gene. *23 Greatest Hits* (Red Dog Express 2636492).
Charles, Ray. *Greatest Hits* (ABC 415).
————. *Tell the Truth* (Charly CRB 1071).
Cooke, Sam. *You Send Me* (RCA ACL 10445).
Dominoes. *All Their Hits (1951–1965) Vol. I* (King 5005X).
Foreigner. *Agent Provocateur* (Atlantic A2 81999).
Franklin, Aretha. *30 Greatest Hits* (Atlantic A2 81668).
Graham Central Station. *Now Do U Wanta Dance* (Warner Bros. BS 3041).
————. *Release Yourself* (Warner Bros. BS 2814).
Green, Al. *Call Me* (Hi XSHL 32077).
————. *Gets Next to You* (Hi SHL 32062).
————. *Let's Stay Together* (Hi SHL 32070).
————. *Livin' for You* (Hi ASHL 32082).
Hammer, M. C. *Please Don't Hurt 'Em* (Capitol CDP 7928572).
Hayes, Isaac. *Best of Isaac Hayes* (Enterprise ENS 7510).
Isley Brothers. *Forever Gold: A Collection of Their Greatest Hits* (T Neck PZ 34452).
The Jones Girls. *At Peace with Woman* (Philadelphia International 36767).
————. *The Jones Girls* (Philadelphia International 35757).
Little Anthony and the Imperials. *Little Anthony and the Imperials* (Sunset SUS 5287).
Mayfield, Curtis. *His Early Years with the Impressions* (ABC ABCX 780/2).
Millinder, Lucky, and His Orchestra. *Let It Roll* (MCA 1357).
The O'Jays. *Greatest Hits* (Liberty LN 10119).
The Orioles. *Best of the Orioles Featuring Sonny Til Vol. One* (Murray Hill M61234).
Pickett, Wilson. *Wilson Pickett's Greatest Hits* (Atlantic SD 2 501).
Porter Sisters. *Tambourines to Glory* (Folkways FG 3538).
Rawls, Lou. *The Best of Lou Rawls* (Capitol SN 16096).
Redding, Otis. *History of Otis Redding* (ATCO SD 33 261).
Robinson, Smokey. *Blame It on Love and All the Great Hits* (Tamla 6064TLB).
Ross, Diana. *Greatest Hits* (Motown M6 869S1).
Sam & Dave. *20 Greatest Hits* (AAD 2462245).
Staple Singers. *Be Altitude: Respect Yourself* (Stax STS 3002).
Staton, Candi. *House of Love* (Warner Bros. BSK 3207).
Warwick, Dionne. *20 Greatest Hits* (Phoenix 20 611 A).
Washington, Dinah. *Golden Hits: Volume II* (Mercury SR–60789).
Williams, Deniece. *Special Love* (MAC MCAD–6338).

ANNOTATED BIBLIOGRAPHY
OF AFRICAN AMERICAN
GOSPEL MUSIC

Lisa Pertillar Brevard

BOOKS

Brooks, Tilford. *America's Black Musical Heritage*. Englewood Cliffs, NJ: Prentice-Hall, 1984.
Includes musical analyses of spirituals, ragtime, jazz, and gospel music. Brooks's section on gospel music focuses on Thomas A. Dorsey's career. With discography and listing of composers' works.

Broughton, Viv. *Black Gospel: An Illustrated History of the Gospel Sound*. New York: Poole, Dorset, Blandford Press, 1985.
Discusses the development of gospel music forms from a sociohistorical perspective. Includes a chapter that focuses on Thomas A. Dorsey and Sallie Martin and a section on the development of gospel music in Britain. Discusses American popular artists such as Sam Cooke, Aretha Franklin, Ray Charles, Dionne Warwick, and others.

Brown, Sterling, Arthur P. Davis, and Ulysses Lee, editors. *The Negro Caravan*. New York: Citadel Press, 1941.
A collection of short stories, novel portions, poetry, dramatic literature, biographies, and essays on aspects and essential components of Black American culture through the eyes of influential African American writers. Section on folk literature includes spirituals and jubilee quartets.

Courlander, Harold. *Negro Folk Music, U.S.A.* New York: Columbia University Press, 1963.
Contains few references to gospel music but discusses African American folk music styles, in-

strumentation, and dances. Music discussed includes field cries and hollers, anthems and spirituals, work songs, blues, Louisiana Creole songs, and children's play songs.

de Lerma, Dominique-René. *Reflections on Afro-American Music.* Kent, OH: Kent State University Press, 1973.
Compilation of colloquia proceedings held at Indiana University's Black Music Center, focusing on curriculum development, Black composers, soul music, and jazz. With discography
and videography on African American gospel music; chapter on Thomas A. Dorsey; listing of
Black music artists and their managers; listing of some college texts that include discussions on
African American music.

Dixon, Robert M. W., and John Godrich. *Blues and Gospel Records 1902–1943.* 3rd ed., Essex,
England: Storyville Publications and Co., 1982.
Lists African American blues and gospel records and related recordings between the years 1902
and 1943. Does not include arranged spirituals but includes some of the earliest gospel singers
recorded.

Dje Dje, Jacqueline Cogdell. *American Black Spiritual and Gospel Songs from Southeast Georgia: A Comparative Study.* Los Angeles: University of California Center for Afro-American
Studies, 1978.
A study of vocal techniques in spiritual and gospel song. Dje Dje defines, compares, and dis-
tinguishes between the two music forms based on their development and function in relation to
historical, social, and economic factors. Dje Dje illustrates the role of the spiritual in shaping
African American gospel music and the role of African American gospel music in shaping popular vocal performance. The author transcribes, analyzes, and compares performance techniques of a select group of vocalists from Jessup, Waycross, and Gardi, Georgia, and
Jacksonville, Florida. Bibliography and glossary.

Epstein, Dena J. *Sinful Tunes and Spirituals: Black Folk Music to the Civil War.* Chicago: University of Illinois Press, 1977.
Traces the development of Black folk music as an African-based art form. Epstein, a librarian
by profession, allows the reader to look at portions of cited materials to judge their validity and
value. Epstein bases her work on personal letters, journals, drawings, and other documents that
present Black folk music as seen by observers prior to the Civil War.

Floyd, Samuel A., Jr., and Marsha Reisser. *Black Music in the United States: An Annotated
Bibliography of Selected Reference and Research Materials.* White Plains, NY: Kraus Interna-
tional Publications, 1983.
A comprehensive listing and annotation of many of the most important sources on Black
American musics. Contains relatively few references to gospel music but cites references to
James Cleveland, recordings, discographies, and other related works.

Goreau, Laurraine. *Just Mahalia, Baby!* Gretna, LA: Pelican Publishing Co., 1975.
A probing, provocative look into the trials and triumphs of Mahalia Jackson. Chronicles Jackson's rise from New Orleans poverty to wealth and international acclaim. Largely based on
personal interviews and correspondence with Jackson, her relatives, and colleagues.

Haydon, Geoffrey, and Dennis Marks. *Repercussions: A Celebration of African American Music.*
London: Century Publishers, 1985.
Doug Seroff's chapter "On the Battlefield: Gospel Quartets in Jefferson County, Alabama"
traces the history and development of the African American gospel-quartet tradition, starting
with a detailed profile of the Fisk Jubilee Singers and their repertoire of classically styled Black
spirituals. Selected bibliography and discography.

Heilbut, Anthony. *The Gospel Sound.* New York: Anchor Press/Doubleday, 1985.
A useful introduction to African American gospel music pioneers, including Thomas A. Dor-

sey, Sallie Martin, Lucie E. Campbell, Professor Alex Bradford, Reverend Charles Albert Tindley, Roberta Martin, and others. Also focuses on trailblazing male gospel quartets, such as the
Dixie Hummingbirds, and discusses the powerful influence of gospel music on popular music
forms and performance styles. Largely written in the vernacular, at times with vague references
to interviewed persons. With photos and selected discography.

Jackson, Irene V. *Afro-American Religious Music: A Bibliography and Catalogue of Gospel Music*. Westport, CT: Greenwood Press, 1979.

Lists books, theses, dissertations, journals, articles, and discographies on Black gospel music
and related topics. Also contains a short guide to identifying printed gospel music.

Jones, Ralph H. *Charles Albert Tindley: Prince of Preachers*. Nashville: Abingdon Press, 1982.

A biographical study of the gospel hymn composer Reverend Charles Albert Tindley, written by
a journalist and editor and a lifelong member of the Tindley Temple United Methodist Church
in Philadelphia. Largely based on interviews, the recollections of the author, and literature
written by Tindley himself.

Levine, Lawrence W. *Black Culture and Black Consciousness: Afro-American Folk Thought from
Slavery to Freedom*. New York: Oxford University Press, 1978.

Captures essential elements of African American folk thought and the many ways in which it is
manifested in, preserved by, and transmitted through oral culture, music, and dance. Includes
a strong section on nineteenth-century sacred music.

Licht, Michael. *D.C. Gospel Groups 1989*. Washington, DC: Folk Arts Program, D.C. Com-
mission on the Arts and Humanities, 1989.

A catalogue of names, addresses, founding dates, and anniversaries of African American harmony groups and quartets in Washington. Also contains a listing of broadcast and print media
that include or are devoted to gospel music. Brief introduction on the development of Black
American gospel music.

Lornell, Kip. *"Happy in the Service of the Lord": Afro-American Gospel Music Quartets in Memphis*. Urbana: University of Illinois Press, 1988.

Traces the development of the African American gospel-quartet tradition, from jubilees, Black
minstrelsy, and Black barbershop quartets to the present. Largely based on interviews.

Maultsby, Portia K. *Afro-American Religious Music: A Study in Musical Diversity*. Springfield,
OH: The Hymn Society of America, Wittenberg University, 1986.

A sociocultural and historical survey of African American sacred musical expression, including
Black spirituals and gospels, relating their connections to European, Euro-American, West African, and African American musical traditions. Discusses the impact of slaves' conversion to
Christianity on the development of Black sacred music forms; characteristics and roles of religious musical expression in traditional West African culture, and their connections to those of
African American churches; and connections between African American religion and preaching and traditional West African religious world views and expressions. With sociocultural and
musical analyses of textual components of African American sacred musics.

National Baptist Convention, U.S.A. *Gospel Pearls*. Nashville: Sunday School Publishing Board,
National Baptist Convention, U.S.A., ca. 1921.

The first book to use the word *gospel* to refer to the religious music contained therein. Contains
musical compositions by Reverend Charles Albert Tindley and Lucie E. Campbell. Printed in
shape-note style.

Newman, Mark. *Entrepreneurs of Profit and Pride: From Black Appeal to Radio Soul*. New York:
Praeger, 1988.

Illustrates the tremendous impact of Black music on all aspects of the radio industry. Traces the
history of the relationship between Black American recording artists and (primarily white) ra-

dio, from Black radio minstrelsy to soul music radio programming. Newman's chapter "Blues to Soul" focuses on commercial elements related to the development and popularization of blues, soul, rhythm and blues, and gospel music. Discusses the lyrical content and function of blues, gospel, soul, and rhythm and blues. With bibliography.

Odum, Howard W., and Guy B. Johnson. *The Negro and His Songs: A Study of Typical Negro Songs in the South*. Westport, CT: Negro Universities Press, 1968.
Although biased toward European musical traditions, this work offers some important insights into the sociocultural significance of Black American music forms from spirituals to jazz.

Oliver, Paul, Max Harrison, and William Bolcom. *The New Grove: Gospel, Blues and Jazz (with Spirituals and Ragtime)*. London: Macmillan, 1986.
Discusses and gives examples of vocal traditions and lyrics used in race recordings. Contains discography and guide to reissued race recordings. Focuses on blues recordings of the 1920s but also includes chapters on the song-sermons of preachers, song traditions of the Sanctified church, and singing evangelists.

Reagon, Bernice Johnson. *In Search of Charles Albert Tindley*. Washington, DC: Smithsonian Institution, National Museum of American History, Program in Black American Culture, 1981.
Describes the worship and song tradition at the Tindley Temple United Methodist Church, founded in Philadelphia by pioneering gospel music composer Reverend Charles Albert Tindley.

Reagon, Bernice Johnson, editor. *Black American Culture and Scholarship: Contemporary Issues*. Washington, DC: Smithsonian Institution Press, 1985.
Collection of papers presented at Smithsonian Institution conferences, including two essays by the author on history of Smithsonian Institution's involvement in research and several articles on gospel music by Horace Clarence Boyer and Pearl Williams-Jones. Includes essays on gospel music, jazz, storytelling, and other history- and culture-transmitting methods utilized in Black communities and in the mass media. Also includes essays on Black African–based cultures in Appalachia and the Caribbean.

Reagon, Bernice Johnson, and Linn Shapiro, editors. *Black People and Their Culture: Selected Writings from the African Diaspora*. Washington, DC: Smithsonian Institution Press, 1976.
Essays document innovative programs created by African American scholars under the leadership of Bernice Johnson Reagon. Includes two articles on gospel by Pearl William-Jones and by Jane Sapp and Reagon.

———. *The Roberta Martin Singers: The Legacy and the Music*. Washington, DC: Smithsonian Institution, National Museum of American History, 1982.
Collection of papers presented during Smithsonian colloquium and concert performance tribute to gospel music pioneer Roberta Martin. Contains extensive biographical information on Roberta Martin. Writers include Pearl Williams-Jones, Horace Clarence Boyer, Portia Maultsby, Irene Jackson, and others.

Ricks, George R. *Some Aspects of the Religious Music of the United States Negro: An Ethnomusicological Study with Special Emphasis on the Gospel Tradition*. New York: Arno Press, 1977.
Describes and classifies spirituals, jubilees, and the following types of shouts: moanin' songs, songs for the dead, and song narratives. Delineates the relationship between demographics and religious expression through music. Compares gospel songs and jubilees and describes characteristics of Black choral traditions. With a discussion on the history and development of African American spirituals, folk hymns, and gospel music.

Seroff, Doug. *Birmingham Quartet Scrapbook: A Quartet Reunion in Jefferson County*. Washington, DC: Smithsonian Institution, National Museum of American History, 1980.

A companion text to the 1980 Grammy-nominated recording *Birmingham Quartet Anthology—Jefferson County, Alabama (1929–1953)* (Alabama Traditions 001), which contains an accompanying booklet.

———. *Gospel Arts Day*. Nashville: Fisk University, June 19, 1988.
Program booklet accompanying Nashville's first national-scale celebration of the African American gospel-quartet tradition. Focuses on the development of the quartet tradition, from spirituals to jubilees and gospel. Discusses pioneers who helped increase the popularity and respectability of the Black spiritual. Performing artists included in the celebration: the Singers, the Fireside Singers, the Voices of Nashville, and the Fairfield Four. With photos and footnotes.

———. *Gospel Arts Day*. Nashville: Fisk University, June 18, 1989.
Booklet that accompanied Nashville's annual celebration of the Black quartet tradition. Discusses the history and development of the Black quartet tradition, from the spiritual to the jubilee, and includes profiles of the Alabama Quartet; the Fisk Jubilee Singers; the Weary Travelers (of Mobile, Alabama); the Golden Gate Jubilee Quartet; and others.

Southern, Eileen. *The Music of Black Americans: A History*. 2nd ed. New York: W. W. Norton & Co., 1982.
Discusses instruments, songs, celebrations, and music performance traditions used by Blacks in both sacred and secular settings in West Africa and the New World. Covers eighteenth-century congregational singing, urban and rural musics in the antebellum era, spirituals, concert music, Broadway and off-Broadway musicals, ragtime, jazz, gospel, soul, rock-and-roll, and popular music. Southern's section on gospel music covers major composers, performers, and gospel quartets. With photos, discography, and extensive bibliography.

Tindley, Reverend Charles A. *Book of Sermons*. Philadelphia: Reverend Charles Albert Tindley, 1509 Christian Street, Philadelphia, PA, 1932.
A collection of sermons written and preached by gospel music pioneer Reverend Charles Albert Tindley.

———. *New Songs of Paradise!* Philadelphia: Paradise Publishing Co., 1916.
A collection of gospel hymns by Reverend Charles Albert Tindley.

Walker, Wyatt Tee. *"Somebody's Calling My Name": Black Sacred Music and Social Change*. Valley Forge, PA: Judson Press, ca. 1979.
A sociohistorical study of Black sacred music. The chapter "'The Lord Will Make a Way Somehow'—Gospel: Historic and Modern" defines gospel music, discusses it in relation to blues and jazz, and makes reference to gospel music pioneer Thomas A. Dorsey.

ARTICLES

"Black American Gospel Music: A Twentieth-Century Song and Performance Tradition." Washington, DC: Smithsonian Institution, National Museum of American History, May 12, 1988.
Program booklet that accompanied Smithsonian conference on the African American gospel music tradition. Includes lead article on quartet tradition by Doug Seroff.

Bontemps, Arna. "Rock, Church! Rock!" In *International Library of Negro Life and History: The Negro in Music and Art*, ed. Lindsay Patterson, 74–81. New York: Publisher's Company, 1967.
Highlights Thomas Andrew Dorsey's musical transition from blues composer to "father of gospel music."

Boyd, Joe Dan. "The Sacred Harpers and Their Singing Schools." In 1970 Festival of American Folklife, 38–39. Washington, DC: Smithsonian Institution, Office of Folklife Programs, 1970. A short introduction to the Sacred Harp singing tradition (also called shape-note, four-note, and fasola music). Describes desired sound qualities and designation of "parts" used in Sacred Harp singing. Notes geographical areas in the United States where Sacred Harp remains an important element of Black folk culture.

Boyer, Horace Clarence. "An Overview: Gospel Music Comes of Age." Black World 23, no. 1 (Nov. 1973): 42–48, 79–86. Focuses on the widespread impact of gospel music upon popular artists and both secular and nonsecular audiences. Makes important distinctions between spirituals and gospel music forms and shows how white audiences gradually adopted African American gospel sounds.

———. "An Analysis of His Contributions: Thomas A. Dorsey, 'Father of Gospel Music.'" Black World 23, no. 9 (Jul. 1974): 20–28. Highlights the accomplishments of pioneering Black gospel music composer Thomas A. Dorsey; provides insights into the role of Dorsey and others in creating, popularizing, and publishing classic and contemporary gospel music.

———. "Contemporary Gospel Music: Sacred or Secular?" First World 1, no. 1 (Jan./Feb. 1977): 46–49. Delineates similarities and differences between sacred and secular gospel music forms, performance styles, and recordings. Boyer questions whether gospel music, with its ever-changing, contemporary sound, will eventually cease to be the domain of the church.

———. "Gospel Music." Music Educators Journal 64, no. 9 (May 1978): 34–43. Chronicles the development of gospel music as an art form in its own right and highlights Black classic and contemporary gospel music composers and song stylists who developed gospel music along sacred and secular paths.

———. "Contemporary Gospel Music, Part 2: Characteristics and Style." The Black Perspective in Music 7, no. 1 (Spring 1979): 22–58. Defines Black gospel singing and instrumentation styles. Discusses the role of the gospel singer and the congregation within the context of the church service. Makes important distinctions between gospel and quartet singing and accompaniment. Includes musical and notational analyses of major elements of the Black gospel song.

———. "Defining, Researching, and Teaching Gospel Music: A Contemporary Assessment." In Black American Culture and Scholarship: Contemporary Issues, ed. Bernice Johnson Reagon, 33–40. Washington, DC: Smithsonian Institution Press, 1985. Defines gospel music and offers suggestions on how to conduct research on and transmit information about gospel music. Also includes a helpful introductory bibliography on gospel music that includes books, articles, theses, dissertations, discographies, and recorded anthologies.

———. "The 'Old Meter Hymn' and Other Types of Gospel Songs." Views on Black American Music 2 (1984–85): 41–46. Delineates several kinds of Black gospel songs, including the shout, the Baptist lining hymn, the gospel blues, the gospel ballad, and the jubilee. Analyzes compositions and recordings that exemplify these song types.

———. "Kenneth Morris: Composer and Dean of Black American Gospel Music Publishers." In Classic Gospel Song: The Music of Kenneth Morris, ed. Niani Kilkenny and Robert Selim. Washington, DC: Smithsonian Institution, National Museum of American History, 1986. Highlights the life and works of African American gospel music pioneer Kenneth Morris. Program booklet article of Smithsonian Institution conference on Morris.

———. "Tracking the Tradition: New Orleans Sacred Music." Black Music Research Journal 8, no. 1 (1988): 135–47.

Noting the difficulties in conducting scholarly studies of locally known, short-lived gospel groups, Boyer focuses on the gospel tradition in New Orleans from 1930 to the present. Includes sections on gospel quartets, accompanied gospel groups and choirs, promoters, agents, composers, and publishers. Notes popular singers such as Lou Rawls, Bessie Griffin, and Mahalia Jackson, whose musical styles are rooted in the New Orleans Black gospel tradition.

Brown, Roxanne. "The Glory of Gospel: Will the Message Be Lost in the Contemporary Sound?" *Ebony* (May 1988): 60, 62, 64, 66.
Traditional and contemporary gospel music artists discuss the financial merits of blending older and newer gospel music forms to gain widespread audience appeal.

Burnim, Mellonee. "Gospel Music Research." *Black Music Research Journal* 1 (1980): 63–70.
Acknowledges the lack of a single, complete source of information on African American gospel music. Burnim surveys a number of scholarly and popular sources for individuals interested in studying Black gospel music. Also highlights the importance of continuing such studies in order to gain a greater understanding of the components and artistic expressions of Black culture.

———. "The Black Gospel Music Tradition: A Complex of Ideology, Aesthetic, and Behavior." In *More Than Dancing: Essays on Afro-American Music and Musicians*, ed. Irene V. Jackson, 147–67. Westport, CT: Greenwood Press, 1985.
Illustrates how the Black gospel music tradition is part of ongoing processes in Black music that incorporate a variety of themes and musical techniques and traditions. With diagrams and a bibliographical listing.

———. "Functional Dimensions of Gospel Music Performance." *Western Journal of Black Studies* 12, no. 2 (1988): 112–21.
Details four major functions of African American gospel music: expressing sociohistorical aspects of Black culture—assessing present concerns and offering solutions for the future, reinforcing the meaning of life, transmitting individual feelings through collective means, and sustaining both spirituality and cultural identity. Includes statements made by John Wesley Work, III; Thomas Andrew Dorsey; Mahalia Jackson; Clara Ward; and James Cleveland. Describes technique, mannerisms, and wardrobe in gospel performance. With bibliography.

———. "The Performance of Black Gospel Music as Transformation." *Concilium: International Review of Theology* 2 (Mar./Apr. 1989): 52–61.
An ethnomusicological and sociohistorical treatise on performance styles in African American gospel music. Introduces, defines, and discusses two ground-breaking concepts in regard to the Black gospel music tradition, "transformation of personae" and "transformation of space," and their essential function in enabling worshipers to access and complete the spiritual communications process. Dimensions discussed range from physical appearance to body movement; successful communication of sincerity; and the concept of the "invisible" church of Black slaves in which God is omnipresent, strongly rooted in the multidimensional, West African religious tradition. With bibliography.

———, and Portia K. Maultsby. "From Backwoods to City Streets: The Afro- American Musical Journey." In *Expressively Black*, ed. Geneva Gay and Willie L. Barber, 109–36. New York: Praeger, 1987.
Discusses the history and development of the African American music tradition from spirituals to popular music, making reference to the relationships between textual, thematic, and performance reinterpretations and socioeconomic change in the United States. Defining conceptual continuums that link all Black music forms, Burnim discusses the apparent paradox in reinterpreting religious songs within a popular vein, offering historical and sociocultural examples in the process. With bibliography.

de Buclet, Linda. "Redefining the Gospel Sound: Wesley Boyd's Choir Combines Classical, Traditional, Contemporary Music Forms." *Washington Post*, Sept. 28, 1985, G10.

Wesley Boyd's Choir preserves older Black gospel traditions and creates new ones to appeal to a wider audience. Highlights the professionalism exemplified by the Wesley Boyd Choir in regard to concert performance.

Dyer, Doris J. "New Directions in Sacred Harp Singing." In *Folk Music and Modern Sound*, ed. William Ferris and Mary L. Hart, 73–79. Jackson: University Press of Mississippi, 1982.
Focuses on the ways in which increased studies and audiovisual documentation of the Sacred Harp tradition change both the tradition and its transmission.

Epstein, Dena J. "Myths about Black Folk Music." In *Folk Music and Modern Sound*, ed. William Ferris and Mary L. Hart, 151–60. Jackson: University Press of Mississippi, 1982.
Explodes several myths about Black folk music, including these concepts: Blacks came to the New World lacking culture and secular music forms; the banjo and the spiritual were originally European inventions, merely adopted by Blacks in the New World; and it was virtually impossible for Blacks to transport African instruments to the New World.

Feintuch, Burt. "A Noncommercial Black Gospel Group in Context: We Live the Life We Sing About." *Black Music Research Journal* 1 (1980): 37–50.
Discusses the noncommercial aspects of gospel music; features the Cross family of Russelville, Logan County, KY.

"'First Lady' of Gospel—Shirley Caesar: New Album, New Contract, New Methods for Gospel Music Industry." *Ebony* (Sept. 1977): 98–100, 102, 106.
Evangelist Shirley Caesar enjoys twenty-five years of success as a professional gospel singer; signs million-dollar contract; discusses new promotional thrusts and gospel music styles that increase her growing numbers of fans among secular and nonsecular groups.

Funk, Ray. "Bill Spivery: A Real Operator." Washington, DC: Smithsonian Institution, National Museum of American History Archives, gospel clipping file, n.d.
A biographical and career sketch of gospel music composer Bill Spivery, whose 1959 gospel song "Operator" was popularized in 1974 by white jazz vocalists the Manhattan Transfer. Traces Spivery's musical ties to the Friendly Brothers, the Sons of Truth, and the Operators. Funk makes reference to James Cleveland, Roberta Martin and the Roberta Martin Singers, the Wings over Jordan Choir, the Angelic Gospel Singers, the Kings of Harmony Gospel Quartet, the Staple Singers, Bobby Womack, the Swan Silvertones, and the Davis Sisters. Includes discography (1959–70).

———. "Wings over Jordan." Washington, DC: Smithsonian Institution, National Museum of American History Archives, gospel clipping file, n.d.
An overview of the Wings over Jordan Choir and its weekly radio broadcast during "The Negro Hour" on WGAR in Cleveland (1939–47). With photographs of James Lewis Elkins (conductor); Charles King (co-conductor); Esther Overstreet (soprano; lead singer of "I Will Trust in the Lord"); Cecil W. Dandy (tenor; lead singer of "It's My Desire"); Dorothy Clark (contralto; lead singer of "I'm Gonna Die with the Staff in My Hand"); and Mildred C. Ridley (business manager). Also contains reproductions of Wings over Jordan performance memorabilia.

———. "The Imperial Quintet." Washington, DC: Smithsonian Institution, National Museum of American History Archives, gospel clipping file, n.d.
A brief historical overview of the Imperial Quintet *a cappella* group of Savannah (1922–ca. 1940). With photo of Willie Robinson (tenor); Clarence Robinson (tenor); Benjamin Bryant (first tenor); Henry Singleton, Jr. (baritone and manager); and Frank Jackson (bass). With discography of recordings issued on the Victor label, including "Michael, Hand Me down My Robe"; "Sweet and Blessed Story"; "Don't Let Nobody Turn You Around"; and "We Pray to the Peace of Jerusalem."

———. "Let's Go out to the Programs (The Peacock Gospel Years)." In *Duke/Peacock Records:*

An Illustrated History with Discography, ed. Galen Gart and Roy C. Ames, 37–50. Milford, NH: Big Nickel Publications, 1989.
A detailed historical overview of Black gospel music on Duke Records and Peacock Records, with special emphasis on Peacock Records and its owner, Don Robey. Funk describes the multitude of gospel quartet groups and solo artists on the Peacock label whose musical innovations influenced recorded gospel during the 1950s and 1960s. With photos and historical background of the Original Five Blind Boys (Jackson Harmoneers), Sister Jessie Mae Renfro, the Sensational Nightingales, the Spirit of Memphis Quintet, Reverend Cleophus Robinson, the Gospelaires, the Mighty Clouds of Joy, Inez Andrews and the Andrewettes, and the Melody Kings of Los Angeles.

George, Luvenia A. "Lucie E. Campbell and the Enduring Tradition of Gospel Hymnody." In *The Songs of Lucie E. Campbell: Gospel Music Composer*, ed. Niani Kilkenny and Rebecca E. Curzon, 6–15. Washington, DC: Smithsonian Institution, National Museum of American History, 1984.
A biographical sketch of gospel music composer Lucie E. Campbell. With photos.

Harrington, Richard. "Onward, Christian Choir: D.C.'s Richard Smallwood Singers Taking Gospel in New Directions." *Washington Post*, Feb. 6, 1989.
Focuses on the Richard Smallwood Singers of Washington, DC, and discusses the contemporary gospel sound. Also discusses the growing popularity and financial gains of gospel music.

Landes, John L. "WLAC, The Hossman, and Their Influence on Black Gospel." *Black Music Research Journal* 7 (1987): 67–82.
Argues that radio historically has been the most important of all media with regard to bringing together commercial and noncommercial aspects of Black gospel music. WLAC's fifty-thousand-watt Black radio program in Nashville, created in 1939, reaches more gospel music listeners than any other. Highlights the importance of this radio program to gospel artists, their record companies, and their listeners. With photos of the Fairfield Four and Bill "Hoss" Allen ("The Hossman"), longtime WLAC disc jockey. Largely based on an interview with Bill "Hoss" Allen.

Maultsby, Portia K. "The Role of Scholars in Creating Space and Validity for Ongoing Changes in Black American Culture." In *Black American Culture and Scholarship: Contemporary Issues*, ed. Bernice Johnson Reagon, 11–26. Washington, DC: Smithsonian Institution Press, 1985.
Notes that scholars of Black American culture must continue to shape the direction of Black studies, especially with regard to researching and transmitting information on the African American gospel music tradition.

———. "The Use and Performance of Hymnody, Spirituals, and Gospels in the Black Church." *The Journal of the Interdenominational Theological Center* 19 (Fall 1986/Spring 1987): 141–59.
Argues that the varying degree to which African Americans have participated in the historically white Protestant tradition has led to the development of two distinct genres of Black religious music: one influenced by the Protestant hymn tradition and one virtually unaffected by the Protestant tradition, strongly retaining elements of traditional West African musical expression. Maultsby details each with respect to ideology, worship, and musical styles, discussing the degree to which each genre has been influenced by West African, Black American, European, and Euro-American musical developments. Details the origin, development, and function of hymns, spirituals, and gospel songs in relation to the sociocultural contexts in which they were created. With extensive bibliographical listing.

———. "Africanisms in African-American Music." In *Africanisms in American Culture*, ed. Joseph E. Holloway, 185–209. Bloomington: Indiana University Press, 1990.
Argues that West African concepts of collectivity and innovation in the face of conflict are

reflected in the music of African Americans. Describes music forms between the seventeenth and twentieth centuries, including folk spirituals, blues, jazz, gospel, soul, funk, disco, and rap. Illustrates how the socioeconomic status of Blacks in the United States is reflected in sacred and secular song forms. Draws important parallels between the musical expression of the freed Blacks and Civil Rights Movement song. Discusses blues and gospel music as manifestations of Black identity in the twentieth century. Makes reference to gospel music composers Reverend Charles Albert Tindley and Thomas Andrew Dorsey. Contains extensive bibliography.

Pinkney, Junette A. "Setting the Issues to Music." *Washington Post*, Jan. 11, 1985, B7.
Carlton Reese, composer of freedom songs, discusses with Pinkney 1960s gospel music styles of Birmingham's Civil Rights Movement campaign.

Reagon, Bernice Johnson. "Notes on the Artists" (Kings of Harmony Jubilee Brass Band, Songs of Grace Quartet, McCullough Youth Choir). In *Smithsonian Black Gospel Music Series: United House of Prayer*. Washington, DC: Smithsonian Institution, National Museum of American History, April 13, 1980.
A brief biographical sketch on the Kings of Harmony Jubilee Brass Band, Songs of Grace Quartet, and McCullough Youth Choir.

———. "Notes on the Artists" (The Harmonizing Four). In *Smithsonian Black Gospel Music Series: The Harmonizing Four*. Washington, DC: Smithsonian Institution, National Museum of American History, April 12, 1981.
A brief biographical sketch of the Harmonizing Four.

———. "Rememberings." In *Song Journey: Retrospective of Gospel Music Composer Rev. William Herbert Brewster*. Washington, DC: Smithsonian Institution, National Museum of American History, 1981.
Introduces the reader to gospel music pioneer Reverend William Herbert Brewster. Reagon shares the contents of an extensive, recorded interview with Reverend William Herbert Brewster.

———. "Black American Urban Culture." In *1984 Festival of American Folklife*. Washington, DC: Smithsonian Institution, Office of Folklife Programs, 1984.
Defines Black American culture and the many ways in which it is manifested and transmitted. Cites the church, with its simultaneous preservation of old traditions and fostering of new traditions, as the major cultural center for many urban Black Americans. Highlights the importance of collectivity, innovation, and self-assertion among African American urban youth. Argues that street games, such as double-dutch, and rap music are important cultural and generation-blending forces in the lives of inner-city youth.

———. "Women in Blues." In *Women in Blues*, program booklet ed. Niani Kilkenny and Robert Selim. Washington, DC: Smithsonian Institution, National Museum of American History, 1985.
Lead article of program booklet that accompanied a Smithsonian Institution program on the blues tradition among Black women. Features two Washington blues singers, Laurie Pettiway and Mary Jefferson.

"Sallie Martin." *Ebony* (Mar. 1986): 76, 78, 81.
Covers the ninetieth birthday of "Mother of Gospel Music" Sallie Martin; credits her for helping composer Thomas A. Dorsey popularize Black gospel music.

Sanders, Charles L. "Gospel Goes to the Holy Land." *Ebony* (Dec. 1983): 36–38, 40, 42.
Covers Barry White's "One Nation Under God First Annual Festival" in Jerusalem. Popular artist Barry White is accompanied on this tour by gospel artists Reverend James Cleveland, Shirley Caesar and the Caesar Singers, Andrae Crouch, and the New World Singers.

"Take 6: Gifted Sextet Serves Up Contemporary Gospel with A cappella Jazz." *Ebony* (Mar. 1989): 74, 76.
Profiles the *a cappella* gospel group Take 6 as they reach sacred and secular audiences with their innovative song stylings.

Weisman, Paul, with Randy Welch. "Gospel Music Rolls Out of the Church, Onto the Charts." *U.S. News & World Report* (Aug. 25, 1986): 56.
Discusses the popularity and profitability of gospel music in comparison to jazz and classical music. Music professor Horace Clarence Boyer discusses the resurgence of gospel music. Black and white gospel music artists reap financial gains.

Williams, Jean. "Gospel Workshop Stresses Growth Through Seminars." *Billboard* (Aug. 22, 1981): 6.
Mentions Gospel Music Workshop of America, which holds workshops to encourage professionalism in gospel music performance and attract secular financial support.

———. "Minimal Gospel Airplay on Los Angeles Black Radio." *Billboard* (Apr. 21, 1981): 41.
States that 50 percent of Black radio stations in Los Angeles play gospel music only during sleeping hours; a few "crossover" gospel artists, like Andrae Crouch, are heard during peak listening hours. Yet gospel music sales continue to rise.

Williams-Jones, Pearl. "Afro-American Gospel Music: A Crystallization of the Black Aesthetic." *Journal for the Society of Ethnomusicology* 19, no. 3 (Sept. 1975): 373–85.
Defines and outlines components of the Black aesthetic. Illustrates how church conservatism helped preserve the African elements present in Black American religious musics, especially African-American gospel music. Also illustrates distinctly Euro-American qualities present in Black gospel music.

———. "Black American Gospel Music." In *Smithsonian Black Gospel Music Series: United House of Prayer*. Washington, DC: Smithsonian Institution, National Museum of American History, April 13, 1980.
An introduction to the Black gospel music tradition. Part of program booklet that accompanied the Smithsonian gospel music series.

———. "Notes on the Artist—Black Gospel Music: Coming of Age." In *Smithsonian Gospel Music Series: Marion Williams*. Washington, DC: Smithsonian Institution, National Museum of American History, October 1980.
A biographical sketch of gospel singer Marion Williams. Part of program booklet that accompanied the Smithsonian gospel music series.

———. "Thomas Andrew Dorsey: Father of Gospel Music." In *Classic Gospel Song: A Tribute to Thomas A. Dorsey*. Washington, DC: Smithsonian Institution, National Museum of American History, 1985.
A biographical sketch and overview of the life and works of gospel music pioneer Thomas Andrew Dorsey.

———. "Toward the Inclusion of Black American Gospel Music in the Curricula of Academic Institutions." In *Black American Culture and Scholarship: Contemporary Issues*, ed. Bernice Johnson Reagon, 27–32. Washington, DC: Smithsonian Institution Press, 1985.
Contests the prevailing American notion that Black musical forms, including gospel, are substandard. Advocates the teaching of Black gospel music in both white and Black institutions of higher learning.

———. "Alex Bradford (1926–1978): 'Singing Rage of the Gospel Age.'" In *Too Close to Heaven: The Music of Professor Alex Bradford*, ed. Niani Kilkenny and Robert Selim. Washington, DC: Smithsonian Institution, National Museum of American History, 1987.
A rare article that focuses on the life and works of Black gospel music pioneer "Professor" Alex

Bradford. Part of program booklet that accompanied a Smithsonian colloquium on Bradford at the National Museum of American History, November 7, 1987.

———. "Roberta Martin: Spirit of an Era." In *Roberta Martin and the Roberta Martin Singers*, ed. Bernice Johnson Reagon and Linn Shapiro, 12–21. Washington, DC: Smithsonian Institution, National Museum of American History, 1981.

Lead article in program booklet for Smithsonian Institution's tribute, colloquium, and performances on gospel music composer Roberta Martin.

———. "Washington, D.C./Gospel Music City, U.S.A.: State of the Art." In *1987 Festival of American Folklife*, 16–21. Washington, DC: Smithsonian Institution, Office of Folklife Programs, 1987.

Highlights the sociocultural importance of Black gospel music to Black communities in Washington, D.C. Describes essential elements of the African American gospel music tradition and discusses gospel music as a reflection of Black rural-to-urban life experiences. Includes a section on Black female and male gospel quartets in Washington. Discusses the role of radio programming in helping gospel artists and preachers gain exposure to wider audiences. Lists popular African American gospel groups in the Washington area.

RECORD ALBUM NOTES

Funk, Ray. Record album annotation for *Little Axe: So Many Years*. Gospel Jubilee Records RF–1403 (Vingaker, Sweden).

Focuses on legendary Black gospel-quartet lead singer Wilmer Broadnax (best known by his performing name "Little Axe") and his strong influence in shaping gospel-quartet lead singing during the 1940s and 1950s (gospel's golden era). Details Broadnax's affiliation with the following great gospel quartets: the Southern Gospel Singers, the Golden Echos, the Spirit of Memphis Quartet (throughout various personnel changes), and the Fairfield Four. Album cover contains photographs of Broadnax.

———. "Jefferson County, Alabama Jubilee Quartets: An Introduction." Record album annotation for *Birmingham Boys*. Clanka Lanka 144.

Focuses on the distinctive jubilee singing style of African American gospel quartets of Jefferson County, Alabama. Briefly describes the *a cappella* jubilee gospel style characteristic in the Birmingham area prior to World War II. Discusses the influence of jubilee- quartet vocal trainers Charles Bridges and R. C. Foster. With special emphasis on the era of "race" recordings and radio broadcasting. Jubilee quartets mentioned include the Birmingham Jubilee Singers, Charles Langford and the Marvel Quintet, the Four Eagle Gospel Singers, the Bessemer Harmony Four, the Bessemer Sunset Four, the Dunham Jubilee Singers, the Famous Blue Jay Singers, and the Ravizee Singers. With photos of the Five Silver Kings, the Famous Shelby County Big Four, and the Famous Blue Jay Singers.

———. "The Pilgrim Travelers." Record album annotation for *Stand Up and Testify! 14 Songs of Soul and Inspiration from Gospel's Heavenly Stars* by the Pilgrim Travelers featuring Lou Rawls. Solid Smoke Records SS 8034, 1984.

A historical and discographical background of the Pilgrim Travelers from its inception in 1936 to its end during the late 1950s.

———. "Golden Age of Gospel Singing." Record album annotation for *The Golden Age of Gospel Singing*. Folklyric Records 9046, 1985.

A survey of African American gospel music's most influential artists between the years 1940 and 1950. Groups profiled include the Sensational Nightingales, the Southern Harps, Bessie

Griffin and the Gospel Pearls, the Nightingale Jubilaires and Madame Ernestine, the Davis Sisters, the Angelic Gospel Singers, the Dixie Hummingbirds, Archie Brownlee and the Five Blind Boys of Mississippi, the Bells of Joy, and the Zion Travelers. Lead singers profiled include J. C. Ginyard (of the Royal Harmony Singers, the Dixiaires, and the DuPropers); and Robert Harris (best known for his work with the Soul Stirrers and the Christland Singers).

————. "Norfolk Jubilee Singers." Record album annotation for *Norfolk Jubilee Quartet, 1927–1938*. Gospel Heritage Records HT 310 (West Sussex, England), 1985.
Detailed historical background on the Norfolk Jubilee Singers of Virginia (1919–40). Details the quartet's progression from a 1921 jazz vaudeville group to later fame as a gospel group. Listed members include: Len Williams (bass); Buddy Butts (tenor); Otto Tutson (second tenor); Delrose Hollins (baritone); Clarence Hare (tenor); Norman "Crip" Harris (tenor, guitarist); Melvin Colden (baritone); and Raymond Smith (tenor). Makes reference to other Norfolk-based groups, including the Golden Gate Jubilee Quartet, the Excelsior Quartet, the Norfolk Jazz Quartet, and the Monarch Jazz Quartet. Also mentions the Selah Jubilee Singers. Mentions Norfolk Jubilee Quartet recordings on OKeh Records and the quartet's extensive live radio performances during the late 1930s.

————. Record album annotation for *Get Right with the Swan Silvertones*. Rhino Records, 1986.
Chronicles the history of the Alabama-based Swan Silvertones from (ca.) 1948 to 1978, with special emphasis on their recordings for Vee Jay between 1956 and 1964. Personnel changes within the group are also detailed. Listed as original members of the group are: Reverend Claude Jeter, Johnny Myles, Peter Connors, Lynn Hargrove, Leroy Watkins, and Eddie Borroughs. Funk updates the reader on the current status of the group and its former members.

————. "*A cappella* Gospel Singing." Record album annotation for *A cappella Gospel Singing*. Folklyric Records 9045, 1986.
Introduces the reader to the dynamic world of traditional Black *a cappella* gospel music between the years 1930 and 1950. Begins with a short definition of African American gospel music and the importance of *a cappella* singing within that tradition. Includes brief and insightful data on the following groups: Georgia Peach; Mitchell's Christian Singers; Wright Brothers Jubilee Singers; Five Soul Stirrers; the Pilgrim Travelers (all of Texas); Bright Moon Quartet (of Durham); Heavenly Gospel Singers (of Spartanburg); and the Jubalaires (of Jacksonville).

————. Record album annotation for *Cleveland Gospel*. Gospel Heritage Records HT 316 (West Sussex, England), 1987.
Highlights the rich Black gospel music heritage in Cleveland from 1928 to 1957. Funk offers brief but detailed historical background on the following gospel singers: the Friendly Brothers, the Shield Brothers, L and N Gospel Singers, the Elite Jewels, the Angels of Harmony, and the National Kings of Harmony. Makes reference to popular artists steeped in the gospel tradition: the Womacks (including Bobby Womack) and Sam Cooke.

————. Record album annotation for *The Five Blind Boys of Alabama*. Gospel Heritage Records HT 315 (West Sussex, England), 1987.
Provides detailed historical background on the Five Blind Boys of Alabama, from the group's humble beginnings circa 1944 to original member Clarence Fountain's performances as Oedipus in the Broadway show *The Gospel at Colonus*. Details personnel changes within the group and updates the reader on members' current undertakings. The following are listed as original members of the Five Blind Boys of Alabama: Velma Trailer (lead singer); George Scott (tenor); Clarence Fountain (lead singer, baritone); George Scott (tenor); Olice Thomas (baritone); and Johnny Fields (bass). Based largely on interviews.

————. "Atlanta Gospel." Record album annotation for *Atlanta Gospel*. Gospel Heritage Records HT 312 (West Sussex, England), 1987.

Details the history and development of African American *a cappella* gospel quartets in Atlanta during the 1940s and 1950s, with special emphasis on the live radio broadcast work and recordings of the following groups: the Reliable Jubilee Singers, the National Independents, the Echoes of Zion, the Starlight Spiritual Singers, the Five Trumpets, and the Golden Gospel Singers. With photographs and a listing of group members.

————. Record album annotation for *Dixiaires: Let Me Fly*. Gospel Heritage Records HT 317 (West Sussex, England), 1988.
Chronicles the history of the Dixiaires of Los Angeles. Details personnel changes from the group's inception circa 1947 through its demise in 1955 and reveals information about Dixiaires members through 1988. Members discussed include: J. C. Ginyard (lead vocalist), Joe Floyd (tenor), Jimmy Smith (baritone), and musicians Johnny Hines (bass) and Abe Green (guitar). Based on interviews with J. Caleb Ginyard and other primary sources.

————, and Marv Goldberg. "Goodbye to the 40's, Hello to the 50's." Record album annotation for *Goodbye to the 40's, Hello to the 50's*. Apollo Records 8018, 1989.
A survey of the most influential gospel music artists and their recordings between 1940 and 1950. Quartets highlighted include the Striders, the Larks, the Melody Masters, the Four Blues, the Rivals, and the Rhythm Kings. Album cover includes photographs of the Striders, Rhythm Kings, and Four Blues.

————. "Goodbye to the 40's, Hello to the 50's, Vol. 2." Record album annotation for *Goodbye to the 40's, Hello to the 50's*, Vol. 2. Apollo Records 8019, 1989.
An overview of the following gospel quartets and their recordings: the Striders, the Melody Masters, the Rhythm Kings, the Three Riffs, and the Four Blues between 1940 and 1950. Album cover contains photographs of all groups except the Rhythm Kings.

THESES AND DISSERTATIONS

Allen, Robert Raymond. "Singing in the Spirit: An Ethnography of Gospel Performance in New York City's African American Church Community." University of Pennsylvania, 1987.
Presents, from a sociocultural and religious perspective, the important functions of the gospel music tradition within African American communities in New York City. Begins with a history of African American gospel music, with reference to and critique of related scholarly and popular texts; discusses the roles of gospel music pioneers Reverend Charles Albert Tindley, Thomas Andrew Dorsey, Sallie Martin, Mahalia Jackson, Roberta Martin, Willie Mae Ford Smith, the Ward Singers, the Davis Sisters, the Golden Gate Jubilee Quartet, and the Norfolk Jubilee Quartet. Provides a historical account of African American settlement patterns in New York City—especially as they relate to the development of Black churches, religious musics, and related social networks. Draws important parallels between community-based and professional Black gospel singers and their musical influence on one another in New York City, and suggests that such theoretical parallels may have wider applications within the United States. With extensive, selected bibliography.

Allgood, B. Dexter. "A Study of Selected Black Gospel Choirs in the Metropolitan New York Area." New York University, 1984.
Based on interviews with five Black gospel choir directors in New York City who speak about the gospel songs they consider to be primary teaching tools for choirs. Dexter observes and transcribes gospel song performances by the five choirs the interviewees direct and notes nine areas of performance and practice technique on which choir members and directors should focus in order to maximize the effectiveness of choral performance. Defines and describes: gos-

ANNOTATED BIBLIOGRAPHY 369

pel (traditional, contemporary, and progressive); pop-gospel; soul; city and country blues; the
Black gospel choir; and the "shout." Songs analyzed include works by James Cleveland, Kenneth Morris, Walter Hawkins, and Andrae Crouch. Includes complete musical scores of each
song.

Amos, Alvin E. "The Use of Keyboard Instruments in the Religious Services of Selected Black
Baptist Churches in Central Piedmont North Carolina." University of North Carolina at
Greensboro, 1987.
Describes the level of congregational participation and the use of keyboard instruments in tar-
get churches and notes commonalities among them. Also describes the level of performance
and style technique which pastors, the choir, and the congregation expect from the keyboardist
in these Black church. Discusses five common musical styles in the Black churches: gospel
music, metered hymns, Negro spirituals, strict hymns/classic hymns, and preaching-in-key.
Mentions these musical styles in relation to gospel artists and other musical styles, such as:
Thomas A. Dorsey, Dr. Isaac Watts, the blues, and the call-and-response tradition. With transcriptions and musical analyses of gospel performances during worship service.

Boyer, Horace Clarence. "The Gospel Song: A Historical and Analytical Survey." University of
Rochester, Eastman School of Music, 1964.
This master's thesis chronicles the history and development of gospel music and illustrates,
through musical analyses, major elements of authentic Black gospel music. Boyer draws important distinctions between Negro spirituals, evangelistic hymns, and gospel music. Boyer focuses
his work on music written, performed, published, and recorded by gospel music pioneers in
the twentieth century, focusing on the 1940s to the 1960s. Based on recorded interviews and
correspondence with Roberta Martin, Kenneth Morris, Thomas Andrew Dorsey, "Professor"
Alex Bradford, James Cleveland, Albertina Walker (of the Caravans), and Dorothy Love (of the
Original Gospel Harmonettes). Also contains a discussion of gospel quartets. True-to-perfor-
mance transcriptions of recorded gospel songs include: "Certainly Lord," "Ride on King Jesus,"
"He's Right on Time," "Surely God Is Able," "Too Close to Heaven," ""Step by Step," "Amazing Grace," and "Peace Be Still." With an appendix on gospel composers, performers, agents,
and recording and publishing companies. Bibliography includes books, recorded interviews,
published music, and gospel recordings.

———. "An Analysis of Black Church Music with Examples Drawn from Services in Rochester,
New York." University of Rochester, Eastman School of Music, 1973.
Boyer's pioneering study notes the importance and viability of studying Black sacred music, as
it is the wellspring of the blues, the Negro spiritual, jazz, and rock and roll. Boyer transcribes
and analyzes music used in fifteen denominational services and notes the connections between
sacred music performance traditions, worship service structure, and the ethnicity of church
members. Notes the "gospelization" of standard hymns. With a sociohistorical survey of the
Black church and related musical development and usage; appendices listing Black churches in
Rochester, New York; charts of the geographical locations of congregations used in the study; a
listing of worship services recorded on audiotape; and an outline of Rochester noting highly
concentrated Black church areas. With extensive bibliography.

Buchanan, Samuel Carroll. "A Critical Analysis of Style in Four Black Jubilee Quartets in the
United States." New York University, 1987.
An important survey of the history of the gospel quartet tradition, from Black minstrelsy to
professional groups. Focuses on four pioneering quartets: Norfolk Jubilee Quartet and Golden
Gate Quartet (of Norfolk, VA); Mitchell's Christian Singers (of Kingston, NC); and the Selah
Jubilee Singers (of Brooklyn, NY). Based largely on interviews with former and current mem-
bers of the quartets, as well as interviews with relatives, accompanists, promoters, and researchers of the Black gospel quartet tradition. Traces the quartet tradition through historically Black

colleges and universities. Among the many famous and popular Black American musical artists mentioned with quartet backgrounds are Paul Robeson, Roland Hayes, Scott Joplin, W. C. Handy, Leonard De Paur, Bayard Rustin, Cabel "Cab" Calloway, Ray Charles, Sam Cooke, Lou Rawls, Jerry Butler, Jackie Wilson, Isaac Hayes, and Brook Benton. With selected discography of the four quartets upon which this study is focused. Contains extensive bibliography and priceless photos.

Burnim, Mellonee Victoria. "The Black Gospel Music Tradition: Symbol of Ethnicity." Indiana University, 1980.

States that gospel music remains dominated by Black Americans for two reasons: it has remained nonaccessible to the non-African American population, and the extent to which it is recorded and promoted is not comparable to the extensive means used to popularize other forms of music in the United States. Notes that because of the manner in which it communicates Black values, experiences, and beliefs, as well as the Black religious experience, African American gospel music is supported not only by persons with a strong background in the Black church but also by secular institutions and places, including college campuses, concert halls, and, on occasion, nightclubs. Burnim utilizes photographs, audio and visual recordings of gospel performances in worship services, concerts, and rehearsals to document the sociocultural and historical role of gospel music in Black America.

Franklin, Marion Joseph. "The Relationship of Black Preaching to Black Gospel Music." Drew University, 1982.

Arguing that Black exclusion from Euro-American Christian organizations led to the development of separate Black forms of sacred music and religious expression, Franklin traces the development of, and draws parallels between, Black sacred music and preaching styles. His analysis includes a discussion of the following sacred-song forms: common meter, short hymns, lining-out hymns, prayer phrasing, and "moaning songs." Noting the similar functions of Black preaching and gospel music—-interpreting biblical texts within the context of the struggles of day-to-day life—Franklin states and discusses their common African roots in the oral tradition. He also illustrates the musical function of various Black vocal techniques in singing and preaching.

Gilchrist, Charles H. "An Assessment of the Preparation of North Carolina Public School Music Teachers in Performance Practices of Black Gospel Music: Implications for Curriculum Revisions in Higher Education." University of North Carolina at Greensboro, 1980.

Based on a random-survey questionnaire administered to public-school music teachers in North Carolina, Gilchrist concludes that the primary reason for the lack of curricular attention to Black gospel music is the teachers' lack of exposure to the field. Extensive information on gospel music performance practices. Contains musical analyses comparing traditional and gospelized melodies. Defines and discusses the origin of sacred and secular gospel musics, in comparison to Black spirituals.

Harris, Michael Wesley. "The Advent of Gospel Blues in Black Old-Line Churches in Chicago, 1932–33: As Seen Through the Life and Mind of Thomas Andrew Dorsey." Harvard University, 1982.

Based largely on seventy-five hours of recorded interviews with blues and gospel music composer Thomas Andrew Dorsey and his musical colleagues. Stating that the blending of blues and gospel music aided in the popularization and secularization of Black gospel music, Harris focuses on Dorsey's life and accomplishments and notes the composer's pivotal role in blending blues and gospel music and popularizing the gospel blues.

Jackson, Irene V. "Afro-American Gospel Music and Its Social Setting with Special Attention to Roberta Martin." Wesleyan University, 1974.

Defines and discusses music of the Black folk church; illustrates the function of gospel music outside the church. Offers extensive biographical information about gospel music pioneer Roberta Martin. Contains a listing of gospel compositions covering the years 1938–65; a guide to identifying printed gospel music; and photographs of the following artists: Roberta Martin, the Swan Silvertones, Evangelist Shirley Caesar and the Caesar Singers, Bill Moss and the Celestials, and Charles Johnson. Delineates and defines gospel music, spirituals, and blues, and notes their sociohistorical function in and demographic relation to Black American life. With discography.

Mapson, Jesse Wendell. "Some Guidelines for the Use of Music in the Black Church." Eastern Baptist Theological Seminary, 1983.
Discusses the African world view and its influence on the African American ministry of music. Discusses Black sacred music from a sociohistorical standpoint and makes distinctions between historical and modern gospel music. Also focuses on the secularization of music in the Black church, with description of the uses of music in the Old and New Testaments. Research partially based on questionnaires given to pastors and church musicians in regard to their views on the proper forms and performance practices of church music. With extensive bibliography.

Raichelson, Richard M. "Black Religious Folk Song: A Study in Generic and Social Change." University of Pennsylvania, 1975.
Discusses how sociocultural and historical factors relate to the development of Black religious folk song. Illustrates the effects of urbanization on African American folk song tradition. Section on gospel quartets includes the Dixie Hummingbirds, the Fairfield Four, the Five Blind Boys of Alabama, the Mighty Clouds of Joy, Five Soul Stirrers, the Swanee Quintet, and the Violinaires, and an extensive bibliography. Notes the limitations of studying Black gospel music from an exclusively historical, literary, or performance/structure perspective, and advocates the utilization of all three approaches.

Reagon, Bernice Johnson. "Songs of the Civil Rights Movement 1955–1965: A Study in Culture History." Howard University, 1975.
Discusses the Black tradition of using songs as a means of transmitting oral histories. Notes the historical base of Civil Rights Movement protest songs. Based on a variety of sources, including interviews of song leaders, songwriters, and song collectors. Also includes eyewitness accounts of Civil Rights Movement activists. Traces the development of the American protest movement and usage of related folk songs, lyrics, and melodic themes from slavery to 1965, with special emphasis on the songs of the union labor movement during the 1930s and 1940s. Discusses the historical role of the song leader in changing, redefining, and reapplying existing songs and related themes for use in the Civil Rights Movement.

Taylor, Frederick J. "The Development and Evaluation of a Black Music Course of Study Designed for Junior High Students." Temple University, 1981.
Advocates the inclusion of Black music studies, particularly gospel music, in the general curriculum of students at the junior high level. Taylor considers how students' ethnic background and level of formal training and/or musical aptitude can affect their level of learning and performance in such a course. Taylor begins his study with a survey of standardized musical tests, such as the Iowa Test of Musical Literacy, and finds that Black students profit far more than their non-Black counterparts when studying Black forms of music and also finds that students who are more musically inclined, in general, benefit more from such a course than those who are not so inclined, regardless of ethnicity. Music styles in the course design include: work songs, blues, ragtime, spirituals, jazz, classic and contemporary gospel, folk songs, soul, African American rock music, and the lining-out tradition in hymn singing. With an extensive bibliography and a sample test for student evaluation.

Thomas, Andre Jerome. "A Study of the Selected Masses of Twentieth-Century Black Composers: Margaret Bonds, Robert Ray, George Walker, and David Baker." University of Illinois at Urbana–Champaign, 1983.

Of particular interest to researchers of the African American gospel music tradition is Thomas's discussion of Robert Ray, whose best- known work is titled "Gospel Mass." The aforementioned work blends Euro-classical and African American gospel music. With a musical analysis of "Gospel Mass"; bibliographies follow each chapter.

Tyler, Mary Ann Lancaster. "The Music of Charles Henry Pace and Its Relationship to the Afro-American Church Experience." University of Pittsburgh, 1980.

A sociohistorical study of the multifaceted career of African American/German Jewish Charles Henry Pace (1886–1963), a composer, musician, arranger, publisher, printer, musical director, and photographer who aided in the development of African American sacred song traditions, recording, and related media promotion. Tyler notes Pace's 104 original sacred music compositions, written between 1935 and 1958; his talents as an arranger; and his musical associations with W. C. Handy, Thomas Andrew Dorsey, Sallie Martin, Lillian M. Bowles, Theodore Frye, and James Cleveland. Also mentions Charles Albert Tindley, Professor Alex Bradford, the Five Blind Boys of Alabama, Edwin and Walter Hawkins, and Andrae Crouch. Defines African American spirituals, gospel music, gospel songs and Pace's "Spiritual Anthems." With copies of Pace's songs in print, a discography of the Pace Jubilee Singers, transcriptions and musical analyses of fourteen of Pace's original gospel songs as performed in churches and concert halls, and photos. Based on interviews with family members and musical associates.

CONTRIBUTORS

Horace Clarence Boyer, Ph.D., scholar, singer, composer, pianist, is associate professor of music at the University of Massachusetts. With wide-ranging interests in African American music and Western classical forms, Boyer is a pioneer in the musical analysis of written and performed gospel compositions. As a gospel singer, he has performed with his brother, James Boyer, as the Boyer Brothers, with recordings on the Savoy and Nashboro record labels.

Lisa Pertillar Brevard is an Emory University graduate student in African American studies. A recent graduate with honors from Smith College, she is already a serious student of cultural studies. Pertillar Brevard completed three Smithsonian Institution internships, from which one of her projects resulted in her contribution to this study.

Luvenia A. George is a music educator and pioneer in the development of materials and techniques that incorporate ethnomusicology in music education curricula. She is a Ph.D. candidate in ethnomusicology at the University of Maryland. She is an author, lecturer, and clinician whose continuing interests are African American music and culture and multicultural education.

Michael W. Harris, Ph.D. in music and American church history from Harvard University, is an associate professor of history and African American world studies at the University of Iowa. His book *The Rise of Gospel Blues: The Music of Thomas Andrew Dorsey in the Urban Church* was published by Oxford University Press in 1992.

Anthony Heilbut, Ph.D., is the author of *The Gospel Sound: Good News and Bad Times*, the first book-length study of gospel music. He has also produced numerous gospel albums, including winners of the Grammy Award and the Grand Prix du Disque. Heilbut has taught at New York University and Hunter College. He is working on a biography of Thomas Mann, to be published by Alfred A. Knopf, Inc.

Portia K. Maultsby, Ph.D., is professor of Afro-American studies and ethnomusicology at Indiana University, Bloomington. She received her Ph.D. in ethnomusicology from the University of Wisconsin–Madison. An authority on the music of African Americans, Maultsby is currently working on a book on the popular music tradition of African Americans.

Bernice Johnson Reagon, Ph.D., is a culture historian specializing in African American oral, performance, and protest traditions. Reagon is a curator in the Smithsonian Institution, National Museum of American History, Division of Community Life, and the founder and former director of the Smithsonian's Program in African American Culture, where she conceptualized and implemented the research, conference, and performance components on gospel music history that are the basis for this volume. Reagon is the founder and artistic director of the internationally acclaimed *a cappella* singing group Sweet Honey in the Rock.

Reverend Charles Walker is an established pianist, composer, and conductor, and he is pastor of the Nineteenth Street Baptist Church in Philadelphia. Reverend Walker is chairperson of the Foreign Missions Board, National Baptist Convention U.S.A., Inc. He is working on a biography of Lucie E. Campbell.

William H. Wiggins, Jr., Ph.D., associate professor of Afro-American studies and fellow of the Folklore Institute at Indiana University, teaches a course on the Black church in America. His research in African American religious drama includes numerous articles and two documentary films, *In the Rapture* (1978) and *The Rapture Family* (1978).

Pearl Williams-Jones (1931–1991) was a singer, pianist, composer/arranger, and scholar. Williams-Jones made a major contribution in identifying the language with which to write and teach African American gospel music history and aesthetics theory. Her performance style was a reflection of her roots in African American culture and her training in Western European art music. She was associate professor of music at the University of the District of Columbia and toured frequently, performing at colleges, universities, and churches throughout the United States.

Index

"Power of the Holy Ghost" (Morris), **327–28**; harmonic analysis, 326
Praise houses, 11
"Praise Ye the Lord" (Campbell), **88–94**, 95
"Pray" (Hammer), 32
Praying ground, 165
Preaching techniques: influence on soul music, 29
"Precious Lord, Take My Hand" (Dorsey), 15, 82, 143, 145, *146*, 298; pitch changes in, **146**
Presley, Elvis, 31, 201
Price, Leona: memories of Roberta Martin, 288–90, 293–96
Program in African American Culture, National Museum of American History, 7
Prophet Jones, 302
Publishing houses, 15, 265, 310
"Pure Gold" (Brewster, Jr.), 244
Purlie Victorious (musical, Davis), 246

Quartets. *See* Jubilee quartets

Radio stations, 20, 21; gospel music on, 24–26
Ragtime, 118, 286
Rainey, Gertrude "Ma," 118, 143, 145, 176
Raised hymns, 84. *See also* Lining hymns
Rap, gospel, 32
Rawls, Lou, 28
Recitative and aria song style, 220, 224
Reconstruction concerts: Roberta Martin Singers, 256–57
Reconstruction period, 186
Record companies, 6, 22, 24, 259, 304; independent, 27
Redback Speller, 187
Redding, Otis, 29, 244
Reese, Della, 17, 23
Rejected Stone, The (drama, Brewster), 249
"Release Yourself" (Graham), 32
Return (album), 32
Revivals, 271, 274
Rhythm and blues, 28
"Ride on, King Jesus," 276, 280
Righteous Brothers, 31
"Right Right Time" (Charles), 31
Riley, Teddy, 32
"Ring It out with a Shout" (Person), 82

Ring shout, 178, 247
"Riverside Blues (Dorsey), 175
Robbins, Caroline Miller, 42
Roberta Martin Singers, 16–17, 23, 264, 270–71, 274; gold records, 293; ministry of, 297; public concerts, 270–71; reunion and roundtable, 7, 287–90, 293–306; revival services, 271; sound, 7, 258. *See also* Martin, Roberta
Roberta Martin Singers: The Old Ship of Zion (album), 266
Roberta Martin Studio of Music, 212
Roberts, Lawrence, 9; memories of Roberta Martin, 304–6
Robinson, Cleophus, 27
Robinson, Smokey, 30
"Rock Me." *See* "Hide Me in Thy Bosom"
Rosemond, Connie, 114, 132
Ross, Diana, 30
Rowing songs, 11
Ruffner, Elmer, 82
Run, Little Chillun (Johnson), 247
Russell, Diz, 28

Sacred Harp, 167
Saint Paul Baptist Church Choir (Los Angeles), 318, 325–26
Sallie Martin Singers, 16, 313, 315. *See also* Martin, Sallie
Sanctified church. *See* Pentecostal church
"Satisfied," 280, 285
Saunders, Howard, 23
Savoy Records, 9, 27, 270, 293, 304, 305
Say Amen, Somebody (film), 145, 158
Scales, in Roberta Martin arrangements, 277–78
Scott, Myrtle, 288
Screaming Jay Hawkins, 30
Scripture paraphrase, 314
"Search Me, Lord" (Dorsey), 149, **150–51**
Secular music industry: impact of gospel music on, 19–33
"See See Rider" (Baker), 30
Selah Jubilee Singers, 24
Set songs, 212
Seward, Theodore F., 11, 12
Seymour, William J., 56
Shape-note singing, 4, 114, 171, 172, 194; origin of, 166, 167

Sheet music, 15, 118, 143, 160, 259, 264–65, 311, 333, 339; Black sheet music not sold in white stores, 333; impact of recordings and photocopying, 333
Shelby, Thomas, 82n, 118, 122
Shepherd, Anna, 272, 283, 299
Sherwood, William Henry, 81, 142, 314
Shiloh Baptist Church (Chicago), 288, 289
Shouting, 28, 29. *See also* Pentecostal church
Shout songs, 13, 30, 95, 166, 224, 258
Silvertones, 202
Simmons, Harry Mae, 117
"Since I Met Jesus," vamp style, 285
Singing and praying bands, 39
Singing technique, 29–33, 209, 243, 326; arpeggio, 286; melisma, 30, 77; slides, 30
Slabtown Convention (drama, Burroughs), 246
Slave music. *See* Spirituals
Slavery, 4–5, 11, 42, 61, 118, 186
Smallwood, Richard, 17
Smallwood Singers, 17
Smith, Bessie, 176
Smith, Eugene, 9, 256, 257, 264, 274, 280, 286, 290, 301, 302; memories of Roberta Martin, 303–4; narrations, 270, 287–88
Smith, J. H. L., 180
Smith, Mamie, 174, 176
Smith, O. C., 30
Smith, William D., 61
Smith, William Henry, 114
Smith, Willie Mae Ford, 285
Smithsonian conference on pioneering gospel music composers, 7–10, 38; participating scholars, 8
Smithsonian Festival of American Folklife, 8–9
So Glad I Know (album), 32
"Somebody's Been Using That Thing" (Dorsey and Whitaker), 180
"Some Day" (Tindley), 65, **68–69**
"Someone Is Hitting the Home Trail Tonight" (Person), 82
"Something Within" (Campbell), 15, 51, 53, 85, 114, *115*, 116,